CONTENTS

THE GUIDE TO
MYSTERIOUS GLASGOW

THE GUIDE TO
MYSTERIOUS
GLASGOW

GEOFF HOLDER

The History Press

Dedicated to the memory of Ron Holder

First published 2009

The History Press
The Mill, Brimscombe Port
Stroud, Gloucestershire, GL5 2QG
www.thehistorypress.co.uk

Reprinted 2009, 2010, 2011

British Library Cataloguing in Publication Data.
A catalogue record for this book is available from the British Library.

ISBN 978 0 7524 4826 8

Typesetting and origination by The History Press
Printed in Great Britain

ACKNOWLEDGEMENTS

I would like to thank: John Braithwaite for the burned boots urban legend; Samantha Cooper of 23 Enigma; Mark Pilkington of *Strange Attractor Journal;* composer Drew Mulholland; Siusaidh Ceanadach of Tuatha de Bridget; Grahame Gardner of the Geomancy Group, especially for the tour of the Castlemilk labyrinth; Duncan Lunan for Sighthill and much more; Judith Bowers of the Britannia Music Hall; Pauline Reid of Bewitching Beauty; Mike Hall, former head flyman and acting stage manager, Theatre Royal, for his research into theatrical history; Gary Painter of the Theatre Royal; Ronnie Scott, our man in the Necropolis; Matt Baker, artist (www.mattbaker.org.uk); Arlene Russo of *Bite Me* magazine; Stevie Allan and Linda Cameron of Provan Hall; Mhairi Douglas and the curators of the Hunterian and Zoology Museums; the stalwart Local Studies staff at the A.K. Bell Library, Perth; my editor Cate Ludlow for patience and enthusiasm; Jenni Wilson for the maps; Paul Revell of www.revellution.co.uk for his website work; and Ségolène Dupuy for digital reworking and insights.

I am also grateful to the many staff of Glasgow Museums who were unfailingly helpful in dealing with my strange requests: Jane Flint, curator (Archaeology) at Kelvingrove; Fiona Hayes, curator (Social History) and Andrew Pollock, technician, at the People's Palace; Simon Eccles, senior curator, (Ancient Civilisations) at the Burrell Collection; Isobel McDonald, project manager and Kevin Kerrigan, research assistant, Regional Framework for Local History and Archaeology; Pat Allan, curator of World Cultures; and Anthony Lewis, curator of Scottish History.

Unless otherwise stated, all photographs are by the author.

For more information visit www.geoffholder.co.uk.

Green Man. One of the
Tontine Faces, Provand's
Lordship.

Foundry worker as the god
Vulcan. University of Glasgow.

'HALF THE LIES WE TELL AREN'T TRUE'

After a few beers and a late night out a man waiting for a train on Kelvinbridge underground station got caught short. Desperate, he sneaked into the narrow service platform that ran into the darkened tunnel. There, although he was an electrician – and therefore should have known better – he carelessly urinated on the live rail. Several thousand volts of electricity followed the arc of liquid and vaporised him instantly, leaving only his boots burned into the concrete – and they're still there to this day.

You may have heard this story, or something like it. The details may differ, but the essence remains the same: the illicit urination, the electrical nemesis, the burned boots. But no matter how ardently the person who told it swore the story is true, it's not: it's a completely fictional story, an urban legend. And I know this to be the case because I've spoken to the man who invented it.

Sometime in the mid-1960s, a student named John Braithwaite accepted a bet that he could invent an urban legend. The criterion was that the story was to be propagated at the start of the weekend and had to be heard being repeated by the Sunday. John and half-dozen of his friends went to pubs in different parts of the city on Friday night and loudly told the story to whoever would listen. On Sunday evening someone in a pub told one of the group the story, swearing it was true, because he had heard it from one of *his* friends who knew someone who

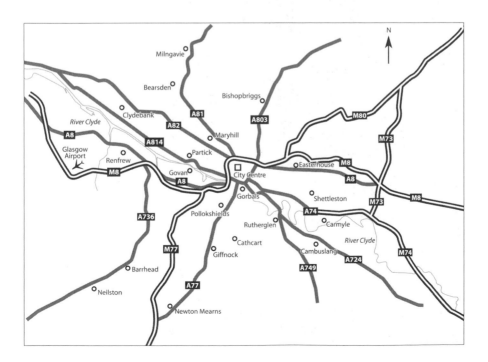

knew someone who'd actually seen the charred boots. The story then continued to circulate, taking on local flavours (the boots were in Buchanan Street or St Enoch, or any of the other underground stations) and gaining circumstantial details (the man was not an electrician but a burglar hiding from the police, so he *deserved* his fate).

The episode highlights both the joys and pitfalls of writing a book like this about Glasgow. On the one hand I have collected fascinating and mind-warping tales of the mysterious and marvellous from medieval annalists, historians, enthusiastic amateurs, specialist journals, newspapers and online forums. On the other hand, Glasgow is, and always has been, a city of born storytellers, with probably a higher concentration of yarn-spinners per square mile than any comparable metropolis. So how is it possible to tell whether all, or most, or even some of the stories contained here are actually true? The answer is that it's not. Just because a respected chronicler or a distinguished academic has written something down, doesn't make it true. Just because it's printed in a newspaper, or circulated on the internet (*especially* if it's circulated on the internet), doesn't mean it's real. Reality, in all its chaos and untidiness, gets translated into a *story,* often helped along by propaganda, partiality, selective memory, bias, exaggeration, whimsy and fantasy. Paranormal events, which are often random and confusing, quickly become transformed into a *ghost story* with a nice neat narrative.

Or, as a character in Terry Pratchett's incomparable *Discworld* series puts it: 'It's true … for a given value of truth.' So, don't worry. Prepare yourself for tales of child-eating vampires, rogue stone circles, chip-shop witchcraft, cantankerous ghosts and resurrected murderers. As they say in Glasgow: 'Half the lies we tell aren't true.'

INTRODUCTION

At the most basic level, this book covers seven main topics:

Dealing with the Dead – ghosts, graveyards, mediums and bodysnatching.

Dealing with the Gods – a term I interpret broadly, to include demons, fairies, deities, religious visions, saints, relics, miracles, holy wells and aliens.

Magic – including magical practitioners, witchcraft, 'superstitions' and healing and protection charms.

Powers of the Mind – telepathy, precognition, dreams and other mental phenomena.

Weird Nature – fireballs, big cats, etc.

Weird Humans – strange behaviour, peculiar crimes, coincidences, urban legends, oddball beliefs, and extremes of human experience.

The Silent Watchers – the countless gargoyles, gods, demons, monsters, saints, legendary figures, creatures and tutelary humans carved on Glasgow's buildings. You may not notice them as you rush past – but they're watching you. There is a glossary of gods, goddesses and other divine beings at the end of this introduction.

Mysterious Glasgow is organised geographically. You can find everything wonderful and weird concerning a street or area in the same place. Cross-references to other locations are shown in SMALL CAPS.

THE TOP TEN

If you want to skip to the ten top 'mysterious' sights to visit, see:

1. Kelvingrove Art Gallery & Museum (pages 99-105).
2. The Hunterian Museum and the Zoology Museum (pages 113-118).
3. The St Mungo Museum of Religious Life and Art (pages 35-36).
4. The Necropolis and the Ladywell (pages 37-42).
5. The modern stone circle at Sighthill Park (pages 142-144).
6. Provan Hall, 'Glasgow's most haunted' (pages 134).
7. Glasgow Cathedral and Graveyard (pages 27-34).
8. The Spiritualist Church Museum on Sauchiehall Street (pages 81-83).
9. The Auld Wives' Lifts near Milngavie (pages 147-148).
10. The 'Angel' sculpture in Gorbals (pages 154-156).

A FEW USEFUL CONCEPTS FOR THE JOURNEY

Apotropaic – That which protects against evil. Apotropaic actions include making the sign of the cross, speaking a charm or wearing an amulet. There are many apotropaic items in the KELVINGROVE, ST MUNGO'S and BURRELL museums.

Liminality – That which is betwixt and between, a transition, a threshold. A liminal time or place can either make a supernatural event more likely to occur, or it can provide the right conditions to make an act of magic more powerful. Liminal times are typically dusk and midnight, as well as dates such as Hallowe'en, Hogmanay, the solstices and equinoxes, and Beltane (1 May). Liminal events in our lives typically encompass first menstruation, marriage, childbirth, and the approach of death. Liminal places include caves, bogs, rivers – and, very importantly, boundaries.

Magical Thinking – This is the thought process that anyone who believes in magic, charms or witchcraft goes through. (Without 'scientific thinking' there would be no evidence-based research which allowed technology to advance; without magical thinking, there can be no magic.) In magical thinking, certain items – a saint's relics, water from a special source, an unusual stone – are regarded as possessing power. The benefits of this power can be transferred to you if you touch the object, or drink or wash in the water (or consume your husband's ashes – see HUNTERIAN ART GALLERY). This 'sympathetic magic' is based on the 'sympathy' between objects that are connected by physical proximity or similarity of form. This 'sympathy' is retained by objects, so if for example the clay figures at the heart of the POLLOK witchcraft case are tortured, the person depicted will feel the pain.

'Tradition' – Also known as 'it is said that' or 'they say that'. The term is often used to imply that the origins of the story concerned are lost in the mists of time, and that this antiquity is somehow a guarantor of truth. But traditions can be easily manipulated, or even manufactured out of thin air. Generally, I'd trust a tradition as far as I could throw a piano.

ARCHAEOLOGY

Relentless urban development has meant that most of Glasgow's archaeology is, to use a technical term, buggered. Few ancient ritual and funerary archaeological sites remain, although there are some examples of prehistoric rock art, particularly cup-and-ring-marked stones. The real purpose of these sometimes spectacular carvings remains speculative – they could be agricultural tallies, directions, tribal markers, illustrations of altered internal states, astronomical maps or means of communication with the dead or the gods – and that's just a few of the current theories. Glasgow has several enigmatic earthworks, the purposes of which (and even their dates) are not clearly understood (*see* POLLOK PARK, QUEEN'S PARK and RUTHERGLEN). I have barely touched on the Roman monuments of the Antonine Wall World Heritage Site, as although they are splendid, they are well covered in other works and there is little inherently 'mysterious' about them; Roman altars and religious inscriptions are described in the HUNTERIAN MUSEUM. Both the Hunterian and KELVINGROVE museums have significant local archaeological collections.

Archaeological terms:
Neolithic, *c.* 4000-2500 BC – The period of the chambered burial cairns.
Bronze Age, *c.* 2500-800 BC – Although stone circles and standing stones were being erected in the Late Neolithic, the Bronze Age was their apogee.
Iron Age, *c.* 800 BC-early centuries AD – Period of the historical Druids.

Dark Ages – The more familiar term for what archaeologists now call the Early Historic Period, roughly fifth to tenth century AD. In the centuries following the withdrawal of the Roman legions the Welsh-speaking Kingdom of Strathclyde rose to prominence in west-central Scotland, later to be carved up by the Angles or Northumbrians from the south-east, the Picts from the north, the Scots (who had moved over from Ireland) in the north and west, and the Vikings or Norse.

Much of the archaeological information here is taken from the excellent online 'Canmore' database of the Royal Commission on the Ancient and Historical Monuments of Scotland, www.rcahms.gov.uk. The West of Scotland Archaeology Service WoSAS website, www.wosas.org.uk, is also recommended, as is www.themodernantiquarian.com, the freewheeling user-generated site set up in the wake of Julian Cope's book *The Modern Antiquarian*. A most useful book is *Archaeology Around Glasgow* by Susan Hothersall (for further research, Hothersall's bibliography is on the website of the Glasgow Archaeological Society, www.glasarchsoc.org.uk).

A SUMMARY OF KEY HISTORICAL EVENTS

Glasgow's beginnings in the Dark Ages are usually stated as being tied up with the (semi-fictional at best) story of St Mungo (see below), but as Neil Baxter notes in *A Tale of Two Towns: A History of Medieval Glasgow*, 'In historical reality, Glasgow has no origins legend worth speaking of.' There were also early Christian sites at GOVAN and Inchinnan. Moving on to better-documented times, from the twelfth century Glasgow was a small hamlet established around the cathedral and stretching down the hill along Castle and High Street to a crossing of the Clyde at Saltmarket. The later medieval Glasgow bishops were Princes of the Earth, mighty rulers both spiritual and temporal of a vast diocese stretching to Cumbria, with powers akin to a minor King. After the Protestant Reformation of 1560, secular wealthy citizens acquired the lands of the church through a spectacular land-grab, and the centre of economic and political gravity shifted from the bishops to the merchants. Through an accident of geography the main conflict zones of the wars of the seventeenth and eighteenth centuries, from the Covenanters to the Jacobites, lay further east or north, and, for its size, Glasgow was relatively untouched by battle (the canny Glasgow merchants thought war and occupation was bad for business; when Bonnie Prince Charlie turned up they simply bought him off). The geography was dominated by the tidal River Clyde, which was both trade route and barrier, although it was much shallower than it is today – as late as the 1720s Daniel Defoe reported that he crossed the river at low tide 'dry-footed without the bridge'.

> Glasgow is a place of great extent and good situation; and has the reputation of the finest town in Scotland, not excepting Edinburgh.
>
> Revd Thomas Morer, *A Short Account of Scotland* (1702)
>
> Glasgow ... the beautifullest little city I have seen in Britain.
>
> Daniel Defoe, *A Journey Through Scotland* (1723)
>
> Glasgow ... launching its aerial cataracts towards the blue heavens from a thousand artificial volcanoes, which vomit forth their black Tartarean vapour in one continuous torrent.
>
> Unnamed nineteenth-century writer quoted in James J. Berry, *The Glasgow Necropolis*
>
> The Cancer of the Empire.
>
> William Bolitho, pamphlet title (1924)

These quotes demonstrate the transition of Glasgow from a prosperous and leafy eighteenth-century trading centre to an industrial megalopolis celebrated for its engineering and manufacturing, and at the same time infamous for its overcrowded slums, disease, crime and pollution.

TIMELINE

c. **603 or 614** Death of St Kentigern.

c. **1115** David I makes Glasgow the centre of the Church in the West of Scotland. Roughly the origin of Glasgow.

1136 First cathedral consecrated, built over Kentigern's grave.

1161 Pope Alexander III decrees that everyone within the vast diocese of Glasgow should make an annual pilgrimage to the shrine of St Kentigern.

1170s Glasgow granted Burgh of Barony by William the Lion. The town can now hold its own markets and impose tolls, removing it from the control of the royal burghs of Dumbarton and Rutherglen, who are not happy with the loss of revenue.
Population: around 1,500.

1175-1199 Bishop Jocelin. Like all the bishops, he is the political and financial leader and has great influence, appointing the burgesses and burgh officers (the people who run the town).

1180s The monk Jocelin of Furness writes his *Life of St Kentigern*.

1189 First cathedral destroyed by fire.

1197 Second cathedral consecrated.

1233 Work begins on the present cathedral.

1286 First mention of a bridge over the Clyde.

1349 The Black Death. Perhaps two-thirds of the population are wiped out. The plague returns in 1380 and 1381.

1451 The university established.

1492 Glasgow elevated to an Archbishopric.

1516 First crafts guilds founded.

1530s Two young Protestant martyrs are burned near the cathedral.
Population: 3,000.

1544 The Earl of Arran besieges and slaughters the Earl of Lennox's troops in the Bishop's Palace. Battle of the Butts between the Earl of Glencairn and the Earl of Arran. Arran's victorious army pillage Glasgow.
Population: 4,500.

1560 The Protestant Reformation – Roman Catholicism is removed as the state religion and its practice made illegal. The cathedral is damaged but the fabric is saved.

1568 Mary Queen of Scots defeated at the Battle of Langside.

1626 Tollbooth built.
Population: 7,500.

1636 Glasgow created a royal burgh. Merchants get richer.

1639 Glasgow is third in income of Scottish burghs.

1647 Plague. The university temporarily relocates to Irvine.

1652 Fire destroys a third of the town. A second devastating fire hits in 1677.

1707 The Act of Union with England opens up trade with the colonies in the New World. Boom time and the era of the super-rich Tobacco Lords. Glasgow is deeply involved in the triangular slave trade; goods are sent to Africa, exchanged for slaves, who in turn are traded for American tobacco and cotton which is then shipped back to Glasgow.

1740 Start of dredging of the Clyde to create a deepwater port. The task takes decades.

1745 Bonnie Prince Charlie and his Jacobite army extort £5,000 from the council in exchange for not sacking the city.

1746 The Jacobites, in retreat north, are bought off with £10,000 and an army's worth of shirts, waistcoats, stockings and trousers. The Prince holds a review on Glasgow Green, attracting only one recruit.
Population: 24,000 (1755).

1758 Glasgow's trade becomes the largest in Britain, eclipsing London.

1768-1790 Construction of the Forth and Clyde canal.

1776-1779 The American War of Independence closes the tobacco trade. Cotton becomes a major industry. The population soars with immigration from the surrounding counties and the largely Catholic West Highlands.

1780 First anti-Catholic riot.

1783 Chamber of Commerce formed – the first in Britain, and the second in the world after New York.

1785 First of many violent actions by organised groups of workers. More immigrants from the Highlands and Ireland.

Population: 64,000 (1791).

1800 The 'big bang' starts. Coal, iron and shipping industries take off.

Population: 80,000 (1801).

Population: 110,000 (1811).

1816 onwards: poverty caused by mill closures results in increased worker militancy, with strikes and riots.

1820 The 'Radical War' fiasco, an abortive working-class insurrection, suppressed with excessive brutality. Two leaders are executed in Stirling, others are transported. James Wilson, a weaver, is hanged and beheaded before a crowd of 20,000 on Glasgow Green.

Population: 200,000 (1831).

1840s Mass immigration from Ireland due to the potato famine. In the last half of the century 10-20 per cent of Glasgow's population originate from Ireland.

Population: 365,000 (1846).

Population: 550,000 (1889).

1900 20 per cent of the Scottish population now live in Glasgow. Sixteen people die of bubonic plague in Gorbals.

Population: over 760,000 (1901).

Population: 1 million (1914).

1920s and '30s Mass unemployment.

1941 The Blitz annihilates Clydebank. Other parts of Glasgow are also bombed.

1950s Start of inner-city communities being moved out to new towns.

Population: 1,100,000 (1951). The population has officially declined by about 25 per cent since, but boundary changes have made comparisons difficult.

1990 Glasgow is European City of Culture.

ST KENTIGERN (ST MUNGO)

St Kentigern was a late sixth-century holy man who was credited with kickstarting Glasgow as both a physical and a Christian community. But initially his cult and his fame were limited. Bishop Jocelin (1175-1199), one of the city's first entrepreneurs, and a visionary when it came to urban development and wealth creation, had grand plans for the nascent Glasgow. He wanted to build a great cathedral. He wanted to create a politically powerful diocese. And he wanted Glasgow to achieve fame throughout Christendom. To achieve all of this, he needed to appeal to the religious imagination of all classes of society. He needed bums on seats. Pilgrims visited the shrines of saints looking for both spiritual salvation and physical healing – and pilgrims meant donations, as well as economic spin-off benefits in the form of accommodation, meals, souvenirs, and so on. Jocelin had a saint (although he had yet to be officially canonised, which was a slight problem that needed to be addressed); all he needed now was a marketing campaign.

The man for the job was another Jocelin, a monk from Furness Abbey. Jocelin was a hack – a learned, conscientious hack, but a hack nonetheless. He had already written the biographies of King David I and saints Helen and Patrick. His *Life of Kentigern*, written around 1185 – 600 years after Kentigern flourished – pushed all the right buttons when it came to twelfth-century saint-making: Kentigern's birth, life and death are all accompanied by miracles; his behaviour

St Kentigern/Mungo letting Glasgow flourish, McNeil Street.

is exemplary and instructive; Roman Catholic orthodoxy is emphasised and Christianity is very clearly shown to triumph over its enemies. As a work of both persuasion and propaganda it is a *coup de théâtre*. Glasgow joined the list of must-see pilgrimage hot-spots around Europe. Pilgrims poured in, as did the money. The bishop got his cathedral, and his successors used the continuing revenues to aggrandise it. The Diocese of Glasgow became one of the largest in the land, stretching as far as the English border. And Kentigern received the official nod from Rome and became a *bona fide* saint.

Kentigern's potted biography, as featured in numerous websites and guidebooks, treats the standard episodes of his life as if they were indisputable facts, but almost nothing is known for certain about the man. Several ancient references give his death as variously occurring in AD 603, 612 and 614. Other than this, apart from a few brief references in Welsh manuscripts, we are in the realms of Jocelin of Furness's propagandist *ur*-text, to which all later elaborations are beholden. Jocelin tells us he based his work on two other works: a fragmentary *Life* written at the request of Bishop Herbert about twenty years earlier, which is included in Jocelin's work, and a possibly older Gaelic text which has not survived. He also admits rewriting these works to ensure conformity with current orthodoxy. The Roman Church had only triumphed over Celtic Christianity in Scotland in the previous century, and the original texts, Jocelin says, contained 'something contrary to sound doctrine, and to the Catholic faith.' They were 'tainted with what was perverse or opposed to the faith,' so he deliberately 'seasons what had been composed in a barbarous way with Roman salt.' Kentigern is one of the great legend-accumulating saints: the *Life* incorporates Arthurian lore and also contains stories and themes that may have been borrowed from other saints or even pre-Christian figures.

The *Life* begins with the older fragment. Thaney (Thenew), the Christian daughter of Leudonus, the half-pagan King of Leudonia (Lothian), was wooed by Ewen, the son of the King of Rheged. Owen, as he is more usually called, is identified by some as a Knight of the Round Table, Gawain's cousin, and King Arthur's nephew and possible successor (subsequent events make Kentigern Arthur's grand-nephew). The girl, however, had her mind on higher things. Enraged at her rejection of a good match, Leudonus had her enslaved to a swineherd, who treated the princess chastely because he was secretly a Christian. Owen then raped Thaney, who became pregnant and in punishment was thrown over a cliff. Her prayers ensured her survival, so she was then cast adrift in a coracle without oars on the Firth of Forth.

In a series of miraculous events the tiny craft travelled 30 miles (48km) to land on a beach at Culross, Thaney gave birth, and the boy was adopted by St Serf, who lived nearby and had been warned of the child's coming in a precognitive dream. At this point the fragment of the older *Life* ends and Jocelin's work continues the narrative, starting with a brief 'Previously in the Life of the Saint' recap, in which the sordid details of Kentigern's conception are glossed over and his pious mother is just said to be with child by means and father unknown. This is emphasised 'because the stupid and foolish people, who live in the diocese of S. Kentigern, go so far as to assert that he was conceived and born of a virgin.' The child is named as both Kyentyern, a status term perhaps signifying 'head-lord' or 'hound-lord', and Mungo, an informal name possibly meaning 'dear one' or 'gentle one'.

Once a man, Kentigern left Serf's school and in the area of Stirling arrived at the door of Fergus, a holy man who made Kentigern his executor just before his death. Kentigern yoked two wild bulls to the funeral cart and relied on the guidance of the Lord to take the body to the appropriate place, which turned out to be a small cemetery consecrated long before by St Ninian. The place was called Cathures, later known as Glasgu. The local elite, apparently already Christian, persuaded Kentigern to remain as their bishop, and he established a monastery on the site beside the Molendinar burn. During his residence, Kentigern is described as being ascetic and self-mortifying in the extreme. However, he was still a worker of miracles, as during a dispute between the Church and the local kinglet over food supplies, the Clyde miraculously rose and swept all the royal stores into the Church's granaries. Kentigern then travelled – possibly to get away from a hostile pagan ruler – and established Churches in Cumbria and Wales.

In later life Kentigern exchanged pastoral staffs with St Columba, who had travelled from Iona to greet his fellow missionary. At the age of 185, Kentigern prepared for death. In the pre-dawn:

> … an angel of the Lord appeared with unspeakable splendour, and the glory of God shone around him. And for fear of him the guardians of the holy bishop were exceedingly astonished and amazed, being but earthly vessels, and, unable to bear the weight of so great glory, became as dead men. But the holy old man, comforted by the vision and visit of the angel and, as it were, forgetting his age and infirmity, being made strong, experienced some foretastes of the blessedness now near at hand, and held close converse with the angel, as with his closest and dearest friend.

As instructed by the angel, Kentigern had a warm bath prepared, in which he calmly passed away. There now follows one of the strangest episodes in the *Life*: Kentigern's followers 'eagerly strove with each other to enter the water; and so, one by one, before the water cooled, they 'slept in the Lord in great peace, and having tasted death along with their holy bishop, they entered with him into the mansions of heaven.' Cultists commit mass suicide following death of charismatic leader? Where have we heard that before? Kentigern was buried to the right of the church altar in his church, and his followers interred in the cemetery in the order in which they had died. Jocelin tells us that King, Rhydderch, died the same year, and was buried in the same cemetery, where '665 saints rest.' Miracles occurred at Kentigern's grave, with the saint posthumously punishing the wicked.

Kentigern, in common with other saints from the Dark Ages, is portrayed as being a potent user of Christian magic. He resurrects a dead baker. People are cured by his shadow passing over them; rain, snow or hail does not wet his robes. He makes barren Queens fertile and curses hostile Kings with blindness, madness and gout. He parts the water of a river. He harnesses a compliant stag to the plough. The wicked are struck dead. When some of Columba's followers kill one of Kentigern's rams, the headless animal runs back to the flock while the head becomes as stone and is stuck to the miscreants' hands until Kentigern forgives them. Jocelin notes:

The bell, bird, tree, fish and ring on a lamp-post at Glasgow Cathedral.

'But the head turned into stone remaineth there unto this day, as a witness to the miracle.' (This is said to be the origin of the name RAMSHORN.) When milk gifted by Kentigern to a 'skilled artificer' accidentally spills into the Clyde it is not washed away but is shaped by the waves into blocks of cheese.

With supernatural assistance, Kentigern erects crosses of power at Glasgow and Lothwerverd (now Borthwick). Of the Glasgow cross, Jocelin says: 'Many maniacs, and those vexed with unclean spirits, are used to be tied of a Sunday night to that cross, and in the morning they are found restored, freed, and cleansed, though ofttimes they are found dead, or at the point of death.' When Kentigern is preaching to a multitude the ground on which he is standing rises up into a mound so everyone can see him – the event giving rise to the motto of the city, 'Let Glasgow flourish by the preaching of the Word and praising Thy Name!' The Victorians found the phrase too unwieldy so it became the shorter (and of course more business-friendly) 'Let Glasgow flourish!' (The only recent appearance of the full motto was when it was spelt out in lights on the Kelvin Hall during Billy Graham's evangelical campaign.)

None of these miracles, however, achieved the popular currency of the elements that made it to the arms of the city of Glasgow:

> There's the tree that never grew,
> There's the bird that never flew,
> There's the fish that never swam,
> There's the bell that never rang.

During his tutelage under St Serf, some fellow students, jealous of the teacher's pet, extinguished a fire Kentigern had been charged with maintaining. 'A wonderful and remarkable thing followed. Straightway fire coming forth from heaven, seizing the bough, as if the boy had exhaled flames for breath, sent forth fire, vomiting rays, and banished all the surrounding darkness.' This is 'the tree that never grew.'

The same men killed a favourite tame robin. Kentigern made the sign of the cross over it and restored it to life.

The fish is from a later period – Languoreth, good King Rhydderch's Queen, bedded a courtier and gave him a ring that had been a present from her husband. Rhydderch discovered the affair and surreptitiously removed the ring from the sleeping swain's finger and threw it into the river. He then accused Languoreth of unfaithfulness and demanded she show him the ring. She could not, and was incarcerated with instructions to produce the ring within three days or, if she insisted on proclaiming her innocence, face a trial by ordeal. Kentigern, responding to a supplication from the Queen, sent a messenger to fish the Clyde and return with the first catch. He was duly presented with a large salmon, which proved to have swallowed the ring.

This is an unusual case of a saintly tolerance of adultery, although the moral may be, as the narrative informs us, that thereafter Languoreth remained a faithful wife and good Christian. Many commentators have seen these stories as descending from pagan originals: the sacred fire, the sacrifice and rebirth of the oracular bird, the treasure in the belly of the beast, the ring of power (related to King Solomon's ring), the Irish myth of the Salmon of Wisdom. The 'bell that never rang,' however, is never mentioned in Jocelin's work. Later writers surmised it had been gifted by the Pope on one of Kentigern's seven (and most probably spurious) visits to Rome. One intriguing suggestion is given in Robert Craig MacLagan's *Scottish Myths*. In Jocelin's *Life*, an Irish bard visits Rhydderch's court and as a gesture of hospitality is offered a gift of his choosing. He requests a dish of fresh mulberries. This causes confusion in the court, because it is mid-winter, and yet they do not wish to insult an emissary from a fellow King. Kentigern miraculously obtains the fruits and the bard becomes a Christian. MacLagan suggests 'mul' means 'bell', although I am unable to confirm this. The tree, bird, fish and bell are a gift for designers, and have been endlessly reproduced around the city in stone, metal, logos, artworks and graphics.

Then there's Merlin. When Kentigern dies, King Rhydderch's 'fool' Laloecen prophesises that both Rhydderch and one of his chiefs will die in the same year, a prophecy which is later fulfilled. This appears to be Jocelin's expurgated version of a text known as *Vita Merlini Silvestris* which may have been written by whoever quilled the earlier *Life of Kentigern* commissioned by Bishop Herbert. In this, Kentigern befriends a wild man named Lailoken who comes to Glasgow and disrupts a church service with a prophesy of his own three-fold death later that day, to be followed within the year by the deaths of 'the most outstanding of the Kings of Britain, the holiest of the bishops, and the noblest of the lords.' That same day, Lailoken is at Drumelzier on the banks of the Tweed (having covered a mere 60 miles/96km in the interim) when, in fulfillment of the triple-death prophecy, he is mortally wounded by shepherds, thrown into the river, impaled on a stake of a fish-trap, and drowned.

Contemporary Welsh stories name Lailoken as Myrddin or Merlin, a Scottish prophet who went mad after witnessing a fratricidal battle he had instigated. At this point the sources become very muddied: this Myrddin is not the Arthurian magician, but a different individual altogether. However, Kentigern's *Life* was being composed at a time when stories of King Arthur were becoming widely circulated, and there seems to have been some form of cross-pollination, two popular figures absorbing aspects of each other's mythos. The Kentigernian Myrddin seems to have become transformed into Merlin the magician in works such as Geoffrey of Monmouth's *Vita Merlini*. The two Merlins became one (or perhaps two aspects of the same seer).

Kentigern is also associated with one of Scotland's few werewolves. The old ballad 'Kempion' or 'Kemp Owyne' tells how the fair maiden Isabel was transformed by her stepmother (it's always stepmothers, isn't it?) into a vile monster. In some versions she becomes a slimy sea beast, in others a fire-breathing dragon. The hero Prince Kempion – who seems to be Owen, a cultural hero of Scotland and northern England, and Kentigern's father (through rape) – gallantly kisses the repulsive creature three times and she returns to her comely self. As punishment, the stepmother is turned into a werewolf:

> Her hairs grow rough, and her teeths grow lang
> And on her four feet shall she gang;
> Nane shall take pity her upon,
> But in Wormeswood, aye, she shall be won;
> And relieved shall she never be
> 'Til Saint Mungo comes o'er the sea.

Wormeswood, or Wormie Wood, may be related to 'Wurm', the old word for a great serpent or monster. The ballad can be found in several publications, such as *English and Scottish Popular Ballads* by Francis James Child.

In *Buddhism in Pre-Christian Britain* (1928), Donald Mackenzie claimed that Buddhist missionaries sent westwards by the Indian emperor Ashoka had passed on their teachings to Druids in Celtic countries, and that this knowledge eventually made it to the form of Christianity practiced by Kentigern, with the motto 'Let Glasgow Flourish' deriving from a Buddhist mantra. Madness or genius, you be the judge.

PSYCHOGEOGRAPHY

There are as many definitions of psychogeography as there are psychogeographers. I define it as the way the physical environment has an unexpected, even spooky, effect on the mind. It's something about the ways the power of place – of specific places – seeps into the parts of our brains that conjure fear, imagination, wonder, curiosity and the sense of the uncanny. It's about why certain places are haunted, and others are haunting. It's about memory and surprises. It's about seeking out places where extraordinary events once happened. It's about walking the streets of the city and accidentally spotting a carving of an owl on a tenement lintel or finding a love letter chalked on a flagstone. It's about the unexpected, the hidden, the obscure and the ignored. It's about what this whole book is all about.

THE GLASGOW NETWORK OF ALIGNED SITES

It's virtually impossible to venture far into exploring Glasgow's strange geography without encountering the Glasgow Network of Aligned Sites, a concept put forward by the late Harry

Bell in his 1984 book *Glasgow's Secret Geometry* and elaborated on the website www.geocities. com/alignedsites. Bell's 'prehistoric site alignments' (or PSAs) are sites that are aligned on hilltops fringing the Clyde basin. His theory is that they were the means by which prehistoric peoples orientated themselves in the low-lying forested land of the valley, setting up domestic or ritual sites on viewpoints that were aligned on the prominent surrounding peaks. Initially, the idea goes, the sites were on a line of sight between intervisible points, while four key places – Carmyle, Camphill, Crookston and the Necropolis – became nodes which themselves became foci for alignments from other sites. Bell's notion is that the alignments were purely practical devices, used by people who employed skyline markers in the local topography for navigation purposes. There was no grand plan, no 'structure', and no priestly class setting out sacred lines. Bell rejected the idea that the alignments were tracks – their straight lines crossed bogs, rivers without fords and other obstacles – or that they had any connection with ley-lines, energy lines, spirit paths, underground water, or anything else mystical (which hasn't stopped shamanic flyers, dowsers and ley-line enthusiasts falling in love with Glasgow's 'secret geometry'.)

Bell claimed that the PSAs ran through not just central Glasgow but also ancient sites in Rutherglen, Castlemilk, Carmunnock, Bothwell, Hamilton, East Kilbride, Govan, Renfrew, Inchinnan, Paisley, Dumbarton, Old Kilpatrick, Drumchapel, Easterhouse and Kilsyth. At the core of the network was an unintentional triangle, with the base running through Carmyle Fords, Gallowflat Mound, Rutherglen Church, Camphill earthwork and Crookston Castle, and the other two sides stretching diagonally up from Carmyle and Crookston respectively to cross at the Necropolis; another PSA ran from Camphill to the Necropolis.

Bell's original and thoroughly-researched ideas may have merit; it's fair to say that they also come in for much criticism, some of which Bell himself acknowledged as possibly valid. Some of the alignments could be coincidental, or simply a case of drawing too many lines on a map with the eye of faith. In many cases he also includes medieval sites constructed long after the prehistoric period – here he plausibly argued that these were reused sites built over more ancient structures, which in some (but only some) cases has indeed been proven to be the case through recent excavation. The weakest link is the notion that Carmyle Fords is a key node. Unlike Crookston, the Necropolis and Camphill, the fords are on low ground, and if there were ever prehistoric structures higher up in the immediate area, urban development has long eradicated them.

The section entitled 'Confessions of a New Age Publisher' on the website contains some of Bell's wryly amusing reflections on his past. In 1977 he cobbled together then-current fringe ideas on ley-lines – 'Are they psychic telegraph wires? Flying-saucer flight lanes? Prehistoric trading routes?' – and self-published a short book on Scottish sites, *Forgotten Footsteps*. Bell writes, 'It could truthfully have been described as a crime against archaeology ... Nothing I have written since has been so poorly researched or so profitable.'

May Miles Thomas has explicitly followed in Bell's footsteps with www.devilsplantation.co.uk, a project to 'explore the Secret Geometry of Glasgow and find magic in ordinary places.' The 'Devil's Plantation' of the title is Bonnyton Mound, a prehistoric burial south-east of NEWTON MEARNS, the spot where Bell began his exploration into PSAs. The paranormal drama series *Sea of Souls* adapted some of the 'aligned sites' concepts for one of its episodes, including the triangle (*see* RIDDRIE).

DRUIDS

There is joy in footing slow across a silent plain
Where Patriot Battle has been fought when Glory had the gain,
There is a pleasure on the heath where Druids old have been,
Where Mantles grey have rustled by and swept the nettles green.
John Keats, 'There is joy in footing slow across a silent plain.' (*c.* 1818)

There are three kinds of Druids: the historical Druids described by the Classical writers and Early Christian chroniclers who encountered these formidable cultural leaders in the centuries either side of the birth of Christ; those who follow one of the several paths of modern Druidry; and figments of utter, outright, bonkers fantasy. It is these latter who supposedly built Stonehenge and other stone circles (which were actually constructed by much earlier peoples). Seventeenth- and eighteenth-century antiquarians invented these Druids, and saw themselves as the lineal intellectual descendents of the Druidic elite – learned, wise, sagacious. The Druids' appeal for antiquarians was not just this, however: Druids were *cool*. They were not mere fusty academics, they were respected and feared, they communicated with the gods – and they went in for human sacrifice. From the safety of a scholarly study, this was very cool indeed. And as they were so clever and cool, it must have been them who erected the megaliths, which were 'obviously' used for blood sacrifice. This series of mistaken assumptions and enthusiasms has been a heady and popular brew for centuries now, and is proving difficult to shake off. Stone circles and standing stones are not Druidic. Historical Druids from the Iron or Dark Ages do not leave archaeological traces; there is no actual evidence to associate Druids with any specific ancient sites in Glasgow, and any attempts to do so merely tell us about the Druidic fantasies of the claimants (*see* AULD WIVES' LIFTS, KILBOWIE, GOVAN and THE NECROPOLIS).

FICTION

Where possible I have included references to Glasgow-related works of science fiction, horror or fantasy – such as those by Grant Morrison and Bram Stoker – in the geographical chapters. Space precludes a full list of works of the fantastic, but for a taster try:

Mr Alfred MA (George Friel, 1972). A disappointed schoolteacher meets the Devil in the form of a man who intends to bring down civilization by generating graffiti and gang violence.

Lanark (Alasdair Gray, 1982). *The* Glasgow novel of the fantastic, with unlovely, realistic Glasgow somehow related to the insane, nightmarish city of Unthank.

Poor Things (Alasdair Gray, 1992). *Frankenstein* in Victorian Glasgow. Sort of.

So I Am Glad (A.L. Kennedy, 1995). An emotionally-frozen woman living in Partick finds her new flatmate is the resurrected Cyrano de Bergerac.

Strange Weather Lately (Metaphrog, 1999). Bonkers graphic novel in which Glasgow natives encounter hallucinatory divinities, trickster spirits and Surrealists.

RECOMMENDED FILMS AND TELEVISION SET IN GLASGOW

Deathwatch (1980). Moody dystopian film set in a society where death is taboo. An undercover journalist starts a relationship with a dying woman and secretly films her final days for a voyeuristic television audience.

Urban Ghost Story (1998). A troubled adolescent living in a tower block has a near-death experience and apparently brings something back from the other side. Loosely influenced by real poltergeist incidents.

Sea of Souls (2005). BBC drama series in which a team from the Department of Parapsychology at 'Clyde University' investigate paranormal cases, including curses, poltergeists and reincarnation.

The Silent Watchers #1: Mercury, god of trade and thieves, merchandise and magic, with his winged helmet, Bothwell Street.

The Silent Watchers #2: Athena, goddess of wisdom, valour and the arts, 40 St Enoch Square.

The Silent Watchers #3: Green Man, University of Glasgow.

SOURCES

A few books I return to again and again, because they are unbeatable: Hugh Macdonald's *Rambles Round Glasgow* (1854), in which Mr Macdonald peregrinates and pontificates with equal pleasure, and Robert Alison's *Anecdotage of Glasgow* (1892), which is stuffed with endlessly quotable anecdotes. For help in identifying the Silent Watchers, I have had frequent recourse to Ray Mackenzie's indispensable *Sculpture in Glasgow* and *Public Sculpture of Glasgow*, as well as the Glasgow, City of Sculpture website, www.glasgowsculpture.com, and *The Buildings of Scotland: Glasgow* by Elizabeth Williamson *et al.* Much useful background material was viewed online from Virtual Mitchell (www.mitchelllibrary.org/virtualmitchell) and The Glasgow Story (www.theglasgowstory.com), while several contemporary reports came from the Hidden Glasgow forum (www.hiddenglasgow.com).

All other sources are mentioned in the text, with oft-referenced works being Tom Rannachan's *Psychic Scotland*, in which the medium discusses his contacts with the dead, and the various sightings of strange things in the sky logged in Ron Holliday's *UFO Scotland*. If you want to delve further, all the works consulted are included in the bibliography.

GLOSSARY – THE SILENT WATCHERS

Symbols are oracular forms – mysterious patterns creating vortices in the substances of the invisible world. They are centers of a mighty force, figures pregnant with an awful power, which, when properly fashioned, loose fiery whirlwinds upon the earth.

Manly P. Hall, *Lectures on Ancient Philosophy* (1929)

By and large, Glasgow's amazing public sculpture is an epiphenomenon of the triple obsessions of the Victorian elite – commerce, industry and religion. There are hundreds of allegorical figures personifying virtues such as Prudence, Thrift, Progress and Charity, or activities like Engineering, Shipbuilding, Agriculture and Science, so in the pages that follow I only mention the best of these. There are, however, more interesting members of the Silent Watchers collective, including:

Amphitrite – Greek goddess of the sea and wife of Poseidon (the Roman version of Neptune).

Angels – Biblical angels are male (or perhaps more accurately non-gender), but many Glaswegian angels are bountifully female.

Apollo – Greek god of the sun, oracles, medicine and the arts. He is always seen with his lyre, and often associated with solar imagery.

Athena – Greek goddess of wisdom, rationality, heroic endeavour and the arts. Identified by her helmet, shield and owl.

Atlantes – The plural of Atlas, the Greek giant who supported the heavens.

Aurora – Roman goddess of the dawn.

Beehive – Symbol of both industry and co-operation, and hence adopted by both elite and workers' organisations.

Caryatid – A supporting column sculptured in the form of a female figure. The original caryatids were priestesses of the Greek goddess Artemis.

Cybele – The Greek and Roman goddess of the fertile Earth.

Europa – A woman who was seduced by the Greek god Zeus disguised as a bull.

Four Evangelists – The supposed authors of the Christian Gospels, each with their own iconography: Matthew (represented by a man or angel); Mark (a lion, often winged); Luke (a bull, ditto); and John (an eagle).

Green Man – A male face either composed of leaves (a 'foliate head') or spewing vegetation from its mouth, nose, eyes etc. Its possible pagan/fertility origins are much debated. In a Christian context it may represent Adam, Christ or resurrection. Variants include Green Lions (who may represent St Mark), Green Demons etc.

Griffin/Gryphon – Half-eagle/half-lion mythological creature, noted as a guardian of secrets or hidden treasure.

Hippocampus – A marine creature from Greek mythology, with the front of a horse and the rear of a fish.

Mercury – Roman god of trade and profit (hence his popularity with Glasgow's merchants), but also protector of gamblers, liars and thieves (hmmm…). The swift messenger of the gods, guide of the recently dead, and patron of magic. Identified by his caduceus or wand, a short, winged staff entwined with serpents in a double helix, and his winged sandals and hat.

The Silent Watchers
#4: Unhappy bishop,
St Mungo's Church,
Townhead.

Neptune – Trident-carrying Roman god of the sea (the Greek Poseidon).

Pelican – Early Christian writers thought the pelican fed its young with its own blood; it is a symbol of charity or of Christ himself.

Serpents/Snakes – In Christian contexts, a symbol of evil. Elsewhere can mean wisdom, knowledge or healing. A snake biting its own tail usually signifies eternity, rebirth or the endless cycle of the universe; it can also refer to the Worm Ourobourus, an alchemical symbol.

Titans – Giants who ruled the world before the advent of the Greek gods of Olympus such as Zeus, Apollo, Athena etc.

Triton – A Greek sea deity, the son of Poseidon and Amphitrite, usually identified by the conch shell he used to control the waves.

Vulcan – The blacksmith god of the Romans.

Zephyr – Greek god of the west wind.

1

CITY CENTRE: NORTH & EAST

GLASGOW CATHEDRAL

Cathedral Square. Cared for by Historic Scotland. Open all year: Monday to Saturday, 9.30 a.m. to 5.30 p.m. (4.30 p.m. in winter), Sunday, 1 p.m. to 5 p.m. (4.30 p.m. in winter). Good wheelchair access to upper church, access to lower church by asking steward.

> The pile is of a gloomy and massive, rather than of an elegant, style of Gothic architecture; but its peculiar character is so strongly preserved, and so well suited with the accompaniments that surround it, that the impression of the first view was awful and solemn in the extreme.
>
> Walter Scott, *Rob Roy* (1817)

The cathedral is the *omphalos* of Glasgow. It is where the city effectively began, and is claimed to be sited over three ancient Christian sepulchres – a fifth-century graveyard consecrated by St Ninian, the sixth-century grave of St Fergus, and the tomb and shrine of St Kentigern. The first cathedral was dedicated in 1136, only to be destroyed by fire forty years later. The present building dates from the thirteenth to the fifteenth centuries. Despite having been knocked about a bit, it is the only cathedral on the Scottish mainland to have survived the Reformation intact (for much of the following centuries it was known as the High Church). It consists of two levels, the upper church and lower church or crypt, with the latter being built into the steep slope at the east end. A guidebook is available, so here I will concentrate on the areas of our particular interest.

The keynote of the cathedral is that it functioned as the great shrine of the cult of St Kentigern. Pilgrims rich and poor poured into the church, seeking access to the relics of the saint. It is this factor which influenced the architecture, in both managing the pilgrim footfall, and creating a theatrical semi-subterranean enclosed space for high-drama scenes of miracles and healing. What is so special about Glasgow is that the current architecture still allows the modern visitor to reconstruct this medieval wonder-space. (This section owes much to Peter Yeoman's excellent *Pilgrimage in Medieval Scotland*, in which he notes, 'the siting of the crypt was determined by the desire to create the most splendid pilgrimage site in the country.') The pilgrims entered from the west and walked through the north and south aisles of the choir to the feretory bay behind the high altar. Here was the elaborate shrine containing the saint's bones, which Bishop Jocelin had removed from the actual tomb. The atmosphere would have been heady – there was probably a tapestry illustrating Kentigern's life and miracles, as well as incense, and candlelight reflecting off the gold, silver and precious stones of the reliquary.

Via a one-way crowd-control system the pilgrims descended darkened steps into the crypt where natural light fell on the richly arcaded tomb, which stood directly below the shrine in the feretory. Even though the tomb was empty, it remained a focus of power. At busy times the crypt would have been hot and claustrophobic, which, combined with the emotionally aroused state of the pilgrims, probably created intense, overwhelming experiences which contributed to outbreaks of 'miraculous' cures.

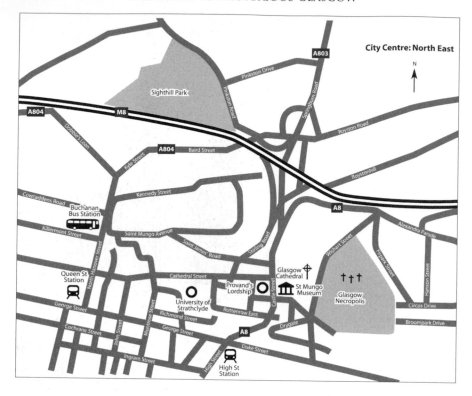

Relics

Glasgow was one of the twenty-one principal places of pilgrimage in Scotland. Yeoman speaks of 'the power which leaked from shrines, which was the power of the Holy Spirit on earth contained in relics.' Through sympathetic magic (usually involving miracles of healing or conception), saintly relics strengthened the faith of the newly converted and valorised the beliefs of the suffering faithful. Relics were powerful totems of Christian magic, and as a great pilgrimage destination, Glasgow had an extensive stock of them. Cleland's *Annals of Glasgow* includes a list from the fifteenth century:

> A splinter from the True Cross.
> The Blessed Virgin Mary's girdle, breast milk (acquired during the Crusades) and some of her hairs.
> Part of the Holy Manger.
> The scourges and combs of St Thomas Becket and St Kentigern and a part of the latter's hair shirt.
> Sundry bones of Saints Kentigern, Thenew, Bartholomew the Apostle, Thomas Becket, Ninian, Magdalene, Eugene and Blaze, as well as several other saints.
> A small phial containing a saffron-coloured liquor, 'which flowed of old from the tomb of Kentigern.'
> Part of St Martin's cloak, which he had cut up to give to a pauper.
> Part of the tomb of St Catherine the Virgin in the Sinai desert, said to be the most remote in Christendom.
> And numerous crosses, containers and images wrought in precious metals and stones.

The several relics of Becket of Canterbury hint at Bishop Jocelin's political agenda. The early Christian saints were martyrs, but in more recent centuries holy men had not usually been murdered for their faith. Becket, killed in 1170 on the orders of Henry II, was the first

Glasgow Cathedral from the Zen
Garden of St Mungo's Museum
of Religious Life and Art.

martyr for hundreds of years, and his powers of intercession were deemed to be especially
strong. Jocelin promoted Kentigern by associating him with the popular Becket. He visited
Canterbury to forge links, clearly obtaining some relics in the process, had a chapel dedicated
to Becket in Glasgow, and constructed Kentigern's shrine in a similar underground manner to
Becket's, which sits in the crypt beneath the choir at Canterbury. In 1560, one month before
the Catholic Church was officially displaced in Scotland, Archbishop Beaton took all the relics
to France to protect them from the wrath of the Reformers. The treasures remained in the
Scots College in Paris until the French Revolution, at which point they all vanished.

Exterior

The walls of the nave have double rows of wonderful boar's-head gargoyles, with their lower jaws
elaborated into griffins, monkeys and human caricatures. The walls of the projecting Blacader
Aisle to the south are decorated with very worn carvings of Adam and Eve flanking the serpent
winding round the tree, what appears to be the Devil hosting a pointed spear like a javelin, a
unicorn, three different dragons and a spotted beast which may be a pard. The pard is described
in early medieval bestiaries as having a spotted coat and being fierce and swift. It is clearly a
leopard, but the bestiaries insist the latter beast is the degenerate offspring of a pard and a lion.

The buttresses and walls of the little-visited north-east corner opposite the Necropolis
hosts one of Glasgow's little mysteries: an argument concerning the existence of God, carved
in stone. The inscriptions are worn; I have inserted the missing words in square brackets.
One block reads. '[The] Philosopher says "When Death is, we are not; the body dies, and
with it all. There is No Future; Mortal is the Soul. Hence Ancient [fools are] superstition's
prey".' The 'Philosopher' is presumably the Roman writer Lucretius, from whom the quote is
taken, but it could equally apply to Voltaire, who popularised it in his *Philosophical Dictionary*.

A religious argument in stone; the mysterious inscriptions on Glasgow Cathedral.

Voltaire (1694-1778) was one of the foremost European thinkers in the cause of intellectual and political liberty; his works were widely read by radicals, atheists and freethinkers.

Immediately below it in another hand is carved: 'The everlasting God who created all things [is equally] present [in all places throughout] the whole extent of infinite space.' This is from Joseph Addison (1672-1719), English essayist and the founder of *The Spectator* magazine. The quote is in his 'Letter No. 580' (13 August 1714), but was widely reprinted in later 'improving' literature of the Georgian period. So we appear to have two anonymous eighteenth- or nineteenth-century individuals having a theological dust-up and carving their respective arguments into the fabric of the cathedral. Another stone has the eroded carving: '[?] well with all the vanitys of time may all my Friends be servants of the living God [?] after I [?]ring in the dust.' If this is a quote I have been unable to identify it. The inscription below is too worn to make out a single word. Nearby are simple names or memorials ('JAs.C McG.1797 1816') and the standard cheery gravestone legend: 'O Man Remember That Thou Must And Shall Die'. This motley collection is the only example I know of vernacular inscriptions on a cathedral.

Upper Church

Pairs of figures on the rood screen represent the Seven Ages of Man. The eleven men in cassocks on the altar platforms are probably the Apostles, Judas having been unavoidably detained. The bullet holes in the oak door of the sacristy probably date from one of the foiled attempts by the Reformers to sack the cathedral. A plaque to the 74th Highlanders in the nave is carved with a sphinx, commemorating their Egyptian campaigns. One memorial features a skull and crossbones with an hourglass rising on gold-painted wings, while on another a brass-winged figure holding the medical caduceus shelters a young woman who is treading on a lively serpent. The underside of a canopied chair is carved with a tiny full-colour ladybird, a memento from the crew of a Second World War motor torpedo boat – shortly after they found the 'lucky' ladybird on board they survived an enemy attack. Several archaeological investigations since the 1990s have uncovered dozens of burials throughout all parts the building, dating from before the first cathedral of 1136 right through to the nineteenth century. The south transept had many redeposited bones scattered in an unceremonial manner – it is not known why this was so. In 1837 a hoard of 130 gold coins was uncovered, probably deposited about 1380.

Lower Church

An extensive range of low-browed dark and twilight vaults … [with] darker and more extensive caverns yawning around waste regions of oblivion.

Walter Scott, *Rob Roy*

The empty tomb remains the focus of the vaulted crypt. Nearby is St Mungo's Well, which may have been sacred before the cathedral was built, as it is deliberately included in the fabric. Little is known of how this holy well was used, although Peter Yeoman suggests it was either associated with miracles of healing, or it supplied the pilgrims' ampullae (souvenir containers) with holy water. In 1614 it was described as the 'idolatrous well'. T.C.F. Brotchie's 1914 article 'The Holy Wells in and around Glasgow' claimed that 'Mungo adopted this well from the pagans, and changed its purpose from evil to good.' Brotchie also relates a personal experience of the continuing veneration for the well. He and a friend saw 'a poorly clad woman with a child in her arms pass by, and seat herself on the stone ledge of the saint's well. She was young, but care and sorrow had obviously broken her spirit, and left their traces on her features. After resting herself she evidently engaged in prayer.' Asked why she came there, she replied, 'Oh sir, I just come to wish. My man's no' very guid to me, and when he's bad I come to the guid well and wish, and aye after I wish my man's kinder to me.'

Excavations in 1978 uncovered a second water feature elsewhere in the crypt, a circular stone-lined basin or cistern with a lead-pipe supply. It may have functioned as a store for the well's holy water, or might be a drain from a piscina, where the ceremonial vessels were washed, or it may have had some other ritual function.

The door, carved with very worn figures and animals, leads to the Chapter House, where excavation found five early nineteenth-century skeletons, a remnant of the time when the heritors of the Barony parish, who had used the crypt as their church after the Reformation, used parts of the lower church as a graveyard. The burial ground was only reclaimed for the cathedral in 1835.

The vaulted Blacader Aisle (no wheelchair access) was probably the site of the grave of St Fergus, which Jocelin records having seen in his *Life of Kentigern*. A spandrel facing the entrance is carved with the two-wheeled cart and wild bulls that brought Fergus' body to the site, and an inscription reads, 'This Is Ye Ille Of Car Fergus.' The carvings here are the best in the cathedral. On the roof bosses, vegetation spews from the mouths of long-haired Green Men and monsters, griffons and dragons. Kings, beatific faces, boars, human-headed birds and composite monsters stare down at us. Grotesques grimace from capitals and corbels, accompanied by animals, running figures, more ugly faces spewing vegetation and a strange triple-faced head, while a man in a painted blue jerkin stands on (or urinates upon?) a ruddy demon.

In *Glimpses of old Glasgow* (1894) Andrew Aird describes 'a well-known Glasgow myth regarding an ill-fated piper and his dog, lost in the maze of the Subterranean Way, popularly believed to exist between the vaults of the cathedral and those of the old kirk of Rutherglen.' The 'Piper in the Tunnel' tale is one of the most widespread folkloric motifs in Scotland, being found in dozens of places from Edinburgh to Arran and the Highlands. Usually the piper's music is heard from above ground until *something awful* gets him in the tunnel, and the dog is eventually found, often half-starved and hairless. Aird ascribes the tale to the masons who stayed south of the river while building the cathedral:

The ancient brethren of the mystic tie, therefore, formed a rude path over the Gallowmuir, in their daily journeys between the two little towns, crossing the Clyde at one of the fords. To this circumstance, aided by the superstitious fancies of a rude age, impressed with awe at the mystic Masonic ceremonies and processions attendant on the great work going on in Glasgow, may be ascribed the above myth; just as another myth, probably from the same cause, associates the builders of the 'Hie Kirk' with a race of pigmies.

LEGENDS OF THE GLASGOW BISHOPS

After his death, the body of Bishop Baldred, supposedly Kentigern's successor, was miraculously triplicated to satisfy the demands of three churches that claimed his remains. In *The Book of Glasgow Cathedral*, however, George Eyre-Todd shows that Baldred died on the east coast in 756, a century and a half after the time of Kentigern, and had no connection with Glasgow.

In 1525, as part of the ongoing political turmoil between Scotland and England, Archbishop Gavin Dunbar (1524-1547) issued a formal holy curse on the reivers who were bringing murder and destruction to the Borders region on the southern edge of the Strathclyde diocese. The 1,069-word curse was read out by priests in every parish. Highlights of the curse include:

> I curse their heid and all the haris of thair heid … The thunnour and fireflauchtis [lightning] that set doun as rane apon the cities of Zodoma and Gomora … rane apon thame, and birne thaim … I condemn thaim perpetualie to the deip pit of hell … first to be hangit, syne revin and ruggit [then ripped and torn] with doggis, swyne, and utheris wyld beists, abhominable to all the warld.

Crikey. In 2000, as part of Carlisle's millennium celebrations, the city commissioned a piece of art, a 14-ton granite boulder with 363 words of the curse inscribed on it. Within weeks of the installation Kevin Davis, vicar of Scotby, wrote, 'This stone, whatever the council's intention, is a lethal weapon. Its spiritual violence will act like a cancer underneath the fabric of society.' By 2005 councillor Tim Tootle had blamed the malediction for bringing disasters of 'Biblical proportions' to Carlisle, citing the foot-and-mouth outbreak, floods, fire, mass redundancy and the relegation of Carlisle United from the Football League. Psychics and healers travelled to Carlisle to exorcise the boulder, the local bishop was reported to have asked his Glasgow counterpart to lift the curse, and Uri Geller offered to help. The story was widely reported in March, in *The Times*, *The Guardian*, the BBC News website, and in the *Carlisle News & Star*. Carlisle Council debated a motion to have the stone destroyed or put outside the city boundaries, but only two councillors voted for the motion, and the Curse Stone remains in place – as one wit remarked, 'from Glasgow, with love.'

The Anecdotage of Glasgow describes Archbishop Leighton (1670-1674) being waylaid *en route* to Dunblane by two chancers, one of whom pretended to have been killed in a recent lightning strike, while the other begged money from the prelate to bury his friend. When the man returned with the coins Leighton had generously handed over, he found his prostrate companion had actually died. 'Oh, sir, he is dead! Oh, sir, he is dead!' he exclaimed, on which the archbishop, having thus been alerted to the fraud, gravely intoned, 'It is a dangerous thing to trifle with the judgments of God!' For a legend associated with the fifteenth-century Bishop Cameron (*see* BISHOP'S LOCH).

THE CATHEDRAL GRAVEYARD

> The broad flat monumental stones are placed so close to each other, that the precincts appear to be flagged with them … these sad records of mortality, the vain sorrows which they preserve, the stern lesson which they teach of the nothingness of humanity, the extent of ground which they so closely cover, and their uniform and melancholy tenor.
>
> Walter Scott, *Rob Roy*

In *A Historical account of the belief in Witchcraft in Scotland*, Charles Kirkpatrick Sharpe notes an episode which occurred in around 1720. A man passing through the churchyard at midnight saw a neighbour, lately buried, rise out of his grave and dance a jig with the Devil, who played the air 'Whistle o'er the lave o't' on the bagpipes. The episode apparently struck the city with such horror that the town drummer was sent through the streets the next morning to forbid anyone to play, sing or whistle the tune. The older part of the graveyard contains tombstones carved with skulls, winged hourglasses, crossed bones, sexton's tools, a winged head and two leoform sphinxes flanking a pair of coiled snakes.

Ted Ramsey (*Don't Walk Down College Street*) notes that many of the city's poor were buried in the area without any gravestones on the north-west side of the graveyard. He describes a continuous trench being dug, with the fresh soil being used to cover the most recent graves. The common grave zigzagged through the area until it reached its starting place, for the cycle to begin again. Old bones or coffin remnants were burned or thrown back in. In his booklet *The Glasgow Necropolis*, James Berry quotes a letter written to the lord provost: 'There were, not long ago, in the St Mungo's new burying ground, a pit or common grave for persons who died in the infirmary. This receptacle was covered by a few planks, and the stench emitted in hot weather was insufferable.'

In 1997 an archaeological dig outside the graveyard wall uncovered an adult skeleton, an infant's skull and a fragmented adult skull. These may have been the mad and the unbaptised, who were forbidden interment in consecrated ground.

The proximity of the cathedral graveyard to the medical schools meant that freshly buried bodies were often stolen for the anatomists' dissecting tables. In 1803 the magistrates offered twenty guineas for information on the person who had stolen the corpse of a woman. In an article from 1867 delightfully titled 'Reminiscences of Body Lifting', Dr G. Buchanan goes to great lengths to justify the actions of the anatomists (the cutting is unsourced – see the bibliography for details). He describes the typical raiding party – four medical students armed with a dark lantern, an old carpet, a sack and tools, and two who acted as lookouts. Once one-third of the coffin lid was exposed, the strongest of the team descended into the grave with a crowbar to wrench the lid open, while the carpet was thrown over the pit to hide the lantern and deaden the noise. A noose was put around the corpse's neck and the others pulled it onto the surface and into the sack. The grave was then refilled and tidied up. Buchanan states that these details were 'related to me by one who was not unfrequently present at these predatory excursions.' He also notes that until recently 'a pistol used to be fired in one of the graveyards near the High Church at midnight, to give notice that the watch is set, and firearms are kept on the premises.' Buchanan notes that the dead were protected with lethal weapons, but at night the living had to make do with 'a set of lazy old men, armed, not with guns and pistols, but only with stout sticks.'

The Anecdotage of Glasgow describes how two watchmen in the churchyard found a body in a sack while the grave robbers were making sure the coast was clear. One watchman changed places with the corpse and was lifted up on the shoulder of a brawny student, who then in the dark asked his companion for directions. The suddenly-animated corpse grabbed him by hair and in deathly voice intoned 'doon the Rottonrow, ye scoundrel!' This may be something of a bodysnatching urban myth, as almost exactly the same story is told elsewhere in Scotland (in Perth, for example, where the 'corpse' comes alive in an old barrow). Robert Southey, the Poet Laureate, watched a grave being dug here (from *Journal of a Tour in Scotland in 1819*):

> A frame consisting of iron rods was fixed in the grave, the rods being as long as the grave is deep. Within this frame the coffin was to be let down and buried, and then an iron cover fitted on to the top of the rods, and strongly locked. When there is no longer any apprehension of danger from the resurrection-men, the cover is unlocked and the frame drawn out: a month it seems is the regular term. This invention, which is not liable to the same legal objection as the iron coffins, is about two years old. The price paid for its use is a shilling per day … I see that hearses in Scotland are ornamented with gilt death's-heads and cross-bones!

The extract is in *Glasgow Observed* by Simon Berry and Hamish Whyte. Iron cages can still be seen around some graves. In 1823 medical student Alexander McGowan of County Down was caught stealing the just-buried corpse of weaver Thomas Seggie. Ramsey says that he was beaten unconscious by a mob from the Drygate, who then proceeded to loot two schools of anatomy and pile up all the bodies found there outside the police station. McGowan was charged but skipped bail and fled to Ireland, so he was declared a fugitive and an outlaw.

On another occasion nineteen-year-old John Carmichael was apprehended in the graveyard itself, his accomplices having fled. He was charged with violating the sepulchre of building worker John Dempster, although the case was never brought to trial (possibly after the Dempster family were bought off by the wealthy Carmichaels).

THE ROYAL INFIRMARY

Titanic-helmeted and wreathed female heads loom out of the south façade of this imposing building, and a large bronze of Queen Victoria presides over the entrance. Binoculars will reveal the tiny cameo of her beloved Albert on her tunic. In 1860 Joseph Lister had responsibility for wards twenty-four and twenty-five, and was puzzled at the number of deaths in ward twenty-three. Investigation revealed that ward twenty-four lay over a part of the burial ground filled with the hastily-buried and heaped coffins and bodies from the cholera epidemic of 1849 (in retrospect, it probably wasn't a good idea to build a hospital right next to the city's most overcrowded and unsanitary graveyard). Ward twenty-three was closed and carbolic acid and quicklime was poured over the corrupting mass, followed by a new layer of earth. Lister went on to be the pioneer of antiseptics. Bodies continued to have a value for the unscrupulous – infirmary gravedigger William Robertson stole the teeth from a woman who had died of fever in the infirmary, and sold them to a manufacturer of false teeth. He was incarcerated for sixty days.

The hospital is renowned for its several ghosts. *The Guardian* for 22 December 2004 quotes Judith Whalley, who as a young nurse at the infirmary saw a ward sister coming towards her on a top floor corridor. 'As she walked by, I said, "Evening, sister." Then I realised I could see her only from the knees up.' Whalley, now a risk manager at City Hospital, Birmingham and a NHS professional for thirty years, believed the building had been altered: 'She seemed to be walking along an older floor level.'

In *Psychic Scotland*, Tom Rannachan mentions meeting an old man in a pub in High Street who had worked as a hospital night porter in the 1950s or '60s. He claimed to have twice seen a grey figure, and also a stern-looking ward sister who would float through the corridors oblivious to the living staff, although Rannachan couldn't tell if he was having his leg pulled for a pint. Dane Love's *Scottish Spectres* says that, at some unknown date, staff were caring for a patient with an excitable nature. He escaped from his bed into the corridor and was about to jump over the banister. A nurse attempted to stop him, but she herself ending up plunging down the stairwell. Despite attempts at resuscitation she died shortly after, and she appears to be the Green Lady, a helpful spirit who has been reported many times. Then there is also supposedly 'Archie' (who has acquired a nickname for no other reason than he looks like an Archie), an elderly man in a bonnet who chats to dying patients in ward twenty-seven, and an unprovenanced report of a hurrying doctor being asked by a patient to point the way out; when he arrived just too late at his cardiac arrest case, he realised the dead man on the bed in front of him was the patient who had just requested directions. North of the infirmary at No. 92 Castle Street is the former Royal Asylum for the Blind, with a sculpture of Christ restoring the sight of a blind child.

THE BISHOP'S PALACE

The medieval palace or castle of the bishops stood on a spot now occupied by Cathedral Square and the Royal Infirmary. It fell into dereliction after the Reformation and in the late eighteenth century the courtyard became the execution site. When the gibbet was not in use it was stored in the cathedral crypt. In 1789 the ruins were removed to make way for the hospital. A memorial pillar in the square shows what the building may have looked like. It is best known for its association with 'the Battle of Bell o' the Brae' in 1300 when an English garrison was defeated by a pincer movement headed by William Wallace (coming up High Street) and the Laird of Auchinleck (attacking from the rear along Drygate). Or, at least that's what Blind Harry, Wallace's first but not entirely-reliable chronicler, says. The battle may have taken place, or it may not have. No other Scottish or English historian mentions the encounter. In Harry's favour, the geography is correct, and he emphasises the truth of his account by the phrase 'as weyll witnes the buk,' an expression he uses when he is referring to some (unnamed) written source. On the other hand, he claims the English numbered 1,000 troops – this at a time when the entire population of the burgh barely topped 1,500 – and the Castle itself was bijou. Of course, exaggerating numbers has long been a part of military propaganda, and as the Scots are said to have had only 300 men, the story serves again to aggrandise Harry's hero Wallace through his defeat of a greatly superior force.

Exaggerations aside, Harry may have recorded a genuine skirmish – or he may have confused his bishops. The Castle was supposedly held by Bishop Beck of Durham, a vassal of Edward I of England. But in 1297, Bishop Wishart of Glasgow, having previously supported Wallace's rebellion, found it expedient to submit to Edward (in this he was not alone: Robert the Bruce, Douglas and other nobles did the same). Wallace accused the bishop of treachery and burned his Castle. It is possible Wallace's unsporting assault on a former colleague was transformed by Harry into a patriotic triumph.

ST MUNGO MUSEUM OF RELIGIOUS LIFE AND ART

No. 2 Castle Street. Admission free. Monday to Thursday and Saturday, 10 a.m. to 5 p.m., Friday and Sunday 11 a.m. to 5 p.m. Wheelchair access.

I would argue this is the best museum in Glasgow after Kelvingrove and the Hunterian. It describes its purpose as to explore 'the importance of religion in people's lives across the world and across time.' As such, it is replete with objects that illuminate belief systems, folklore, magic, relations with the dead, the gods and the spirits, and much more. In most museums you have to search hard for the 'items of mystical weirdness'. Here they're all around. Highlights include:

Various apotropaic charms: 'Lammer' or amber beads (rheumatism); a sheep's bone (drowning); ash twigs (fits); and mole's feet (toothache).

A crocodile oracle used by the Kuba of Zaire to discover the identity of a thief or sorcerer, or to find a cure. The diviner oils the croc's back and rubs it with a wooden knob while reciting names. When the knob sticks the oracle has spoken.

A Chinese dragon robe, with dragons coiling amidst clouds, cranes and bats. It was worn in the film *The Last Emperor*.

An awesome four-armed figure of the Hindu god Shiva, Lord of the Dance. His whirling hair holds flowers, snakes, a skull and the goddess Ganga. He is adored by two sages, one with the lower body of a snake, while the other has tiger feet. I really love those tiger feet.

A dancing skeleton from the Mexican Day of the Dead.

A spirit image from Vanuatu, carved from a tree fern. According to the Christian missionary who donated it, it was 'the first idol given up on the island of Malekula by the chief Barabuukabuuk about the year 1890.' Also an ancestor's skull decorated with clay and hair to make it more lifelike.

The Bodhisattva Avalokiteshvara, with ten heads (the eleventh is missing) and forty-eight arms. The ribbons and scrolls of his cloak transform into serpents.

Stained glass by the Pre-Raphaelite artist Edward Burne-Jones, showing St Stephen and three angels, Moses, Enoch and David, and Elijah and the Ravens; there is also Elijah with the fiery chariot that appeared just before he was transported to heaven in a whirlwind.

One of the Tontine Faces,
Provand's Lordship.

A Chinese baby boy doll dressed as a girl to trick evil spirits.

A divinatory bronze mirror from Islamic Turkey or Iran, decorated with sphinxes of good fortune from pre-Islamic traditions.

A late nineteenth century St Brigid's Cross, made from reeds to commemorate the cross the fifth century saint used to convert an Irish chieftain.

A spectacular charm necklace with a large bird's skull, used by a healer in West Africa.

A Yoruba smallpox spirit, a bald man with spots who represents the spirit of the disease.

A tiny Guatemalan trouble doll for taking away people's worries … and much, much more, with items relating to saints, ancestors, fertility, healing, the Blessed Virgin Mary, Joan of Arc, divine Kings, totemic animals, Egyptian magic, feng shui, headhunting, death masks, demons, hell, shrines …

PROVAND'S LORDSHIP

No. 3 Castle Street. Admission free. Monday to Thursday and Saturday 10 a.m. to 5 p.m., Friday and Sunday 11 a.m. to 5 p.m. Wheelchair access to garden and the ground floor.

Once this area was filled with almshouses and accommodation for pilgrims, and the town houses of the canons of the cathedral chapter, but this is now the only house to survive from the clustered hamlet of medieval Glasgow. Dane Love, in *Scottish Spectres,* reports hauntings, supposedly of the victims of the hangman who lived here or nearby, but there are no details. A wooden armorial wooden panel features a *Wizard of Oz*-type human-headed lion. Behind the house is the St Nicholas medicinal garden, dating from 1997 and containing herbs used in medieval healing. The walls are lined with the amazing Tontine faces, a series of large grotesque masks that have finally, and happily, ended up here having resided variously in Trongate,

Buchanan Street and the People's Palace. They cover the range of expressions, from grim and scary to comic and caricatured.

THE NECROPOLIS

> There is no cemetery in Britain as spectacular as the Glasgow Necropolis ... it is literally a city of the dead.
>
> James Stevens Curl, *A Celebration of Death* (1993)

> Who is not made better and wiser by occasional intercourse with the tomb?
>
> George Blair, *Biographic & descriptive sketches of the Glasgow Necropolis* (1857)

For centuries people were buried in their parish graveyards at the cathedral, Govan, Cathcart, Rutherglen, Shettleston and Tollcross. The vast increase in population from the eighteenth century put immense pressure on these traditional sites. In the 1830s over 5,000 people were dying in Glasgow each year, many from typhus, cholera and other infectious diseases, and they were being buried in increasingly fetid churchyards. Necessity uncoupled sentiment from sacred location, and hence there was a movement towards creating new, hygienic graveyards unconnected with older religious sites. The Necropolis was the first of this new wave of sanitary sepulchres. It was initiated by the Merchants' House in 1832, and rapidly became a Victorian theatre of the remembered dead. The monuments cover every architectural neo-style – Classical, Norman, Gothic, Renaissance, Baroque, Moorish and Celtic, as well as Art Nouveau. It is a must-see sight – grandiose, inspiring, sad, grotesque, and occasionally eerie.

The Père Lachaise cemetery in Paris, on which the Necropolis is modelled, is noted for the grave of rock singer Jim Morrison. And talking of belligerent drunks, be cautious in the quieter areas of the Necropolis, which can be home to the intoxicated and the volatile. Vandalism is also an obvious problem (count how many headless statues you pass). The Necropolis is open free of charge during daylight hours. Wheelchair access is presently limited as the paths can be a bit ropey. The main entrance is off Cathedral Square through a set of elaborate wrought-iron gates decorated with the ship and trading motto of the Merchants' House, *Toties redeuntes eodem* – 'So often returning to the same place', which of course can have an entirely different meaning in the context of a cemetery.

You cross the road on the Bridge of Sighs, which spans the canyon of Wishart Street, underneath which is the Molendinar Burn, the river on which Glasgow was founded. It has long since been culverted and abstracted from sight. The semi-circular entrance façade was intended to be the entrance to a grand tunnel driven right through the hill to provide rows of tiered catacombs, secure against the depredations of the bodysnatchers. But the grave-robbing trade vanished with the 1832 Anatomy Act – clearly an early example of the nanny state driving self-employed entrepreneurs out of business – and the vaults flooded, and no one wanted to be buried in the Stygian gloom. The tunnel was abandoned and the space now holds a fine collection of lawnmowers.

To describe the Necropolis in detail would take up half this volume. Two splendid books have been recently published – Ruth Johnston's *Glasgow Necropolis Afterlives* and Ronnie Scott's *Death by Design: The True Story of the Glasgow Necropolis,* which between them will tell you everything you need to know – Scott's is a particularly handy pocket guide. The Friends of the Glasgow Necropolis organise popular walking tours (*see* www.glasgownecropolis.org). Here are just a few highlights:

The *Monument to Corlinda Lee*, the Queen of the Gypsies, who once read Queen Victoria's palm at a Gypsy Ball in Dunbar. Her husband George faked his own death in Edinburgh to get out of paying creditors. The memorial service was packed. Three months later, one of the mourners met George in Edinburgh's Princes Street ...

The badly damaged monument to *William Motherwell*, a minor poet with a thing for Scandinavian heroic deeds. The frieze shows 'Halbert the Grim' ensnared by snakes and fiends: 'Sheer downwards! Right downwards! Then dashed life and limb/As careering to hell sank Halbert the Grim.' The monuments didn't spring up overnight. In the case of a sudden death, it could be a year before the grand sepulchre was ready. Hence the spooky *Egyptian Vaults*, where corpses were temporarily stored behind cast-iron gates decorated with four pairs of inverted torches and a winged hourglass.

The doorway and eaves of the circular Neo-Norman *Monteath Mausoleum* are home to dozens of grotesque faces. The huge structure holds just two brothers, and has not a single inscription or date anywhere. In 2008 it was noted that the lid of the unremarkable tomb of *Alexander Dunlop Anderson* had slid down. Then a short while later it had been moved back by hands unknown. On the whole, I think this was more likely to be a prank, or a hiding place for drugs or other valuables, than evidence for a revenant. The memorial to *Sam McCalden* features a relief of a speedway rider and the inscription, 'See you later glamour boy'.

Parts of the arthouse science fiction film *Deathwatch* are set in the distinctive landscape of the Necropolis. In Lin Anderson's crime thriller *Easy Kill*, a prostitute's body on a monument leads to the discovery of another woman secretly buried in a hidden grave. And in Alasdair Gray's *Lanark*, the apocalypse comes to a juddering halt on the slopes of the city of the dead.

Tom Rannachan relates how as a student he accepted a £20 bet to spend thirty minutes in the Necropolis at midnight. Whilst there he heard singing, and saw a very beautiful young woman with waist-length dark hair. She was barefooted, had a posy of daisies in her hand, and was wearing a long white gown or shroud – he couldn't tell if she was of the living or the dead. She saw Tom and ran away, disappearing behind a gravestone. One night a week later he returned but saw nothing. A year a so later on another visit he picked up her voice at the same grave, but had no sight of her. Each year he visits and leaves a rose for her. I've also been told in a third-hand way of a little girl who points people towards a grave saying, 'That's my place.' I can't tell if this is a separate spirit or a new version of Tom's story.

I've lost track of the number of times I've been told that the hill on which the Necropolis stands was once a Druid college or centre. Apparently it's a 'well-known fact'. It may be well-known, but

The Necropolis: pair of magnificent bronze angels, Alexander Allan Monument.

I beg to differ on the 'fact' aspect. The earliest reference I can find is in Andrew Brown's 1797 *History of Glasgow*. James Cleland followed Brown closely in 1816 with his *Annals of Glasgow*: 'in the year 601, before Paganism had been completely extirpated, and Christianity established, the DRUIDS had a TEMPLE where Glasgow now stands. The priests lived in cells, said to be near the place where the Black Friars Church was afterwards erected.' Probably the most influential work on the topic came in 1898, with George Eyre-Todd's *The Book Of Glasgow Cathedral*: 'The original consecration of a cemetery by St Ninian, and the subsequent foundation of a church by St Kentigern, at Glasgow, were owed to the fact that the neighbourhood was already a great religious centre.'

Later writers have regarded these authorities as, well, authoritative, and their speculations – for that's what they are – as hard facts. But sadly there is not a shred of archaeological or documentary evidence for the presence of Druids in this area. It's *possible* there was a sacred Druidic grove here in pagan times; it's just that there's no evidence for it. Several eminent historians speculating learnedly about something do not constitute evidence.

Part of their thinking drew on the continuing fascination with Iona and St Columba. The sixth-century Columba had documented dealings with Druids in Ireland, and the belief was that he had founded his great monastery on Iona precisely because it was a hotbed of Druidism.

The Necropolis: headless angel, Aitken of Dalmoak Mausoleum.

The Necropolis: winged hourglass, Egyptian Vaults.

The Necropolis: one of several Green Men adorning the John Henry Alexander monument.

The Necropolis:
The Butterfly of
Resurrection and
the tail-biting Snake
of Eternity.

The Necropolis: city of the dead, city of the living.

As in Iona, so in Glasgow … a great holy man had founded a Christian community here; and reading between the lines of Jocelin's *Life of Kentigern* there was clearly a conflict between paganism and Christianity in sixth-century Strathclyde. Hmmm, paganism, a disputed Christian foundation … it can only mean one thing: Druids woz 'ere! QED. Learned lilywhites were fascinated by Druids because the cowled ones were powerful, dark and dangerous. Glasgow historians *wanted* there to be a Druid colony near the Molendinar. And so, in their writings, there was.

The *Herald* for 11 May 2007 put the conspiracy cat among the hidden-agenda pigeons when it asked, 'Does Necropolis hold the key to Freemasonry's secret history?' The answer to that question is probably 'no', but the topic has managed to ruffle some feathers. The basic argument – as suggested, perhaps not entirely seriously, by Ronnie Scott, *pandit* of the Necropolis – is that the location and layout of the cemetery mirrors the Freemason's personal spiritual journey. Masonic iconography shows the individual travelling from west to east, over a bridge, beside an arch, through two pillars and up a hill. Visitors to the Necropolis enter from the west over the Bridge of Sighs, and ascend a hill past monuments which include pillars and arches. And most of the big kahunas who started up the cemetery were themselves Freemasons. And many of the monuments have Egyptian stylings, which are also a major part of Masonic symbolism. And the monument to ironmaster Walter Macfarlane resembles a Royal Arch, the emblem of the fourth degree of Freemasonry. Put it all together and do you get a 'symbolic Freemasonic landscape'?

Well, maybe. But there is a tendency to over-conspiricise our world: sometimes a bunch of dead Freemasons on top of a hill is an act of gargantuan landscaping manipulation secretly perpetuated over decades to achieve a mystical symbolic arena of meaning accessible only to an initiated few, and sometimes it's just the result of a self-perpetuating socio-economic elite rising in the world partly through the use of semi-covert networking opportunities. I look forward to someone coming up with an argument that the cemetery is designed on the Zodiac, or a pentagram, or an alien sigil … the Necropolis is that kind of place.

LADYWELL STREET

This unprepossessing cul-de-sac at the foot of the Necropolis, off Wishart Street, leads to the Lady Well, a holy well also known as the Well of Our Lady and dedicated to the Virgin Mary.

The Lady Well.

In a paper for the Old Glasgow Club in 1914, Alexander Fowler mentions two accounts of the well, one that it was a 'physic' well with a rather sulphurous taste, and the other than it was a normal public well: the council records from 1700 required Andrew Whyte, hammerman, to 'keep the ten public wells of the city in good condition, to lock and open them every night and morning in good time, and to furnish the wells known as the Four Sisters and the Lady Well with iron ladles, for a period of five years.' For this Whyte was paid 500 merks. When the cemetery was built the water became polluted and the well was closed.

The plain Classical-style niche on the north bank of the street was constructed in 1836 and rebuilt in 1874 by the Merchants' House. A plaque states that it was further restored by Tennent Caledonian Breweries in 1983 (their giant brewery is just a few yards away). In a paper to the Society of Antiquaries of Scotland in 1882, Russel Walker noted it was sometimes also known as the Lady Love Well. Sadly we have no records of what rituals were carried out at the pre-Reformation well, but it continues to be venerated in modern times – roses have been left, and cremation ashes scattered on the bank.

DRYGATE

An article contributed by 'W.G.' of No. 11 Hill Street, Anderston, to *The Scottish Journal of Topography, Antiquities, Traditions* in 1848, tells of Saunders Finlay of the Gawfell, a farm between Kirkintilloch and Kilsyth, and his bewitched cows. So many of his cattle were dying he got on his horse and consulted a 'celebrated Witchdoctor, who resided in the garret of an old tenement in the Drygate.' This individual complained that witches were more numerous since burning at the stake had ceased (the tale is set in the 1760s or 1770s) and charged Saunders two merks for a charm, telling him to follow his instructions or the witches would '*rive you to pieces, like the peelins o'ingins!*'

That night at home the farmer blocked up the chimney and windows and barricaded the doors. Then he put a pot on the fire and poured in the ingredients of the charm, which included three or four large pins. The stink and the smoke were abominable, but worse was the howling from outside, and the screams of someone imploring him to remove the pot. Saunders took to his bed, hiding under the blankets until the noise died down. The next day Bessie MacTavish – whom he had suspected of being the witch – took to her sick-bed and died, and Saunders' cattle were healthy thereafter. The witchdoctor, by the way, said that from his window each morning he could see '*mae than twenty lums reeking, and every one o' them is the lum o' a Witch!*' The Drygate must have been like Diagon Alley.

CATHEDRAL SQUARE

The Barony (Glasgow Evangelical) North Church looks like it has been teleported straight from Michelango's Rome, with Renaissance statues of Saints Peter and Paul and the four Evangelists, each with their symbols peeping out from behind their robes. The Cathedral House Hotel at Nos 28-32 is a former hostel for prisoners released from the now-demolished Duke Street prison. Dane Love (*Scottish Spectres*) notes that apparitions of two children have been sighted by both guests and staff. On 9 October 2005 Ghost Finders Scotland conducted an investigation in the hotel. Several phenomena were recorded in the restaurant, with knocks that appeared to answer questions, footsteps, a chair being jerked backwards during a communication board séance, and several alleged EVP (Electronic Voice Phenomena) recordings. Bangs were heard in the attic space, running footsteps above bedroom three, and knocks in bedroom seven, and the latter also produced flashes of light and several apparent spoken phrases on digital voice recorders. The report is on www.ghostfinders.co.uk.

CASTLE STREET

23 Enigma at No. 258 is Scotland's oldest occult shop, set up in 1995 by Samantha Cooper and her partner. It stocks products and books, runs occult arts events, offers Tarot readings, and acts as a semi-formal networking locus for many involved in witchcraft, Paganism and similar areas. The shop has hired occult items to film and television productions and collaborated with the KELVINGROVE MUSEUM on their display of healing charms (*see* www.23enigma.com). Within the Victorian former Barony Church on the corner with MacLeod Street can be found carvings of the four evangelists, a wonderful fresco of Christ in Majesty worshipped by two gold-haloed angels, and excellent modern stained glass which uses letters, numbers and symbols to cryptically tell the story of science and Strathclyde University, who own the building. Once you've de-crosaworded 'Jolly Jack Phosphorus', the rest should be easy. The Barony is occasionally open for guided tours.

DUKE STREET

In *Gazetteer of Scottish Ghosts* one veteran ghost-hunter, Peter Underwood, related a story he had been told by another, Elliott O'Donnell. O'Donnell had visited an unnamed house in Duke Street which had a supernatural reputation. A solicitor had told him he had wished to rent the place, but almost as soon as he entered he heard footsteps that followed him as he climbed the stairs and explored the rooms. The house was cold on a warm and sunny summer's day. Walking along a passage lit by an uncurtained window he saw on the wall ahead the shadow of man with arms outstretched and missing the left hand. The solicitor fled, but eventually was persuaded by the low price to move in. One morning his children were playing with something in the nursery that appeared to be a dog. The solicitor saw the blurred outline of a large dog come out of the room. The kids were delighted although they said it was a 'funny dog' because it never wagged its tail and they could not touch it. That night as he went to switch off the light he found his hand caught by something large and soft which had no fingers. The light went off and he screamed in surprise. The thing released his hand and then there came a loud crash from the bedroom above. He rushed upstairs to find his wife apparently asleep but talking to a vague dark shape crouched at the foot of the bed. As he approached it seemed to disappear into the wall. His wife awoke and implored him to take her away from the house. She had dreamed of a murder being committed in the room and described the murderer approaching her with outstretched hands. Next day the terrified family moved out.

O'Donnell obtained the key and was poking around at night when he was interrupted by a policeman suspicious of his actions in the empty house. O'Donnell explained his purpose in being there, and the officer said he obviously had nothing to fear when he had with him 'a dog like that'. O'Donnell turned and saw a huge shadowy dog-like shape halfway up the stairs. As they watched it seemed to retreat and disappear into the wall, exuding a feeling of great evil. O'Donnell was utterly terrified and hurriedly left with the policeman, and did not return.

UNIVERSITY OF STRATHCLYDE

The attractive campus is home to several examples of modern art, including 'Callanish', sixteen steel shapes 16ft (4.9m) high loosely based on the prehistoric stone circle and rows at Callanish on Lewis. Inevitably, the sculpture is dubbed 'Steelhenge'.

2

CITY CENTRE: SOUTH & EAST

COLLEGE STREET

The coffin was forced, the cerements torn and the melancholy relics, clad in sackcloth, after being rattled for hours on moonless by-ways, were at length exposed to uttermost indignities before a class of gaping boys.

Robert Louis Stevenson, *The Bodysnatchers*

When it comes to dastardly deeds carried out over a lengthy period, one of the key elements is often the combination of necessity and simple proximity. For several hundred years, until the profs and studes relocated to the more salubrious West End in 1871, this area was occupied by the University of Glasgow. In the early eighteenth century there were several hundred medical students at the university – Edinburgh and Glasgow were at the time premier among the few centres of learning offering medical degrees.

To obtain their degree the students needed a certificate stating they had been taught anatomy. Anatomy classes were conducted using cadavers as teaching aids. There were far too few bodies available through legitimate channels, such as via official executions. And so the laws of supply and demand forged an unholy union between some medical professionals, and people who were prepared to supply their needs: the resurrectionists. Necessity worked spade-in-hand alongside proximity: the nearest graveyards were at the CATHEDRAL (known then as the High Church), Blackfriars on HIGH STREET, and Ramshorn Kirk on INGRAM STREET. During the height of the bodysnatching fashion, roughly from 1800 to 1830 or so, fresh graves were frequently violated in all these sites.

In many cases medical students did the 'lifting'; other times the bodies were supplied by others. In 1805 John Burns, founder of the first College Street medical school, was banned from teaching anatomy because of his involvement in a bodysnatching case. His brilliant sixteen-year-old brother Allan took over the classes. In 1809 Allan appointed as his assistant and demonstrator Dr Granville Sharp Pattison; when Allan died in 1813, Pattison went into business with surgeon Andrew Russel. And so the stage was set for one of the most notorious bodysnatching cases of all time.

The most detailed description of what is normally regarded as the accepted version of events is in *The Anecdotage of Glasgow*. On 13 December 1813 two recently-interred corpses were stolen from the cathedral graveyard, but an expedition to Ramshorn was disturbed. The next day the graveyard was overrun with anxious relatives and it was discovered that the grave of Mrs McAllister – the wife of a well-known wool merchant in Hutcheson – was empty. An enraged mob smashed the windows of the house occupied by Dr James Jeffrey, the professor of anatomy (and later 'star' of the Matthew Clydesdale episode, see below).

Police officers, armed with a search-warrant, and accompanied by the dead woman's dentist and two of her close friends, searched Pattison's rooms in College Street. Pattison was the perfect host, letting them roam at will. The emptying of a suspicious tub of water revealed a jawbone with several teeth still attached, some fingers, and other parts of a human body. The dentist identified the teeth as those he had himself fitted into Mrs McAllister's mouth, and someone

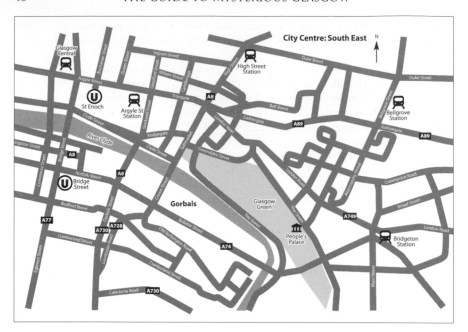

else picked out the dead woman's wedding ring finger. After Pattison and his companions were arrested – and barely escaped being lynched by the mob – the police dug up the floorboards, discovering the remains of several bodies. All the grisly evidence was sealed in glass bottles and duly presented at the trial in Edinburgh on 6 June 1814. It seemed an open and shut case, but the defence proved that none of the body parts found *actually belonged to Mrs McAllister.* The defendants had obviously been stealing corpses, but by the letter of the law they could not be convicted on the specific charge. Russel and medical student John McLean were found 'not guilty', while Pattison and student Robert Munro received 'not proven' verdicts. Public feeling was so strong that Pattison quickly emigrated to America, where he founded anatomy departments at Jefferson College in Philadelphia and at the University of New York.

That, at least, is the standard account. However, in a little-known book published in 1985, *Don't Walk Down College Street,* Ted Ramsey put forth an alternative narrative. In his reading of the events, Pattison was set up. Ramsey's theory is that the hundreds of bodies the medical schools needed each year were supplied not by robbing graves, but by simply not burying some people at all. The scam worked like this: paupers who died without means (and there were a great many of them in Glasgow) were buried in simple unmarked graves with the city council picking up the cost. Where there were no mourners, the gravedigger, undertaker and the beadle of the graveyard pocketed the fee from the council and then made an additional tidy profit selling to the anatomists the fresh corpse.

Ramsey speculates that Pattison refused to pay the high prices demanded for corpses. Instead, he set up his own independent supply chain – by hiring as his doorkeeper the beadle of the High Church graveyard. No business cartel likes a rebuff, and so, Ramsey surmises, the bodysnatching closed shop stole Mrs McAllister's body and set up a series of false clues leading directly to Pattison. Pattison, of course, did have illegal body parts on the premises – but they were from one or other of the corpses taken from the cathedral graveyard by his own team. The two 'close friends' who took part in the search were in fact James and Donald McGrigor, the dead woman's brothers, both rich and powerful merchants. Although they were as much victims of the conspiracy as Pattison, they were convinced the doctor had stolen and dismembered their sister's body, and such men's convictions carry force. The dentist, for example, otherwise an innocent party, was overawed by their presence, and consequently demonstrated his worth by positively identifying the dental work. It was the various members of the conspiracy who were responsible for finding many of the body parts and putting them together in a grotesque jigsaw puzzle, the result of which they identified as the body of Mrs McAllister.

After Pattison was arrested, the body parts were given a second funeral, although the genuine corpse had almost certainly been taken to one of the cartel's trusted customers, another anatomy school. The 'Mrs McAllister' reburied at Ramshorn was probably the remains or two or three other individuals. In a parallel but unrelated conspiracy, the Establishment did not favour a respected doctor being found guilty of dissection – a technically illegal but scientifically necessary act that was committed by many medical professionals each day. The case could not be dropped because of the machinations of the powerful McAllister brothers, but the charge was deliberately framed in such a way that it had to result in an acquittal. Ramsey admits he cannot prove his theory, but it does plausibly answer some nagging questions about the case, such as why Pattison would have dug up the corpse of such a prominent individual. The poor could disappear without question, but a merchant's wife – in a city where the wealthy captains of trade were a power in the land – was another matter.

Ramsey also suggests there was no mob smashing windows in the college – no newspaper reports of 1813 mention this – and believes the episode was grafted on from an earlier incident on 24 January 1803, reported in the *Glasgow Courier*. A mob had entered the college on the pretext of searching for a body. Nothing had been found, but they smashed windows and threatened to wreck the place. It is entirely possible, then, that the popular and much-repeated story of 'Pattison the bodysnatcher who got off on a technicality' may be a farrago of deceit, invention and confabulation. On the other hand, in his evidence to the Select Committee in 1828 Pattison openly admitted he had organised raids, dispatching groups of up to eight students to harvest the graveyards, and was unrepentant about doing so, because there were so few official cadavers available from executions.

Which brings us to Mathew Clydesdale. On 27 August 1818 this unlovely man brutally beat eighty-year-old Alexander Love to death. He was sentenced to be hanged and his body dissected. So horrified was Clydesdale at this that he tried to slash his arms with a bottle. The suicide attempt was thwarted and on 4 November he was duly hanged at Saltmarket. Clydesdale appeared to expire straight away, unlike Simon Ross, hanged on the same day on the same gallows, who had died only after a fierce struggle. Clydesdale's corpse was taken to the anatomy hall and placed semi-upright in a chair in front of an audience of medical students, teachers and genteel visitors, all eager to view an example of the latest sensation in medical science, Galvanism. And then:

> A light air tube, connected with the Galvanic battery, was soon placed in one of his nostrils. The bellows began to blow in that nostril in solemn reality. His chest immediately heaved! He drew breath! A few more operations went swiftly on – which really we cannot very well describe – but at last the tongue of the murderer moved out of his lips, his eyes now opened widely – he stared, apparently in astonishment, around him; while his head, arms and legs actually moved; and we declare he made a feeble attempt as if to rise from the chair whereon he was seated. He did positively rise from it in a moment or two afterwards, and stood upright; at seeing which a thrill ran through the excited and crowded room ... that he had now actually come to life again through the extraordinary operation of the Galvanic battery!

Students screamed, people fainted, the lead demonstrator plunged a lancet into Clydesdale's jugular, and the reanimated corpse 'instantly fell down upon the floor like a slaughtered ox on the blow of the butcher.'

Dramatic, terrifying stuff indeed, and the source of a story that continues to be repeated and elaborated to this day. Unfortunately, it's only partially true. The quotes above are taken from the main source, Peter McKenzie's *Reminiscences of Glasgow*, written in 1866 when he was sixty-seven years old, recalling an event he had witnessed when he was only nineteen – if he had indeed witnessed it at all – and deliberately omitting some key facts. A much more sober, but far less well-known, account appeared as 'An Account of Experiments on the Body of a Criminal after Execution' in *The Journal Of Science And Arts* in 1819, less than a year after the event. The author was Dr Andrew Ure, one of the participants in the experiment.

McKenzie's lightly glossed over 'few more operations ... which really we cannot very well describe' turn out to rather major: incisions were made into various parts of the body to drain the blood, and a section of the atlas vertebra supporting the skull was removed – after these actions, Mathew Clydesdale was very definitely dead. However, Ure noted that when Clydesdale's corpse arrived at the anatomy theatre it was not as damaged as most bodies that had been hanged; there is a distinct possibility that at this stage he was actually still alive. As Ure says, if the Galvanic wires had been applied to the phrenic nerve before all the surgery, 'we are almost willing to imagine that ... there is a probability that life might have been restored.'

After the draining of blood, Ure cut into the chest, hip, heel, fingers and forehead, and applied electrical wires to the various exposed nerves. Fingers moved and seemed to point at members of the audience. Stimulating the nerves in the forehead caused the face to contort into a smile, frown or scowl. A Galvanised leg kicked out, almost knocking over one of the assistants. The chest rose and fell – but, like all the other actions, this ceased when the wires were withdrawn. Everything that took place was as the result of electrical stimulation of exposed nerves on a corpse. The dead man never drew breath, never achieved self-animation, and never stood up. And Dr James Jeffrey certainly did not plunge a scalpel into the neck of the lurching murderer, an addition which probably owes much to McKenzie's fifty-year-old memories, very likely influenced by the most famous Galvanic episode in literature: *Frankenstein*.

In 1791 Luigi Galvani experimented with dissected frogs' legs, which twitched when he applied metal rods. He wrongly assumed the nerves themselves were the source of the electricity – the rods simply 'released' the animal electricity, a form of 'vital force'. Alessandro Volta later showed the electricity was in the rod and in 1796-7 developed the first electric battery, the Voltaic pile. Volta won the scientific honours, but the word 'Galvanism' got the popular vote and became the term for all experiments using electricity and living matter.

On 17 January 1803 Luigi Aldini, Galvani's nephew, wired a huge Voltaic pile to the ear and mouth of Thomas Forster, who, for murdering his wife and child, had been hanged at Newgate just one hour before. The result, according to Aldini's *Account of the Late Improvements in Galvanism*, was that 'the jaw began to quiver, the adjoining muscles were horribly contorted, and the left eye actually opened.' Later when Forster's thumb was wired up, the electrical charge 'induced a forcible effort to clench the hand.' This public demonstration at 'Mr Wilson's Anatomical Theatre' in London almost gave 'an appearance of re-animation.' It was even possible that 'vitality might have been restored, if many circumstances had not rendered it possible.' The report in *Pantalogia: A New Cyclopaedia* of 1813 noted that, 'It appeared, to the uninformed part of the by-standers, as if the wretched man was on the eve of being restored to life.' Furthermore, 'the result of this experiment promises great advantages to the interests of humanity, especially in cases of apparent death by drowning, and other cases of asphyxia.'

Aldini's and similar experiments were reported in the press and the scientific literature, and stimulating corpses with electricity became something of a vogue among medical men. The idea of Galvanic reanimation was 'in the air', and almost certainly these experiments were discussed at the Villa Diodati in Switzerland where four bohemian intellectuals gathered in June 1816. In the famous genesis of the famous novel – one of the best accounts being in Christopher Frayling's *Nightmare: The Birth of Horror* – Lord Byron suggested they all write a ghost story. Byron's effort was a minor work, Percy Bysshe Shelley soon gave up, and Dr John Polidori wrote *The Vampyre* – whose main character many saw as based on Byron. The teenager Mary Wollstonecroft Godwin, later Shelley's wife, was troubled by nightmares and visions:

> When I placed my head upon my pillow, I did not sleep, nor could I be said to think ... I saw – with shut eyes, but acute mental vision – I saw the pale student of unhallowed arts kneeling beside the thing he had put together. I saw the hideous phantasm of a man stretched out, and then, on the working of some powerful engine, show signs of life, and stir with an uneasy, half-vital motion.

During my research I was twice told by tour guides that Mary Shelley got the idea for *Frankenstein* from attending the supposed 'reanimation' of Matthew Clydesdale. It's a great story, but I'm afraid it's yet another urban legend. Mary wrote the first draft of the novel in 1816, and it was published in the spring of 1818. The Glasgow Galvanism spectacle did not take place until November of that year.

In a grim coda, shortly after Mary completed the first draft of the novel, Shelley's first wife, Harriet, drowned in London. When her body was retrieved from the water, resuscitation was attempted using smelling salts, vigorous shaking, artificial respiration – and electricity. None of it succeeded in reviving Harriet.

HIGH STREET

The friary of the Dominican or Black Friars was founded in 1246, more or less where High Street station is now. It was secularised following the Reformation and some parts were incorporated into the College. *The Anecdotage of Glasgow* describes how a would-be resurrectionist was killed by a grave-protecting tripgun in Blackfriars churchyard. He was taken back to his lodgings by his two desperate companions, who each tied one of his legs to theirs, and then staggered home singing and shouting as if they were a typical trio of drunken students. The next morning they circulated the story that during the night the man had committed suicide, and it was not until many years later that the truth came out.

The railway company demolished the church and graveyard around 1875. A splendidly grotesque face currently sits high up on a new building on the east side of High Street, with a plaque stating that it was donated by the university to mark the 400 years during which it

Grotesque head on former site of the University, High Street.

occupied the site. Nos 252–84, on the corner with Duke Street, have pairs of foliate eagles' and lions' heads, and a dynamic full-length lion. Cheeky bare-bottomed winged cherubs crawl all over the former British Linen Co. Bank at No. 215, on the corner with Nicholas Street. The oriel window has a stained glass of a Greek ship and the word Argosy, written in reverse as seen from outside. Clearly this is supposed to be the *Argo*, the ship that took Jason and the Argonauts on their adventures, but this is a common mistake – the two words have different etymologies, an 'argosy' being a merchant fleet or a rich supply.

ALBION STREET

Excavations in 2003 on the site of the Franciscan friary (founded 1473–6, destroyed round 1559) revealed eighteen graves containing twenty adult skeletons (twelve male, seven female, one undetermined). The remains were re-interred in the Southern Necropolis.

INGRAM STREET

Ramshorn Theatre at No. 98 is in the former Ramshorn Kirk, built in neo-Gothic style in 1824 on the site of the previous St David's Church of 1720. Its graveyard, in the heart of the Merchant City, became the most fashionable place to be buried in Glasgow until the advent of the Necropolis. It fell out of use at the end of the nineteenth century and the last interment in the church's large vaulted crypt was in 1903. Dane Love, in *Scottish Spectres*, notes that shortly after conversion to a theatre in 1982 there were sightings of a female ghost in the building's toilets, which occupy the spot of the former vestry. The apparitions were always accompanied by a strong smell, and strange footsteps were occasionally heard. For no obvious reason the ghost was dubbed 'Edie'.

In 2008 the West of Scotland Archaeology Service (www.wosas.net/news.html) reported that on 23 April fragmentary human remains had been dug up during works at the top end of Candleriggs. These were on the site of the graveyard of the earlier church, which had been built over when the street was upgraded and widened and the new church constructed. The Special Collections section of Glasgow University Library (reference Sp Coll Bh14-x.8) has a coloured cartoon from the first edition of the *Glasgow Looking Glass*, 11 June 1825, showing skeletons and ghosts in death-shrouds rising from the old graveyard to terrify the citizens of modern Glasgow for daring to build over their graves. It can be viewed on www.theglasgowstory.com. The walls of the church have at least a dozen carved heads sporting a variety of headgear, hairstyles and expressions (from blootered to bug-eyed), several with open mouths raging, screaming or singing.

The current graveyard is – the occasional drunk notwithstanding – an oasis of peace in the busy city. None of the graves have carvings, but several are of interest nevertheless. Mrs McAllister was buried (once, if probably not twice) in the north-west corner, the place being marked by a stone on the west wall named for McGrigor – the woman's family name. There are several large 'cages' of iron railings, which are usually said to have been placed around graves to prevent 'another McAllister', although Ted Ramsey is convinced many were erected *after* the bodysnatching scare, not to prevent the illegal removal of bodies, but the illegal burial of bodies by people seeking a free interment in someone else's costly lair. Some of the flat gravestones, meanwhile, are truly massive, probably a deterrent to the pick-axe and shovel. In *Reminiscences of Body Lifting*, Buchanan states that a young man patrolling his relative's grave was shot in the chest when a pistol accidentally went off. He was taken to the infirmary, but died soon after. On another occasion a watcher in the graveyard let off a round, the bullet lodging in the window-shutter of a house on George Street. A tombstone named 'Kennedy' covers the otherwise unmarked grave of Pierre Emile L'Angelier, the alleged victim of Madeleine Smith (*see* Blythswood Square).

Anti-bodysnatching cage, Ramshorn kirkyard.

WILSON STREET

This street was the site of the former Hangman's Rest pub. Much folklore was attached to the name, some of it collected by the inimitable Jack House in his 1972 book *The Heart of Glasgow.* It was said that the hangman was not allowed in any of the pubs near the Tollbooth, so he skulked through the country lanes to this little tavern, where he could spend his tainted money freely. At one time the pub had murals illustrating this tale. By 1972 the murals had gone, replaced by windows showing the hangman's rope and the gallows tree, and a sign stating the Hangman's Rest was 281 years old and was the designated accommodation for visiting executioners. This last claim is not true – all Glaswegian hangmen lived locally – so perhaps the first story had more grains of reality contained within. In later years the pub had a 'real' noose hanging from the ceiling.

GLASSFORD STREET

The Green Man and monstrous face on Nos 61-5 are clearly salivating at the fine fare on sale at Peckham's Deli.

BRUNSWICK STREET

One morning in June 1977 Mrs McCarron went shopping in J. & P. Harris, Outfitters, which formerly stood on this street, and had an experience so perplexing that she wrote to the Midland Association of Ghost Hunters about it. After walking up the left side of premises and finding nothing suitable, she was on her way to the other side when her attention was caught by a man reading a newspaper and sitting with legs crossed on a chair in the centre aisle. It seemed an odd place to do this. He was well-built, middle-aged and clean-shaven, and was wearing an old-fashioned suit that was too heavy for the season. She approached him but when she was only a few feet away, both man and chair vanished. A few weeks later she returned to the store and made enquiries. The proprietors said they used to provide a chair for elderly customers, but it was placed nearer the wall. In retrospect she realised there was no space for a chair where she had seen it. The episode is related in Andrew Green's *Ghosts of Today.*

TRONGATE

The Tron Theatre has a history of persistent alleged supernatural events. The site was originally occupied by the Collegiate Church of Our Lady and St Anne, founded in 1525. After the Reformation it was reworked as the Protestant Tron Church, and a tower added in 1628. On 15 February 1793 the church was burned to the ground, only the tower remaining. Robert Reid's *Glasgow, Past and Present* (1851) gives great detail on the events. The church housed the session-house (the room where the Presbytery met) and doubled as the guard-house of the city guard. The watch left at 3 a.m. to do their rounds. Some members of the local Hellfire Club, having participated in the taking of alcohol, passed by and popped in, only to semi-accidentally burn the place down. The Hellfirers fled abroad:

> … where, as was said, most, if not all of them, died miserably, which might have been predicted by any one who was aware of their vicious habits. Prior to the burning of the church, a party of said club went to one of the church-yards at midnight, and, with a trumpet, &c., endeavoured to turn into ridicule the doctrine of the resurrection of the dead.

Hellfire Clubs were an upper-class late eighteenth-century phenomenon arising partly out of changes in the intellectual climate which meant that the elite were no longer necessarily beholden to the church. The *ur*-club, held under the auspices of Sir Francis Dashwood in the caves of West Wycombe, combined political radicalism, atheism and sexual liberation (the latter for men only, of course). They believed that by freeing themselves from strictures on sex and other indulgences, a similar liberation would extend to the social and political realms. Ridiculing the dogmas of Christianity was part of the programme.

Other well-bred young men set up clubs around the country, with varying degrees of emphasis on politics and pleasure. The Glasgow posse can easily be dismissed as Hooray Henrys, toffs just out for a shag and a pint of claret, but Reid has one sneering comment – he calls them 'disciples of Tom Paine' – which may hint at a parallel political agenda. Paine was the author of *The Rights of Man,* one of the key texts in the revolutions against the *anciens régimes* worldwide. One reveller, Hugh Adamson, returned to Glasgow, eventually coming to a bad end when he was hanged at the Cross for forgery on 5 June 1805.

In 1794 the present church was built, and this building is the basis for the current theatre. The separate tower, one of Glasgow's most recognisable landmarks, has a modern full-length statue of St Mungo on the west face, his black metal robes casting him as Darth Vader without the helmet. The vaulted porch has more conventional painted representations of the saint and his symbols, and a golden chubby camp cherub poses in a niche on the east side. In June 1997 building works uncovered part of a human skull on the north side of the building, the site of the graveyard of the collegiate church. Possibly as a reference to this, an oversized carved skull sits high up in a niche near the stage door on Parnie Street.

The theatre has an extensive programme of alleged supernatural phenomena throughout the building, including in the auditorium itself, especially the back two rows. Several paranormal groups have stayed up past their bedtimes to investigate the place. SPI visited for the third time in July 2005 – see the full report at www.scottishparanormalinvestigations.co.uk. A staff member stated that he felt a presence above his head in the box office, and had heard a door handle being opened in an empty office. A breezeblock wall in the basement was described as having been constructed after an architect had a strange experience in the room, which is the former crypt. A large man was glimpsed walking past the kitchen door. The group's psychics contacted several spirits, including: an unhappy man named Tom Winson or Whinstone dressed in a town crier's costume who pointed meaningfully to the box-office area; a camp, theatrical type called Arthur, aged fifty to sixty-five; a small boy of about eight years old, possibly named Simon; a teenage girl called Lisa with a missing right hand; and a tall military man.

The Ghost Club investigated on 18 February 2006, with Derek Green as team leader. There were several incidents relating to a small child – Derek thought he saw her on the east stair,

St Kentigern, Tron Theatre.

Skull, Tron Theatre, Parnie Street.

one of the psychics picked up her presence, one member heard a child whimpering and a faint, possibly childlike noise was found on the EVP (Electronic Voice Phenomena) recording. Other people elsewhere have reported the apparition of a little girl on the east stair, seen through the window from outside. A psychic picked up the name Robert Adam(s) – the 1794 church was designed by James and Robert Adam, although there may have been prior knowledge of this. Brand new batteries and fully charged walkie-talkies drained very quickly, and cameras and camcorders played up in the boiler room, a space where staff members have reported strange feelings and seeing a sinister dark shape. When everyone was present in the foyer, and the rest of the building empty, a tape recorder recorded what sounded like someone moving around the auditorium over about twenty minutes.

The Ghost Club returned on 27 January 2007. A medium picked up on the 'dark shape' seen in the boiler room – one of the building's more persistent phenomena – and stated it was responsible for an accident involving a ladder. There had indeed been an incident logged in the theatre's accident book eight months previously, when a technician working alone in the room had fallen off a ladder, which he had felt had been pushed. One of the experiments carried out by the group involved placing objects on a dusting of flour to record any movement – and the tray containing the flour itself appeared to have moved. Three people heard a child's giggle – which may be consistent with the 2006 investigation and previous reports of a sound of a child – and a tape recorder in the empty auditorium recorded a single sound in forty minutes of silence: a noise similar to a large book being closed. A psychic sensed a noose and prisoners, which may relate to a time when the building was used for police and justice purposes. The admirably detailed and cautious reports can be found at www.ghostclub.org.uk/tron.htm and /tron2.htm. I have no doubt further investigations will take place at the Tron.

William Hone's bucolic *The Every-Day Book* of 1827 quotes a letter written by a Mr Roots, relating to a visit he made to Glasgow in 1801. Roots saw between twenty-five and thirty women queuing at a public pump. But although the pump had two spouts, only one was used, the other being plugged up:

> I was informed by an intelligent gentleman residing in the neighbourhood, that though one and the same handle produced the same water from the same well through either of the spouts, yet the populace, and even better informed people, had for a number of years conceived an idea, which had been handed down from father to son, that the water when drawn from the hindermost spout

would be of an unlucky and poisonous nature; and this vulgar prejudice is from time to time kept afloat, inasmuch, as by its being never used, a kind of dusty fur at length collects, and the water, when suffered from curiosity to pass through, at first runs foul; and this tends to carry conviction still further to these ignorant people, who with the most solemn assurances informed me, it was certain death to taste of the water so drawn, and no argument could divest them of their superstitious conceit, though the well had been repeatedly cleaned out, before them, by order of the magistrates, and the internal mechanism of the pump explained.

The pump may have been drawing water from St Ninian's Well, mentioned in 1433 as being on the south side of St Thenaw's Gate (Trongate).

Hidden upstairs beyond Mitchell's Amusements at Nos 113-117 Trongate is one of Glasgow's great treasures – the Britannia Music Hall, also known as the Panopticon. The full story of this exceptional building is told in Judith Bowers' highly recommended book *Stan Laurel and Other Stars of the Panopticon*, from which many of these notes were taken. Having been one of the city's most popular entertainment venues, the Britannia closed in 1935 and was for decades forgotten and just used for storage, until Judith rediscovered it in 1997. Although much of the fabric is still in a delicate condition – the amazing church-like sweep of the U-shaped balcony, for example, is too dangerous to enter – the venue is regularly open for music-hall events, jazz bands, and Laurel and Hardy film shows. A visit on one of these occasions is not to be missed (*see* www.glasgowmerchantcity.net/britanniapanopticontrust.htm).

The Britannia in late Victorian times was a vulgar, smelly, rough-and-tumble place, frequented by prostitutes, filled with a choking fug of cigarette smoke, and so lacking in basic facilities that the seating areas were soaked with urine (which may be why, almost uniquely among Glasgow theatres, it never caught fire). And what the audience wanted was spectacle, such as the 'séances' conducted by Professor Holmes and Madame Lena in 1895. Such acts took their influence from the mysterious afterlife communications and physical mediumship of spiritualism, but burlesqued them out of the controlled, darkened room and into the hurly-burly of the arena. 'Spirits' walked across stage via the mirrors of the technique called Dr Pepper's Ghost. A 'volunteer' from the audience (actually an accomplice) would be hypnotised and bound hand and foot and placed behind the curtains of the Spirit Cabinet. The auditorium would become silent and the tension rose. Suddenly plates, cups, balls and tambourines would erupt from the cabinet. The curtain was pulled back to reveal the bound victim still in a trance. The ghosts must have done it! A 'medium' would sink into a trance, the lights dimmed, and then an invisible assistant would use a string to pull luminous ectoplasm from the medium's mouth – very, very slowly so everyone could get a good view. The ectoplasm was muslin soaked in glowing phosphorous, which may not have done the medium's health much good.

In 1904 a brash Yorkshireman named A.E. Pickard bought the run-down Fell's Waxworks at No. 101 Trongate, two doors east of the Britannia. Inspired by P.T. Barnum's famous travelling show, he renamed the attraction the American Museum and Waxworks, and used his mercurial talent for publicity to make the business a success. By the following year he was manager of the Britannia. He bought up the various curiosities in Macleod's Waxworks and Museum at No. 155 Trongate, combined all his assets, and in 1906 reopened the Britannia as the Grand Panopticon (from the Greek 'to see everything'), an entertainment 'department store' where all the attractions were under one roof, and all available for the one price.

The live and cinema shows remained in the auditorium on the first floor. The attic was home to the freaks, of whom there were many over the years: Princess Cristina, the Illustrated or Tattooed Lady, who had her 'tattoos' painted on before each show; Harold Pyott from Stockport, known as Tom Thumb, the Smallest Man in the World, who was 23in (58cm) tall and weighed 24lbs (10.8kg); the Bearded Lady, Maud Temple from County Monaghan, who went from being a recluse to a minor celebrity; Mary Ann Bevan, the Ugliest Woman on Earth, whose masculine looks had won her several Ugly Contests, which in turn had enabled her to travel the world and do things she would never normally have been able to experience given her class position; Alice Bounds, the Bear Woman of Texas, who walked on all fours and was covered in thick hair, which may have been a bearskin; Miss Lucy Moore, 'the American Fat Girl', supposedly the heaviest lady in the world at 46st 12lb (298kg); the Human Spider, who was actually an usherette called Flora who had volunteered to pretend to be a spider – she had no deformities, and just ate rubber bugs all day. And finally, Ida Campbell, the Human Trunk or Half Lady, who was born without legs and had one complete arm and hand. Many of the 'freaks' supplemented their income by selling short autobiographies to visitors. In hers, Ida claimed that her condition was caused by her pregnant mother witnessing the mauling to death of her lion-tamer husband, an example of the common but erroneous 'imprinting' belief about traumatic events during pregnancy (the Elephant Man, John Merrick, had a similar reason for his disfigurement). Like many of the freaks, Ida earned good money from being exhibited and so achieved an independence that would have otherwise been denied her.

In *The Heart of Glasgow* Jack House described his encounter with the Armless Wonder. He was a refined-looking gent with a waxed moustache, a high collar and a plain tie. His cloak concealed his torso, so it was not clear whether he was actually armless. With his bare feet he threaded a needle, hammered a nail into a block of wood and signed copies of his autobiography at sixpence a time. 'It was a most impressive performance. You felt it didn't really matter whether he had arms or not.' Images of many of the freakshows are on display in the Trongate window of the amusement arcade.

In 1906 crowds queued round the block to see a man not eat. Monsieur Victor Beaute, clearly the David Blaine of his time, was on display twenty-four hours a day as the Fasting Man. On 1 October he weighed 11st 7lb (73kg) and thereafter was allowed nothing but cigarettes and aerated water. His wooden cage had windows on both sides and was divided in two by curtains. One part had a bedstead, the other an armchair, a small chair and a chest of drawers. Pickard's publicity machine claimed the aim was to beat the world record of forty days without food. After thirty-nine days Beaute weighed 8st 11lb (55kg) and the magistrates apparently told Pickard he would be responsible if Beaute died. The fast stopped that night, just short of the record. For years it was claimed that Beaute was sustained by protein pills hidden in his cane, but Judith Bowers has found that the stage manager's wife would pop in after midnight, when the building was quiet, and surreptitiously hand over a hot steak pie.

Perhaps the strangest denizen of the freak shows was the Irish Leprechaun: 'Have you seen the Leprechaun? – The Mullingar Fairy – The only one ever captured alive', said the poster. The story was that in 1908 some children in County Westmeath had discovered a leprechaun, which was caught and held in the Mullingar workhouse, where he refused to wear clothes. Pickard heard about it from his agent in Dublin, sent a representative to view it, and after some negotiations brought the creature back to Glasgow, although there was still anxiety about the tendency towards naturism. Carol Foreman's *Glasgow Curiosities* describes the leprechaun as a dwarf-like figure sitting in a cage rocking himself to and fro or picking the works out of clocks, which he kept in the several jackets he had been eventually persuaded to don. He was rude and abusive, had a strange way of talking like a cross between a grunt and a squeak, and puffed on a corncob pipe. This sad individual may have been a mentally disabled dwarf, although it is hard to tell exactly.

The waxworks included torture scenes and a rogues' gallery of murderers, including what was claimed to be the embalmed body of Mary Bateman, 'the Yorkshire witch' who was hanged in 1809 for poisoning. Thousands paid to view her corpse and strips of her skin were sold as apotropaic charms. Her skeleton is in the Thackray Museum in Leeds.

From 1908 the basement was home to the zoo, named Noah's Ark, where forty-two cages held beasts and birds in what must have been appallingly cruel conditions. One of the star attractions was Solomon the chimpanzee, called the Man-Monkey or Darwin's Missing Link. He was never seen without clothes, stood upright like a man when there was an audience, and was portrayed on posters going to church wearing top hat and tails. On 31 October 2006, as part of its Hallowe'en coverage, the *Evening Times* interviewed psychic researcher Jackie Jones-Hunt, who saw the spirits of animals in the building without knowing about the zoo. She was quoted as saying: 'Where we had been told the figure of a woman had been seen near the stage, I saw a monkey.' This is just one of several incidents at the building.

Judith Bowers believes that the spirit of Solomon continues to wreak mischief. When the BBC television programme *Psychic Detectives* (2005) was recorded in the building, the sound engineer picked strange noises circling the séance being conducted in the basement (the site of the zoo). Back at the studio the sounds were identified as those of an angry chimp. During another vigil in the basement the darkened room was dimly lit only by glowlights. The no-nonsense sports editor of a national newspaper was seated on a platform on which the cages once stood when he felt the sensation of a wet finger in his ear. He immediately switched on his torch to check if it was a practical joke, but no one was nearby. When he turned the flashlight off, he was shoved off his chair. Exit editor, at speed.

On another occasion the chairs in the bingo area were moved into the arcade section so that an object test could take place – various items were placed on the floor and their outlines chalked round. When the team returned later to see if any of the objects had been moved, none had – but all twelve chairs had been returned to the bingo area. And during a bingo session the main prize was announced as a toy zebra. An old lady shouted, 'F*** the f***ing zebra, I want the f***ing cash prize', at which the zebra launched itself across the room and landed at her feet. Later, every time she visited the loo, the toilet flushed as she arrived, which so unnerved her she swore never to visit the toilet in the building again.

Derek Green of the Ghost Club, on a visit in 2001, sensed the spirit of a soldier in a Boer War-era uniform on the rear section of the balcony. Other psychics have mentioned a man dressed in scarlet in the area, usually around the second row. In February 2007 photographer David Shrigley was in this area when he heard a voice right in his ear: 'You right there big yin?' Not only was David alone, he is also very tall. It could have been noise carried from the Trongate, but …

With the lights low, the dark, rickety, time-faded cavernous auditorium has a distinct atmosphere. Judith believes the building has its own personality, which expresses itself in several ways. When she is out, the unlocked door to her office will not open to visitors, but when she is in the building it opens easily. The building assesses newcomers and if they are not *simpatico* they are treated unwelcomingly. In contrast, it loves performance and crowds, and Judith told me that it seems to amplify positive feelings: a fairly ordinary show can become an acme of enjoyment for both audience and performers. The building also enjoys a bit of sport with objects, which are frequently found out of place. One day a piano tuner was working on the pianola by the side of the stage. He asked Judith for a saw, but then said, 'Oh, don't worry, there's one here,' and picked up the building's saw, which was always kept in a toolbox in the basement. On my visit we were gingerly walking across the rear balcony when Judith found a pair of scissors that normally lived in her office: the balcony is a very dusty area, but the scissors had not a speck of dust, and no one had been up in the balcony for days. There are of course possible – and more prosaic – explanations for such events, but maybe the Britannia does like to kick up its psychic heels every now and then.

No. 177 Trongate has a gaunt-looking Neptune with a trident and a horse of the sea, and a goddess with a leafy branch looking benevolently at a tiny figure of Mercury standing on a plinth carved with his caduceus. Below the Olympians are a sailor in distress and a crippled woman, between them a miniscule figure of a bishop, presumably Mungo.

STOCKWELL STREET

There was a well on this street called the Ratton or Rotten Well. Folk etymology has excelled itself here, combining the foul taste of the water with a legend of William Wallace to derive the street name in a spectacularly ridiculous union: after the Battle of the Brae, the slain English were said to have been thrown down the well, with Willie saying 'Stock it well, lads, stock it well.' The Scotia Bar, built in 1792 and prime contender for the disputed title of 'the oldest pub in Glasgow', is another drinking den with a long but vague history of hauntings. *Scotland on Sunday* (11 March 2007) had a feature on an investigation conducted by the paranormal investigation group Spirit Finders. The team's psychic picked up a man of medium build moving towards the locked cellar, from within which came rattling noises. This may have been the shade of a former landlord, popularly thought to have committed suicide on the premises and the standard identity given to the manifestations.

OLD WYND

Jack House, in *The Heart of Glasgow,* records a long-held belief that bodysnatchers with pads soaked in chloroform lurked in the lanes off Trongate, especially Old Wynd. House met elderly people who told him their parents had warned them never to pass the wynd's entrance at night without putting their hands over their mouths. Hawkie, a well-known street character, lived in a vile slum at the foot of the Old Wynd. His much-quoted comments about the rats – which ate the corpse in the next bed, and could steal whole eggs through carefully-coordinated teamwork – are perhaps simply too bad to be true.

TOLLBOOTH STEEPLE/GLASGOW CROSS

The imposing lone steeple, marooned by traffic, is all that remains of the seventeenth-century Tollbooth used as the courthouse and jail. The turret on the north end used to have spikes to which were affixed the heads of executed traitors and felons, *pour encourager les autres.* All but the steeple was demolished in 1921. In David Crooks' short story 'Spaced Out' the Tollbooth is actually a spaceship. The piece was published in *The Glasgow Herald* (29 March 1986) and reprinted in *Starfield,* a collection of science fiction stories, many set in Glasgow, edited by Duncan Lunan, and with contributions by Janice Galloway and Alasdair Gray.

Hangings took place outside the Tollbooth between 1788 and 1814, when the gallows moved to Saltmarket. In a notorious case of 1797, James McKean was hanged for the murder of Andrew Buchanan. Again the body was handed over for dissection, but in this case the anatomist was approached by a group of city merchants, who offered to buy the skin off McKean's back. The skin was tanned, cut into circles, and distributed as mementos. In 1798 the hangman was too nervous to complete an execution so Lord Provost John Dunlop pushed him aside and pulled the bolt to deliver murderer John McMillan to oblivion. Now that's a politician with the courage of his convictions! Glasgow Cross railway station was in operation from 1895 to 1964, and is still there, a genuine Victorian underground ghost station, possibly contributing much to the 'vanished underground city' myth. The only indication at street level is the ventilation grilles on the traffic island. Kenna and Sutherland's *They Belonged to Glasgow* drily notes that in 1899 a policeman at Glasgow Cross found a dead shark measuring over 8ft (2.4m) long. The creature was placed on the standard 'drunk's barrow' and taken to the police HQ.

ST-ANDREW'S-IN-THE-SQUARE

The coat of arms on St-Andrew's-in-the-Square Church overlooks the grotesque face of a bearded demon. A belligerent bull's head sticks out from the former Tannery Building.

Glasgow's coat of arms and Georgian grotesque, St-Andrew's-in-the-Square.

SALTMARKET

Having being variously located at Gallowgate, the former Bishop's Palace and the Tollbooth, the gallows came to rest here in 1814, outside the High Court in what is now Jocelyn Square, and was then Jail Square. Seventy-one public executions took place here, the last, in 1865, being 'Dr' Edward William Pritchard, hanged for poisoning his wife and mother-in-law in his house in Sauchiehall Street. Pritchard's was the last public hanging in Glasgow; in 1875 the gallows moved behind the walls of Duke Street prison, and from there to Barlinnie Prison in 1928. Pritchard's cold-bloodedness – before he was a suspect, he had the coffin lid opened so he could kiss his wife on the lips one last time – earned him the sobriquet the Human Crocodile. The entire case caused a sensation. 30,000 people came to see him hanged, he had a starring role in the waxworks at the PANOPTICON, and he became a key figure in Jack House's *Square Mile of Murder*. The crimes were examined in the 1950 novel *Flesh and the Devil* by Elbur Ford (aka Jean Plaidy, aka Victoria Holt, aka Philippa Carr, aka Eleanor Burford). What happened to Pritchard's remains, however, is open to conjecture.

There are at least two deeply contradictory accounts. The redbrick building on the north side of the square is the city mortuary, a very busy institution handling some 2,000 horizontal clients a year. House states that when the mortuary was built around 1910, workmen found Pritchard's skeleton in the area where the hanged were known to have been buried, with a small headstone marked E.W.P. He was still wearing his new pair of patent leather boots, which were promptly stolen and sold, so for a time someone was walking round in the murderer's shoes. The skull was also stolen and sold to a discerning collector – although three genuine authentic Dr Pritchard skulls are known to exist.

Donald Fraser, in *Scottish Mysteries,* gives a completely different tale. He states that there was a tunnel leading from the prison in the High Court, below the Saltmarket, to emerge beside the scaffold at the entrance to Glasgow Green. In 1985 the courthouse was renovated and it was decided to fill in the tunnel, which had lain unused for 120 years and might be in danger of collapsing under the weight of modern traffic. About 9–10ft (2.7–3m) into the tunnel from the courthouse side, a niche was discovered. It contained a pair of brown leather button-fastening boots in good condition. In one was a neatly folded piece of greaseproof or tissue paper which disintegrated at the touch. But behind it, in the boot, was some black human hair. Fraser reconstructs the events as follows: the executioner was William Calcraft, who usually took a personal memento from each corpse. Once Pritchard had been hanged and returned to the prison, his hair and beard was shaved off so that Alexander Stewart of the Edinburgh Phrenological Society could cast a death mask. Stewart also took casts of the hands and feet. The magistrates ordered all the shaved hair to be burnt. However, Pritchard's eldest daughter had requested a lock of his hair. This was agreed to, but when the time came for the memento to be handed over, it was said to have already been destroyed. Then Calcraft was discovered in possession of all the hair. An argument ensued, and eventually he was forced to hand it over. To avoid further problems, Calcroft probably then hid the boots and the one bit of hair he had managed to hang on to.

He obviously intended to go back for them, but other factors intervened. Firstly, this was to be the last public execution. And secondly, he was dismissed for his behaviour. So the no-doubt potentially lucrative souvenirs languished in their hiding place until 1985. Fraser notes that the recent expansion of the courthouse has covered over Pritchard's grave and that of other executed felons, and that also there is a rumour of a second, much longer tunnel, running the full length of Saltmarket between the courthouse and the Tollbooth. This may be a tunnel too far. He does not say what happened to the boots. The two accounts are clearly somehow related to the same event – the discovery of, at the very least, Pritchard's boots – but the differences between them are striking: the dates, finds and events all contradict each other, and House's account was published decades before the alleged find in 1985. Perhaps there were two finds? Or perhaps the myth machine is at work again, manufacturing inconsistent testimony to perplex and bamboozle us.

In 1785 Mr Brown's Auction Room advertised 'the Surprising Dwarf … the shortest person that has ever been exhibited to the public,' and, 'A Young Lady from Newfoundland, born without arms.' In August 1828 a mob gathered here after a man was seen leaving a poor woman's house with a newborn infant under his coat; the man was severely beaten and had to be rescued by the police. At the station the baby was examined and found to have been stillborn. The mother, in extremis both financially and medically, had agreed that if the medical student attended her during her illness, he should, in the words of *The Anecdotage of Glasgow,* 'have the body of the dead child for the purpose of using it as he thought proper.' Dane Love (*Scottish Spectres*) notes that one of the regulars in Graham's Bar is the apparition of an old woman wearing a shawl over her head.

When Walter Scott wrote *Rob Roy* in 1817, he created a fictional Glasgow character who was so vivid on the page he made his entry into real life. Bailie Nicol Jarvie is a shrewd, canny merchant, business-minded and cautious, but also likeable, even loveable. The novel is set in 1715–16. When Queen Victoria visited Glasgow for the first time in 1849 she asked to see Jarvie's house. HRH was duly shown an old building in Saltmarket, behind the 'Original Bailie Nicol Jarvie Tavern'. From 1872 the periodical *The Bailie* was published, and for most of the paper's long life the fiction was maintained that it was indeed edited by Jarvie himself. Correspondents (real or equally fictitious) addressed him as 'Dear Bylie' or 'My Magistrate'. In 1922 the paper published a full biography of the man, giving his date of birth, details of his early life, and so on. Talk about yer post-modernism! (All this comes from Moira Burgess's *Imagine a City!*)

Seahorse power: Hippocampus, former Fish Market, Clyde Street.

CLYDE STREET

John Watson in *Once Upon a Time in Glasgow* notes that in 1587 the Kirk Session built a pulley to lower female criminals for ducking in the Clyde, with the law-givers watching from the ramparts of the old Glasgow Bridge. In the early nineteenth century a pair of police officers disturbed a bodysnatcher in Clyde Street burial ground and severed his arm with a cutlass.

The former Fish Market at Nos 64–76 is now Glasgow Sculpture Studios, still retaining its crowned female and bearded grumpy males heads and, above the entrances, two splendid pairs of winged hippocampi.

The corner with Ropework Lane was the site of the mansion of wealthy merchant Robert Dreghorn. With his out-of-proportion massive head, collapsed nose, missing eye and smallpox-scarred face, he was widely regarded as the ugliest man in Glasgow, hence his nickname, Bob Dragon. His very name was a pacifier of misbehaving children, for whom he became a potent bogeyman. His pleasure was to follow pretty women along Argyle Street and Trongate, but despite his wealth, his deformities condemned him to bachelordom, and in 1806 he committed suicide. He then supposedly haunted his empty mansion. *The Old Country Houses of the Old Glasgow Gentry* records how strange lights and sounds were in evidence, although in 1812, when the house was opened, it was found that smugglers had taken advantage of the house's reputation to set up an illicit distillery. Carol Foreman in *Glasgow Curiosities* describes how James Galloway, auditor of the burgh court of Glasgow, eventually leased the house at a knockdown price. His daughter, however, felt scared in the house so the family left. Again the great mansion lay empty until rented by George Provand, an oil and colour merchant. One Saturday night some late revellers dared themselves into peering into the 'haunted house'. In the poor light they spied a table dripping with red ichor and two black, rounded shapes that

City Chambers, George Square.

could only be severed heads. Rumours spread and by the afternoon of Sunday 17 February 1822 a mob had gathered. With cries of 'bodysnatcher' and 'murderer', the house was ransacked and plundered. Provand, an old man, fled for his life. At some point some of the looters may have noticed that the blood and severed heads were spilt red pigment and two large jars of black paint, but it was too late. The mob was quelled by dragoons and infantry with drawn bayonets. A reward of 200 guineas was posted and the ringleaders soon apprehended and sentenced to fourteen years transportation and, in one case, being whipped through the streets of the city. Dreghorn's fine mansion is long gone, replaced by a warehouse. (For more on Bob Dragon *see* RUCHILL.)

3

THE HEART OF THE CITY

GEORGE SQUARE

The spectacular City Chambers doubled for the Vatican in the film *Heavenly Pursuits*, in which a liberal Glasgow schoolteacher, played by Tom Conti, gets caught up in a politico-religious plot to prove the miracles that will elevate a local woman, the Blessed Edith Semple, to sainthood. In the entrance of the Chamber of Commerce stands the statue of Kirkman Finlay, one of Glasgow's alpha entrepreneurs. Foreman's *Glasgow Curiosities* says Finlay's friendly ghost wanders the building. Peter Underwood's *Gazetteer of Scottish Ghosts* describes a scene which took place a few years before the early 1970s. Somewhere in or near George Street, a man walking home from late shift-work at 2 a.m. was joined by two ghosts dressed in eighteenth-century costume. They walked beside him, 'going about their own amicable business' as he put it, and chatted to each other companionably, although the man heard no sound. Within a few seconds they faded and vanished. The down-to-earth workman had enjoyed the experience and hoped it might be repeated. The Auctioneers pub (No. 6 North Court) is rumoured to be haunted by a female ghost (there is the briefest of mentions in the *Evening Times*, 31 October 2001, but I have no further details).

Ron Halliday's *UFO Scotland* tells of two strange encounters. In November 1979 a Mr McDougall was walking in George Square when he was almost hit by a grey football-shaped object which let out a high-pitched hissing sound and emitted a pungent smell of sulphur. He felt it was moving as if under some kind of intelligent control, although it may well have a) a prank or b) an example of ball lightning, one of the most fascinating and least understood of natural phenomena. A decade later a couple crossing the east quarter of the Square saw an octagonal object hovering above them. Despite being some 30ft (9m) across, everyone else in the square was oblivious to it. It vanished in a blue flash.

WEST GEORGE STREET

Among the multiple sculptures on Connal's Building at No. 34 are hands bearing garlands creepily emerging from the walls, and figures who seem to be struggling out of the fabric, as if the building was a portal transforming these troubled figures from stone to flesh. High up in the south-west corner of Nelson Mandela Place, two monstrous griffons stand guard over the former Stock Exchange. The Royal Faculty of Procurators, on the corner with West Nile Street, has several truly monstrous faces on the upper keystones. Nos 105-111 has several wonderful – and mischievous-looking – Green Men carved, unusually, in profile. The former Sun Life Building at 117-121 has one of the most amazing collections of ancient mythological motifs in Glasgow. The punning solar theme starts with Aurora in a chariot drawn by a pair of dynamic horses, and continues with six planetary gods, the Zodiac, Apollo (on Renfield Street) surrounded by naked male and female sunbathers, and an astonishing Medusa-like sun at the top. Just to the left of the main entrance is Mithras, the Persian solar deity worshipped in Roman times via a bull-sacrificing cult. Angels, Green Men, demons, grotesques and gargoyles abound. Unmissable.

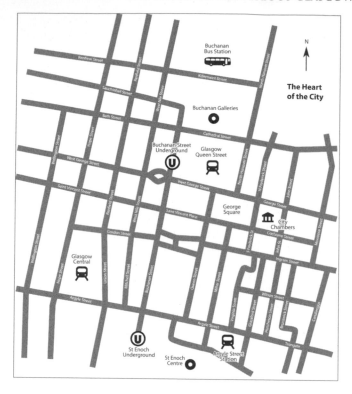

Griffon guarding
the Stock Exchange,
Nelson Mandela Place.

Mischievous Green Man,
Nos 105-111 West George
Street.

Mithras, the Persian-Roman sun god, to whom bulls were sacrificed, Nos 117-121 West George Street.

Personifications of Exchange and Security, Royal Bank of Scotland, St Enoch Square. Note the ship of trade, cornucopiae, Mercury's winged caduceus, snakes, keys and piggy-bank.

ST VINCENT PLACE

The former Anchor Line Building at Nos 12-16 berths marine symbolism, with sea monsters, anchors, conches and masks of Neptune and Mercury, the latter having a helmet decorated with tiny sphinxes. The Clydesdale Bank (No. 24) features pelicans, lions and mythical creatures. Sailors fish from a Viking longboat on the former Scottish Amicable Building (Nos 31-39) while on Nos 30-40 decorous ladies representing Sowing, Reaping, Industry and Commerce dispense their graces on the working classes. Over the entrance arch, fish swim through the beard of Father Clyde.

ST VINCENT STREET

Phoenixes, both massive and modest, are arrayed all over the former Phoenix Assurance Co. Building at No. 78. Naked children cheerfully undertake trade, navigation and wealth creation on Nos 81-91 and 93, while at Nos 84-94 chained dolphins plot delphine revenge on humanity.

BUCHANAN STREET

Around 2004, whilst working in a coffee shop on the first floor of No. 235 (the Virgin Megastore) David McCabe, one of the 'sensitives' working with Ghost Hunters Scotland, often had a vision of a 'drawing room' and two people in Victorian dress; the building was once the George Hotel.

No. 113 sports dragons, griffins and unicorns as well as a winged bishop and, for some reason, a camel; No. 91 (Bradford & Bingley Building Society) features dolphins, while Nos 63-69 (Jigsaw/Esprit), the former *Glasgow Herald* building, is overrun with urchins acting as journalists and printers. Caxton and Gutenberg keep an eye on their offspring from on high. Jaeger (Nos 60-62) is ornamented with allegorical female figures of Justice (sword and scales) and Truth (removing blindfold and holding mirror). Higher up, angels recline and winged griffons glower. Industry and Art sit back to back on Fraser's (No. 45) while on Argyle Chambers (Nos 28-32) one woman spins yarn while another holds a caduceus.

For decades, staff at upmarket Sloans Restaurant, No. 62 Argyll Arcade, have claimed the premises are haunted by the spirit of Myron, a former waiter who plays piano and brushes against staff in corridors.

ST ENOCH CENTRE/SQUARE

'St Enoch' is a corruption of St Thenew, she being the unmarried single mother of St Kentigern (at least according to Jocelin's *Life of Kentigern* – see introduction). Thenew's well and reliquary chapel were secondary but still important destinations for pilgrims visiting Kentigern's relics at the cathedral. McUre's *History of Glasgow* (1736) describes the ruins as standing 'in a solitary spot in the country surrounded by cornfields', but urban development has annihilated all traces. The well was clearly used for healing – Andrew MacGeorge's *Old Glasgow* reports that when it was cleared out several votive offerings were found. These were shaped in the form of the afflicted part of the body and fixed to the tree which shaded the well.

The Royal Bank of Scotland building (No. 22-24 St Enoch Square) has winged caducei and cornucopia along with excellent female figures personifying Exchange, Security, Prudence and Adventure, the last an uncharacteristically impetuous attribute among the usually more conservative banking allegories. No. 40 has a wonderful head of Athena wearing a winged helmet bearing a cat's face.

Ron Halliday (*UFO Scotland*) reports that in December 1990 a woman standing at the bus stop outside British Home Stores in the shopping centre saw a silver shape with a belt of amber lights across its middle. It was 4.30 p.m., already dark, but the skyline was clear. She and a fellow bystander watched the object cross the city centre at rooftop height for about five to ten minutes, after which it drifted out of sight to the south.

ARGYLE STREET

The entrance to Nos 134-156 is supported by two massive stooped Atlantes. In 1981 roadworks on the south side of Howard Street uncovered at least four bodies, probably from the site of the burial ground of the town hospital – actually a poorhouse – which stood on Dunlop Street from 1733 to 1850. Two more skeletons were found in 2004 slightly further south during the Metropole Development. One of the skulls had been opened after death, a common fate for the insane.

GORDON STREET

Naked infants print money and carry bags of coins on the former Commercial Bank of Scotland at Nos 2-16. Athena presides over No. 46. At Nos 60-79 semi-naked, joyful Summer contrasts with the austerely hooded Winter. Below them, a bare-breasted female warrior drives a chariot, while a lion, elephant, bear and kangaroo represent the colonies, and grotesque keystones glower above windows.

Load-bearing Atlante, Nos 134–156
Argyle Street.

CENTRAL STATION

One of Glasgow's persistent myths is that an entire street – complete with still-existing shops and houses – is buried beneath the station. Variants of the story include a supposedly long-forgotten but still complete Victorian railway station, and a secret tunnel leading north from the station along Hope Street to be used in a crisis for the evacuation of VIPs. The idea of the 'Lost Underground City' has a strong appeal to the imagination, as shown in examples as diverse as Edinburgh's City of the Dead tours and Neil Gaiman's *Neverwhere*, set in a fantastically-realised magical subterranean London. The Glasgow version has a few obvious sources. When Glasgow Central railway station was built, it swept away the village of Grahamston – sadly for the story, the entire area was flattened, so there are no dark abandoned streets to be found. There does appear to be a tunnel of some sort beneath Hope Street, but it is almost certainly part of the Post Office's communications network – the kind of mundane thing that is found under many city streets in highly developed urban areas. And not only does Glasgow have a subway system, but the part of the suburban rail network within the city centre is subterranean; I suspect this daily chthonic experience of underground railway stations and tunnels unconsciously contributes to the continuing idea of the 'Secret and Lost' beneath the city.

The underground platforms at Glasgow Central are also the locus of a series of sightings of a man dubbed 'the undertaker' because he is dressed in formal black clothes and wearing a top hat. A post by 'nuttytigger' on the forum at www.hiddenglasgow.com for 28 April 2004 is typical of the experience: the man was seen walking down the track both before and *after* a train came through. David McCabe of Ghost Hunters Scotland told me he used to work in a café in the curvilinear line of shops on the west side of the station. He often encountered the

Relaxing angel, former Liverpool, London and Globe Insurance Building, No. 116 Hope Street.

The Angel of Insurance, No. 116 Hope Street.

Gent with marine
moustache, Mercantile
Chambers, Bothwell
Street.

spirit of a caretaker in the service corridor behind the shops, and in the storage area – to which he had the only key – he frequently found the boxes disturbed.

HOPE STREET

No. 116 is richly endowed with grotesques, lounging angels, griffins and male and female torsos. Lion Chambers at No. 172 has some of the most unusual sculptures in the city – a pair of massive concrete bewigged judges, projecting boldly out from the first floor corners. The building once housed a suite of law chambers.

4

CITY CENTRE: SOUTH & WEST

ST VINCENT STREET

No. 123 has four Green Ladies whose striking hairdos are made out of vegetation, a stern-looking fellow (probably unhappy because he's got a cogwheel stuck in his hair) and a beatific agricultural beauty. No. 142, the 'Hatrack' building, delights in goat's-head keystones, winged figures and sunbursts, with a stained-glass oriel window showing a stately galleon supported by some kind of dragon. The amazing Sun Alliance building at No. 200, formerly home of the North British & Mercantile Insurance Co., features a monumental St Andrew on a ship's prow; a young man in seaboots holding a boat, and his wife, a pouting temptress awaiting his return; a fierce winged and webbed lion-amphibian beast; a Triton blowing a trumpet and riding a seahorse; other seahorses supporting tridents; an animal-headed oar-propelled Greek trireme; an Elizabethan man o'war; and coiled marine monsters.

The Royal College of Physicians and Surgeons of Glasgow was founded in 1599. Its current headquarters at No. 232-242 holds a vast library of medical, anatomical and surgical texts from the sixteenth to the twentieth centuries. One of their treasures, an anonymous *Book of Herbal Remedies* from lowland Scotland, has been published online at www.rcpsg.ac.uk/herbal. It contains the following suggestions for nosebleeds: 'put a pice of hot hoggs turd as it comes from the gig up in your Nose' or 'hold a living toad Near Nose it stops the blood instantly'.

Elsewhere it gives hints how the 'sons of Art' can amaze and bamboozle the rubes. Magnetic lodestones can make metal objects move as if by magic. Coals or metal tongs can be taken straight from the fire into your mouth without burning, and an accomplice can even use bellows to pump up the heat in your mouth – but only if you first anoint your mouth with liquid Storax, a balsam obtained from the Near East. Secretly inserting some quicksilver (mercury) under the shell of a boiled egg will cause the egg to 'capper and dance upon the floor as if ther were an evel spirit in it'. Quicksilver inserted in an inflated sheep's bladder will have a similar effect. Apparently spontaneous fire effects 'which will be very admirable to beholders' can be achieved by covertly using phosphorus. A tiny amount on the edge of a glass will re-ignite an extinguished candle, or a dry wick impregnated with phosphorus will light up if just touched by anything warm and metal. There is also a discussion of the Philosopher's Stone, which through rubbing will turn brass to silver, and transform silver to gold. Sadly, the herbal does not describe where such a stone can be obtained. The library and archives are open to the public by appointment.

Alexander Thomson's extraordinary church at No. 265, with its Greek Temple accompanied by Egyptian and Assyrian motifs and statuary, is a must-see. Egyptian designs continue in the splendid interior. Altogether an appropriately spooky venue for the spiritualist church, which used to contact the dead here (the church now operates on SAUCHIEHALL STREET). One of the strangest things about this church is that it was built for the Free Presbyterian Church, a group more usually associated with austere architecture. St Columba's Church of

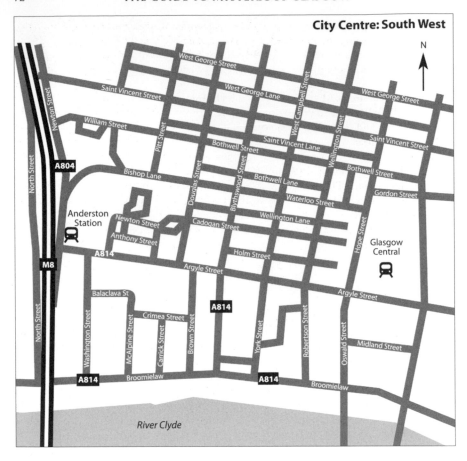

Scotland at No. 300 has, among the usual praying angels and human masks, a head of Moses sporting horns. This is a remarkably common depiction deriving from a mistranslation of Exodus 34:29-35: when Moses came down from Mount Sinai with the Ten Commandments he is described as having rays of light shining from his face, but in some versions 'rays of light' becomes 'horns'.

BOTHWELL STREET

The wonderful Art Deco building of the Scottish Legal Life Assurance Society (Nos 81-107) is graced by allegorical figures and capitals featuring scales and crossed swords, crossed staves tied by a rope, lions confronting a pillar of fire, horses flanking a sword, cornucopia, a beehive, an hourglass, a sword and breastplate, and a striking image of a hand grasping a snake. The company's name is symbolically set out on the Blythswood Street side – a lion rampant (= Scottish), a judge's wig (Legal), a fountain (Life) and a castle (Assurance). Add to this a stunning quasi-Egyptian carving of a woman with a headdress-neckpiece composed of a mean-looking double-bodied single-headed snake, and you've got one of the more imaginative commercial buildings in Glasgow. Mercury lounges insouciantly in the centre of the Mercantile Chambers (Nos 35-69), surrounded by strange and mysterious sculptures: monstrous heads with fish moustaches; a Green Man with hair and moustaches of foliage; an unhappy man wearing a hat of fishes; a semi-Green Man crowned with a crescent and a double cornucopia dispensing fruit; another man with a winged and starred helmet; two lizards crawling high up the stonework; a dragon crawling down; an Oriental turbaned head inside a ring of snakes; another turbaned head; a winged female torsos; a sea monster; and swords, guns, lions, mudskippers, eagles, ships' prows, compasses, and cornucopiae dispensing coins.

A ribbon deconstructs Mungo's symbols in both words and images – Trees Grow, Birds Fly, Fish Swim, Bells Ring – and Prosperity, Prudence, Industry and Fortune look down over the Four Elements. And one of the smaller sculptures – a bird with clawed feet, human breasts and bat wings – bears a strong resemblance to the 'Queen of the Night' figure in the British Museum, a Babylonian carving that is either Ishtar (goddess of sex and war), Ereshkigal (ruler of the Underworld) or Lilitu, aka Adam's first wife Lilith, mother of demons.

The former Central Thread Agency at Nos 36-62, opposite, sports: a bearded man with a crown to which a fish is attached; a Native American chief with headdress; an Egyptian pharaoh with a winged sun-disc on his chest; a turbaned, bearded man; a crowned, clean-shaven King; and a winged cherub with an Elvis quiff, alongside all of which the deities Mercury and Athena seem quite mundane.

WATERLOO STREET

The former United Distillers building at No. 64 is a sculptural billboard for Walter Scott's popular romance 'The Lady of the Lake'. The poem's two rivals, Roderick Dhu (buoyant in a kilt with fox-headed sporran – the company produced a whisky named after him) and James Fitzjames (jauntily kitted out for the hunt) snub each other over the entrance, while the heroine Ellen Douglas stands on a small waterfall on the corner tower holding the paddle which got her across Loch Katrine. Elsewhere a dragon and a griffon snack on a sheaf of corn, two dragons bite their own tails, heads are draped in grapevines, and *trompe l'oeil* cannons poke out, while the best carving is a bizarre bat-thing with whiskers.

A snake charmer, Scottish
Legal Life Assurance Society,
Bothwell Street.

Alexander 'Greek' Thomson's Church, No. 265 St Vincent Street.

There's a star man waiting on the Mercantile Chambers, Nos 35-69 Bothwell Street.

Dragon, Mercantile Chambers.

The goddess Ishtar? The demon Lilith? Bat-woman on Mercantile Chambers.

Native American chief, Nos 36–62 Bothwell Street.

Pharaoh, Nos 36–62 Bothwell Street.

ROBERTSON STREET

The Clydeport Authority building contains some of the best sculpture in Glasgow. At the top Neptune's ship surges through the waves propelled by multiple horsepower; the pediment has Neptune again, this time being paid tributes by the peoples of the world. Ships' prows thrust through the wall; engineering alumni gaze benevolently down; comically moustachioed grotesque faces decorate the dome; and, best of all, Europa leads a massive bull by a chain while Amphitrite urges on her seahorses with a trident.

A dragon and a griffon have a healthy wholefood snack. No. 64 Waterloo Street.

Europa stepping out with the bull, Clydeport building, Robertson Street.

BROOMIELAW

By 1812 the price of a corpse for the anatomist's table had soared and so cheap foreign imports became popular. Poverty in Ireland meant that for a time cadavers could be obtained for a very reasonable rate. That year a cargo marked as 'linen rags' was unloaded at the Broomielaw quay but, as the story recounted by Peter McKenzie has it, the addressee, a huxter in Jamaica Street, refused to pay the excessive freight charges. After having lain for several days in a dockside shed, the cargo gave off a terrible smell. Investigation showed it contained the bodies of men, women and children. They were buried in Anderston.

On 7 May 1990 a man's body was recovered from the Clyde near Broomielaw. He was about thirty-forty years old, with brown wavy hair and a dark moustache. All he had on him was a lighter with the initials 'J.C.' and a black leather wallet containing a three-figure sum of money. Following publicity, the police were contacted by a New Jersey couple who came to Glasgow and identified the body as their son John Crawford. The body was flown to the US, but then the real John Crawford turned up, alive and well. The now unidentified corpse was returned, leaving the Glasgow police back at square one. The strange tale is in the *Sunday Post* (24 June 1990). During the first chaotic weeks of the First World War, one of the many rumours sweeping the country was that thousands of Russian troops had landed in Scotland, and were passing through Britain on their way to the Western Front. James Hayward, in *Myths & Legends of the First World War,* notes that dozens of eyewitness reports were generated by word of mouth, and everyone knew the story. The Russians were seen landing at Broomielaw, as well as at Aberdeen and Leith. They were fed at York, Crewe, and Colchester, seen smoking cigars in closed carriages and stamping snow from their boots on station platforms, and spotted in Carlisle, Berwick, Durham, Stoke, Oxford, Bristol, Stroud and Folkestone. The source was always an anonymous railway porter. After a few weeks the reports ceased and the entirely fictional Russian saviours gently faded from public consciousness.

HILTON HOTEL

Dane Love's book *Scottish Spectres* states that the modern hotel on William Street has been haunted since it was built. A male spirit in the bar moved glasses, switched lights on and off, threw things across the room, groaned at men and wolf-whistled at female staff. A barmaid became so scared of the constant attention she fled from her work. The apparition of an attractive woman has also been seen. She has long blonde hair over her shoulders and wears a low-cut shimmering blue dress. Staff said they often received bookings for rooms on the thirteenth floor in the hope of meeting this particular ghost.

ANDERSTON

In 1828 thirty-year-old Henry Gillies or Gilles was jailed for nine months for graverobbing from Anderston churchyard. He had lost his job as a gravedigger for stealing and reselling grave furniture, and was banned from the churchyard because during funerals he had shown an unwelcome interest in the depth of the graves, measuring them with a sharp-pointed cane. He was apprehended at 3 a.m. on 17 March by the night watch, who had seen him dumping suspicious parcels in a garden. Three other men with him escaped. The baggage turned out to be an elderly pauper woman, and Margaret McNeil, a small child recently killed by whooping cough. Margaret's mother was a poor seaman's widow. A woman from a higher station offered to rebury Margaret in the grave of her own recently deceased child, but when the lair was opened, it was found this body too had been stolen. It is not clear what happened to Gillies.

Most of Anderston was wiped out when the M8 was built. David Glenday's *Anderston As It Was* notes that North Street Burial Ground contained a statue which, according to local children's folklore, was actually a little girl who had been turned to stone because she had swallowed chewing gum. The small graveyard was little used after 1870 and removed in the 1960s. The marooned section of Argyle Street west of the motorway has two intriguing sets of sculpture. No. 650, now the Buttery Restaurant, has a panel with distinctively Masonic insignia (Quick! Call the Conspiracy Police), as well as five busts and a deer's head. The delightful Art Nouveau former Glasgow Savings Bank at No. 752, now the Art House, features mock-medieval scenes of angels and knights, Saints Andrew and Kentigern, two angels with astonishing cowl-like batwings, and, above the doorway, a bust of Henry Duncan, founder of the Savings Bank movement, sagely tapping his forehead and clutching his bulging moneybag filled with well-gotten gains.

5

CITY CENTRE: NORTH & WEST

BLYTHSWOOD SQUARE

> Murder has a magic of its own, its peculiar alchemy. Touched by that crimson wand, things base
> and sordid, things ugly and of ill report, are transformed into matters wondrous, weird and tragical.
> Dull streets become fraught with mystery, commonplace dwellings assume sinister aspects, everyone
> concerned, howsoever plain and ordinary, is invested with a new value and importance as the red
> light falls upon each.
>
> William Roughead, *Classic Crimes*

'The Square Mile of Murder' is the coining of legendary Glasgow journalist and author Jack House, in his 1961 book of the same title. It covers four murders committed between 1857 and 1908 within a relatively small part of the city, from this Square, north to Sauchiehall Street and south and west towards Charing Cross. Some of the 'Square Mile' is now on the other side of the M8. The accused were Madeleine Smith (verdict: not proven), Jessie McLachlan (guilty, although she was almost certainly innocent), Dr Pritchard (guilty, hanged) and Oscar Slater (guilty, but later released – his conviction was a miscarriage of justice). All are still part of the living mythology of Glasgow, and hence are included here.

Madeleine Smith lived at No. 7 Blythswood Square, an upmarket address then and now. An inscription marks the house. In 1857 she was accusing of murdering her inconvenient lover Pierre Emile L'Angelier by lacing his cocoa with arsenic. *The Anecdotage of Glasgow's* introduction describes why the case attracted so much attention: 'on account of her sex, youth, beauty, standing in society, and the romantic incidents in the case.' The sexually explicit letters between Pierre and Madeleine were read out in court. Pierre was poor, Madeleine's new beau was rich, Pierre was deliberately withholding the letters, possibly for blackmail when he realised the affair was cooling. Madeleine had motive and opportunity, and although she had purchased arsenic, it was proved to be a different type to that found in Pierre's stomach. It is possible Pierre committed suicide as revenge on Madeleine, hoping she would be both stricken with remorse, and implicated in the crime. It is possible she was involved in the poisoning in some way. We will never know. Not surprisingly, after what was revealed in court, Madeleine's wealthy fiancé broke off the engagement, but the 'notorious temptress' went on to live a full life. Pierre is buried in RAMSHORN GRAVEYARD.

The *Daily Express* (26 January 2001) reported that the headquarters of Melville Craig employment agency in Blythswood Square was haunted by the ghost of ... Madeleine Smith. Kettles were switched on and off, strange noises were heard, and one of the rooms was always freezing cold – supposedly the very room where Madeleine was claimed to have poisoned Emile. There was even the vaguest of suggestions that her spirit was seen wandering the corridors. Staff were said to run out of the door at 5 p.m. Marketing consultant Melanie Harvey was quoted as saying: 'Nobody wants to be the last one in the office, especially during the dark and dreary nights. It is a scary thought to be in here yourself knowing that Madeleine could be standing right behind you.'

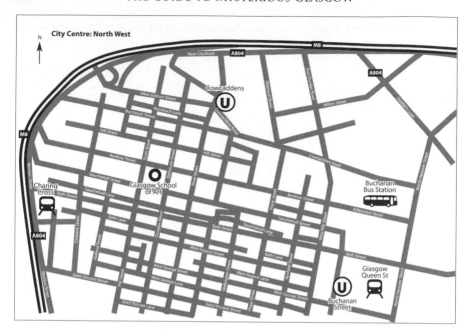

The tale of another haunting in the area is told in Elliott O'Donnell's *Scottish Ghost Stories*. Captain W. de S. Smythe took _____ House, unidentified except that it was near but not in Blythswood Square. The bathroom had a grim atmosphere, to the point where Smythe refused to wash. Eventually necessity required he ablute. Naked in the bathroom, he fell over, the candles went out, and he heard a large person washing in the bath. He then saw a beautiful but malignant dark-haired woman dressed in silk skirt and petticoats open the door of the cupboard, walk past him, and strangle the person in the bath. Smythe sat up, the darkness lightened and suddenly he was face to face with the luminous white face of the murderess. She smelled of violets. After staring at him, she vanished, and in horror Smythe fled in 'Adam's costume'.

Another day the eldest boy, Ronald, saw the dead, bloated body of an old man in the bath. His screaming brought his mother and the servants, who did not see the corpse, but all glimpsed the dark evil-eyed woman. Her clothes and jewellery were costly, and she glided past the astonished group before vanishing by the cupboard. Within a week the family had quit the house, the rumour getting about that it was haunted. The landlord threatened the Smythes with an action for slander of title, and in exchange for not going to court the family agreed to contradict the report they had originated. The Smythes discovered that a lady of Spanish descent had lived in the house with her wealthy but aged husband. They often quarrelled. One day he was found dead in the bath – the verdict was that he had fainted and drowned. His widow inherited his wealth and went abroad.

In 2004 there were reports of a tree in the Square being festooned with cuddly toys, a rather creepy sight at night. The general opinion was that it was a prank initiated by the cycle couriers who congregate in the cafés on West Regent Street.

PITT STREET

The Strathclyde Police Museum in Police HQ presents an endlessly fascinating set of displays on crime and policing from 1800 – when the City of Glasgow Police, Britain's earliest police force, was founded – to the present day. Among the exhibits are the bloodstained footprint on a wooden floorboard that helped erroneously convict Jessie McLachlan of the Sandyford Place murder, and, contained within jars of formaldehyde, a piece of a watchman's ear cut off during a crime, and the tip of a woman's nose bitten off in a moment of passion. A crystal ball from 1936 illustrates the inter-war campaigns against fortune-tellers and 'false mediums'. In 1922 a Glasgow fortune-teller told an undercover policewoman 'you will marry a tall, dark man and live to a good old age'. A few minutes she gave an identical reading to a second undercover cop. There's also much on developments in modern forensic detection, and details of various grisly and shocking murders. The museum is open to anyone, either singly or groups, but visits must be booked in advance on 0141 532 2822. Wheelchair access is available. The museum also sells a useful guide which expands the stories of some of the exhibits: *In Custody,* by Rudolph Kenna and Ian Sutherland.

WEST REGENT STREET

Or 'West Freemasons Street' as I like to think of it. No. 79 has Masonic emblems such as dividers and the mason's gavel, while the former Masonic Halls at Nos 98-104 has a brilliant blazing sun, stars encircling a crescent moon, and two statues, one of which is St John the Baptist dressed in an animal skin and cradling a lamb, while the other is presumably St John the Evangelist, the other saint much venerated by Freemasons. Curiously the Evangelist, usually associated with an eagle, is here instead shown holding something which you may choose to interpret as a lamp, cup … or grail. Sovereign House, Nos 158-60, the former Institute for the Adult Deaf & Dumb, has carved dragons, mice, lizards and snails, and, most obviously, a panel showing Christ healing the dumb man. The inscription EPHPHATHA is Aramaic for 'be opened', the healing word said by Jesus (Mark 7:34). I'm not sure what message such imagery communicates to those who are mute – 'if you're lucky, you might be cured by a passing miracle-worker,' perhaps?

SAUCHIEHALL STREET

Ron Halliday, in *The A-Z of Paranormal Scotland*, mentions a phantom tram that was regularly seen here. Someone tried to hail it but the driver simply nodded and smiled as he drove by, before the vehicle vanished in a gentle mist. A life-size alien warrior from the *Predator* films

Nos 98-104 West Regent
Street: Masonic sun?

'Let me put my hands on you ...' The faith healer, Nos 98-104 West Regent Street.

stands in the window of the Red5 gadget shop at Unit 2 Buchanan Galleries. The 8ft (2.4m) high fully-armoured figure is yours for a mere £10,000. The Savoy Centre (Nos 128-152) has colossal heads of Mercury and Athena above nine female figures, associated respectively with a flaming torch, palm frond, released doves, cockerel, dough paddle and scroll, sailing ship, book and lamp, trumpet, and mirror and compass. In the middle is a soldier with a shield and axe or standard, and a cheery sun rises from behind an arch. What does all this arcana mean? Another golden sun beams down from atop No. 154.

The Empire Theatre formerly stood at the corner of Sauchiehall Street and West Nile Street. The Ghost Club website has two accounts from Daniel Fernie, whose trade as an apprentice sign-writer took him to a contract at the Empire in August 1960. He was on the upper balcony when he experienced 'a feeling of electricity in the air' and saw on the stage a faint apparition of singers dressed as nuns. At the same time he distantly heard the Easter Hymn from *Cavalaria Rusticana*, a piece with which he was familiar. The lead soprano had a powerful voice. The name Marion popped into his head. Daniel sat and watched the performance for about three minutes while his trainer, who had heard and seen the same things, went to (inconclusively) investigate. Back at home Daniel told his mother what had happened and she connected 'Marion' with Charlie Chester, although he could not remember any further details. This might be Marian Miller, born in Tynemouth in 1931; after touring in various shows she was discovered by Chester and became a regular in his revue and variety shows on stage and television. She was always billed as 'the Golden Voice of Marian Miller'.

The Scottish Theatre Archive at the University of Glasgow has a programme for the Charlie Chester Show at the Empire for 19 November 1956, but there is no detail about whether a sketch involved singing nuns. About a week after this first incident, both men where on the stage behind the fire curtain when the stage boards moved as if responding to stamping and dancing; Daniel also heard some unfamiliar 'foreign' music. Some years later he happened to buy a record by the Red Army Choir and Dancers. Listening to it he identified the music he had heard as a balalaika ... and then found out the Soviet ensemble had once appeared at the Empire. The theatre closed in 1963.

Rising sun and allegorical figure; some of the many curious sculptures on Nos 128-152 Sauchiehall Street.

Harry Bell describes an out-of-body-experience (OOBE) as a child attending Glasgow Dental Hospital. After the anaesthetic was administered, he saw the whole operation from the ceiling. Interestingly his perspective switched from being in the chair to looking down several times. His post-extraction insistence of 'Mammy, mammy there's two me's' met with parental scepticism.

The Royal Highland Fusiliers Museum at No. 518 hosts the Delphic Sibyl and Isaiah, both famed for predicting the future through divine inspiration. Two Muse-caryatids each raise a lamp. The winged figure playing two flutes simultaneously on the attic is Harmony, probably a frustrated prog-rock musician. Charing Cross Mansions (No. 2-30 St George's Road) is a meditation in stone on the passage of time, with a great clockface surrounded by symbols of the Zodiac and Michelangeloesque figures representing the four Seasons and Dawn and Dusk, while Old Father Time peers beardily from the centre.

RENFIELD STREET

Castle Chambers (Nos 59-69) has the usual protection from Mercury and Athena, as well as four dreamy maidens sheltering under the shade of a ledge and a cherub skipping with a rope while four of its fellows set up a swag of flowers.

Harmony playing the pipes above
No. 518 Sauchiehall Street.

The Pavilion Theatre is home to an entire variety show of spooks. In *Psychic Scotland* Tom Rannachan writes that when he was a member of the chorus at a show in 1994, he was standing in the lower corridor of dressing rooms, waiting to go on stage, when a pretty young girl wearing a bright blue dress and tiara smiled at him. He stepped aside to let her pass, quickly glanced the other way – and she had vanished, except for the strong scent of her perfume. This was possibly a dancer who, *it was said,* died in the top dressing-rooms when her dress brushed against an open fire. One afternoon Tom was sitting on the stage an hour or so before last the show, when, from the box-seat to the right of him, he saw a large grinning man leaning towards him. Years later he saw a photo of the comedian Tommy Morgan – and recognised the face. Morgan's ashes were scattered on the roof of this, his favourite theatre. The Pavilion is also allegedly home to several other phenomena, as noted on The Ghost Club's website: the apparition of a woman in one of the boxes in the auditorium, phantom piano music, a seat in Row F of the stalls which goes down by itself, and items of equipment which spontaneously disappear.

The Theatre Royal is another in Glasgow's long list of venues that are claimed to be haunted. The first theatre here dates from 1867, rebuilt in 1895 after two fires. From 1957 it was the studios of STV. Scottish Opera bought it in 1973. The first phenomenon was in the upper circle, with moaning, banging of doors, and a sense of presence behind people. At some unknown point the spirit has acquired the name 'Nora' and something of a biography. She was supposed to have been an aspiring actress who took a job as a cleaner. She was either mocked off the stage during a try-out or went through a 'casting couch' audition and became pregnant, possibly having the baby. In both cases she was so shamed that she jumped from the upper circle, possibly after drinking bleach. Unfortunately no one knows when this story first started, other than it has been circulating around the theatre staff for many years.

The Zodiac clock and Old Father Time, Charing Cross Mansions.

It may, however, have a theatrical rather than a supernatural origin. Mike Hall, who worked at the theatre and has researched its history, has tracked down a play that transferred from London's Drury Lane to the Royal in 1894. The central character of *A Life of Pleasure* is named Norah Hanlan. The villain, the despicable Colonel Chandes, seduces and then abandons her. She becomes a strolling prostitute in the promenade of a London music hall. Ultimately, Chandes is struck by remorse and poisons himself in the music hall. So we have a tale of seduction, betrayal and suicide in a theatre, and a woman called Norah. It is therefore possible the story of Nora the cleaner is a case of art creating folklore. But the strange phenomena still continue. Gary Painter, who works at the stage door, told me that in 2006 or 2007 a contractor working alone in a roof space reached by a hatch from the upper circle was hit on the back of the head with a brochure, and several staff members have commented that the nearby vestibule and corridor have an unpleasant atmosphere.

One night, possibly in the late 1970s, a member of the Scottish Opera orchestra asked a colleague why there was a fireman sitting in the corner of a back room. The answer was, of course, 'what fireman?' The apparition was described as staring into space and wearing a slightly old-fashioned uniform, the kind of black serge jerkin in use in the 1960s. On Monday 2 November 1969 an electrical fault started a fire in a sub-stage area filled with flammable magnetic tape and film. Smoke drifted into the STV studios during a live interview. It took ninety firemen almost twenty-two hours to extinguish the slow smouldering fire. Sixteen people were injured. One died, who Mike Hall has identified as thirty-five-year-old Sub-Officer Archibald McLang of the Southern Division in Queen's Park. The place had been pumped with foam, and it was dark and smoke-filled. Archie was one of a group of firemen who entered from Hope Street and walked across the stage. Either it gave way or he fell through a trap door; his body was recovered the next day.

As a result of the accident, Sub-Officer John Jameson invented an inertia-saving device, which warned others if a fire officer was stationery for too long, and became standard issue, saving many lives. The basement where the apparition was seen continues to generate phenomena. Gary Hall told me that around 2004 a plumber stacked his tools before going to another part of the area. When he returned, the tools were scattered across the floor. He restacked them, only later to find them once more dispersed.

In his *Guide to Ghosts & Haunted Places*, veteran ghost-hunter Peter Underwood described visiting the STV studios for an interview in the early 1970s. He found it was considered unlucky to talk about the ghost (presumably 'Nora'), and that the building had both poltergeistic phenomena – 'as I can personally testify' – and apparitions, one of whom was recognized as that of a former manager.

ROSE STREET

In 2008 St Aloysius' Church received a copy of the famous Black Madonna of Montserrat, the original of which is venerated by pilgrims in the Monastery of Santa María de Montserrat in Catalonia. This wooden Romanesque carving shows both the Virgin and the infant Jesus with dark faces. Black Madonnas are widespread in Catholic Europe and have generated numerous theories as to their genesis and meaning. There may be a link to Egyptian statues of the goddess Isis suckling the infant Horus on her lap, and perhaps from there to an earlier African earth deity, or other pre-Christian Mediterranean mother goddesses. Perhaps the colouring is meant to represent the original Middle-Eastern skin tone of the Holy Family. Perhaps a dark-skinned Madonna represents feminine power, in a way that the submissive, obedient standard pale-skinned images of Mary cannot. Perhaps it is all, or none, of these things.

In July 1999 hundreds of 'vampires', many in costume, turned up at the Glasgow Film Theatre to attend the launch of *Bite Me!*, Glasgow's still-thriving magazine dedicated to all things vampiric. Editor Arlene Russo went on to write *Vampire Nation,* in which she discusses various kinds of contemporary aficionados – the 'lifestylers' who enjoy the look and sub-culture, the 'psychic vampires' who drain the energy of others, and 'sanguine vampires', who actually exchange blood in various ways.

RENFREW STREET

And talking of vampires, the Glasgow School of Art, Charles Rennie Mackintosh's Art Nouveau masterpiece, has an intriguing link with *Dracula*. In 1903 the author Bram Stoker gifted a gold

The dressing room in the Theatre Royal where the apparition of a fireman has been reported.

Guardian spirit, China Town gate, New City Road.

Fairy mural, Woodside.

medal to the school, and each year since it has been awarded to the student producing the best imaginative work. Only a rubbing is actually handed over – the Bram Stoker Medal itself is kept secure in its crypt. No one really knows how Stoker came to donate such a gift, as he had no obvious link with the GSA, although part of his short story *A Dream of Red Hands* is set in Glasgow, with a guilt-ridden murderer finding redemption through a self-sacrificing act after a terrible accident in a gasometer. On 7 May 1987 *The Sun* reported that eight statues of Greek gods at the School 'had their willies chopped off.' A 'mystery crackpot' was suspected. A colossal bust of Beethoven frowns intensely atop No. 321, the rear entrance of a former piano warehouse.

GARNETHILL

Two fiercesome guardian creatures flank the Chinatown gate on New City Road, while dragons writhe along the roof tiles. Nos 101-103 Shamrock Street demonstrate its former function as a savings bank with a barrage of sculpture, including chained keys, cornucopiae, coiled serpents around a winged flaming torch, lions, and winged heads and cherubs.

6

THE WEST END

ST GEORGE'S CROSS

In 1978 workers constructing St George's Cross underground station found a medieval coal mine worked by monks who had 'carved it out in such a way that pillars of coal were left to support the cavities,' according to *The Sunday Post* on 20 August. The narrow seam of 'Possil Wee Coal' stretched as far as the River Kelvin half a mile (800m) away. Digging during their lunch hours over five months, the workmen excavated 16 tons of coal for their personal use. The mine is now covered by the station.

A powerful sculpture of St George slaying the dragon sits on a plinth in the open space behind the station, although the saint has lost his dragon-puncturing spear. Panels in the Oscar Slater's pub at No. 129 St George's Road tell the story of Slater's 1909 conviction for the murder of elderly spinster Marion Gilchrist at No. 49 West Princes Street, his reprieve from the gallows two days before the execution, and, after nineteen years in prison and a long campaign headed by the likes of Arthur Conan Doyle, his eventual pardon. This miscarriage of justice is a cornerstone of Jack House's *Square Mile of Murder*. At the time of the murder Slater lived at No. 69 St George's Road. The entire sad and sordid story is also told in Richard Whittington-Egan's *The Oscar Slater Murder Story*.

The Glasgow Lodge of the Theosophical Society meets at No. 17 Queens Crescent. Theosophy can be thought of as a mixture of Eastern religion and Western occultism. One of its co-founders, Helena Blavatsky, remains one of the most controversial, revered – and reviled – figures in esotericism. The building is a centre for all manner of talks and courses on esoteric subjects, including dowsing, astrology, yoga, meditation, mystical philosophy, and much more.

GREAT WESTERN ROAD/KELVINBRIDGE

Lansdowne United Presbyterian Church has demonic gargoyles and female angels on either side of the front entrance, with several carved heads elsewhere. St Mary's Episcopal Cathedral has impressive statues of the Virgin and Child, Saints Margaret, Andrew, Kentigern and George (the latter with expired dragon) and four bishops – Trower with a votive model of the church itself, Jocelin with a miniature Glasgow Cathedral, Leighton with book and palm frond, and Turnball with a scroll and seal reading STUDIUM GENERALE, the medieval term for a Rome-approved university, and the phrase used on Glasgow University's founding Papal Bull of 1451. Somewhat more fun are the comic-demonic faces on the corbels, and fourteen heads of recent ministers, slightly caricatured.

WOODLANDS ROAD

St Jude's Free Presbyterian Church (No. 133) has four unidentified Biblical figures, angels, a pair of dogs, two fierce big cats, and massive rainspouts with crocodilian or Native American Thunderbird stylings.

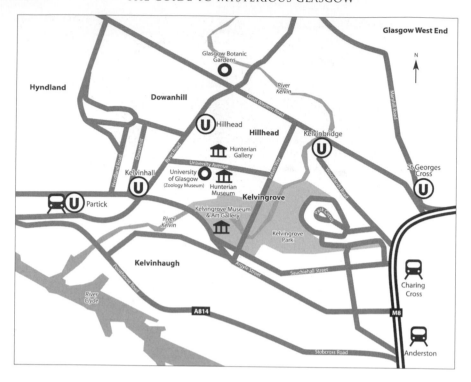

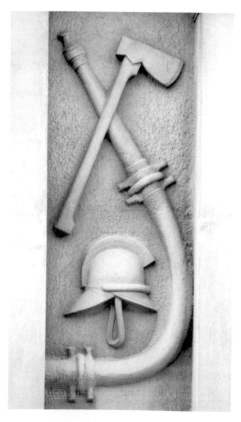

Fire Brigade symbols, St George's Road.

Esoteric graffiti on St Mary's Episcopal Cathedral, Great Western Road.

Clerical corbel,
St Mary's Episcopal
Cathedral.

The delightful Lobey Dosser statue at the junction with Lynedoch Street commemorates the popular – and surreal – cartoon creation of Bud Neill. Lobey is sheriff of Calton Creek, and is shown on his two-legged horse El Fideldo (Elfie) taking in Rank Bajin, the bad guy. At the unveiling ceremony in 1992 everyone who had donated to the costs was sworn in as a deputy. Two self-satisfied cats sit on the ledges of a tenement on the corner with West End Park Street. Four literal Green Men – their bodies composed entirely of metal leaves – clamber up the walls at 20 Ashley Street.

SAUCHIEHALL STREET (WEST OF THE M8)

In *Scottish Ghost Stories*, Elliott O'Donnell relates the tale of 'The Choking Ghost of _____ House, near Sandyford Place', told to him by his friend Hely Browne. Browne, a comedian and performer, lodged on the second floor of the hotel. For three nights in a row he had nightmares. On the fourth night he was woken by a loud crash. Groping for matches in the pitch darkness he encountered a noose, with its cord terminating in thin air. Unable to move, he felt the noose tighten round his neck while cold clammy hands lifted him up and let him drop. The pain caused him to faint.

The next night he lit candles but later woke up in darkness. A powerful chemical smell filled the air and he could feel something cold and flabby. Falling out of bed, he saw on the pillow the face of his brother Ralph, who was living in New York. Ralph's eyes bulged in their sockets, his tongue swelled in his open mouth, and his complexion was black and terrible. He rasped some words: 'I have been wanting to speak to you for ages, but *something,* I cannot explain, has always prevented me. I have been dead a month; not cancer, but Dolly. Poison. Good-bye, Hely. I shall rest in peace now.' With a rush of cold air and the smell of chemicals and bodily decomposition, the face on the pillow vanished. In the morning Browne received a black-edged letter from his mother saying that Dolly, Ralph's wife, had written her that he had died from cancer of the

Big cat, St Jude's Church, Woodlands Road.

Small cat, tenement, Woodlands Road.

throat, but fortunately before his death he had ensured she was well provided for. Browne told O'Donnell he later heard the hotel had developed a further reputation for being haunted, with guests reporting strange noises and nightmares.

In July 1862 Jessie McPherson was found brutally murdered with a meat cleaver at No. 17 Sandyford Place. Servant Jessie McLachlan was found guilty and sentenced to death, but at the last minute her sentence was mysteriously commuted to life imprisonment. She served fifteen years, being released in 1877 and travelling to America (where she died in 1899). Although her testimony was full of contradictions and lies, she almost certainly was not the murderer – the culprit was probably James Fleming, aged eighty-seven, known as 'Old Fleming', who had a reputation for forcing himself on younger women. This is another 'Square Mile of Murder' case, and the bloody footprint that helped convict McLachlan is on show in the POLICE MUSEUM on Pitt Street.

The Glasgow Association of Spiritualists holds services at Nos 6-7 Somerset Place at 11.30 a.m. and 6.30 p.m. on Sundays, 7.30 p.m. on Monday and 2 p.m. on Tuesday. All are welcome. The services in the brightly-lit hall usually include a medium on stage delivering messages to the audience from their deceased loved ones or, in spiritualist terminology, from 'spirit'. With the singing of hymns accompanied by a piano, the flowers on stage and the reading out of notices from a lectern, the service has at times something of the feel of a modern, utilitarian Christian denomination meeting in a secularised 1970s-era space. The shop sells kitsch figures of guardian angels, fairies and buddhas, and copies of *Psychic News*, but the unmissable feature for anyone interested in the paranormal is the small museum, which can be visited thirty minutes before services. A brief history of the Association in Glasgow notes that it started in 1866 and over the years was based in several different addresses. The first regular meeting place was at No. 164 Trongate, where public weekly Sunday services were held, although the mediumship itself was confined to the private séance room. From 1939 to 1964 the Association owned 'Greek' Thomson's extraordinary church in ST VINCENT STREET. The displays feature a number of items of abiding interest: original glass lantern slides showing mediums producing ectoplasm; a psychograph (an example of automatic writing) in seven languages; a skotograph (a psychic image obtained without use of camera or lens by holding unopened packets of photograph plates in the hand); infra-red photographs taken in his flat by Dr J. Winning of the spirit guide 'Abdul'; pictures of the infamous Fox House in America; photographs of materialised forms at séances; and numerous credulity-stretching images of Victorian sitters surrounded by their beloved dead in suspiciously formal poses, as if they had been transferred from portraits (look out for famous medium David Dugald 'surrounded by spirit friends', Conan Doyle with his deceased son Stanley, and one sitter who is visited by the shade of Abraham Lincoln).

There is also a small section of photographs on spiritualist martyr Helen Duncan, who was imprisoned in 1944 under the Witchcraft Act of 1735. Duncan remains a controversial, mercurial figure: despite being exposed as a fraud several times, some of her séances in pre-D-Day Portsmouth produced sensitive wartime information – hence her sentence. In the early 1930s J.B. McIndoe, president of the Spiritualists' National Union, invited Duncan to give sittings in Glasgow, where she apparently astonished sitters. On 5 January 1933 she performed at the spiritualist church in Holland Street, where she filled the room with the scent of roses and materialized a woman who returned the red rose her husband had placed in her coffin. Afterwards Helen was told that while she had been in a trance her spirit guide Albert had warned her to be careful that evening. She then travelled to Edinburgh where she was caught in a blatant fraud and was prosecuted and fined. In the late 1940s she was due to perform at Glasgow. At Waverley station in Edinburgh she had a premonition and refused to take her granddaughter with her. Just before the train arrived in Glasgow it crashed. Seconds earlier, Helen had clairaudiently heard Albert's warning and had fled into a vacant lavatory, the walls of which protected her from the force of the impact. She was taken to hospital and discharged after a few days. All these details are in Malcolm Gaskell's excellent biography *Hellish Nell: Last of Britain's Witches*.

MITCHELL LIBRARY

The entrance on Granville Street is enlivened by two Titans at the door, caryatids in the attic, and groups representing Literature (Homer, Shakespeare, Dante), Visual Art (Michelangelo, Leonardo, Raphael), Ancient Art (Athena holding a small winged female figure bearing a frond, with a sculptor and an architect) and Music (Apollo with his lyre and two female musos). Anti-pigeon spikes give them the look of Clive Barker's Pinhead. Wisdom sits enthroned above the North Street entrance and the personification of Literature (jocularly known as Mrs Mitchell) stands on the great dome, possibly wondering whether her library books are overdue.

Glasgow Association
of Spiritualists,
Sauchiehall Street.

The eye in the semi-circle, Hindu Community Centre, La Belle Place.

LA BELLE PLACE

The sculptures on the Hindu Community Centre, originally the Queen's Rooms concert hall, are some of the strangest in Glasgow. Striking though the extended frieze is – noble savages progress through taming horses and yoking oxen to agriculture, industry, seafaring and commerce, culminating in the arts overseen by the architect's wife portrayed as Athena – it is the panels on the east side that intrigue the most. A helmeted woman works with dividers, a telescope and scrolls. Truly weird foliate decoration centres on a penetrating single eye. A Masonic compass and setsquare stand beneath an owl. A naked winged male figure with elaborately coiffed long hair holds a set of tools and an armless figure, possibly the Venus de Milo. A helmeted Mercury holds a caduceus and ship while nearby is the partially-obscured word [?]NOPIA. Elsewhere there are musical instruments, sea monsters and a swan/phoenix. At the back the building is 'signed' by all those who had a hand in designing and building this puzzling structure.

PARK CIRCUS

In *Empathy is the Enemy* and *The Red Right Hand,* Denise Mina's take on the *Hellblazer* supernatural graphic novel series, this architecturally iconic hilltop becomes the testing site for an Empathy Accelerator, a magical device which enables people to experience other humans' emotions, including their darkest feelings. Glasgow consequently becomes a dead zone where most of the inhabitants have committed suicide, and the empathy plague threatens to end the world. KELVINGROVE MUSEUM becomes the last stand for chainsmoking magus John

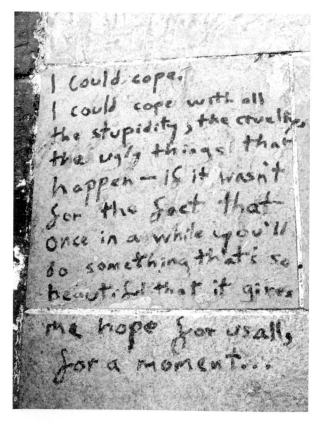

Message written on pavement, Park Terrace.

Dragons on the banister, Park Terrace Youth Hostel.

Constantine and his motley crew as they attempt to fend off an invasion of misery-eating Praexis demons and turn off the Empathy Accelerator before the military eliminate Glasgow. Mina's puckish approach to apocalypse prophylaxis involves distracting the demons with porn and sweets and focusing on the positive feelings generated by the museum's Joan Eardley paintings (although most of them are actually in the Hunterian and the National Art Gallery in Edinburgh). In the end the fate of the world hangs on whether England win a World Cup match (they don't, but mass annihilation is avoided because the soldiers are delighted – they're from Scotland).

KELVINGROVE PARK

Then as for Kelvin Grove, it is most lovely to be seen,
With its beautiful flowers and trees so green,
And a magnificent water-fountain spouting up very high,
Where people can quench their thirst when they feel dry.

William McGonagall, 'Glasgow' (1889)

The magnificent Stewart Memorial Fountain commemorates the bringing of Glasgow's water supply from Loch Katrine in the Trossachs. The main figure represents the fair Ellen, heroine of Walter Scott's *The Lady of the Lake*. Elsewhere there are gargoyles, monsters, signs of the zodiac, fish and aquatic plants, birds and animals. The equally splendid equestrian monument to Lord Roberts, the iconic hero of the British Empire, is bookended by War (garbed in ancient armour and sitting on an arsenal of edged weapons) and Victory (seated on the prow of the Ship of State). The memorial lists Roberts' extensive achievements, titles and awards, including the Victoria Cross. But no mention of any 'O' Grades.

Nearby is the statue of *The Royal Bengal Tigress with a Peacock*, which, yes, is a tiger eating a peacock. The four sets of superb much-photographed bronze figures on the Kelvin Way Bridge represent Philosophy and Inspiration (north-west), War and Peace (north-east), Navigation and Shipbuilding (south-east) and Commerce and Industry (south-west). Gary Nisbet and Tim Gardner of the www.glasgowsculpture.com website suggest that the group contains esoteric and Masonic symbolism. In particular, they see Philosophy and

Kelvin Way Bridge:
statues of War and Peace.

Inspiration as embodying the following Masonic concepts: the *Philosopher* or *Alchemist*, represented by the portrait of Leonardo Da Vinci pondering mortality (skull, closed book and rosary beads); the Masonic *Volume of Sacred Law* (the open book on the lectern); *Duality* (the central pillar and the small architectural column, representing the Jachin and Boass columns from the original Temple of Solomon in Jerusalem and seen in all Masonic lodges); and *Enlightenment* (the eagle, which, like true knowledge, is obscure and hard to find).

KELVINGROVE ART GALLERY & MUSEUM

Admission free. Open Monday to Thursday and Saturday, 10 a.m. to 5 p.m., Friday and Sunday 11 a.m. to 5 p.m. Wheelchair access.

In *Fortean Times* (March 2008) Anna Kelvin (a pseudonym) described experiencing a timeslip in 1985 or '86. One day in either early autumn or late spring she was passing the museum when, for a split second, she saw the scene as it would have been in the late nineteenth century, complete with horse-drawn carriages, men in top hats, and women in bustles carrying parasols. She could not remember if the architecture was different. The scene vanished quickly, leaving her slightly breathless, chilled and puzzled. 'I'm not sure if I was actually there or seeing it at one remove, as if on film,' she said.

Kelvingrove is not only the best museum in Glasgow, it's one of the best in the country. A recent refurbishment has revitalised many galleries and displays. The pleasures start with the exuberant architecture, with the pinnacles, pavilions and façades adorned with a riot of sculpture

Kelvin Way Bridge. Philosophy and Inspiration: a Masonic code?

and symbolism. Highlights on the exterior include, on the north entrance, a great bronze St Mungo as patron of the arts, 'The Empire Salutes Glasgow' (trumpet-blowing babes praising a miniscule Mungo carrying a bright copper staff), 'The Industries of Glasgow at the Court of Mercury' (with the winged god of trade looking slightly bored with the adulation) and 'Love Teaching Harmony to the Arts'. Elsewhere there are giant winged heads, multi-oared ships ferrying the symbols of Glasgow, personifications of arts and sciences, lions' heads, and much more. Muriel Gray's highly recommended book *Kelvingrove Art Gallery and Museum* shows that there are sculptures on the topmost towers around the steeply sloping roof of the centre hall, even though they cannot be seen by anyone. Gray also mentions Jonah, a 59-ton blue whale

The Industries of Glasgow at the Court of Mercury, north entrance, Kelvingrove Museum.

caught off Trondheim in the 1950s. With its viscera removed and its lungs inflated, it sat in a refrigeration unit in the museum car park. Thousands of people paid to walk through the belly of the whale.

You could spend days in the museum, which is structured under two themes, 'Life' in the west half, and 'Expression' in the east. The subheadings refer to the galleries or courts. Here are some of the more unusual highlights.

Ground Floor West

West Court (look for the Spitfire)
'Return to Sender,' a fibreglass figure of Elvis Presley with a neon halo. Statues of 'St Elvis' have already been spotted being worshipped in churches in New Mexico.

The skeleton of a porpoise. Gray notes that in the 1960s the fully fleshed original was found in a sack in the gents' toilet of Glasgow Central. I'm sure we've all had that 'Where did I leave my porpoise?' moment.

A collection of biological superlatives, including biggest ever bird's egg (elephant bird), longest penis relative to body size (barnacle), longest sperm (fruit flies), biggest egg in relation to body size (little spotted kiwi), most poisonous UK plant (monkshood), most venomous reptile (Gila monster) and most venomous British mammal (the terrifying … water shrew).

Glasgow Stories
A full-size statue of St Patrick, with a snake coiled around the base of his pastoral staff.

A seventeenth-century German scold's bridle in the shape of a devil with horns, and a set of sixteenth-century Scottish branks.

Ancient Egypt

The sarcophagus of Pa-ba-sa, the Great Steward of Princess Nitocris, was donated by the estate of the Dukes of Hamilton. At his death Alexander, the 10th Duke, a noted eccentric and Egyptophile, was mummified and buried in a sarcophagus. Unfortunately, at 6ft 3ins (1.9m) he was too tall for the tomb so his legs had to be broken before he could fit in. During the museum's refit, the sarcophagus was cleaned out. The gap between lid and base had attracted generations of chewing-gum balls – as well as a carefully-folded girlie magazine. Perhaps someone was trying to fend off Praexis demons. Other Egyptian items include two wonderful monumental black granite statues of the lion-headed goddess Sekhmet, a scene of one pharaoh worshipping another, deified, pharaoh, and four mummies.

Creatures of the Past

Icthyosaurs, prehistoric desert crocodiles, pterosaurs, fossil footprints, a life-size model of a Jurassic *Ceratosaurus,* the skeleton of giant Irish deer, and a model of a dodo.

Environment Discovery Centre

A large ammonite carved with a snake's head. A 1905 article in the journal *Folklore* by Edward Lovett, 'The Whitby Snake-Ammonite Myth', describes how the persistent belief that ammonites were snakes turned to stone (often via the intercession of a saint) created a cottage industry of people carving snakes' heads onto the fossils.

Scotland's Wildlife

A real genuine authentic haggis, *Haggis Scoticus*, a composite beast created by museum staff in 2005 from various creatures of the earth, water and air – a nod to the fake creations such as Feejee mermaids, Jenny Hanivers, Jackalopes and Wolpertingers that lurk on the fringes of collections, as well as a send-up of legends of the wild Highland Haggis.

Ground Floor East

East Court

Look for the forest of hanging faces, source of various 'ghost' photographs. The small charms and healing case is the most fascinating display in the entire museum, containing as it does items dealing with magic, divination, witchcraft, destiny, the afterlife and much else. Do not omit to open the drawers below the case, for they too are filled with treasures. The case includes:

Four orishas, figures of beings worshipped in the Santeria religion of Cuba. Santeria is a syncretic belief system, bringing together ideas from Roman Catholicism and the Yoruba in West Africa. Orishas are always paired – the case contains St Francis of Assisi and Orula, the orisha of divination and wisdom, and St Anthony of Abad, paired with Osain, the god of forests, herbs and healing.

Charms from the First World War: a holed stone worn by Private White of the Northants Regiment in the trenches, a homemade woollen poppet carried by a soldier from East London, a cowrie shell and compass charm used by a Japanese soldier, and a necklace of spent bullet cases with a 'medicine' charm, from the Kikuyu culture in Kenya.

Other charms, including: a Mankwala or mjuti charm against gunshots (Malawi, 1897); an amuletic necklace from Saudi Arabia with twenty-seven attachments of wood and glass beads, fruits, nuts, coins and a large tooth; a Tibetan printed spell to ward off sickness, scorpions and dog bites; a photograph of a *makishi* costume made by a shaman to magically protect a fellow prisoner in a Zambian jail; a fifteenth-century maize bangle countering the evil eye, from Peru; a replica rowan cross of the type used against witches, a gift from the Museum of Witchcraft in Cornwall; an amulet necklace worn by a mummy for protection in the afterlife, an Eye of Horus, and an amulet of the Egyptian dwarf spirit Patek for protection in the home.

Others include a Turkish 'eye of envy' charm to absorb evil wishes, and Islamic charms with Qu'ranic quotations and hand and eye amulets against the evil eye; a Palestinian headdress with charms of St Joseph and the Hand of Fatima; a Taiwanese bell with Buddhist prayers for protection, for hanging in a car; uncut garnets, a charm against sickness from Northern India; a modern deer bone, 'Celtic symbol of death and rebirth', a pentacle, and a 'witch's claw', symbol of protection. Many of these contemporary items were sourced from the 23 Enigma shop on CASTLE STREET. Other items on display include:

A Chinese fortune-teller's book for casting horoscopes, and *Chiao pei* – bamboo roots for divining the future.

An Iro-Ifa divination tapper, used to greet the god of fate in Yoruba Nigeria.

Western divination tools – a Tarot deck and a quartz crystal ball.

A fourteenth-century brass vessel decorated with the signs of the Hindu Zodiac.

A rabbit's foot – and in a similar vein, a Japanese paper charm against bad luck, and a Daruma doll for granting wishes.

A St Brigid's cross – each reed stands for a hope or dream.

A Maneki Neko 'beckoning cat' to increase business, from Thailand.

Funeral banknotes burnt to ensure prosperity in the afterlife, from Singapore.

A nineteenth-century Scottish brooch inscribed with a prayer to God, inscribed DVS? EXIV 'DEO' RVM (circle?) ESV SNA EAR.

A green toad, an old Gaelic cure for whooping cough, and a modern Chinese turtle charm for support and protection; see also a jade dragon-headed tortoise amulet for long life, from the Han dynasty.

A Mala, a Hindu rosary to improve spiritual health, made from the sacred tulsi plant.

Pachamama, a spirit of the earth who brings health and fertility. From the Mercado de Hechizeria (Witches Market) in La Paz, Bolivia.

A green vine snake, a South East Asian symbol of fertility.

Modern fads – a copper band for rheumatism, lapis lazuli to help mental clarity, and gemstones for stress.

The superb display opposite includes initiation, spirit, masquerade and secret society masks, models and costumes from Africa and the Pacific, the best being the 'Firespitter' helmet mask from Ivory Coast, which looks like a scary black antelope dragon. As the display text says: 'Masks are powerful, transform, are mysterious, heal, protect, perform, deceive.'

The sculpture collection includes: *The Harpy Celaeno*, a marble bust of the Greek female monster with wings on her head and one of her reptilian-clawed hands clutching her naked breast; *William Wallace,* with strange winged fish on his helmet; *Achilles*, with a helmet featuring griffons and an androform sphinx; and the *Eight Immortals of Taoism*, who were all once human, but attained immortality and supernatural powers.

The 'Beauty and Ugliness' display includes a set of jougs from Stirlingshire, a Neolithic stone ball, a wooden carving with healing powers from Sierra Leone, and a superb prehistoric cup-and-ring-marked slab.

Looking At Art
Sir Joseph Noel Paton's *The Fairy Raid, Carrying off a Changeling – Midsummer Eve,* one of the great touchstone paintings of Victorian fey supernaturalism. This endlessly fascinating piece has at least seventy beings, many hidden in the trees and foxgloves, lilies and ivy. The Fairy Queen holds the abducted baby, while a cavalcade of butterfly-clad lords and ladies ride grandly past the hayricks and standing stones, accompanied by dwarves offering armour for sale, elves, goblins, winged beings, a hag, and four human children with small chains on their ankles, the victims of a previous raid.

Scottish Art

George Henry and E.A. Hornel's Symbolist masterpiece *The Druids – Bringing in the Mistletoe* features the Wise Ones clad in red and goldleaf, wearing gold torcs and magi-like cloaks, with two bulls carrying mistletoe. The frame itself adds to the piece's power, with its Celtic knotwork topped with a lunula enclosing three snakes. Bill Smith's book *Hornel* says that as part of their research Hornel and Henry examined skulls reputed to be of Druids, to ascertain their features, and visited the Duke of Hamilton's herd of ancient Caledonian cattle.

Hornel was interested in archaeology and may have got the idea for the painting on a search for cup-and-ring stones, as noted in A.S. Hartrick's *A Painter's Pilgrimage Through Fifty Years*. Hornel took Hartrick and another friend to visit an old man called Sinclair who knew the location of some of the stones. At his cottage Sinclair picked up a small bean-like bluish stone and after a few minutes went into a kind of trance, describing, 'like a wireless announcer of today, a vision of a procession of priests with sacred instruments and cattle which somehow were connected with the cup-and-ring markings.' Hartrick could not remember all the details, but he thought the vision appeared to be genuine. After a time Sinclair returned to himself, and refused to discuss the subject further.

First Floor West

Scotland's First People

There is much that hints at prehistoric ritual and religion in this gallery and the exhibits include:.

Three different Neolithic carved stone balls, all from Aberdeenshire. These balls are truly mysterious – great effort was required to carve them, but they have no obvious function. Suggestions include symbols of status (chiefship or priestship), some sort of magical device, or 'talking stones', where you can you only speak at a tribal gathering, or address the gods, if you are holding the stone.

An excellent cup-and-ring stone from Bowling, with three major ring features plus central and peripheral cups and interconnecting channels.

A model of a cist burial at Temple Wood with four stone slabs, a man in the foetal position and a beaker.

Three bronze swords and one rapier, all found as ritual deposits in rivers and bogs (which are classic liminal sites). The Late Bronze-Age sword from the Isle of Shuna, Argyll, was one of three found thrust point down into a peat bog.

The Peelhill Hoard, from Strathavon, Lanarkshire. Many of the bronze items were 'ritually killed' by being heated until the metal started to melt, then twisted or broken, and finally thrown into a bog.

Cinerary urns and grave goods from various prehistoric cremation sites,.

A cist slab from Badden, Argyll with sixteen carved diamond shapes.

A cast of one of the tenth-century hogback gravestones from GOVAN.

Corridor

Salvador Dali's incomparable *Christ of St John of the Cross*, painted in 1951 from the viewpoint of someone looking down on the Crucifixion from above. Legend has it that Dali hired Tom Saunders, a Hollywood stuntman, to spend all day suspended on a cross so he could get the perspective right. It's a painting that arouses strong emotions. Muriel Gray notes it has been twice attacked, once by a man with a sharp stone who then ripped it with his hands, and at later date by someone with an airgun which dented the new protecting Perspex.

Conflict and Consequence

Finds from the BATTLE OF LANGSIDE. The display mentions the legend of the 'Devil's Kirkyard' – the ghostly return of those killed at Langside.

A helmet made for the film *Willow*, in the shape of fierce fanged monster's skull.

Something which looks equally as if it belongs in the realm of fantasy, but was all too real – the formidable martial garb of a warrior of the I-Kiribati, once described as the most war-like people in Micronesia. The armour is coconut fibre, the sword is edged with shark teeth and the helmet is made from the skin of the spiked and poisonous puffball fish.

Cultural Survival

Two ceremonial turtle posts from the Torres Islands, each carved with three human faces, while one has a turtle and the other a clamshell. They were found in a cave, long forgotten. The elders told the Europeans that once upon a time the posts were used as part of a ceremony to thank the turtles for coming ashore and providing eggs, meat, and shells. The posts were decorated with flowers and human bones. In recent years two islanders visited the museum and took back three of their ancestors' skulls for ceremonial reburial.

A memorial head of the Oba god-king of Benin, decorated with dogs, arms, legs and crocodiles, and a bell to call the spirits of the ancestors.

An Inuit wolf spirit mask from Alaska.

Study Centre

A modern Ghost Dance shirt, made by the Lakota and exchanged for the museum's original, which may have been worn at the massacre of Wounded Knee. The original was repatriated in 1999 and is kept by the South Dakota Historical Society. The shirt is venerated by some visitors who feel a connection with Native Americans.

First Floor East

Scottish Identity in Art

Short sections on the myths of Robert the Bruce, Mary Queen of Scots and Bonnie Prince Charlie.

Several Jacobite items – a chair supposedly made from a tree at Culloden where Jacobite officers were hanged, an anamorphic portrait of Bonnie Prince Charlie with the glass cylinder that reveals the secret on the canvas, and a lock of Charlie's hair treated as a relic.

Another 'relic' is a quaich made from a yew at CROOKSTON CASTLE where Mary Queen of Scots met Lord Darnley.

A snuffbox showing the cavorting witches from Burns' *Tam O'Shanter*.

The Brownie of Blednoch by E.A. Hornel, in the corridor outside. The painting illustrates William Nicholson's poem, which tells the story of Aiken-Drum, 'a wild and unyirthly wight' who strikes terror in the hearts of all:

> His matted head on his breast did rest,
> A long blue beard wan'ered down like a vest;
> But the glare of his e'e nae bard hath exprest,
> Nor the skimes [glance of relected light] o' Aiken-drum.

> On his wauchie [clammy] arms three claws did meet,
> As they trailed on the grun' by his taeless feet;
> E'en the auld gudeman [the Devil] himse' did sweat,
> To look at Aiken-drum.

A witch on a broomstick flies past, some kind of creature lurks in the clouds, the moon seems to echo the cup-and-ringmarks of ancient rock art, and the Brownie himself is a gaunt figure with incandescent eyes. As a contrast to all this hellishness, Burne-Jones' sublime *Angel* is nearby.

THE MUSEUM OF TRANSPORT

Admission free. Open Monday to Thursday and Saturday 10 a.m. to 5 p.m., Friday and Sunday 11 a.m. to 5 p.m.

The museum at Kelvinhall houses an extensive and nostalgic collection of trams, steam engines and motor vehicles as well as what is for many the prize exhibit, 'Kelvin Street,' a recreation of a 1930s Glasgow street, complete with shops, cinema and underground station. In the 1990s Bill Mutch, who worked the night-security detail, started reporting strange phenomena centred on the street. These included sounds – running footsteps, a limping man dragging his foot on the ground, children's voices – balls of light moving at great speed, the sensation of someone tapping his shoulder, and apparitions, such as a man wearing a trilby hat standing outside the Clyde Model Dockyard shop. The sightings were reported in Ron Halliday's *The A-Z of Paranormal Scotland* and *Evil Scotland* and elsewhere, and staff continue to record strange occurrences – such as a man seen sitting in one of the cars, and a headless female figure in the Regal Cinema.

In *Psychic Scotland* Tom Rannachan records meeting a very solid-looking chap wearing a coat and hat in the cinema. He sat a few seats away from Tom exuding a smell of dampness and pipe tobacco and his clothes looked soaked. Tom turned to him to ask him about the rain, but he had disappeared. In recent years several paranormal groups have undertaken research on the site, and the Ghost Club in particular has undertaken four investigations. Here I have summarised their main findings on a site-by-site basis. As ever, their meticulous highly-detailed records can be found on their website (www.ghostclub.org.uk).

The Street
Sounds of children crying and of an old-fashioned car horn. At five o'clock one evening the security guards were checking the building before locking up when they heard a noise. One of the guards called out 'Hello' – and a child's voice said 'Hello' back.

The Cinema
The most persistent phenomenon appears to be minor poltergeist activity which persistently flips the seats down when no one is present. This has been frequently noted by investigators, cleaners and other staff, and recorded on audio. Psychics have picked up presences and a strong floral odour in the second row. On one occasion the recorded temperature late at night rose from 60.8°F (16°C) to 78.6°F (25.9°C) in twelve minutes, but all the investigators felt the cinema remained very cold.

The Underground
Staff, visitors and investigators all report an unpleasant feeling here, although some of this could be simple claustrophobia. Links have been made with the electrical box, which was brought from Merkland Street underground station, site of a dramatic suicide from the platform in the 1950s. During one attempt at contact with the dead it was noted that the spirits seemed to be communicating through the temperature by raising it (for 'yes') or lowering it (for 'no').

Elephant Walk
This is a maintenance workshop and is not open to the public. It is the former backstage area for the circus which was once based here. Staff have reported sudden cold spots and shadowy shapes moving about. During a Ghost Club investigation a door appeared to open by itself, thuds were heard, and camera and torch batteries were drained.

Much of the attempted communication with the spirits is predicated on the building's history – during the Second World War it was used as a morgue during the Clydebank Blitz – although there is also a strong suggestion that the exhibits themselves are somehow integral to the phenomena. In 2009 the museum will be moving premises – will the phenomena make the same move?

Kelvin Street, Museum of Transport – site of alleged hauntings.

Large-lugged grotesque, Pearce Lodge, University Avenue.

NAIRN STREET, YORKHILL

The *Evening Citizen* for 19 August 1971 reported that a two-roomed flat at No. 12 was haunted. The tenant, Mr Towson, who lived there with his mother, her friend Mrs Hedley, his sister and nephew, recognised the apparitions as those of his grandfather, grandmother and aunt. The eleven-year-old nephew had been pulled by an unknown force and the boy's mother said she had sensed a presence and she got 'a funny prickly feeling.'

THE UNIVERSITY OF GLASGOW

The older part of the campus on University Avenue, with its signature bell tower visible as a landmark for miles around, is the second-largest example of Gothic-revival architecture in Britain after the Palace of Westminster in London. This atmospheric grove of old school academe, with its twin quadrangles and vaulted undercroft, dates from 1871 when the university moved from its original site near the cathedral.

The university has probably the single most concentrated cluster of strange sculpture in the entire city. Above the main doorway of the McIntyre Building on University Avenue, on the side gates of the Quincentenary Gates at the main entrance, and on a building in University Gardens nearby, are the heraldic emblems of the Hogswartian 'four nations' into which the academic staff and students were divided according to their place of birth: Glottiana (Glasgow and Lanarkshire), Rothseiana (the former counties of the Clyde Coast, Ayr, Bute, Renfrew), Transforthana (the west of Scotland generally and the country north of the Forth) and Loudoniana (south-east Scotland). I invite anyone to use these as names for their fantasy novel or roleplay game set in an 'alternative history' of Scotland.

The Pearce Lodge dates from 1656 and was transported stone by stone from the original site across the city to be rebuilt here in 1888. The four upper windows have grotesque faces with enormous ears and the symbols of Scotland, Ireland and Wales. Norman Adams in *Haunted Scotland* records an incident from February 1989. A university porter saw an old lady approach the entrance to the lodge. She was wearing a grey coat and a round grey hat and her face was 'shiny-like.' He expected her to ring the front doorbell, so he went and opened the door to greet her – but she had vanished.

University of Glasgow: man versus snake.

University of Glasgow: man versus dragon.

University of Glasgow: man versus book.

University of Glasgow War Memorial
Chapel: Lovecraftian pelican.

The astonishing outer west face of the main buildings is home to more than 100 carvings. These include, on the northern section: a man waving a cross at a fanged snake which has him trapped him in its coils; a knight fighting off a spectacular dragon which is biting his Crusader's shield; two Green Men, one spewing vegetation, the other made of leaves; a foliate lion-like monster biting its own reptilian tail; a foliate reptilian lion with two tails; a long-haired robed man singing from a book; a nun with model of a church; a fruit tree with the words 'IN 1727'; a trowel-wielding brickie in a cap walling himself in; a Mr Punch mask and comedy mask; the crescent moon with stars; a setsquare and dividers; a sun with a human face; a ring and crossed oakleaves; vegetation supporting a big cat, a basilisk, and a squirrel with nuts; St Mungo's fish, ring, bell, bird, tree and mitre; a knight's helmet; a winged wheel; several avian species; a sailing ship; a panther; and a fierce, toothed fish.

On the north wall of the war memorial chapel, birds, trees and thistles support letters which spell ODO. The chapel's west face is dominated by a giant St Mungo, and a pelican feeding its young, although this looks more like a Lovecraftian alien god; elsewhere a chunky angel removes something – presumably a ring – from a fish's mouth, another angel with a spooky expression reads a book, herbage protects a Green Man, a Green Lion and a basilisk, birds eat fruit, and the symbols of the four Evangelists wing about. Inside the chapel can be found a spider and owl, female faces poking out of vegetation and crops, a helmeted warrior holding a scroll above a serpentine dragon, and a stag with a cross between its antlers. This last is a clear reference to the legend of King David I, who in 1128 was supposedly attacked by a spectral cross-bearing stag; after grabbing the cross David had a dream which led to the founding of Holyrood Abbey in Edinburgh, a defining moment in Scottish Christianity.

The southern part of the building gets even stranger: there's a Green Man spewing vegetation and fruit, a pair of Green Lions, and two Green Demons; two Aladdin's lamps; a human-headed reptile; a beast face with protruding ears; a man reading with a finger on his forehead; a Mayan head spewing blocks of symbols; a wheel firing off arrows; a sceptre encircled by a lion-headed snake; a greybeard with a saw and carpentry tools; a stylised eagle in a Native American idiom;

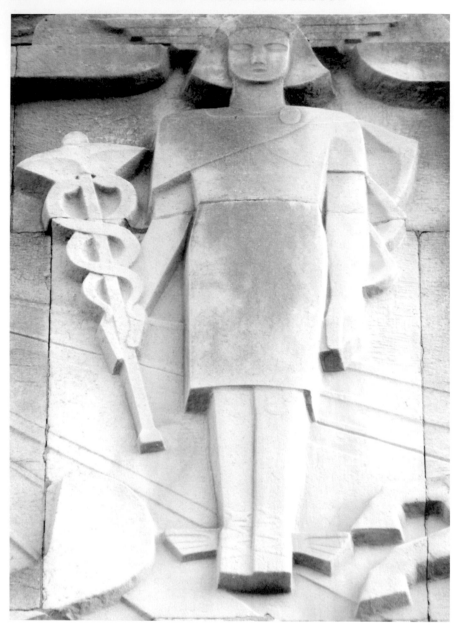

University of Glasgow, James Watt Engineering Building: androgynous Mercury.

a helmeted winged man bearing a flaming sword and a shield with the symbols of justice; a fisherman with a net, boat and fish in hand; a stonecarver carving a capital; a winged ring; flowers in a boat; a mortar and pestle; and a motley collection of fruit trees, iguanas, owl's eyes, owls, other birds, swords, scales, scrolls, fruits, fishes, bells, frogs and hourglasses. My guess is that this entire argosy of arcana is meant to represent every subject taught at the university, from anthropology to zoology; this deserves the attention of some art-historical researchers.

The Lion and Unicorn Staircase, dating from 1690, was transported from the original site in the city. The lion – which looks more a toothy toad – sits on a fat-cheeked grotesque face.

Vulval sculpture,
University of Glasgow.

In the west quadrangle, pairs of demonic and human heads adorn the south side, and winged gargoyles project from the spire of the chapel. In the east quadrangle, a single gargoyle sits forlornly in the north-west corner, with two coiled foliate monsters alongside a nearby arched niche. An owl and monkey lurk in the tympanum over the entrance to the Randolph Buildings, and the east side has faces of a bear (?), ape and eagle (?), as well as two human-headed monsters. A massive bas-relief on the south side of the James Watt Engineering Building conceives the university's contribution to science and engineering in mythological terms, with a Vulcan-like blacksmith, androgynous Mercury, winged Pegasus and lever-pulling Cronos, god of time, presiding over an amalgam of blast furnaces, metallurgy, James Watt's linkage, parachutes, and marine and bird life. Comic faces leer out of the arches nearby. The uppermost ring of the bell-tower framework is the eyrie of nine carved eagles.

The Gilmorehill G12 building has two tiny dragons coiling out of the vegetation on the entrance arch. And the Kelvin Building has a six-armed starfish within a triangle enclosed by a snake swallowing its own tail – scientific and esoteric at the same time.

Like most great universities, the library here has a great many historical works that touch on areas such as magic and the supernatural. One of the most significant is the Ferguson Collection of works on alchemy, a vast resource covering everything to do with the ancient art of the supposed transformation of metals, the enlightenment of the magician, the symbolism of the physical and chemical universe, the Philosopher's Stone, and much else occult and magical. The starting point for this often difficult and abstruse area is the library's special collections website, http://special.lib.gla.ac.uk/ferguson.html.

Archie Roy is one of those maverick figures universities are sometimes lucky enough to attract. On the one hand he is Professor Emeritus of Astronomy at Glasgow, with a long and distinguished career of astronomical research and achievements: the International Astronomical

Union recently named an asteroid after him. On the other hand, he is the Founding President of the Scottish Society for Psychical Research (SSPR), and has had an equally impressive history of academic investigation of the paranormal. His books *A Sense of Something Strange* and *Archives of the Mind* are highly recommended.

He has investigated many cases, including the troubling incidents at MAXWELL PARK, publicly supported Gordon Smith, the famous 'Psychic Barber', and helped to found PRISM (Psychical Research Involving Selected Mediums), a project in which SSPR president Patricia Robertson evaluates the accuracy and reliability of mediums. Three papers using statistics to test the sceptical hypothesis that 'All mediums' statements are so general that they could apply to anyone' have been published in the *Journal* of the Society for Psychical Research. Robertson was quoted in *The Times* for 9 April 2005 as saying:

> We are convinced that some mediums can impart to a sitter information about people who have died that they couldn't possibly know in any normally accepted way. I'm not saying that it comes from the dead, but the most plausible explanation is that the information is coming from the deceased personalities.

Robertson also commendably notes: 'With psychics a lot of it is nonsense … most in this country are guilty of what psychologists call 'cold reading' (a set of techniques used by alleged professional mediums to get a subject to believe in their supernatural abilities) and wishful thinking; people tend to believe what they want to.'

The SSPR holds monthly public lectures from September to April at the Boyd Orr Building in the university. Guest speakers have included Rupert Sheldrake, Maurice Grosse (one of the investigator on the Enfield Poltergeist case), and Colin Wilson (author of dozens of books on the paranormal, including the highly influential opus *The Occult*). The organization also publishes a newsletter called *The Psi Report,* and in 2007 the university's Department of Adult and Continuing Education ran a twenty-week course entitled 'An In-Depth Study of Psychical Research', which covered apparitions, haunted places and people, poltergeist activity, telepathy, mediumship, psychic surgery, paranormal healing, possession and reincarnation (*see* their website, www.sspr.org.uk).

The Times for 14 February 1985 noted that a medical student at the university was so exasperated by the computer he was using that he typed in the word JESUS. The computer promptly responded ERROR: JESUS DOES NOT EXIST.

THE HUNTERIAN MUSEUM

Inside the University of Glasgow, with an entrance off University Avenue. Admission free. Monday to Saturday, 9.30 a.m. to 5 p.m. Closed Sundays and public holidays. Wheelchair access.

The Hunterian gives Kelvingrove close competition for being the best museum in Glasgow. Its original funding, and the core of its collection, came from the bequest of William Hunter, anatomist, scientist and collector, who died in London in 1783. This is the kind of museum that deserves multiple visits: herein are the highlights, viewed of course from my own particular perspective.

Foyer
A mastodon tooth, possibly acquired from Benjamin Franklin. In proof that human beings can find symbolism in anything, the mastodon became meaningful for American revolutionaries in their struggle against the British. 'What made [Hunter's] assertion so powerful, especially among American patriots, was his linking of extinction to the idea that the *incognitum* [the mastodon] had been a monstrous carnivore whose disappearance was God's blessing on the human race.' Thus spake Thomas Jefferson (1743-1826) the third President of the United States.

First Room

Six skulls with gaping holes showing various degrees of bone damage due to tertiary syphilis, 'the great pox'. There are also grotesquely malformed skulls warped by cancer and TB. The sarcoma cancer has turned one skull into a coral-like structure.

Some of Hunter's teratological specimens are also here. As part of his attempt to understand developmental anatomy, Hunter was fascinated when things went wrong and collected nature's 'sports' or freaks. His own system of labelling body parts used the letters A-Z then AA-RR, with the letters cut into the specimen jars. The designation 'MM' stood for 'monsters'.

There is a 'MM' in the 'Medical Preparations' section, on the back row of the first shelf from bottom: a chick with eight limbs. This may prepare you for the full range of animal deformities: three little pigs, one with a single head, two bodies, eight limbs and four ears; another with a single central eye; the third has one head and upper body, two rear ends and four rear legs. Three fallow deer, one exhibiting two heads and upper bodies, four forelimbs, two rear limbs and one rear body; a second with one head, four ears, two rear ends, four rear legs and four forelegs; and the last, labelled 'a monstrosity of the fallow deer', a single-headed specimen which diverges at the chest, creating two rear ends and two sets of forelimbs (one set part-fused). The section also contains a 'monstrosity of the sheep' with two complete heads, two forelimbs, two rear ends and four rear legs.

The museum also houses the leg and foot bones of Owen Farrel, an Irish dwarf, known from his attire as Leather-Coat Jack, plus a portrait from around 1717. Farrel was a well-known London character famous for his strength. Sometime before his death he sold his body to a surgeon for a weekly allowance.

Other exhibits include intestinal worms looking like great strips of pasta; a 'Carpenter's Heart', from 'a carpenter who, in dovetailing a piece of wood, ran a chisel through his heart and died suddenly', and a 'Honeymooner's Heart', 'a portion of the ruptured right ventricle of the heart of an old man who married his maid, and died suddenly the first night after'; the skull and enormous antlers of a Giant Irish Deer, an extinct species sometimes mistakenly called the Irish Elk; two pre-Ice-Age elephant teeth, possibly found underwater off Dogger Bank, dating from the time Britain was joined to the Continent – a now-submerged area archaeologists call Doggerland.

Also to be seen are a cow hairball 8in (20cm) across and an inflated porcupine fish; a trephine (a tool used for trepanation, the opening of a hole in the skull for supposed medical benefits, a widespread practice up until the eighteenth century); part of the HIGH POSSIL meteorite, a giant ammonite and a Neolithic carved stone ball.

Roman religious items such as a statuette of Fortuna, goddess of good luck, (shown with a cornucopia, rudder and wheel) found in the bathhouse at Castlecary Fort, and an altar from near Kirkintilloch, dedicated to Jupiter and Victory.

Penis simulacrum, Hunterian Museum.

Thylacine, Hunterian Museum.

There is also a section entitled 'Weird and Wonderful': 'Most of the items in our collections have obvious scientific, historical or artistic value. However, some of the most intriguing items seem to have been acquired simply because they look odd, or have strange stories behind them.'

These curios are some of the best things in the museum, and include: a life-size human penis simulacrum, a river-worn pebble of greenish sandstone from Scotland; the baculum (penis bone) of a walrus which is 18in (46cm) long – compared with a 1in (2.5cm) long weasel baculum; a mineralised bird's nest with an egg, encrusted with calcite from limestone spring-water; a stalagmite formed of slag from a nineteenth-century blast furnace; naturally weathered sandstone showing 'desert varnish' resembling a human face; plaster death masks of Isaac Newton and Charles XII, King of Sweden 1682-1718, and a bronze death mask of Chopin – and finally, a cast of the musician's hand.

Main Collection – Ground Floor

Paleontology

In 2001 a full-size T. Rex was installed in the university grounds to publicise a 'Walking with Dinosaurs' exhibition, the monster quickly attaining the status of a popular local landmark. Although the increasingly decrepit creature finally became extinct in 2005 – long after its anticipated sell-by date – the museum has a fine collection of prehistoric monsters and other fossils:

The exhibits include a *Triceratops* skull; a complete plesiosaur skeleton; Jurassic crocodiles; four icthyosaurs; six Upper Cretaceous dinosaur eggs from China – electronic scanning shows that one contains small bones; the world's smallest dinosaur footprint, a blackbird-sized fossil found in 2005, and a set of theropod dinosaur footprints from Skye; skulls of *Velociraptor, Allosaurus* and *Diplodocus,* and a massive leg of the latter; the 330-million-year-old Bearsden shark, showing the remains of its last meal, and three other shark fossils found near Glasgow.

It has other highlights too, including a block of red desert sandstone from the Permian period (300-250 million years ago), found in 1997 near Elgin (MRI scanning of the curious hole in the rock revealed a complete skull of a mammal-like reptile called *Dicynodon*), fossils of amphibia, fishes, trilobites, ammonites and a bat; three casts and a skull of the 'missing link' feathered bird-dinosaur *Archaeopteryx*; a model of *Arthropleura,* one of the largest-ever creepy-crawlies, a gigantic millipede-like arthropod whose tracks have been found on the Isle of Arran – and finally, a complete set of 1920s British Museum dinosaur models, and two 1870s prints by Waterhouse Hawkins of the dinosaur figures at Crystal Palace, all exuding period charm.

Natural History

This section houses a mounted specimen of a thylacine or marsupial wolf. This is the exhibit that will make cryptozoologists' hearts beat a little faster. The thylacine, occasionally called the Tasmanian tiger because of its distinctive stripes, was exterminated in Australia in the early twentieth century – many of their skins being made into leather waistcoats – with the last representative dying in a zoo in 1936. Nevertheless, there have been numerous unconfirmed sightings of thylacines in the outback, and there is a possibility that some may still survive.

A bluebuck skull. The blue antelope or bluebuck, *Hippotragus leucophaeus,* was almost unknown to Western science when it became extinct in 1799 – the first extinction of an African large mammal in modern times. It was never photographed or properly recorded, and hardly any fragments of it exist. This skull is one of only two left in the world. The Blue Antelope Project runs an excellent website on this tragic case, www.blueantelope.info.

Other natural curiosities include the skeletons of a dire wolf, a false killer whale, and a dolphin, elaborate birds' nests – true avian architecture – and a gobsmackingly large nest of the tropical stingless bee from Costa Rica, weighing in at 44 stone (280kg).

Anthropology

A Native American coat made to honour the spirit of the caribou when hunting. Items from eighteenth- and nineteenth-century Canada and Alaska ('the animals shown on many objects might be protective or might be clan ancestors, zigzag designs might mean powerful serpent-beings, and flowers were often from medicinal plants which brought life.')

The unmissable Kunyu Quantu map of the world. The continents – including Magellanica, the uncharted southern part of the world shown as a large landmass – are illustrated with a superb collection of real and imagined animals, all taken from Konrad Gesner's early zoological catalogue *Historia Animalium*, published between 1551 and 1586. Look for the goat, beaver, turkey, chameleon, spider, seahorse, bird of paradise, lion, rhinoceros, crocodile, quasi-giraffe, sea monsters, unicorn, chimera (?) and a mermaid and merman.

Archaeology

This diverse section includes the Clachaig Skull, found in a Neolithic chambered cairn on the Isle of Arran; a display of prehistoric stone and metal tools, including miniature axes used as charms; twelve Neolithic carved stone balls, each of a different style; the coffin and mummy of 'The Lady Shepenhor', and numerous Egyptian ushabti figures, scarab amulets, and gods; and several Roman inscriptions, altars and carvings from the Antonine Wall.

Main Collection – Balcony

A Healing Passion

Including: a horribly disfigured tumoured skull, and various bladder, gall and kidney stones (some queasily huge at 5-6in/13-15cm diameter).

Kelvin Exhibit

William Thomson, later Lord Kelvin, entered Glasgow University at the age of ten and became Professor of Natural Philosophy (i.e. physics) at the age of twenty-two. His achievements included propounding the Kelvin (Absolute) temperature scale (-273 degrees centigrade), formulating the Second Law of Thermodynamics, patenting over fifty inventions, and working on the first submarine Atlantic telegraph cable. (And to show that not even scientific geniuses get it right all the time, his pronouncements included 'Heavier-than-air flying machines are impossible,' 'X-rays are a hoax,' 'Radio has no future' and 'There is nothing new to be discovered in physics now. All that remains is more and more precise measurement.')

The display contains many fun and interactive exhibits which demonstrate Kelvin's discoveries, the highlights being a wine glass that wobbles in resonance with a variable tone, a spooky box in which a visible electrical spark transmits a voice, and a Tesla coil. Nikolai Tesla was the great (and eccentric and largely unsung) pioneer of electricity, and when he gave a demonstration in London in 1882 he created an illumination in sparks which spelt out the word 'Kelvin' – the scientist Tesla most admired. As an echo of this, the Hunterian Tesla coil uses high voltage sparks to spell 'William'. There is also what looks like just a dull piece of wood – which is actually the longest-running scientific experiment in the world. Kelvin wanted to show the behaviour of aether (the substance through which light was once thought to travel, a theory now discarded). As part of the theory, the aether needed to be very rigid for fast motions while at the same time not impeding slow motions. If you hit cobbler's wax hard it will shatter, yet sit it at the top of a stair and it will slowly slide down, like a fluid. Kelvin made a wooden slide and poured pitch at the top. The pitch 'glacier' was set going in 1887 and has been slowly flowing ever since – it may take another 100 years before it all reaches the bottom.

Robert McLaughlan's *Gifted: Personalities and Treasures of the University of Glasgow* gives a Kelvin-related anecdote. During one of his lectures Kelvin, to make a point about physics, famously fired an elephant gun. In 1951, during the celebration of the university's first 500 years, a scientist decided to recreate Kelvin's stunt. The chosen venue was the splendid lecture theatre of 1907, and the occasion a joint lecture to students and the public, thus, as the lecturer stated, 'killing two birds with one stone'. At the right moment the weapon was fired. Although not the size of an elephant gun, it was still a substantial discharge, and as

Glasgow mega-snake #1: the Kelvin Building, University of Glasgow.

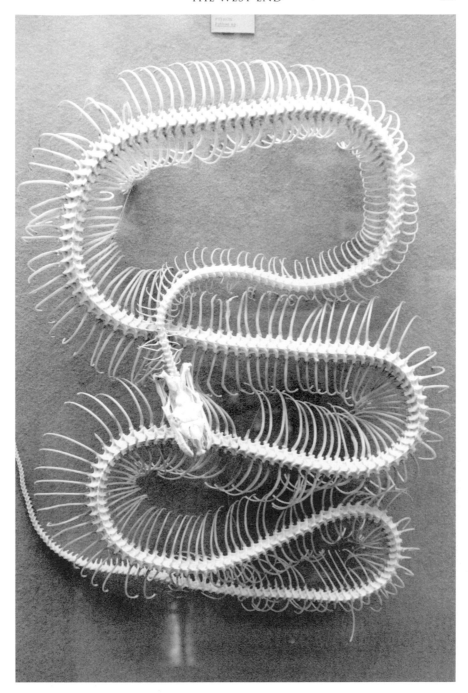

Glasgow mega-snake #2: Python skeleton, Zoology Museum, University of Glasgow.

the echoes from the bang faded, a blood-splattered pigeon fluttered down from the gantry. The lecturer collected himself, and muttered that, well, he had said 'two birds with one stone.' At this point a second dead bird hit the stage, and both audience and lecturer had a good laugh at the practical joke.

ZOOLOGY MUSEUM

In the Graham Kerr building of the Department of Zoology. Admission free. Monday to Friday, 9 a.m. to 5 p.m. Closed Saturdays, Sunday and public holidays. Partial wheelchair access.

While the Hunterian Museum is deservedly popular, its neighbour is virtually a secret. This is a shame as I defy anyone not be impressed with its collection of wonders (and horrors) from the animal world. Here are a few of the sights to be seen:

Skeletons and stuffed specimens of vampire bats, as well as skeletons of echidna, platypus, koala, common seal, mole, fruit bat, sloth, armadillo, flying lemur, common dolphin, dugong, kookaburra, macaw, kiwi, pigeon, grey heron, great cormorant, guillemot, monitor lizard, grass snake, rattlesnake, alligator, ostrich, giant anteater, bullfrog, common frog and tuatara (last living survivor of the dinosaurs).

An overhead model of a giant squid, 32ft (9.7m) long and the skulls of baboon, giraffe, giant anteater, pygmy anteater, tamandua, babirusa, aardvark, hyaena, black Malayan bear, capybara, coypu, African elephant, hyrax, pelican, spoonbill, marabou stork, greylag goose, curlew, albatross, flamingo, macaw, eagle, toucan, hornbill, large python, alligator, gharial, great tortoise, freshwater turtle, walrus and a huge estuarine crocodile.

Stuffed specimens of elephant shrew, tenrec and a truly enormous reticulated python – along with eleven successive moults from a growing Mexican red-knee spider, mounted specimens of a goliath beetle (the largest living insect) and the giant hornet, and displays on insects in art and in forensic investigation.

Casts of *Archaeopteryx*, a narwhal tusk (the likes of which contributed to tales of the unicorn) and whale vertebrae and baleen plates. Other exhibits have also come from animals which are now extinct, including the foot and leg limb (and a rare complete egg) of the giant flightless Elephant bird, *Aepyornis maximus*, a 1,000lbs (454kg) colossus that died out in the thirteenth century and which may have given rise to the legends of the giant roc bird (which snatched Sinbad in *The Arabian Nights*). The ovum inside the egg is probably the largest single animal cell ever known, over 6in (15cm) in diameter. In a similar vein, a 500lbs (227kg) specimen of a New Zealand moa, extinct from the seventeenth century, is also housed here.

Live animals include frogs, harvest mice, California king snake, Jalisco milk snake, royal python, Macleany's Spectre or giant prickly stick insect, Brazilian salmon pink birdeating spider, and a pair of beguiling bearded dragons.

ANATOMY MUSEUM

In the anatomy department. Admission free (but by pre-arrangement only: telephone 0141 330 5871/4292). Visits to this collection are by appointment only for two reasons – firstly, it is a teaching area, and the space is limited, and secondly because it mostly consists of endless jars of 'wet' specimens of dissected body parts from humans and animals, with no interpretation, so unless you are particularly fascinated by a kangaroo's colon, there is little of interest here.

However, within the formaldehyde-filled jars can be found: the stomach, spleen and intestine of a thylacine (*see* HUNTERIAN MUSEUM; a two-headed boy, with two sets of limbs and one body, and the head of a boy born with a single eye in the centre of his face (neither survived past birth). Not on display is 'The Mermaid', the skeleton and skin of a human infant with fused legs. There is no provenance for this stuffed example of human teratology, but it is probably eighteenth century. A photograph can be seen in McLaughlan's book.

HUNTERIAN ART GALLERY

University Avenue (opposite the Hunterian Museum). Admission free (charge for the Mackintosh House). Monday to Saturday, 9.30 a.m. to 5 p.m.; closed Sundays and public holidays. Wheelchair access. Alongside the famous works by James McNeill Whistler and Charles Rennie Mackintosh, there are several works of Fortean interest, including:

Artemesia Preparing to Drink the Ashes of Mausolus (Erasmus Quellinus, Flemish, 1652). The Roman writer Aulus Gellius told the story of the widowed Artemesia who in 351 BC removed the ashes of her husband from the Mausoleum of Helicarnassus and made them into a potion which she then drank. This act of sympathetic magic, similar to the practices of cannibals who seek to absorb the heroic qualities of their defeated enemies through eating them, emphasised her claim to the throne. In the painting a slave is opening a carved chest and Artemisia is holding a gold dish being filled with water.

Tobias and the Angel (Giovanni Francesco Grimaldi, 1650). Tobias, instructed by the Archangel Raphael, catches a fish and cuts out its heart, liver and gall, which he later uses to drive away a demon and cure his father's blindness. The story is from the apocryphal *Book of Tobit.*

Family Conversation Piece (Christine Borland, 1998). A set of skulls (a family of two adults and three children) made from bone china, decorated with sailing scenes in the style of traditional English blue delftware. The sculpture manages to be both charming and creepy at the same time.

Tools for the Shaman (Jake Harvey, 1996-7). Five diorite stones in the external sculpture garden, their shapes reminiscent of standing stones, mushrooms, holed stones and ritual sites. Next to it is Eduardo Paolozzi's *Rio,* looking like the disembowelment of a giant robot.

Tools for the Shaman, Hunterian Art Gallery.

WESTERN INFIRMARY

The hospital dates from 1871 and is alleged to be home to several ghosts. The one most commonly mentioned is that of Sir William MacEwen (1848-1924), a distinguished neurosurgeon who developed brain surgery and pioneered operations for tumours, abscesses and trauma. The suspiciously convenient story goes that he was asked to perform surgery on a young artist suffering from severe migraines. MacEwen refused to operate, and the artist, angry and in pain, jumped down four flights of stairs to his death. Many people have apparently seen MacEwen's regretful ghost – as noted in Dane Love's *Scottish Spectres,* most accounts have him disappearing into thin air outside the operating theatre where he worked (for example, a white-coated figure vanishing at the theatre door, seen by a young nurse and reported in Peter Underwood's *Gazetteer of Scottish Ghosts*).

Andrew Green (*Ghosts of Today*) records another apparition, seen by two people at the same time. One night in 1975, ward sister Mary McLellan was setting up some equipment in a room facing a well-lit corridor when she noticed a 'tall, silver-haired man wearing a blue dressing gown and standing near the doorway of the ward opposite'. After standing silently for a moment, he vanished. McLellan paid little attention, assuming he was a patient who had just gone back to bed. Almost immediately the ward nurse came over, very upset. She had seen the man and recognised him as a patient who had died two days previously.

The entrance to the Gardiner Institute at No. 44 Church Street is topped with a panel of two snakes coiling round a flaming torch above the word *Chirurgia* (meaning surgery); next door is a headmasterly looking eagle, while the Clinical Research and Education Centre at No. 38 is divided thematically into Night (sleeping girl holding a bunch of flowers, an owl snoozing while a mouse scurries about, crescent moon, star) and Day (a boy carrying a spanner, blooming flowers, an awake owl which has presumably just breakfasted on the mouse). The Anderson College of Medicine façade around the corner at No. 56 Dumbarton Road has another Day and Night, this time a pair of female angels trampling on serpents, Day radiant in a sunburst with feathered wings, Night sporting a splendidly nocturnal pair of bat's wings. The main carving is of Peter Lowe taking a patient's pulse in front of a class of Medicine 101 students. The sixteenth-century Lowe was the founder of the Faculty (now Royal College) of Physicians and Surgeons of Glasgow. In the 1922 British Medical Association's *Book of Glasgow*, Dr John Fergus imagined how Lowe would react to his twentieth-century colleagues. The poem includes the lines:

> If Maister Peter Lowe were here,
> Revisiting this earthly sphere,
> What wondrous changes would he see,
> Within his famous Faculty ...
> 'How oft, Sir, do you burn your witches?
> A horrid crew, ill-omened bitches,
> Of Satan's seed a monstrous birth,
> Who are far better off the earth.
> You say you never burn the creatures,
> But search for stigmata their features,
> And 'mid their
> howlings and their squealings,
> You psycho-analyse their feelings ...

HILLHEAD

Sometime in the 1970s, a maintenance worker engaged in track replacement at the (then closed) Hillhead underground station felt a strong sensation of cold and saw a woman on the platform. He went after her but she was nowhere to be found, and the only exit was a locked door barred from the inside. The next day, with another person present, he again felt the cold and saw the woman. Just before the sighting a brand new padlock was found rusted shut. (This interview with the workman was conducted by Drew Mulholland in 2006.) Over the years there have been several other reports of the sighting of a woman, with some mentioning her upmarket clothes and a sound of singing.

Tom Rannachan tells a very funny story of, when he was a lank-haired, heavy metal-loving teenager, meeting at a girl at an Ozzy Osborne gig and agreeing to accompany her to a medium on the top floor of a tenement just off Byres Road. Gallantly, he paid a £45 fee for each of them, a substantial figure in the 1980s. The medium was a huge woman in her fifties with dyed black hair, 'huge gold earrings, a loose-fitting black kaftan and make-up that looked as if it had been applied with a shovel.' She guzzled Irn-Bru and teacakes – the spirits apparently needed a sugar rush – then uttered pathetic, trite messages from the other side before having her hands tied and performing physical mediumship in the darkened room. Tom clearly saw the 'ectoplasm' was nothing but regurgitated cloth and was not best pleased at the associated smell of vomit. He was £90 down, ripped-off and disgusted. And he never saw the girl again.

On the south-east corner of Byres Road and University Avenue is a clock-like sculpture which, when it used to work, showed an animated abstract representation of the moon occulting a sunburst to create a solar eclipse. The splendid Victorian Kelvinside Hillhead Church on Saltoun Street, inspired by the thirteenth-century Sainte Chapelle in Paris, has an excellent selection of animal and demonic gargoyles and angels.

The Oran Mor (Gaelic for 'heavenly voice'), formerly a church, is now a popular bar and venue, with the auditorium featuring a series of murals by Alasdair Gray. The Ghostfinders paranormal investigation group, following up several reports of strange incidents (locked doors being found open, chairs being moved and presences being sensed) conducted an investigation on 10 April 2006. The basement nightclub produced unexplained noises, cold spots, and EVP recordings of a voice apparently saying the name 'Fraser'. A couple of the team experienced strong emotions and were reduced to tears for no obvious reason. At a séance in the auditorium almost all the team reported cold drafts, touches, or a strong sense of something moving around the table, while loud noises were heard and the recorders picked up the spoke word 'Fraser' again. More apparent voices were picked up in the private dining room (*see* www.ghostfinders. co.uk for the full report).

BOTANIC GARDENS

James Napier in *Notes and Reminiscences of Partick* relates the possibly tradition-indebted story of Catherine Clark, who arranged to meet her lover one night at the trysting place of Three Tree Well, also known as Pear Tree or Pea Tree Well. A few days later her body was found buried near a large tree near the well. Her bloodstained ghost was also seen at night. The tree and well were on the banks of the Kelvin, but both were removed by the extension of the Caledonian Railway. The railway itself has now gone, and an abandoned station lurks beneath the lawns. The excellent Kibble Palace hothouse holds a meaty collection of carnivorous plants, and white marble statues of Eve, her escutcheon-besmirching son Cain, the Biblical Ruth, a gamine known as the Elf, and King Robert of Sicily with his monkey, subject of a well-known Christian fable (one day King Bob, an arrogant monarch, found himself transformed into a jester with just a monkey for company; only when he acknowledged Christ as his overlord did he regain his throne).

The Opal Moon shop at No. 120 Queen Margaret Drive sells magical products and offers a diverse range of esoteric services. There are clinics on Tarot, spells, astrology and Neuro-

Linguistic Programming, wand-making workshops, readings with Tarot or Faery Oracle Cards, therapies (Reiki, aromatherapy, spiritual healing, Swedish massage) and channelled artwork of your spirit guide. The spells and astrology clinics are hosted by Siusaidh Ceanadach, Wiccan high priestess of a local coven.

DOWANHILL

Ron Halliday's *UFO Scotland* records a pair of incidents around Westbourne Gardens two decades apart. In the summer of 1955 eight-year-old Emma Roberts (a pseudonym) was with her sister and a group of older children, cooking potatoes over a small fire on a piece of wasteland. First two, then several more, strange identical beings arrived, all looking intently at the ground. They were thin and very pale-skinned with pointed faces and deep penetrating eyes, and wearing long, plain white garments with white caps. They were also floating. Their presence cast a strange spell over Emma, but suddenly one turned towards her, as if becoming aware of the child for the first time, and moved up the slope towards her. It was quickly followed by the rest of the group, who seemed to follow its actions. At this point Emma knew the beings were not human and she fled the scene.

At 3 a.m. sometime in May 1976 Allistair McNeil was sitting in a flat in Westbourne Gardens with two friends when they all saw a large silvery disc hovering about 100ft (30m) above the grassy space opposite the flat. McNeil described it as 60ft (18m) across with round porthole windows on its upper sections. It soared over the rooftops and disappeared from view, buzzing and humming. The incident had a huge impression on McNeil, who described the object as feeling almost divine, and certainly not from this planet.

PARTICK

It seems Partick once had several Viking hogback tombstones similar to those in the church at GOVAN. And they may still be there. The archaeological detective story is told in T.A. Davidson Kelly's article 'The Partick hogback hunt'. Kelly quotes the *Partick Illustrated Journal*, No. 3, 1 November 1854:

> In a field on the west side of the Byres, there lay three long and rounded stones termed the Sow Back Stones. An old tradition existed that these marked the burial place of those who died in the Plague, and a fearful doom was in reserve for the first person who should disturb these relics of the dead; but the stones are now removed, and the tradition has died away.

James Napier, in *Notes and Reminiscences relating to Partick* (1873) has more:

> In a field on Dowanhill Estate, a little east from Dowanhill House, and about 50yds from Byres Road, there were several large stones lying lengthways, half covered with earth … but there was a general fear to go near them … the children were made to believe that any person removing these stones would be seized with the plague, and that it was even dangerous to play near them.

Kelly suggests the stones were probably in the area bounded by Byres Road and White, Elie and Lawrence Streets, and may still be under a garden somewhere in the area.

Napier relates a jokey story about the Relief (West) UP Church. It was built on an east-west axis in line with tradition, but this put it out of line with Dumbarton Road, creating what many saw as an eyesore. It was a common jibe that some local residents were seen early in the morning, jackets off, pushing against the church to align it with Dumbarton Road. This motif, of people trying to push a church into the 'right' position, is widespread across Scotland.

The prolific Napier also published *Folk Lore: Or Superstitious Beliefs in the West of Scotland*, in which he related the traditions practiced at New Year in his father's house in Partick in the 1820s. They are rich in sympathetic magic. On the evening of 31 December the fire was carefully banked – if it should go out it was an ill omen, and no one would give or receive a light or fire from anyone else on New Year's Day – and every piece of ash swept up and taken out of the house. Everyone had to retire before midnight, as it was unlucky not to be in bed as the New Year came in.

In the morning all the children were given an oat bannock that had been baked with great care the evening before – if any of the bannocks broke while being cooked, it forecast illness or death for the specific child in the coming year. During the day no fire, ashes or anything that belonged to the house was taken outside. First-footing took place not after midnight but early in the morning. 'To visit empty-handed on this day was tantamount to wishing a curse on the family.' Flat-footed or pious people were unlucky first-footers: the best sort was a 'hearty ranting merry fellow.' Whatever drink the first-footer brought and poured out had to be drained to the bottom of the glass, and the same applied to the hospitality offered by the host; in either case if any liquid did remain it had to be immediately thrown out.

What happened on New Year's Day omened the coming year: once something was stolen from the house, and Napier's parents were later ill in bed for weeks – 'the cause and effect were quite clear'. On the other hand, one year the first-foot was a man who had fallen and broken his bottle, and who therefore spilled blood in the house when he was being attended to; despite Napier's mother being convinced that this foreshadowed injury or death, everyone in the family had a healthy and prosperous year.

Adam Ardrey's book *Finding Merlin – The Truth Behind The Legend* claims that Merlin, rather than being a legendary wizard, was a historical figure who lived in Partick with his wife Gwendolin between AD 600 and 618. He was apparently an individual of high political status, being the son of a late sixth century/early seventh-century Scottish chief called Morken. Ardrey's interest was sparked when he was researching his own surname, which led him to Ardery Street just off Dumbarton Road, which he then linked to the Battle of Arderydd in 573. Ardery is the modernised form of Arderydd, Merlin (or Myrddin as he was more commonly named) was at the battle, and so it all fits – if you accept the rather dubious idea that a modern placename commemorates the residence of a Dark-Age bigwig through his association with a battle.

The small former Quaker burial ground on Keith Street contains a plate inscribed 'Society of Friends. Burial Ground Gifted by John Purdon 1711. Last used II.XII.1857.' The first person buried here was 'Quaker Meg', the wife of John Purdon. In *Villages of Glasgow: North of the Clyde*, Aileen Smart records the local belief that if you put your ear to her grave at midnight and asked, 'What did you get to your supper tonight Meg?' she would answer back, 'Naething'.

The *Glasgow Herald* (14 November 1979) reported the case of an unnamed elderly couple who had been transferred from a council flat in the west end after suffering a haunting lasting three years. The unidentified flat had apparently been built seven years previously on the site of 'the old haunted house'. The ghosts were apparently a doctor and his wife and three children, one of whom was disabled. The elderly woman not only saw the apparitions, felt the cold as they walked past, and had been pushed by them, but had also been medically examined by the phantom doctor. The couple's married daughter also witnessed the spirits when she came for visits, but the teenage granddaughter, who lived in the flat, had never seen them – although she did notice small objects had been moved without explanation. According to the report, the family had declined to have the flat blessed by a priest for fear of upsetting the ghosts and causing more trouble.

St Simon's Church in Bridge Street has long been popular with the Polish community, ever since Polish troops worshipped there during the Second World War. On Sundays the

Stone Spiral, McPhun's Park, Glasgow Green.

congregation is so large that many worshippers kneel in the street outside. The exterior has a magnificent Polish eagle. A side chapel holds a copy of the Our Lady of Czestochowa, one of the most revered of the Black Madonna icons. The original in Poland is the locus of numerous legends – it was supposedly painted by St Luke the Evangelist on a table top owned by the Holy Family; it miraculously saved a monastery from war in the seventeenth century; it prevented the destruction of a church (but not before the fire darkened the pigments, thus creating the 'Black' Madonna); and the two scars on the Madonna's right cheek were caused by the sword strikes of plunderers, who either died from the act, or fled when the icon began to bleed.

Intriguingly, the Czestochowa Madonna may well be the visual origin of the Voodoo loa Erzulie Dantor, the spirit of motherhood; copies of the icon were carried by Polish soldiers fighting in the Haitian Revolution in 1802. The St Simon's icon used to be surrounded by medals won by Poles fighting against Nazism; sadly, the medals were stolen from the sanctuary, a double sacrilege which one can only hope brought pain and suffering upon the thieves. St Simon's doubled for 'All Souls' Church' in 'Amulet', perhaps the best episode of the television series *Sea of Souls*. The church was supposed to be built on the '2,000 year old foundations of a pagan temple' which the plot suggests may conceal a 'vanishing stone' – although this turns out to be not only erroneous but a red herring.

7

EAST GLASGOW

GLASGOW GREEN

McLellan's triumphal arch at the entrance off Saltmarket has carvings of Apollo (lyre and sunburst) and the Three Graces (jigging to the beat of a tambourine). Tom Rannachan describes as a small boy seeing a filthy old man begging cross-legged in the middle of St Andrew's Suspension Bridge. He asked his mum for some coins, turned back – and the man was gone! Tom also received an email from someone in Gorbals saying he was on his way to work at 6.30 a.m. when, alone on the centre of the bridge, he heard loud cursing right in his ear. The park on the far side of King's Drive has a modern sculpture of boulders which spiral in to a central monolith, all inscribed with key events in the story of Glasgow Green.

PEOPLE'S PALACE

Glasgow Green. Admission free. Monday to Thursday and Saturday, 10 a.m. to 5 p.m., Friday and Sunday 11 a.m. to 5 p.m. The museum tells the story of the people of Glasgow. Displays of interest include:

A list of the sixty-seven men and five women executed in Glasgow between 1814-1865, including the infamous Mathew Clydesdale (*see* COLLEGE STREET). Inside a reconstruction of a cell from Duke Street prison an audio-visual features ex-death cell guard Frank McCue revisiting the now disused execution chamber in Barlinnie Prison.

A pair of huge whale jawbones set over the staircase. They came from the BISHOP'S PALACE, where they formed an archway in the old flower garden.

The shaving mirror and German drill book that took a bullet and therefore saved the life of a Tommy in the trenches. The soldier carried the items as a good luck charm thereafter.

CALTON

This area was considered so dangerous that police officers were issued with cutlasses, so in a tussle with graverobbers in the burial ground on Abercromby Street one of the bodysnatchers nearly had his arm amputated. A broadside of 1827 entitled 'Supposed Murder' told the tale of a destitute young Irishman who died in Calton. After the wake, his uncle, now drunk, attacked the funeral party carrying the coffin, saying that he needed to sell the body of his nephew to the anatomists: 'Have I not a right to make as much of it as I can?' He was heavily fined.

A report in the *Glasgow Chronicle* of 10 February 1829 tells of the ordeal suffered by Margaret Log, wife of the bodysnatcher William Hare, of Burke and Hare infamy. Log had turned King's Evidence, testifying against William Burke in exchange for a pardon. She had walked from Edinburgh to Glasgow and lodged anonymously in Calton while daily trying for a ship to Ireland. In Clyde Street she was somehow recognised by a drunken woman, who shouted out,

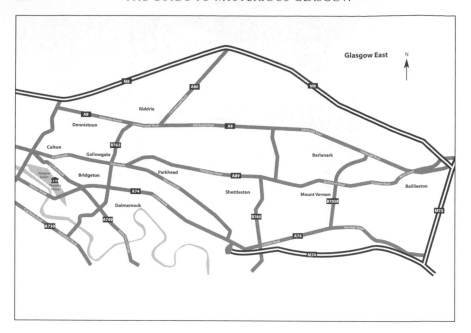

'Hare's wife! Burke her!' – and Mrs Hare was stoned and beaten. She was sequestered in Calton police station for several days for her own safety before being spirited out of Glasgow on a steamer bound for Belfast.

Abercromby Street used to be known as Witch Loan. A.G. Callant, in *Saint Mungo's Bells* (1888), gives his origin for the name. The townsfolk's cattle were struck with a disease said to be caused by witchcraft. Advised to seek out running water and a change of pasturage, the owners drove the animals down to the Clyde via this route. The cure worked, the path hence acquiring its witch name.

GALLOWGATE

The Gallowmuir, an open space formerly north and east from Gallowgate, was the site of the first gallows. The excellent website www.theglasgowstory.com has the story of wealthy merchant John Wallace, who built a carriage road from his Whitehill House mansion in Dennistoun to the eastern end of Gallowgate. The lodge at the entrance to the drive was nicknamed by the local people 'Mount Hooley' and said to be haunted by a husband and wife, he being hanged in 1801 for murdering her.

One of the legends attached to St Kentigern is that when preaching to a multitude on a plain he realised most people could not see him, so he caused the ground beneath him to rise up. This place was later identified as Dow Hill, a spot on the north side of Gallowgate just outside the east Port (gate) of the city, and in 1500 the chapel and graveyard of St Mungo Without the Walls, also called Little St Mungo's Kirk, was constructed on the spot. The trees nearby were St Mungo's trees, the well St Mungo's Well, and the route to it St Mungo's Road. The sixteenth century, however, was a very late date for a new religious venture, and the site appears to have been abandoned after the Reformation.

In 1755 the site became the Saracen's Head Inn, for many years Glasgow's premier inn, where many a distinguished visitor stayed. There was once a sign stating that Adam Smith was ejected from the establishment for calling Dr Johnson 'a son of a b★★★★'. The traditional virtue of the well

Holy gravestone,
Calton Burial
Ground.

was lost, although Alexander Fowler's 1914 paper 'Old Draw and Drip Wells' records the curious fact that during the rinderpest epidemic of 1860, the only cattle to escape the infection were those kept by John Stirling in the stable yard of the inn. When the inn was demolished in 1905, the well was restored by Mr Anderson of the Tron House. Skeletons were also uncovered, presumably from the old graveyard. The current Saracen's Head pub is slightly to the east of the site of the inn.

The RCAHMS 'Canmore' website records a sign still standing in 1951: 'Ancient Well of Little St Mungo. Restored 1906. Near this spot Christian converts met St Kentigern (St Mungo) on his return from Wales. Near this spot also his meeting with St Columbus is said, by some historians, to have taken place.' The sign has long gone and the site of the now-subterranean well, somewhere to the rear of the pub, is difficult to pinpoint.

A cleaned and polished skull sits in a glass case behind the bar. This is supposed to be the last woman burned at the stake for witchcraft in Scotland. As the last such execution was in 1727 in Dornoch, Sutherland, this is unlikely to say the least. It is just another example of a widespread folkloric motif, 'the last witch'. There are dozens of 'last witch' sites around Scotland (just as there are many places claiming the slaying of the 'last wolf') and it is simply a combination of a good story allied with our collective obsession with 'last things'. A more likely candidate for the skull is that it is one of those uncovered during the building works of 1905. A hatch in the cellar, it is said, opens into a tunnel leading to the Necropolis, another manifestation of the 'secret passage to the cathedral' myth.

The Saracen's Head does, however, have a long history of hauntings, many attributed to the spirit of a previous owner named Angus. In the *Daily Record* for 11 May 2005 the bar's licensee, Anne McGuigan, was quoted as saying, 'We always feel Angus when we're in here on our own. There are gusts of wind going past you, footsteps and just the feeling that there is someone there.' Two days earlier the paranormal research group Ghostfinders had conducted an investigation. Motion sensors went off, loud noises were heard in areas that remote video cameras showed were empty,

The Saracen's Head, site of Mungo's miracle, a holy well, and ghostly phenomena.

electromagnetic field machines recorded strong signals, and tape recorders picked up what were claimed to be EVP (electronic voice phenomena) communications from old Angus. Angus turned up during a session with a ouija-type communications board – he was happy with the present way the pub was run, but wanted his portrait hung back up – and then the board indicated there was a spirit present who wanted to speak to BRM – the initials of *Daily Record* reporter Brian McIver. The glass spelled out the initials of Brian's late grandfather. Brian then threw in a red herring – by giving the wrong name for his mother – but the glass moved to his mum's correct initial. The full investigation is reported on the group's website www.ghostfinders.co.uk.

The famous Barrowlands Ballroom is inextricably linked with the horrific murders of three women in 1968-69: Patricia Docker, Jemima McDonald and Helen Puttock. They were picked up at the dance hall and later found strangled. The mystery killer was dubbed 'Bible John' because he called himself John and a witness heard him quote scripture and say, 'I don't drink at Hogmanay, I pray.' The crimes remain unsolved (although there is speculation they may have been carried out by Peter Tobin, a rapist, sexual predator and multiple murderer imprisoned in 2007 for killing another girl). Because Bible John was never caught or even identified, he has joined the exclusive brethren of mystery serial killers, brother in blood to Jack the Ripper. Such mysteries provide fertile ground for outré speculation. Ron Halliday (*Evil Scotland*) suggests John may have been a black magician killing for an unknown ritual purpose. During a taxi ride Helen Puttock's friend Jean Langford thought he muttered something about his surname being Templeton, Sempleton or Emerson. Halliday wonders if John was actually saying 'The Temple of Solomon, Jerusalem.'

Menstrual blood may have been his ritual object. All three victims were menstruating. Did he know this? And if so, how? In the first two cases he took their sanitary towel, and in the last he placed it under Helen Puttock's left armpit. Many years ago, a Glasgow taxi driver told me Bible John had deliberately left his victims at specific places as part of creating an occult sigil over Glasgow, but I confess to have forgotten all the other details of his argument.

In 1991 Glasgow comics writer Grant Morrison penned 'Bible John – A Forensic Meditation' for *Crisis Magazine* (Nos 56–61). The work was not reprinted in book form so I am here relying on the few reviews that appear online. It is said to cover similar ground to Alan Moore and Eddie Campbell's Jack the Ripper graphic novel *From Hell*, being a disquisition on evil and speculating why the killer committed his crimes. The atmospheric artwork appears to use mixed media and highly stylised techniques. The Wikipedia webpage on Grant Morrison claims that Morrison and artist Daniel Vallely used a ouija board to write the script, and that Vallely created the collages while using hallucinogenic drugs before destroying most his work when the project was finished. Vallely's own MySpace page simply says, 'I lost a lot of sweat and blood on this – the rumors were true.'

Morrison's astonishingly prolific output has included revamping mainstream superhero characters – Superman, Batman, the X-Men, and many more – to countercultural freak-outs such as *The Filth* and *The Invisibles*. For the latter – which was supposedly partly communicated through contact with aliens – Morrison, using his noted *agent provocateur* approach, instituted a worldwide event in which orgasms were to be magically focused on increasing sales of the comic. Parts of his *Animal Man* series are set in Anniesland, and Morrison himself appears in the story. His thoughts on everyday magical practices were set out in the article 'Pop Magic!' in *The Book of Lies*. Part-Puck, part-Trickster, part pop-culture Renaissance magus – reading Grant Morrison may blow your mind; you have been warned.

An isolated classical arch on Bellgrove Street hosts a superb carving of the great god Pan. Around the corner, west on Gallowgate, an office building has an insignia decorated with two fine red-painted griffons.

The Great God Pan, Bellgrove Street.

BRIDGETON

Kenna and Sutherland's *They Belonged to Glasgow* notes that in 1823 a Bridgeton parent lost two children; on opening the grave of the first child to bury the second, it was discovered the corpse had already been stolen. Anti-bodysnatching citizens' groups patrolled with pistols and swords. A young man protecting his sister's grave was accidentally killed by his own gun. In 1824 the Bridgeton Grave Protection Society was founded and a fundraising song composed by Alexander Rodger. Entitled 'Ye Who Mourn Your Dear Departed' – and I would suggest, ripe for a folk group to revive – its second verse runs:

> Midnight prowlers bent on robbing,
> Shall no more your dead molest;
> Now, 'the wicked cease from troubling',
> Now, 'the weary are at rest'.
> Soundly sleeps your sire or mother,
> Faithful husband, virtuous wife,
> Son or daughter, sister, brother,
> Safe from the dissector's knife.

Attached to the pulpit of Sacred Heart Church at No. 50 Old Dalmarnock Road is a crucifix which deflected a bullet and saved a soldier's life in the trenches of the Western Front.

PARKHEAD CROSS

Jimmy Black in *History's Mysteries* tells the story of an 'Onion Johnnie' named Pierre – almost certainly not his real name – who supplied onions to Dunn's restaurant in the 1930s.

Carving at Glasgow Gallowgate, eastern Necropolis.

St Michael despatching a
dragon, Gallowgate.

One day the cook, Madge, cut into an onion and found within a man's gold ring engraved
ZEBA. Someone had apparently removed the centre of the onion, squeezed the ring inside and
replaced the core. The following week when 'Pierre' came back, Madge showed him the onion
and the ring. He gave an anguished cry, burst into tears, grabbed the ring, tossed it through the
grating of a drain, jumped on his bike and sped off, never to return.

St Michael's Church at No. 1,350 Gallowgate has a splendid but severe 1960's sculpture of the
titular archangel slaying a dragon (which looks more like a big cat). The Eastern Necropolis
(Nos 1,264-70 Gallowgate) is not as exciting as the other Necropoles, but it does have a small
selection of Victorian angels and statues, many of them vandalised. The sculpture at the very
top of the former Glasgow Savings Bank (No. 1,448-56 Gallowgate, now The Bank bar) is
supposedly 'Prudence strangling Want' but to me it looks like a muscular man feeding a dog.
A female angel reading a (if not the) good book tops Parkhead Library (No. 64 Tollcross Road)
and the robed and garlanded personification of Glasgow stands above the entrance, also with an
open volume, while various bookish cherubs busy themselves round about.

DENNISTOUN

Musician Drew Mulholland (see MOUNT VERNON) told me an episode from his childhood in
the 1960s. His parents, looking for somewhere to buy, visited a three-storey house on Clayton
Terrace which had a very cheap asking price. Just a few paces into the hall his mother and
father paused, looked at each other, realised they had both sensed 'something', and instantly left
without viewing the rest of the house. Later Drew learned lights were frequently seen in the
lean-to greenhouse, even though the house was empty.

TOLLCROSS

On a bright summer's day in 1978 children at St Mark's primary school, Muiryfauld Drive, saw a silvery metal 'Star Trek-type' object hovering about 20ft (6m) above the fence. It then vanished. The group Scottish Earth Mysteries Research investigated in 1993 and witness Euan Riley recalled the event in the Glaswegian: 'It glistened in the sun, about four feet across. It looked weird, like two fedora hats joined together. Although I was young, the memory of the incident has remained vivid in my memory, and I am sure of what I saw.' The incident is recorded in Ron Halliday's UFO Scotland.

RIDDRIE AND RIDDRIE KNOWES

In the 'Amulet' episode of Sea of Souls, the fictional All Souls' Church (see PARTICK) is in Riddrie Knowes at the centre of an equilateral formed by two ley-lines and the Molendinar Burn. Like everything in the story, the geography is fictionalised, with the Molendinar moved several miles east from its actual course, Edinburgh Road renamed as Drygrove Street, supposedly 'the oldest thoroughfare in Glasgow' and Cumbernauld Road becoming Keyne's Loan, 'which before it was rebuilt by the Romans was used to transport the dead to a Druidic temple'.

Much time is spent drawing lines on maps, and there's a glimpse of what looks like Harry Bell's alignments; leys are discussed as representing ancient death roads, and the most potent places for vivid dreams of the past are said to correspond with underground water. The story concerns a young man who mysteriously vanishes then apparently follows an old burial route while possessed by the spirit of his grandfather, whose unburied corpse lies at the end of the route. There is a sense that the production team had fun reworking Glasgow to meet the demands of the script: 'Drygrove' is clearly meant to refer to DRYGATE, which is one of the city's oldest streets, the 'Druidic temple' is probably the AULD WIVES' LIFTS, which is aligned on Dobbie's (rather than Keyne's) Loan, and All Souls' Church is depicted on the map as being where, in reality, you would find Barlinnie Prison.

CRANHILL

The Cranhill water tower at the junction of Stepps Road and Bellrock Street was part of a project in which various landmarks were enhanced with dramatic lighting. According to an article by Catherine Slessor in The Architectural Review (August 1999), Glasgow's nine water towers were paired with the planets of the solar system; Cranhill corresponded with Neptune. With its square bulk supported on a forest of tall legs, when it was lit the tower looked like one of the alien machines from H.G. Wells' War of the Worlds. Sadly the lighting is no longer fully working. In 2001 the theme was continued with the installation under the tower of six wonderful metal sculptures by Andy Scott – a mermaid, three sirens with female heads and bird bodies, a salmon and Neptune himself.

SHETTLESTON

The two stone 'sentry boxes' on either side of the graveyard entrance were used by watchmen looking out for bodysnatchers. In 1830 graverobbers used a duplicate key to open a locked mortsafe and steal a young girl's body.

In 1938 in Yorkshire there was an apparent outbreak of assaults on women by what the News of the World (27 November) termed a 'terrorist with a razor blade.' The 'Halifax Slasher' was said to have cut the clothes of thirteen victims. The town underwent a reign of terror; the maniac was seen everywhere, vigilantism was in full force, and innocent men were rounded on for just being present when someone shouted, 'There he is!' Then the panic spread right across the country: Bradford, Sheffield, Barnsley, Wigan, Settle, Blackburn, Cheshire, Brentford – and Glasgow. In a Shettleston back court a man bumped into Mrs Mary Murphy and cut her leg – the Slasher had struck! Panic in the streets of Glasgow!

After some time, however, it became clear that Britain had been gripped by an exaggerated, not to say hysterical, response to reports of the original 'mystery assailant' – who, it turned out, may not have existed at all. Many of the 'crimes' appeared to have been self-inflicted, fantasised, or maliciously invented, wasting thousands of police hours in the process. Everywhere the panic had struck, people were coming to terms with the demeaning realisation that, for a brief period, they had become subject to an extraordinary popular delusion and the madness of crowds. Mrs Murphy and an Alexander McFarlane, like many elsewhere, were remanded on charges of false accusation. The temporary insanity is collated in Michael Goss' *The Halifax Slasher,* a *Fortean Times* publication from 1987.

MOUNT VERNON

A Bronze-Age burial ground was uncovered in 1928 at the Greenoakhill sand-pit (NS66956280). Several of the cists contained skeletons. In December 1995 James MacLean was taking photographs in the area, during which a compass in his pocket reversed itself. When he had the film developed he noticed two objects in the sky – one discoid, the other shaped like a dumb-bell. The photos are in Ron Halliday's *UFO Scotland*. The area is home to one of Glasgow's more intriguing creative types, *avant-garde* electronic composer Drew Mulholland. His works are inspired by psychogeographical excursions around Glasgow and London, with references to abandoned military sites, closed-down railways, British science fiction, lost placenames and districts, subterranean networks, secret tunnels – an entire urban litany of the forlorn, the forgotten and the fantastic.

In 'Magical Cyrkles', an article in Mark Pilkington's *Strange Attractor Journal,* Mulholland wrote of taking a magical walk from Mount Vernon to discover 'Egypt' – a now lost placename, the area around Ochil and Dalness Streets in SHETTLESTON – leaving subtle symbols for pyramids and Mercury along the way. Mulholland has gone by various *noms de synthesiser* – Mount Vernon Arts Lab released the CD *Séance at Hobs Lane* (which is set in the fictional tube station at the centre of Nigel Kneale's creepy science fiction classic *Quatermass and the Pit*) while Mount Vernon Astral Temple made *Musick That Destroys Itself*. Mulholland also contributed some of the music to the play *Standing Wave: Delia Derbyshire in the 1960s*, an exploration of the pioneering electronic musician who created the *Doctor Who* theme. In 'Magical Cyrkles' he describes using one of Derbyshire's old snuff tins to transport ashes from the remains of the Wicker Man (the one burnt in the film) to a location in Glasgow to achieve a magical rite.

CARMYLE

Hugh Macdonald, a psychogeographer of a different century, recorded the tale of the *Bluidy Neuk* of Carmyle. Two inseparable friends both fell in love with the same girl. They quarrelled, and one killed the other with his sword. When he realised what he had done, he took his own life. They were laid in the same grave where they had fallen.

A ferruginous spring in the neighbourhood was long looked upon with horror by the good folks of the village, who saw in the red oxidised earth around it a mysterious connection with the blood that had been shed. An old lady who was born in Carmyle informed us that the spot was reckoned 'no canny,' and that in her youth he would have been considered a bold individual who would have ventured there alone after nightfall. So regardless of such matters, however, have modern agricul-turists become, that within the last few years the plough has been driven over the spot.

UDDINGSTON

The *Herald* for 12 November 1979 had a letter from a man who had seen a big cat near Uddingston. H.C. Mullin had spotted the creature on the M74 coming out of Honeywells Controls factory at Viewpark. It was early on a Saturday morning in summer, and the visibility was good. 'The animal was grayish in colour, with white tufts of hair on its side. It walked with a peculiar padding motion on big flat feet or paws. It had a very long tail, quite smooth, which swept back in a long upward curve.' He thought it was a mountain lion. 'I actually stopped the lorry and ran across the road to see it going through a thick hedge. Then I realised that this was a big cat and might be partial to a bit of lorry-driver for tiffin. So I ran back to the safety of the cabin and drove off.'

8

NORTH-EAST GLASGOW

GARTHAMLOCK

In the right atmospheric conditions, the two landmark circular water towers on Jerviston Road can easily suggest alien spacecraft.

PROVAN HALL

Auchinlea Road. Admission free. Monday to Friday, 9 a.m. to 4.30 p.m. Partial wheelchair access. Provan Hall is probably Glasgow's most neglected gem. It is the oldest standing building in Glasgow, predating Provand's Lordship by a handful of years. The main building is a fifteenth-century hunting lodge, with an eighteenth-century plantation-style building, Blochairn House, on the south side of the central courtyard. The very active Friends of Provan Hall are seeking funds for a major refurbishment, and also put on spectacular Hallowe'en events each year. Provan Hall is possibly the most haunted location in Glasgow. Since 2005 the Ghost Club have conducted several investigations at the site and Derek Green's exemplary, highly-detailed reports can be found at www.ghostclub.org.uk. I give a brief summary of the findings here.

Provan Hall

On the ground floor are the kitchen (which has a fireplace large enough to roast half an ox), dairy, and hallway, all vaulted. Above are the dining room and master bedroom. The dairy often houses paintings by members of the Alcohol Information Service, an alcoholics' group supported by Provan Hall; in 2008 the exhibition, on the subject of the effects of alcohol withdrawal, included works featuring severed heads on the wall, beetles in the bed, demon dogs, and a hungry mouth emerging from a hand.

Kitchen
Perhaps the most interesting incident came on 23 June 2007 when the investigators spilt into two groups who worked successively in the various rooms, following each other at a distance. During group one's vigil, Derek Green psychically contacted a bearded, unruly-haired man in his early thirties who was armed with a sword. The individual gave his name as Robert. When group two moved into the kitchen, having had no idea what had transpired with the other group, their medium Lisa Bowell was contacted by a soldier who, with some agitation, demanded to know where Derek had gone. The spirit called himself Robert.

On another occasion a spirit named Robert Baillie came through. The Baillie family had owned the estate after the Reformation. A tray dusted with flour to detect movement was found to have been slightly disturbed, with no obvious cause. Two sets of brand-new camera batteries were drained of power – back home they were found to be fully charged, and the camera working perfectly.

Garthamlock water towers advancing over the landscape.

Dining Room

During a vigil the body temperature of one of the sitters dropped by 10 degrees and he had to be taken outside to recover. Mediums contacted Robert Baillie again and another Robert, apparently a fourteenth-century archer in the retinue of a lord. He was interested in the purpose of 'the box making a noise' (the EMF reader carried by one of the team). Another medium reported an aggressive presence. A face was seen at the window by someone in the courtyard, an experience that has been reported several times by visitors.

Master Bedroom

Here low temperatures, tappings (on the first-floor window), bangs, thuds, footsteps, a solid heavy door that frequently opened of its own accord, and an oppressive atmosphere were experienced. A moving shadow was seen by three people during a séance, and one of the sitters felt as if he was encased in ice (while his external body temperature dropped alarmingly). There were also major EMF fluctuations, unexplained breezes, smells of excrement, mediumistic visions of the bodies of a murdered woman and child, and walls and floors splattered with blood – the bedroom seemed to the epicentre of whatever was going on. For years staff have been reporting strange events from this room.

After the investigation, a member of staff revealed that he had discovered that around 1850 a soldier had returned from the Crimean War to find his wife had borne another man's child. He stabbed his wife twenty-eight times and cut the child's throat, both in the master bedroom. None of the Ghost Club team knew this in advance. Derek Green's cautious conclusion was that there was possibly 'some evidence' that the master bedroom is haunted. Certainly the results have persuaded the Ghost Club to conduct several investigations at the site.

Provan Hall, possibly Glasgow's most haunted. Blochairn House is on the left.

Blochairn House

Back Staircase

Sightings by two of the investigators of a 'black mass' and a luminous shape just up from the first landing may correspond with numerous sightings reported by visitors and staff of a white-bearded man dressed in black and wearing a black bowler hat. This is claimed to be Reston Mather, the last owner, who died of pneumonia in 1934. The area became very cold and there were several knocks (apparently in response to questions being asked out loud) which were heard by both groups at the same time but in different rooms. Linda Cameron, a staff member, saw and heard three children and a woman she presumed to be their mother on the stairs. All were dressed in old-fashioned clothing and the children were playing about, sliding down the banisters. Despite the fact that it was night and the lights were off, Linda could see the family clearly. The experience lasted about two to three minutes. On two separate visits a different medium was drawn to the window looking out to the trees and the Fort Shopping Centre, with the sense of someone being hanged. A staff member confirmed that about 2003 a female had been found hanging in the grounds close to Blochairn House.

Office

Various members of the teams reported sounds: a breath or sigh, a noise from outside the door when no one was there, and something being dragged. As part of the investigations various 'trigger objects' were scattered around the site, their position traced around and photographed. Only one object was found to have moved – a box containing two stones on the corridor seat outside the office door. It had shifted off the pencil line by ¾in (1.9cm).

This may not seem a big deal, but Green states, 'I do feel fairly confident that the movement of the box on the corridor seat was paranormal,' and quotes the great investigator Harry Price with approval: 'The paranormal movement of a box of matches one inch is more significant to the psychical researcher than an army of phantoms marching down the hallway of a stately home.'

Stevie Allan, the enthusiastic property manager, has a wealth of stories related to the investigations. On one occasion, during one of the séances, he was apparently 'taken over' by something, and spouted incomprehensible words before the others brought him back to consciousness. Several hours later, in the time before dawn, he was still feeling the after effects, 'trancing out' and losing track of time. For three nights thereafter he was unable to sleep. Only when some of the investigation team performed a 'cleansing' ritual in each of the rooms was he able to have a good night.

On my visit, another member of staff at Glasgow Land Services was taking the tour; she was unable to enter the master bedroom, and felt so uncomfortable just staying at the threshold that eventually she had to leave and return to Blochairn House. She told me that the first time she visited the master bedroom she felt a choking sensation as if she could not breathe. This was long before she knew about the hauntings.

QUEENSLIE

In 1965 John Fagan, a dockworker living at No. 35 Penston Road, was diagnosed with cancer and following unsuccessful operations he was sent home to die. In early 1967 the parish priest at the Church of the Blessed John Ogilvie on Newhills Road, anointed him with the Last Rites; Fagan was going to die within hours. Mary Fagan pinned a medal of Ogilvie to her husband's pyjamas and the family and the congregation prayed to the martyr for his intercession. A short time later Fagan suddenly improved. His GP, followed by several other doctors, confirmed the apparently impossible – the cancer had vanished.

John Ogilvie was raised as a Protestant in north-east Scotland before converting to Roman Catholicism. He was ordained as a Jesuit priest at Paris in 1610, and, as part of the Counter-Reformation strategy aimed at re-Catholicising newly Protestant people, he returned to Scotland in 1613 *ut dedocerem haeresim* ('to unteach heresy'). Disguised as a soldier, he travelled round the country celebrating Mass and spreading the Catholic word. In 1614 he was betrayed to the authorities in Glasgow, sleep-deprived for nine nights, beaten and tortured, eventually being hanged for high treason at Glasgow Cross on 10 March 1615. The treason charge came about because he refused to accept the supremacy of James VI in spiritual matters. Ogilvie the martyr became an important figure to some Glasgow Catholics, and there had long been a campaign to canonise him. The annual Ogilvie Walk was a common sight, and the 1967 march took place just before Fagan's recovery. But without an attested miracle, Ogilvie could not be canonised.

An investigation lasting nine years tried to find a medical reason for Fagan's recovery. The conclusion: 'There was no natural explanation.' In 1976 the case was presented to the Consistory of Cardinals in Rome, who voted unanimously in favour of ratifying the events as a *bona fide* miracle. The Blessed John Ogilvie became St John Ogilvie, the first Scottish saint since Queen Margaret in 1250. Four thousand Scots, including the Fagans, watched Pope Paul VI formally canonise Ogilvie. Also at the event in Rome was Pastor Jack Glass, Glasgow's anti-Catholic blowhard, with a banner reading '4 million Scots are against this Canonisation – Ogilvie was a traitor, not a saint'. John Fagan went on to outlive all those who had supported him during his illness – his GP, his priest and his wife Mary. The full story is told in *Miracle* by Des Mickey and Gus Smith, and in John Burrowes' *Glasgow: Tales of the City*.

The former Gartloch Hospital.

EASTERHOUSE

On 9 November 1979 a woman in Easterhouse saw an unusually bright aerial light. It split into two equally bright objects which moved around before reuniting, and then vanished. The sighting is in Ron Halliday's *UFO Scotland*.

There are two of Andy Scott's iconic 'wirework' sculptures in the area, a phoenix on the approach road into Easterhouse (symbolising the regeneration of the area), and the majestic 13ft (4m) tall *Heavy Horse,* a landmark on the M8. It stands on the south side of the motorway in Glasgow Business Park, of which it has become the emblem.

BISHOP'S LOCH

One of the earlier Scottish chroniclers, George Buchanan (*History of Scotland,* 1582) relates how Bishop Cameron of Glasgow (1426-1446) retired to bed on Christmas Eve in his house in Lochwood only to be summoned by 'a thundering voice out from heaven' which called upon him to suffer judgement for his supposed cruelties and oppressions. He roused his servants and ordered them to light candles and sit with him. Cameron started to read aloud, but the voice was heard again, this time by all present. The bishop groaned terribly and was found dead on his couch with his tongue hanging out and his features horribly distorted. The bishop's country house was destroyed by in 1579. In 1962 its position was located on a mound on the south side of the loch (NS69376698) with a second archaeological dig in

Wistful head, former Gartlock Hospital.

2005 confirming the moat, wall and buildings of a prestigious medieval building. According to *The Old Country Houses of the Old Glasgow Gentry*, one severe winter the stones from the house were carted across the frozen Bishop's Loch to build the mausoleum at Bedlay Castle.

GARTLOCH

The gaunt Victorian buildings of the former Gartloch psychiatric hospital on Gartloch Road have a real Arkham Asylum feel – far from the city, isolated, Gothic – I wouldn't have been surprised if clichéd horror movie lightning and thunder had broken out during my visit. The site is being developed into the residences of Gartloch Village. The arches on the twin towers of the main building have keystones carved with wistful, slightly distracted female heads. Both Dane Love and Martin Coventry record an apparition of a woman dressed in black seen by staff at the hospital. Her patch was the corridor and the top of stairs near ward one, and she had been seen walking through an old doorway that had been boarded up for years.

9

NORTH GLASGOW

MARYHILL

In *Confess and Be Hanged*, Sheila Livingstone suggests that in October 1832 Dr Carlaw of Maryhill took part in a bodysnatching raid on New Kilpatrick. Watchers fired on the party and, although Carlaw had been at a social event until midnight, he was found dead on the path to his house at 5 a.m. He had earlier shown a 'lifting' spade to friends. The funeral took place before the body could be examined, no doubt to protect his reputation.

In 1827 the body of Mrs Purdon was stolen from the graveyard on the corner of Maryhill Road and Duart Street. The now-overgrown burial ground was locked on my visit; through the gates can be seen the foundations of the former parish church. Also gone is a famous cast-iron column, the monument to George Miller, a nineteen-year-old worker stabbed by a strike-breaker in 1834 during a calico printing trade dispute.

Ron Halliday's *UFO Scotland* records the case of Rita Drummond. In 1968 she saw a silvery-grey cigar-shaped object in the sky. At the time she was having dreams in which she would try and hide from strange shapes in the sky, but found it impossible to escape because a round object with antennae would always manage to find her. In October 1997 she saw a fast disc-shaped UFO surrounded by a shimmering heat haze – possibly its propulsion system – and followed by four smaller discs. The main craft was topped with a raised cabin-type structure and had dark patches, possibly windows, all the way round. She has since seen many other fast-travelling objects, often with lights of different colours, as well as something like a red and white 'squiggly worm' which jumped erratically and glowed like a fluorescent light. In a separate case, several people saw bright lights hovering over Maryhill for ten minutes in July 1988.

In 1975 a phantom spectacles-snatcher was active in Maryhill. On 21 July teenager Alex Campbell was standing in Dalmally Street when a man driving a yellow Avenger stopped to ask directions. He wrenched Alex's glasses from his face and drove off. Five similar thefts had been reported in Glasgow that year. (*Daily Mirror* 22 July 1975).

RUCHILL

About 1834 James Napier was walking along the Forth and Clyde Canal when he met a group of well-dressed men, one of whom pointed out the spot which he claimed was the secret grave of Robert 'Bob Dragon' Dreghorn (*see* CLYDE STREET). As Dreghorn was Laird of Ruchill, and as the estate was bought by the council and turned into Ruchill Park, this spot was probably in the Panmure Street/Murano Street area, between the canal and the park. Napier was told that Dreghorn's family did not want his suicide to be revealed as the dead man's property would be forfeit to the Crown. They therefore covertly buried him at this out-of-the-way spot, and obtained another corpse as a substitute (although it is not clear how they acquired a cadaver matching Dreghorn's distinctive physiognomy). Then someone digging beside the canal accidentally discovered Dreghorn's body, which, despite several years having passed, was as fresh as the day it was interred. There was a general belief that the body of a suicide would not decompose until the time arrived when they would have died under normal circumstances – in other words, God allocates to us a pre-ordained moment of death, and suicides cannot cheat this. Dreghorn's family apparently then bought the finder's silence with a handsome recompense, and Bob Dragon was once again secretly buried. Napier did not know what to make of the story, and had no way of knowing whether Dreghorn was indeed hidden on the spot. In his account in his *Folk Lore* he states that in recent years he had heard the same 'undecomposed' story attached to a suicide by drowning.

LAMBHILL

On 5 April 1804 the High Possil Meteorite fell close to Possil Loch. This was the first recorded meteorite in Scotland, and parts were distributed to the HUNTERIAN MUSEUM and research institutions around the world. The original meteorite was about the size of a half brick but the biggest part was thrown away, possibly into the now filled-in quarry. The noise was heard from Falkirk to Glasgow and there were probably other fragments, although none have been reported. Analysis showed the meteorite was 4,500 million years old and originated in the asteroid belt. In 2005 a monument was erected close to where it landed, off Balmore Road.

POSSIL PARK

Tom Rannachan relates the incredible journey of his dog Major. Because the family home in Possil Park was being renovated, Major was moved by bus many miles across the city to a temporary house on the south side, on a route he had never taken. At 1 a.m. that night Major turned up at Possil Park, his coat soaked through and his paws bleeding.

SIGHTHILL

In 1979, gripped by high unemployment, Glasgow Council managed to wangle money from the Manpower Services Commission for the creation of temporary jobs. Someone came up with the wheeze of getting those thus temporarily employed to build a replica of Stonehenge or Callanish in modern materials in one of Glasgow's parks. Science fiction writer and amateur astronomer Duncan Lunan, somewhat reluctantly, became involved, persuaded the powers that be that a stone circle made out of real stones would be a better option, and set about designing a structure based on the celestial alignments suggested by Alexander Thom, the father of archaeoastronomy. So in the early part of 1979, assisted by the Parks Department, quarrymen, temporary labour, and a Royal Navy helicopter (for delivering the really heavy stones), Lunan built a substantial stone circle on a rise in Sighthill Park. It's still there, and it's still fabulous. Sadly, it was never completed, for later that year the newly-elected Prime Minister Thatcher stood up in Parliament and lambasted job creation schemes, particularly a 'ludicrous' stone circle built in Glasgow. Funding for the project was immediately stopped, and in later years, when he was struggling to apply for benefits, Lunan believed his case was deliberately obstructed by orders from on high. So Sighthill is the only stone circle in the country to be condemned by Margaret Thatcher, which must be something to be proud of.

In 1974 Lunan published *Man and the Stars*, a sober examination of the possibility of contacting alien intelligences. In it, he presented his analysis of a set of mysterious radio signals received in the 1920s: they appeared to have been transmitted by an alien space-probe in orbit around the Earth. The communication indicated an origin from a doomed civilisation in the Boötes galaxy. It caused a sensation. For a brief period Lunan became the

Sighthill Stone Circle, unbeloved of Margaret Thatcher.

The circle with its creator, Duncan Lunan.

new Erich von Däniken. But almost as soon as the book was published it became clear to Lunan and others that his analysis was flawed, based on inaccurate and obsolete data; there was no spaceship, no SOS message. So Lunan attempted to publish a retraction – but no one wanted to know. The Epsilon Boötis probe was hot news, and no publisher was interested in a mere mundane explanation.

Eventually Lunan got his new analysis published in an obscure small press magazine. This instructive episode – people believe what they choose to believe, irrespective of the evidence – is recounted in Lunan's contribution to Chris Boyce's book *Extraterrestrial Encounter*. To this day, UFO websites refer to the reality of the Epsilon Boötis probe and Glasgow University receives letters addressed to 'Professor Lunan, Department of Astronomy'. (Lunan is not a professor, a professional astronomer or a staff member at the university).

At the time of writing, Lunan is seeking to complete the stone circle and upgrade the local environment through the Roystonhill Spire and Park Project.

Sighthill Cemetery at No. 201 Springburn Road was opened in 1840 on a dramatic hill site. Although not as exuberant as the Necropolis, it is still worth a visit, partly because relatively few people come here (apart from the terminally intoxicated, of course). The Lodge looks like a miniature Greek temple and there are many fine Victorian monuments. The most famous memorial is to John Baird and Andrew Hardie, leaders of the Radical uprising of 1820. Both had been executed with medieval barbarity in Stirling – after each was decapitated with an axe the hooded executioner held up their heads and declaimed, 'This is the head of a traitor!' – and in 1847 their bodies were secretly exhumed and buried here. In the Middle Ages the godly competed to be buried close to the altar of a church or the shrine of a saint. In a kind of Socialist parallel, Baird's and Hardy's monument became a focus for later radicals, who sought to be buried immediately nearby – the Union of Sighthill Socialist Republicans, perhaps.

There was once another graveyard in Sighthill, now long lost. It surrounded the Church of St Roche, founded about 1500, and stood in the area of Glebe, Castle, Tennant and Kennedy Streets near the canal. In *Mediaeval Glasgow*, Revd James Primrose gives the story of St Roche (also known as Roque, Marrokis, Semirookie, Rowk, Rollack and Rollox) and explains why a chapel was founded here (one word: plague). Roche's *Life* was written in 1478, about 150 years after his death, so is probably semi-legendary at best. It tells how he was born to a wealthy family in Montpellier around 1295, with a birthmark on his breast in the shape of a red cross.

On a pilgrimage to Rome he encountered a city struck by plague and spent many years in Italy tending victims of the disease. Eventually he was infected, but despite being healed by a friend he was so ravaged that when he returned to Montpellier his relatives failed to recognize him and threw him into prison as a spy. Before he died, aged thirty-two, in 1327 he reached an agreement with God: anyone stricken with the plague who invoked him would be healed. This specific power, in a time when plague was sweeping Europe, not surprisingly made Roche a very popular saint, and after the *Life* was written, the plague in France became known as *Mal St Roche*, his body was ceremonially removed to Venice in 1485, and chapels dedicated to Roche were erected throughout Europe, including Edinburgh, Dundee, Stirling, Paisley and Glasgow.

In art he was usually depicted in pilgrim's garb pointing to an ulcer or plague-spot on one of his limbs. In 1502 a French friar sold one of Roche's bones to James IV for £10 10s Scots. The relic was said, inevitably, to ward off plague, hence its price tag.

Around the year 1500 Sir David Lindsay satirised the actions of the plague-anxious:

> Superstitious pilgrimages
> To monie divers images,
> Sum to St Roch with diligence
> To saif them from the pestilence

The Glasgow chapel stood outside the city gates. Plague victims camped in wooden huts or lodges around it, while twice weekly the clergy marched through the streets offering prayers against the 'visitation', as the plague was known. The chapel was ruined after the Reformation and the council feued the land, while reserving the right to bury the dead of the city in the cemetery in all time coming. This proved far-sighted, and the graveyard was again busy during the pestilence of 1645-6. A tombstone from this time, inscribed 'Memory of his brother William 1647' and known as the Plague Stone, can be found in the wall on the west side of the railway a little north of Queen Street tunnel.

In 1665 the area was leased out on the condition that 'The Kirkyard was not to be digged or tilled, but was to lie in grass.' This requirement was, conveniently or otherwise, forgotten, and the St Rollox chemical works were built on the site, bringing a different kind of plague to the lungs of those in the houses nearby.

SPRINGBURN

The Ghost Club website has the fullest details I can find of a much-repeated incident from Stobhill Hospital. In 1955 a student nurse saw a white-uniformed woman she assumed to be the night-sister enter a side ward near the door. The only patient in this ward was due to be discharged the following morning. As the nurse went to ask the sister a question she heard a voice calling – and discovered that the supposedly well patient was alone and unconscious. The immediate treatment the nurse provided saved the patient's life. There was no one in the ward who could have called out, and had the sister been in the area the nurse could not have failed to meet her.

The former North British Locomotive Co. at Nos 110-36 Flemington Street has allegorical female figures of Speed (with an arrow flying away from her) and Science (compass, globe, flaming torch) and a locomotive emerging in the chains that held the engines as they were moved. Gals on No. 11 Millarbank Street personify Locomotive Building (with a model locomotive and wheel) and Engineering (with machinery and anvil).

BARMULLOCH

In 1977 a boy died in a fire on the twenty-third floor of the tower block at No. 10 Red Road Court. After renovation the floor was turned into a common room area, which was said to be haunted. Matt Quinn, a contributor to www.hiddenglasgow.com (16 November 2007) mentioned the place had an 'unearthly' feel about it, and recalled that a foreign student who had just arrived in the UK was using the telephone in the empty room when he felt a tap on his shoulder – and there was no one there.

BISHOPBRIGGS

In 1840 two Irish navvies working on the construction of the Edinburgh-Glasgow railway murdered one of their overseers, John Green. For some reason it was decided to hang the men at the scene of the crime, and so Dennis Doolan and Patrick Redding travelled in carts from the jail on Glasgow Green to Crosshill in Bishopbriggs, their route lined by 50,000 spectators. The executions probably took place near South Crosshill Road, just north of the railway station. Another giant circular water tower looms over Wester Cleddens Road.

10

NORTH-WEST GLASGOW

SCOTSTOUN

Around 1972 Margaret McCulloch was having trouble sleeping, so she regularly decamped into the spare bedroom to watch the night sky from her ninth-floor flat in Kingsway Court. One night she saw 'a huge silvery-grey and metallic object' over the Campsie Hills. From it 'a platform like an elevator started to descend with a very bright shaft of light following in its wake'. She rushed to tell her sleeping husband but he was unresponsive so she returned to bed. The report is in Ron Halliday's *UFO Scotland*.

KNIGHTSWOOD

In *The Book Of Glasgow Cathedral*, George Eyre-Todd, quoting the *Episcopal Church Year-Book* for 1898, repeats a tradition that the placename comes from this being the hunting forest of the Knights Templar. Hmmm.

The Anecdotage of Glasgow has a section entitled 'Weird Stories of Cowdon Mansion House'. The seventeenth-century house, much decayed by Alison's time, stood on the hill, roughly where Cowdonhill Circus is today, and once belonged to the Crawford family. Alison piles on the *House of Usher* descriptions: it is 'a dreary, desolate, and woebegone-looking edifice,' and 'a bleak house' with 'a most ghastly and doleful appearance.'

> A spot is pointed out in the neighbourhood where the grass will not grow, and which, according to tradition, was the scene of some dark deed in days of yore ... a quantity of human bones were, many years ago, found in a portion of the edifice, which was known as Cowdon's Den ... People shake their heads when spoken to on the subject, and hint more than they are willing to express.

The two ghosts he managed to find out about were an old Crawford dowager whose spirit could not rest until it had revealed where she had walled up a pot of gold, and a wicked laird who on his death bed ordered the servants to keep the fire burning hot so he might have a foretaste of what was to come in the afterlife.

A post by 'Macoftheisles' on 16 September 2006 on www.hiddenglasgow.com describes a spooky experience somewhere in Knightswood. A few years previously he and a friend had been planning to go on a ghost hunt in Larkhall. Two days before the trip his friend was talking to a Nigerian student about the expedition when, in classic horror film fashion, the living-room balcony door blew inwards, as did the hall door opposite, and the window curtains were forced flat against the ceiling by the wind. The friend fled the house, the Nigerian locked himself in the bathroom, and the ghost hunt was called off.

As reported in the *Daily Record* for 8 December 2003, the staff of Freddie's Food Club at Nos 21-39 Great Western Road were in the grip of a 'you couldn't make it up' love triangle.

Twenty-three-year-old Carrie Heron believed that her fish-fryer boyfriend of four years, Campbell Kidd, was cheating on her with her colleague, twenty-eight-year-old Denise McEwan. Carrie, supposedly a member of something with the unlikely name of the British Coven of White Witches, then left a curse in the chippy. Denise, a minister's daughter, found the spell – 'it was a bit of pink and green paper with my name written on it and swirly symbols and signs on it' – and asked a friend to pray to God to break the curse. The mini-soap opera ended with claims that Carrie and thirty-eight-year-old Campbell were still an item, and she was flying out to see him in Germany (where, during a visit supporting Rangers, he had been arrested for allegedly passing counterfeit 50 euro notes in a Stuttgart brothel). Heron's mother defiantly claimed, 'Carrie may read tarot cards and stuff but she is no white witch.'

DRUMCHAPEL

At 9.40 p.m. on 5 October 1976 Ben Goodwin, then a recent police recruit, watched from Drumchapel as a silver ball descended over Glasgow to just to the left of Glasgow Airport. As it neared the ground it swung back and forth like a pendulum, then suddenly shot upwards and disappeared. The sighting is in Ron Halliday's *UFO Scotland*. Halliday's *Evil Scotland* briefly mentions John Allan from Drumchapel, whose home was infested with slamming doors and furniture being moved around. When he was in bed the invisible entity – a poltergeist? – would pull his legs, hover over him and even try to enter his body.

BEARSDEN

After war was declared in 1914, foreign waiters and governesses were singled out as possible enemy agents, and in the panic there were many urban legends of the 'treacherous governess' whose trunk contained a false bottom concealing explosives or firearms. These were 'friend-of-a-friend' tales – as James Hayward in *Myths & Legends of the First World War*, points out, 'naturally, everyone knew someone who knew the woman's employer.' A typical, and typically untrue, story was told of a German servant girl at Bearsden, 'caught with a trunk full of plans and photographs.'

MILNGAVIE

Craigmaddie Muir has a substantial range of archaeological monuments covering thousands of years. If driving, park at Blairskaith Quarry, walk back to North Blochairn Farm and ask permission to take the track onto the moor. Near the track is a damaged Neolithic chambered cairn, with part of the entrance façade and the burial chamber visible (NS58597646). The farmland further south has five Bronze-Age cairns, which, when haphazardly dug up in the nineteenth century, revealed urns, bones and a bronze dagger which is now in the HUNTERIAN MUSEUM.

The best site is the truly weird Auld Wives' Lifts (NS58187646), an enormous pile in which two huge boulders support a third. The formation, to the left of the track to the cairn, looks like an artificial cromlech, but is entirely natural. Inevitably such a striking site has attracted folklore. 'A narrow, triangular space remains open between the three stones, and through this every stranger is required to pass on first visiting the spot, if, according to the rustic creed, he would escape the calamity of dying childless.' (Daniel Wilson, *The Archaeology and Prehistoric Annals of Scotland*). Alternatively, it was necessary 'for superstitious young couples to crawl through to ensure that they marry' (Peter Underwood, *Gazetteer of Scottish Ghosts*).

James Pagan's *Glasgow Past and Present* asserts that the action also protected you from 'the pranks of the Evil One'. The origin-story is that the Auld Wives, three old women or witches from Campsie, Strathblane and Baldernock, laid a wager to see who was the strongest; the first two carried the lower stones, but the winner was the third, who placed the highest boulder. Since the nineteenth century the stones have been associated with Druids, and Hugh MacDonald experiences the pleasurable *frisson* that Victorians enjoyed when writing about 'the dark rites of pagan worship' and 'the sacrifice of human victims whose blood was shed at the rude shrine of Moloch' when he describes 'a gruesome but not altogether disagreeable feeling pervading us as we stand upon the stone of blood.' Antiquarians always like a nice bit of human sacrifice. George Eyre-Todd, in *The Book of Glasgow Cathedral*, puts the *sine qua non* of Victorian Druidphilia: 'Probably no better example exists of the rude stone altar of Druid times. Here ... stands the great pagan cathedral of western Scotland.'

Opinions have moved on, and the Lifts are now seen as unquestionably natural. But in 1975 archaeologist Leslie Alcock, poring over the graffiti-covered boulders, discerned nine faint carved and incised heads on the eastern and northern faces. The primitive-looking carvings cannot be dated. Alcock suggested they were of ancient origin and related to the Celtic head cult. Controversy has raged ever since, with the favoured alternative notion being that the heads were *jeux d'ésprit* carved by the quarrymen whose cuttings for millstones are very obvious nearby at NS578676360. The stoneworkers may possibly have also cut the 3ft (90cm) circle on the level top of the upper boulder, the tiny 'fairy footprints' close by, and the apparent 'eye' carved into an adjacent rock. The definitive solution to these enigmatic carvings will probably always remain elusive; but they do add to the strangeness of this strange place.

About two-thirds of a mile (1km) east is the remains of a Second World War Starfish bombing decoy system constructed to divert German bombers from Glasgow (NS595762). The shallow ditches were filled with different kinds of fire to suggest burning industrial targets. The only surviving structure, a decoy system control bunker, is beside the road 765yds (700m) south-east of the farm (NS60507614).

CLYDEBANK

Much of Clydebank was destroyed in the Blitz. In the main foyer of the Town Hall Clydebank Museum has displayed a book damaged by a large piece of shrapnel, its front cover displaying a prominent swastika.

KILBOWIE

> Where once a Druid court was laid,
> Near Knapper farm in recent days,
> Great excavations there, did daze,
> ... A period of five thousand years
> Have come and gone since it was laid,
> And Druid rites with honour paid.
>
> Poem by 'Auld Monk' in the *Clydebank Press*, 28 September 1937

Today there is nothing about the area where Kirkoswald Drive parallels Great Western Road that gives any hint that in the years before the Second World War it was the supposed site of what *The People* (15 August 1937) described as 'the Westminster Abbey of Scottish Druid times'. In 1933-34, workers at Knappers Farm sand quarry uncovered an extensive Neolithic and Bronze-Age cemetery. This was clearly once an important ritual site: thirty-four burials and cremations were found, some in pits, some under cairns, and a wide range of grave goods were recovered, including a bronze dagger, an adze, jet and paste beads, and much pottery. Also found was a stone incised with two double ellipses and other markings. The excavations, which were on the east side of what is now Great Western Road, were supervised by J.M. Davidson, who published a proper archaeological account in the *Proceedings of the Society of Antiquaries of Scotland* in 1935. Little notice was accorded to the discovery by anyone outside the archaeological community.

Then in the summer of 1937 more graves were found, now on the west side of the road (roughly where now stand two blocks of high-rise flats, Garscadden View and Gleniffer View, NS50707130). This time the excavations were conducted by Ludovic Maclellan Mann, an enthusiastic antiquarian. The initial discoveries were certainly curious – arcs and circles of stakeholes surrounding groups of stones, one of which was dubbed 'the Altar'. It is worth noting that most of the stakeholes were tiny – only one-third to half an inch (8-13mm) in diameter, but some holes for more substantial posts were also found.

At this point it all went Druid-shaped. Mann's press releases excitedly mentioned 'a miniature Scottish Stonehenge in wood' and 'a site frequented by Druid astronomer-priests.' *The Bulletin* (2 August 1937), alongside a description of multiple mystical wooden circles, printed a photograph showing Mann 'inspecting the sanctuary and planetarium.' By September Mann had 'found' a circular timber circle with a diameter of 82ft (25m), identified a number of 'serpentine features', and was invoking Egyptian and Celtic myths, as noted in *The Glasgow Herald* (20 September 1937):

> The wide circular area was shown to have been occupied by timber-built serpentine structures, the meaning of which was interpreted by Mr Ludovic Mann on astronomical grounds. The temple, he said, was put up apparently to commemorate the victory of light over darkness – that is, the triumph of the sun god over his arch-enemy, the demon of darkness, at the time of an eclipse. In that crisis the sun god called for the help of his colleagues, the planet deities, who assumed the guise of serpents and surrounded the dark serpent and defeated him. An additional group of serpents was revealed after clearing away the modern surface soil down to the prehistoric level. In this newly disclosed ring there were originally a group of 24 huge serpent figures. Their sizes and aspects could be identified with the different planet divinities, and they had been laid out in a very systematic manner. Reference was made to the analogies between the Celtic and the Egyptian myths, such as the fight between Horus and Set. The arrangement of the temple, Mr Mann stated, resembled a picture of that ancient Egyptian battle where the eclipse-causing demon is referred to by various names, such Apepi and Suti.

Not surprisingly, having an Egypto-Druidic snake cult site on their doorstep grabbed the attention of Glaswegians, and thousands turned up on the site each day.

Mann self-published two books, *Earliest Glasgow: A Temple of the Moon* (1938) and *The Druid Temple Explained* (1939). The former explains how 'the Neolithic philosopher and astronomer' laid out Glasgow on a rigorous clock-like pattern divided into 19 segments whose divisions ran straight through 'loci of prehistoric importance.' Mann also landscaped the site, erecting a circle of white timbers (complete with Stonehenge-style trilithons) in the centre and placing painted stakes in the holes surrounding the banks of the 'serpentine features' (there is a photograph in Susan Hothersall's *Archaeology Around Glasgow*). He established the sacred site as being 245ft (75m) across and 'discovered' a surrounding stone circle of '19 large, hard, white sandstone pillars equidistantly set, and each about 8 feet in height' *(The Glasgow Herald,* 25 June 1938). A model of his interpretation of the site was made for an exhibition held in the McLellan Galleries on Sauchiehall Street, lectures sold out, and some of the exhibits were displayed in America. It was a genuine sensation.

Unfortunately Mann's enthusiasms alienated conventional archaeologists and actually prevented legal protection being granted to the site (irrespective of Mann's idiosyncratic interpretations, Knappers was clearly an important site). James Richardson, inspector of ancient monuments, visited the site on 18 November 1937 and reported that:

> To schedule this ground would only bring ridicule on the Department and give an official stamp of authenticity to the fantastic diagrammatic 'restoration' of a 'wooden temple'. Brightly coloured

stobs in red, blue, yellow, orange, green, black and white delineate the Serpent attacking the Sun and the planets rushing in to save Phoebus from extinction …The evidence of the existence of post holes is inconclusive – some being little more than dark dimples in the sand.

Archaeologists Gordon Childe and Gerhard Bersu examined the site in 1938 and concluded that the holes were made 'not by prehistoric stakes but by recent field mice'! Despite several appeals to save Knappers from development, the Government's response, based on the opinions of senior archaeologists, was expressed on 28 February 1945: there was 'no evidence to justify the placing of any restriction on the development of the area in question on the grounds that it is the site of a Druid Temple'. The site remained visible on air photographs taken in 1949, hemmed-in by new housing, but nothing now remains.

In 1981 Graham Ritchie and H.C. Adamson published a reassessment of the Knappers case in the *Proceedings of the Society of Antiquaries of Scotland* (this article has been my main source, but see also Derek Alexander's 'Knappers, Great Western Road (Old Kilpatrick parish, West Dunbartonshire) Evaluation' in *Discovery and Excavation in Scotland*). Ritchie and Adamson conclude that what Mann may actually have found were timber settings which temporarily marked ground for some ritual purpose before Bronze-Age people built burial mounds over them – there are a small number of analogous finds around the UK.

Alternatively there may have been a henge monument. Certainly people from the Neolithic and Bronze Age were using the site for ritual and burial purposes for at least 1,500 years. While dismissing the elements for which there is no evidence – the outer stone circle, the prehistoric observatory, Egyptian eclipse-eating and, especially, Druids – Ritchie and Adamson note that Mann recovered a considerable number of bones and grave goods, all of which would have been lost if he had not excavated. It's such a great shame that the crankiness of his views tainted the site so much that it was not preserved for us to visit, re-assess and argue over today.

SOUTH GLASGOW

GORBALS

In 1957 work on a pit for a hydraulic car-lift at a garage on Adelphi Street was suspended when the digging uncovered human bones. Initially foul play was suspected, but then it was found the site was on the graveyard of the fourteenth-century St Ninian's Hospital for lepers. The hospital itself stood on the east side of what is now Gorbals Street. In *The Gorbals: An Illustrated History* Eric Eunson relates how the lepers were only allowed into the city on Wednesdays and Saturdays between 10 a.m. and 2 p.m., and had to walk on the edge of the street, cover their faces with veils, and announce their presence with wooden clappers. In return for the charity they received they had to ring the chapel bell every night and pray for their benefactors, this latter act giving rise to the silly but persistent myth that the name 'Gorbals' derives from 'gory bells'. The last remains of the hospital were demolished around 1730.

John Burrowes in *Great Glasgow Stories* tells the harrowing episode of the outbreak of bubonic plague in Gorbals in August 1900. The infection started in Rose Street (later called Florence Street), and spread through the overcrowded slums nearby, with thirty-six cases in total, sixteen of whom died. The source was unknown – possibly an infected rat from an overseas ship, with the virus being spread during wakes for the early victims (where the body would be displayed in a small, crowded room).

The Anecdotage of Glasgow tells the tale of two Glasgow medical students who, tipped off by a country doctor, were determined to acquire the body of a man who had died of an unusual illness at NEWTON MEARNS, but knew they faced at obstacle in the vigilant keeper of the Gorbals toll-bar. They purchased a suit of old clothing in the Saltmarket, raised the corpse from Mearns graveyard, then drove back with the dead man in his new clobber. At the Gorbals toll-bar they stopped the gig; one paid the fee while the other tended to his 'sick friend', telling him to be of good cheer as they would soon be having breakfast in High Street. On seeing the state of the man the toll-keeper simply passed a sympathetic remark and let them through. When the party arrived at the college they were greeted with a round of applause for pulling off their ingenious plan.

In *Discovering The River Clyde*, Innes MacLeod and Margaret Gilroy note that, like on board a ship, women in the School of Nautical Studies on Adelphi Street were thought unlucky and until recently female staff were confined to an annexe. The modernist Church of Blessed John Duns Scotus on Ballater Street has a brass-bound wooden casket containing what are claimed to be the relics of St Valentine. The Franciscan friars in the area had looked after the remains since 1868, when a Belgian friar brought them from France. For more than a century the casket was effectively forgotten about, but it is now on display in the atrium.

Even by the standards of the early Church St Valentine is an obscure figure, with three saints of that name competing for the 14 February feast day. The most likely candidate is a Bishop of Interamna (now Terni in Italy), martyred by the Romans in AD 270. It seems likely that the association between St Valentine and love was created in the Middle Ages, partly by Chaucer.

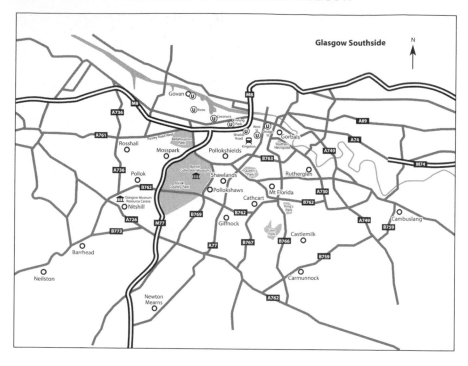

The White Lady,
Southern Necropolis.

Danger: vampires!
Southern Necropolis.

As well as being patron saint of happy marriages, he is responsible for beekeepers and is invoked against fainting, epilepsy and plague. There are other alleged Valetinian relics in Dublin, Roquemaure in France, Vienna and Birmingham.

The Rose Garden on Old Rutherglen Road is the site of the Old Gorbals burial ground (founded 1715, extended 1817), the appalling condition of which prompted the creation of the more sanitary Southern Necropolis. Some of the old gravestones with their trade symbols have been included in the walls of the play area – look for the crossed shovels of a baker, a collier's picks, the paired rinds of a miller, and a stonemason's mallets.

The area abounds in intriguing artworks installed as part of the multi-million pound regeneration of Gorbals. The chimney of the Twomax Building on Old Rutherglen Road is topped with a 'smoke cloud' which turns in the wind like a weathervane. Giant fir cones sprout from corners in Benny Lynch Court. And Lauriston Square sports abstract structures which architectural historian Ray Mackenzie compares to crow's nests, crowns, UFOs or Daleks. More old-school is the former library on McNeil Street, now the Gorbals Economic and Training Centre. The ubiquitous St Mungo stares benevolently from above the entrance, with young ladies cradling the fish, bell, tree and bird (and a ship), while the tower dome has four excellent griffons surrounding an angel representing Learning, absorbed in the latest bestseller.

The year 1954 was the year of the vampire in the Southern Necropolis on Caledonia Street. Rudolph Kenna in *Heart of the Gorbals* tells how in September residents in Caledonia Road complained to the police about hundreds of children – some apparently armed with stakes and crosses – invading the cemetery searching for a vampire with iron teeth which had killed and eaten two small boys. Nine-year-old Margaret Boyle said that she was told by bigger boys that a monster was in the graveyard. Constable Alex Deeprose said:

> When I appeared I felt like the Pied Piper of Hamelin. All shapes and sizes of children streamed after me, all talking at once, and telling me of the 'vampire with iron teeth'. This I could handle, but when grown-ups approached me and asked earnestly 'Is there anything in this vampire story?' it made me think.

The police dispersed the crowds, but some kids were so upset they could only get to sleep with the help of sedatives. Edward Cusick, headmaster of St Bonaventure's primary school in Braehead Street gathered all the pupils together to reassure them that the vampire story was absurd. Bailie John Main claimed that American horror comics such as *Tales from the Crypt* were responsible – this was a common 'moral panic' of the day – and urged city magistrates to ban the evil publications. When the whole episode died down the *Evening Times* printed the immortal headline: 'Vampire with Metal Teeth is Dead.'

Although not up to the grandeur of its namesake beside the cathedral, the Southern Necropolis is still worth a visit. Opened in 1840, it consists of several large rectangles on flat ground, giving wide-open vistas. A trail map and guide is available from www.glasgow.gov.uk and South Glasgow Heritage Environment Trust have published a very good guidebook, *City of the Dead*. Among the more interesting monuments are two modern ones – the 2006 replacement monument for the grave of architect Alexander 'Greek' Thomson, a striking, vaguely Egyptian tombstone and entrance passage made of black granite so highly polished it spookily reflects the memorials around it, and the 2005 grave of twenty re-interred skeletons found during an archaeological excavation on the site of a medieval Franciscan friary on ALBION STREET.

Then there is of course the 'White Lady'. This weathered female statue, a memorial to carpet manufacturer John Smith, his wife Magdalene and their housekeeper Mary McNaughon, is one of the few human figures in the cemetery, which is probably why it has acquired its reputation. She turns her head to follow you as you pass by; to prevent her gaze petrifying you to stone you should run round her three times shouting: 'White lady! White lady!'

Further west along Caledonia Road is one of Glasgow's most extraordinary pieces of public sculpture, The Gatekeeper, focus of the *News of the World*'s headline of 29 September 2002, 'Miracle in the Gorbals?' The cast bronze twice-life-sized figure weighs a ton and a half and is suspended 35ft (10m) up between two blocks of stylish modern flats, above a large, evocative photograph of a woman walking through a columned space. Despite the lack of wings, the sculpture has been dubbed The Angel. The 'miracle' was the appearance of a reddish stain on the palm of the outstretched hand, like a stigmatic wound. And bronze doesn't rust. Inevitably, divine intervention was suggested, although perhaps also inevitably this was interpreted in modern ways: the *News of the World*'s report quoted a twenty-three-year-old resident as saying, 'I do hope it's a sign from God because maybe then my flat will shoot up in value.'

The Big Issue in Scotland for 15-21 May 2003 reported the claims of Share International, an organisation that believes similar signs and wonders – such as Hindu statues that drink milk –

The Gatekeeper, aka the Angel, with its 'bleeding' palm showing.

The Gatekeeper *in situ.*

herald the coming of Maitreya, a pan-religious being who will bring a new global equality to the earth. Share International do seem to opportunistically leap on any new 'miraculous' manifestation, such as lights and images seen on buildings, and moving, bleeding or weeping statues, and so on, but at least for them these are indicators of a positive change, rather than the usual apocalyptic doom-mongering put about by 'The End is Nigh!' groups.

The Gatekeeper was part of the regeneration of Gorbals, previously one of the most blighted urban environments in Europe. The statue's creator, artist Matt Baker, shared his thoughts in an email of 13 June 2008:

> All was new and strange and then out of nowhere one of the newest and strangest things, 'The Gatekeeper', seemed to be connected to the universe in a deeper way. People seem to seek 'connectedness' and here was evidence that this 'new stuff' could have meaning after all. From an initial reaction of 'what is that?' and 'what is it to do with the Gorbals?' I have now had first-hand reports from researchers that local people have said that 'the Gorbals will be OK as long as the Angel is hanging there'... As for the 'real' explanation of the 'stigmata', there is no fully accepted explanation, my best guess (after going up there for a close look and drilling into the bronze) is as follows: When you make a bronze cast there is an outer mould and an inner 'core' (the inner means that the cast is hollow rather than solid through) the two moulds are held in place together with steel pins as the bronze is poured and then these pins are driven out afterwards and the holes patched with bronze. We suspect that part or all of one of the steel pins was missed in the palm of the hand and then that some water is collecting inside the cast and dripping out around the steel pin – making a drip of reddish 'rusty' water. I have to say though, that neither a hole or any iron was visible. Even if this is the 'explanation' it has always been strange to me that a steel pin should have been missed in this particular place on the sculpture.

Matt Baker's work can be seen at www.mattbaker.org.uk. As of July 2008 the hand has stopped 'bleeding', and only a small stain is visible through binoculars.

More evocative modern sculptures (The Attendants) lean out from the new housing around Malta Terrace, providing a suitably otherworldly foregrounding to the roofless but still eerily striking portico and landmark tower of Caledonia Road Church, possibly Alexander 'Greek' Thomson's finest kirk.

The Attendants and the shell
of Caledonia Road Church.

The Citizens Theatre at No. 119 Gorbals Street is allegedly haunted by the apparition of a front of house manager who committed suicide or otherwise died in the theatre. She has been seen wearing pale green in the stalls and circle. There are reports of other apparitions and unexplained noises, and the website of Scottish Paranormal Investigations mentions an occasion when the lights were switched off by mistake and a member of staff was followed down the main staircase by a small boy holding a lantern. In April 2004 SPI conducted an investigation; as well as the sound of footsteps and the numerous psychic contacts made by the mediums on the team, one spectacular event in the auditorium of the upper circle involved the balcony and then the building shuddering, and a powerful rush of air as if something invisible moved quickly through the auditorium.

In *Psychic Scotland* Tom Rannachan recalls that when he was nine or ten years old and visiting an uncle in Gorbals, he, an older cousin and two of her pals climbed a nettled embankment onto a disused railway. They had heard stories of the local phantom train, and were walking along the rusty tracks when one of the group screamed, 'There's a ghost train coming!' They all ran away, and when Tom looked back he was certain there was a steam train thundering towards him. In later life he dismissed it as group hysteria, but recently his cousin told him she too had seen the train.

At 2 p.m. on a hot June afternoon in 1995, twenty-three-year-old Pauline Ford was walking to the city centre from Mount Florida when she saw 'a very large white object spinning through the sky' in Eglinton Street. A drawing she made later was diamond shaped. The case is in Ron Halliday's *UFO Scotland*.

KINNING PARK AND KINGSTON

Shields Road underground station is reputedly haunted by a female spectre who has been seen on the platform and the track. The given story is that she committed suicide in the 1920s by jumping in front of a train. Opposite, the former Scotland Street School (now a museum of education) is the locus of a number of phenomena, including apparitions on the top floor and in the Audio Visual Room, cold spots that remain chilly even when the heating is on full, footsteps, and adults' and children's voices; Tom Rannachan reports sensing the form of an old-fashioned female teacher in a corridor. On 27 October 2007 the Ghost Club conducted an investigation. The results were not spectacular, but did include sounds of sniggering and whispering and something like a chair being dragged across the floor in an empty room, fully-charged batteries draining, and the entire team feeling uneasy in the top-floor corridor. Many of the noises could have been caused by high winds in a draughty old building, a possibility fully acknowledged in the club's exemplary report.

The quasi-municipal grandeur of the former Co-operative Wholesale Society on Morrison Street is ill-served by its surroundings, beset by the titanic piers and off-ramps of the M8 (the best view can probably be obtained when stuck in a traffic jam on the Kingston Bridge). The building is over-ripe with sculptures representing the ethics of the Co-op, with handshakes, Justice and Brotherhood shepherding Commerce, swags inscribed UNITY, Cybele, cornucopiae, Plenty with a plough and a wheatsheaf, and other symbols of bounty and fraternity. Look out for the chaps with baroque sailors' headgear, and the Virgin and Child on a boat.

The Angel Building at the junction of Paisley Road West and Govan Road is topped with a magnificent gilded angel bearing a five-pointed star on its forehead. Andrew McMahon's *A History of Kinning Park* notes that up to about 1900 there was a group of buildings called Standingstone between what are now Fleurs Avenue and Gower Terrace. If there ever was a group of standing stones on the site, no one recorded them before they vanished.

GOVAN

If the Govan stones did not exist, there would be almost no evidence at all that this was an important early Christian site.

Alan MacQuarrie, 'The historical context of the Govan Stones' (1994)

Govan's collection of early medieval stones, one of the finest in the UK, shows that its antiquity is far deeper than Glasgow's – although as the above quote demonstrates, its history in the Dark Ages has largely had to be reconstructed from hints and speculation. The best guess is that in the ninth century it was a royal church and burial ground of the Britonnic (British) Kingdom of Strathclyde, linked by the stepping stones across the Clyde to the royal centre at Partick (Govan remained one of the key dryshod crossing points until the eighteenth century, when the river was dredged).

The Scots of the Gaelic Kingdom of Dalriada to the west then defeated Strathclyde and, as a way of establishing their *imprimateur* as conquerors, established a cult centre for one of their own saints on the site – the relics may have been transferred here from a coastal site that was too exposed to Viking attack, possibly in Kintyre. This saint is named as Constantine but there is no real clarity as to his identity – there are at least seven candidates – and he may have been a conflation of two or more early holy men, a saint from the Dalriadic royal bloodline, or a semi-legendary founder-king.

Constantine remained a popular royal name in Dalriada, and a later King of the same name could re-affirm the status of his namesake predecessor. Whatever the real origin, the shrine of St Constantine seems to have been regarded as a 'royal' tomb. This high status attracted the Vikings, now Christianised Danish settlers, and the Anglians of Northumbria, both of whom buried their prestigious dead here – making eleventh-century Govan something of the

Jerusalem of the Clyde, a sacred site for four different (and competing) cultures. A monastery or something similar was probably established to manage the burials, and the powerful noblemen from the various kingdoms may have commissioned the sculptured stones from the craftsmen associated with the monks.

However, when power shifted to new Scottish dynasties Govan was seen as the unacceptable cult centre of the *ancien régime*. In the early twelfth-century David I established a new diocese at Glasgow and revived the cult of St Kentigern. Deprived of royal patronage, Govan and the cult of St Constantine declined until the latter disappeared completely from view, and there is no evidence of pilgrimage to Govan in later medieval times. At some point – possibly at the Reformation – the sculptured stones were 'damned' and buried in the churchyard, to be accidentally rediscovered in the nineteenth century. For more detail on this complex skein of informed speculation, see *Govan and its early medieval sculpture*, edited by Anna Ritchie.

The stones currently reside in the old parish church at No. 866 Govan Road (telephone 0141 440266 to check the opening hours; poor wheelchair access). In 1899 there were forty-six medieval stones; today there are thirty-one – some were damaged when the demolition of the adjacent Harland & Wolff factory accidentally took down part of the churchyard wall in 1973, while others have just vanished. The group, the third largest in Scotland, dates from the late ninth century to the end of the eleventh century and encompasses four monumental crosses (two still standing), five hogback stones and twenty-one recumbent graveslabs decorated with crosses.

The prize exhibit is 'St Constantine's Sarcophagus', a stone coffin carved from a single block of sandstone and decorated with Pictish-style carvings: a rider and what may be a dog hunting a stag; a backward-facing animal trampling on another beast, possibly a wolf, and a coiled snake, a scene taken to represent the Lamb of God driving out the serpent; two pairs of opposed beasts; and two animals with crossed necks.

My favourite stone, however, is the cross-slab known as the Sun Stone: as well as a pig-tailed rider and a cross decorated with interlace, the monolith bears a strikingly pagan symbol, a large central boss from which spring four animated snakes, whirling as if being spun. The other cross-slab is broken and bears only part of a carving of a man on a scraggy-looking horse, hence its name of the Cuddy Stone ('cuddy' meaning donkey).

Memorial, Govan graveyard.

Gravestone with cross 'burnt in'. Govan graveyard.

The Govan or Jordanhill cross-shaft has interlace and a man on horseback, while the second cross-shaft bears a worn representation of David playing a harp. The five massive hogback gravestones, meanwhile, are carved with zoomorphic figures in the Scandinavian style; the hollow on stone eleven comes from the hogback being used as a whetstone for sharpening the gardener's scythe. The twenty-one graveslabs each have a cross surrounded with interlace, and most are carved with initials from their re-use in the eighteenth and nineteenth centuries.

The 1888 kirk stands on the site of several previous churches in a heart-shaped graveyard which excavation shows dates back to the Dark Ages. There are also several gravestones carved with eighteenth-century symbols of mortality and trade emblems, and extensive evidence of the contemporary leisure pursuit known as churchyard vandalism. In *Psychic Scotland*, Tom Rannachan recalls spending an evening in the graveyard and meeting an entire conclave of spirits, including: a monk-like figure with head bowed standing at a grave; hushed voices speaking in Gaelic; four children; and a pair of forty- to fifty-year-old women, both wearing shawls, one with her hair tied back in bun, the other wearing a black covering on her head – these two remained visible until they were 5-6ft (1.5-1.8m) away.

Then Tom heard an English accent. The chap introduced himself as George from Manchester, and said he was a sailor and that he had died in 1779 – he passed out drunk on the common land known as Fairfield's Land (now Elder Park) and woke up dead. Tom offered prayers to help him 'move on' but George contentedly said he was, 'very happy where I am, thank you very much sir.' He whistled a tune and vanished. Tom called it a night when he heard a broad Scots voice calling him a 'swine'. Sheila Livingstone, in *Confess and Be Hanged*, mentions an undated episode of a medical student who was disturbed attempting to disinter a corpse from the graveyard, and had to swim across the Clyde to evade capture.

Just to the east of the church once stood Doomster Hill, a large mound 148ft (45m) across and at least 16ft (5m) high. The hill was rubbed out in the 1830s and replaced with a dyeworks – the demolition uncovered planks of black oak, small fragments of bone and decayed bulrushes. Antiquarian drawings show it as a flat-topped mound with a wide ledge half way up; T.C.F. Brotchie in his *History of Govan* mistakenly thought it was built by Druids for sun worship. Excavation has shown the surrounding ditch was dug out in the Middle Ages, so the site was probably a moot hill or justice mound. In the late 1820s 'children listened on the turf for the sound of grinding within, and those who asked questions were answered that little babies came from there.' (PM Chalmers, *The Govan Sarcophagus*).

The bountiful website www.theglasgowstory.com displays a ceremonial apron of the Govan Weavers' Society. The proto-trade union was founded in 1756 and apparently instituted rituals that 'not only rivalled but excelled the Masonic mysteries.' Rudolph Kenna and Ian Sutherland's *They Belonged to Glasgow* note the case of a Govan man put on probation for breach of the peace. He claimed, 'the people who stay below me are deliberately pumping hot air into my house by a mysterious apparatus every night when I go to bed.'

GOVAN ROAD

The cast-iron John Aitken Memorial Fountain drips with blood-red alligators, many of them vandalised. A ship powers out of the wall of the Bank of Scotland (No. 816), its sails filled by the mighty lungs of two winged zephyrs, its prow carved with a tiny female figurehead and a pair of dragons. Human figures peep out of foliage on the column capitals, including workers with beehives and tools, a man at a ship's wheel, and one who I swear looks like Margaret Thatcher.

Brechin's Bar, formerly Cardell Hall (Nos 801-5) is famous for its carving of a cat. No one really knows why it is there, but Ray McKenzie (*Sculpture in Glasgow*) list the following theories: 1) Govan Cross was once overrun with a plague of rats that arrived on the flax ships from Europe. One day the heroic cat appeared, killing all the verminous beasts until only the King Rat was left – and in the final showdown both combatants died. 2) The cat was beloved by a lady who lived on the site before the Hall was built; when it fell to its death from a window she left a cash sum for it to be immortalised in stone. There is also a horned monster carved on the door of the other side of the building, and an armorial panel with two club-wielding wild men wearing thongs made from leaves.

Tom Rannachan mentions several incidents in the area. He once witnessed an old man wearing a filthy cloth cap vanish as he stood outside the pub. His grandmother told him the story of an old woman who lived in a flat on Govan Road in the 1950s. Each evening she would smile down at the workers on nightshift, who included Tom's uncle. One night she was not there and the house was empty – and on investigation, Tom's uncle found the woman had committed suicide, not the previous day, but several months earlier.

One lunchtime in the mid-1990s, Tom was sitting alone in the front row of the theatre in the Pearce Institute. After a few minutes he had the feeling of being watched, accompanied by the faint smell of pipe tobacco. He turned around and saw a white-haired old man wearing glasses and good-quality clothes staring blankly at the stage from the fourth row. After a few moments he looked directly at Tom – and evaporated into thin air. When the institute itself was built in 1904 a 10ft (3m) deep stone-lined bottle-shaped well was unearthed by the side of an old path leading into the kirkyard. Brotchie, in 'The Holy Wells in and around Glasgow', found no local memory of the well, but did speak to a very old man who told him that as a boy his granny spoke of the 'guid well' near the church. Brotchie surmises that it was a holy well. The institute is carved with a water monster, a panel containing a sailing ship and a unicorn, and is topped with a bronze model of a three-masted ship.

Tenements in Shaw Street, meanwhile, are decorated at street level with a beehive and an owl with outstretched wings. The dilapidated Kvaerner-Govan Yard offices at Nos 1,030-48 Govan Road are carved with two fine down-to-earth blue-collar fellows, unfazed by their association with mermaids, sea monsters, Norse gods and Neptune. Opposite is Elder Park primary school. Ron Halliday (*UFO Scotland*) describes an event from 1952. Pupil Joan Torrence was leaving at the end of the school day when a shadow obscured the sun and looking up she saw a sombrero-shaped object, tilted a little to one side, rotating above the school steeple. It appeared to be about 100ft (30m) off the ground, and was seen by other children, the teacher and the janitor. 'Time seemed to stand still,' said Joan, then a whining sound was heard and the object shot off towards Glasgow. Halliday also mentions an unnamed witness who during a full moon saw a UFO over Govan 'as big as Hampden Park,' and in 1957 ironmoulder John Anderson, of Culloden Street in Dennistoun, saw two flying saucers from the top deck of a tram near Govan docks. 'They were perfectly round and shone like two silver threepenny bits,' he said.

As a child, medium Tom Rannachan lived in a small flat in Langlands Road, where he was often confined to bed with chest problems. He recalls befriending a spirit-child named Andrew who after a time stopped appearing, to be replaced by a malevolent boy and girl dressed in rags. Their skin was tinged blue and their eyes were spooky and black. The duo tormented him, even trying to throw him out of a window – he was rescued by his mum and granny, both of whom saw the children on another occasion. One night the girl came to Tom, bringing with her a dark atmosphere and a touch 'like an icy feather.' She told Tom her fellow spirit-urchin was going to harm Honey, Tom's mongrel puppy who always barked at them. Two days later the dog died. Before the family moved out Tom saw Andrew one more time; he seemed sad and distant. One year later the building was demolished.

In February 2007 Tom revisited the site. He had a mental vision of two small bodies drowning in the Clyde while a drunken man lay on the riverbank laughing, but could not link this directly with his earlier experiences; it is possible the vision was influenced by his own expectations of revisiting the location of a highly charged childhood experience.

The route east along Govan Road passes post-industrial decrepitude and some fine Victorian sculptures. Nos 577-81 has the stern heads of John and Jane Cossar, publishers of the *Govan*

John and Jane Cossar, Nos 577-81 Govan Road.

Chronicle, and portraits of four evangelists of the writing/publishing game, Scott, Burns, Caxton and Guttenberg (*sic*). The Tower of the Winds at Prince's Dock Hydraulic Pumping Station is an octagonal chimney with each of the cardinal points named for a Wind – East, West, North, South – and cherubs blowing sailing ships across the ocean wave.

In 1966, in the early hours of Hogmanay, nineteen-year-old Alex Cleghorn was walking along Govan Road with his two elder brothers. They were first-footing, arriving at doors in the hope of being invited in for a convivial drink. Suddenly Alex vanished, never to be seen again. The following New Year's morning the two brothers were planning to first-foot along the same route, passing the spot of the disappearance 'in the vain hope that somehow he may return'. The bizarre episode is related in the *Scottish Daily Express* for 27 December 1971.

MOSSPARK

Within two months of moving into No. 14 Airth Drive the Burns family were quickly rehoused a short distance away at No. 14 Arran Drive. The reason, according to the housing department, was that 'a supernatural presence was affecting the family's health,' with an unnamed staff member claiming the house 'had a history of poltergeist activity'. Neighbours also spoke of the Burnses being shaken after seeing 'visions of the Virgin Mary'. As the papers picked up the story (*Evening Times* 14 December 1978, *Glasgow Herald* the next day) Joseph Burns backtracked, rubbishing any notion of visions and ghosts, and saying the rehousing was due to damp and the kitchen floor subsiding. He also denied consulting a local priest, but Monsignor Brendan Murphy spoke of being called in for a blessing. This had apparently worked, as the phenomena had ceased. Murphy was from the Cardonald Church of Our Lady of Lourdes – and Lourdes is famous for visions of the Blessed Virgin Mary.

CROOKSTON CASTLE

Through Crookston Castle's lonely wa's
The wintry wind howls wild and dreary.
Robert Tannahill, 'Crookston Castle's Lonely Wa's' (c. 1806)

No. 170 Brockburn Road. Historic Scotland. 9.30 a.m. to 5 p.m. every day (closes 4.30 p.m. 1 October to 31 March). Admission free. Guidebook available. Partial wheelchair access.

This is one of Glasgow's best-kept secrets: the city's last remaining Castle, and yet little-visited. It stands impressively on a wooded hill, surrounded by a massive ditch from an earlier twelfth-century fortification, the single remaining tower from the fifteenth-century Castle containing a scary pit-dungeon and a prison. Several dubious traditions link Mary Queen of Scots with Crookston. In its later years the Castle belonged to the Stewarts of Darnley, and she is supposed to have become betrothed to Lord Darnley beneath a yew tree slightly to the east of the Castle, and to have held court here after their marriage. Anything associated with Mary tended to achieve the status of a quasi-religious relic.

The famous Crookston Yew was subsequently celebrated in verse and song, and blighted by souvenir-hunters. When the tree was felled, G. Finlay, a Pollokshaws craftsman, cut the wood into tiny square 'stones' and created a perfect model of the Castle, now in POLLOK HOUSE. Excavation has found a circular structure outside the Castle, possibly a Dark-Age ring work or fortified settlement, or even an Iron-Age dun. Dane Love (*Scottish Spectres*) has the story of Duncan Lindsay who as a young boy in the late 1940s lived in one of the houses adjacent to the Castle. On several occasions from his upstairs window he saw phantom soldiers marching up and down the embankments below the Castle.

POLLOK

In the summer of 1987 Mary McShane from Pollok was standing in her front garden at 11 p.m. when she saw a group of lights moving in formation, 'forming two corresponding arch shapes with an inner and outer arch.' They seemed to fade away then reappeared in the same place (Ron Halliday, *UFO Scotland*). The description suggests a ground-based light source rather than anything unusual.

HOUSEHILLWOOD

Househill Park contains a mature tree with a short section of iron chain attached to the trunk. The local legend is that this is where witches were hanged, although there is no evidence of this, and the purpose of the chain is unknown – it's probably something mundane, but it's still a strange sight. Elsewhere in the park is a single fossilized tree stump, its companion having vanished at some point, and itself suffering at the hands of vandals.

THE BURRELL COLLECTION

Pollok Park. Admission free. Open Monday to Thursday and Saturday, 10 a.m. to 5 p.m., Friday and Sunday 11 a.m. to 5 p.m. Tel: 0141 287 2550. Wheelchair access.

This wonderful museum is an art-historical treasury of items from many different cultures and periods. There's far more than you can see in a day. A guidebook is available and there are various guided tours. Highlights include:

Rodin's statue *Age of Bronze*. Muriel Gray's *Kelvingrove Art Gallery and Museum* notes that when it was at Kelvingrove so many female visitors stroked the handsome youth's penis that the bronze patina wore off. This may partly be due to basic naughtiness, but there is an extensive history – from ancient Greece through to modern-day Mediterranean cultures – of the penis, flaccid or otherwise, being regarded as an apotropaic symbol, to bring luck or ward off evil. The Kelvingrove experience may be an example of spontaneous modern superstition (see penis on display at convenient height = rub penis = get good luck). The chap's pudendum has now been restored.

Egyptian items, including: the wooden case of a mummified ibis; shabti figures; a statue of Horus which the god could temporarily inhabit if he so desired; an ichneumon (mongoose) figure worshipping the sun god Ra (ichneumons were seen as Ra's ally because they killed snakes, the enemy of Ra); and the lioness-headed Sekhmet, goddess of health and disease. On once occasion Sekhmet became so enflamed with bloodlust she wanted to slaughter all mankind, so the other gods took her out for a beer or three – when she woke up her hangover made her forget her desire for humanicide.

Medieval stained glass, including a multi-headed beast from the Book of Revelation, and a diamond-shaped panel showing a man falling from a tree, an eye and the word SLIP – the doubly punning device of the Abbot of Westminster, John Islip.

Chinese items, including a pair of fierce and monstrous *fangxiang* tomb guardian figures from the Tang Dynasty, a roof tile with a blue-faced demon, two Ming guardian figures with writhing dragons on their detailed armour, and a jade pendant with a dragon's head at each end.

Tapestries: a thirteenth-century fragment with lozenges filled with monsters and pairs of birds; a sixteenth-century Bible tapestry from Germany with thirty-four episodes from the Old Testament (the expulsion from Eden, Jonah emerging from the mouth of the whale, and so on) and two New Testament scenes; and another German tapestry heavily populated with wild men.

Carpets with patterns revealing angular or abstract dragon shapes.

The various medieval arches built into the fabric of the building as walk-through features include many Fortean features: the French portal from Montron has several Green Men, the arch from Hornby Castle has angels and symbols of the four Evangelists, and the entrance to the museum has several very worn animals. The oak fireplace from the Tudor royal palace at Oatlands in Surrey is carved with caryatids, mermaids, lions, snakes and dragons.

The Hutton Castle rooms, transplanted from Burrell's stately home, are also here. The dining room has numerous grotesques and hybrid monsters created around 1500, while in the hall the oak doorway into the tapestry gallery sports a vignette of a fox dressed as a bishop, preaching from a pulpit to a flock of geese – an obvious symbol popular just before the Reformation. The most bizarre item in these rooms is the 'imprisoning chair', in which two iron pinions are concealed in the wings to entrap the unsuspecting guest. This is a fake, probably manufactured in the eighteenth-century for Gothic enthusiast Horace Walpole to hark back to the previous century, when they enjoyed a certain vogue. Samuel Pepys in his *Diary* mentions seeing one in 1660 in the house of Sir William Batten: 'a chair which he calls King Harry's chaire, where he that sits down is catched with two irons that come round about him which makes great sport.' BDSM fans take note.

POLLOK HOUSE

Cared for by the National Trust for Scotland. Admission fee (free from November to March, except for special event days). Guidebook available. Opening hours 10 a.m. to 5 p.m., all year. Partial wheelchair access. Tel 01416 166410.

This mansion offers a peek into the world of a gracious Georgian country house, built on the site of earlier castles. In 1939 the Maxwell family, after seven centuries' continual ownership, handed over the estate to the National Trust for Scotland. The twelfth-century Pollok church, dedicated to St Conval, the surfing saint who crossed the Irish Sea on a stone, stood somewhere near Pollok House, but it (and St Conval's Well) have long vanished.

Ground Floor

Hall
An astronomical clock from 1764, displaying the current state of night and day in both the northern and southern hemispheres, the constellations currently visible, zodiac signs, the date, the angle of degree from the sun to the earth, the age of the current phase of the Moon in days, and a twenty-four hour dial showing the time of high tide.

The Cedar Room
The walls are lined with original watercolours by William Blake, a religious visionary and communicator with other realms whose poetry was dictated directly to him by the spirits. The paintings are *The Entombment, Christ's Entry into Jerusalem, Adam Naming the Beasts, Eve Naming the Birds,* and *The Pilgrimage to Canterbury.*

First Floor

Family Room
Model of CROOKSTON CASTLE made from 'Queen Mary's Yew'.

Centre Room
Several Chinese pieces – a Buddhist good luck augury from around 1780, consisting of two upright carp; a miniature landscape with a sage pointing to a girl emerging from a shell on the surface of the sea while holding a pearl; an ivory 'Devil's work carving' in the form of a

peach with miniscule monkeys; and an ivory ceremonial fan intricately carved with tiny figures including a dragon, a phoenix, dragon-prowed and bird-prowed boats, warriors, a sage sitting astride a monstrous beast, and an eight-armed deity.

Upper Landing

Portrait of a Royal Infant by the Spanish painter Claudio Coello (1642-1693). The accompanying interpretation reads: 'It is rumoured that there is something uncanny and lifeless about the infant and the picture has been moved around the house, with even the servants requesting that it be removed from their quarters.' Elsewhere there are several full-length portraits of the Spanish Habsburgs, demonstrating the disastrous genetic faults created by inbreeding, culminating in the inwardly collapsing features of Charles II (1673).

POLLOK COUNTRY PARK

In 1676-77 Sir George Maxwell of Auldhouse, owner of the Pollok estate, was struck by an illness that came to be ascribed to witchcraft. A disturbed teenager later known as Janet Douglas allegedly discovered several clay effigies that were supposedly used to torture Sir George remotely, and after a witch-hunt six presumably innocent people were executed. The entire sad, sordid story of the 'bewitched baronet' was dramatised by Anne Downie as The Witches of Pollok, performed by the Tron Theatre Company in 1990.

The park also has a contemporary reputation for magical activities. A local coven is reputed to meet here, although I have no confirmation of this. One of the rangers told me of being out on a winter's day and finding the snow cleared in a circle around a hawthorn tree, as if that tree were somehow special. 'Jim', a contributor to the www.hiddenglasgow.com website, recalled several incidents. On 19 June 2004 he wrote that when aged around twelve he was walking through the 'Witches Wood' (north-west of the Sheep Park Farm entrance). Suddenly the normal ambient insect noise intensified to the point that he panicked and had to leg it. This is a typical reaction of what is known as 'nature panic', an unreasoning fear engendered in a natural environment and, ultimately, deriving from the great god Pan, from whom the word 'panic' is taken.

Jim also recalled playing with an Ouija board in the former tack room of Sheep Park Farm. He and his companions clearly heard a car turning into the farmyard, but when they looked out there was no car there. On 20 February 2004 Jim posted his account of the discovery of a 'witch bottle' in Witches Wood, although he does not indicate the date of the find. The neck was sticking out of the disused and frozen curling pond and was surrounded by several photographs of people and a house. When Jim and his friend unplugged the wax stopper they found seeds, what may have been horsehair, and a parchment mentioning the ninety-ninth degree of Freemasonry (which is doubly bizarre as the highest Masonic rank is the thirty-third). Jim thought he might have intercepted a curse.

On 16 January 2006 'Bex Bissell' posted some anecdotal material he had picked up about a 'Witches Tree' somewhere in the park. The tree was supposed to be a focus of hangings, black magic and murder, and to be a gateway to the underworld. This may be a conflation of several stories – perhaps those springing from the tree with the chains in HOUSEHILL PARK – or rumour, conjecture, storytelling, or even partial truth.

The north of the park is home to two enigmatic archaeological sites. The first is a circular earthwork with an obvious ditch on the north side of the northernmost metalled park road about 440yds (400m) west of the North Lodge entrance on Haggs Road (NS55666263). This has been interpreted as either a Dark-Age homestead (about AD 400-800) or a Norman ring work from the early twelfth century. The Tuatha De Bridget, 'an open Pagan Druidcraft group', perform ceremonies at the site eight times a year to celebrate the festivals of the Wheel of the Year (*see* www.tuathadebridget.co.uk). The possibility that the site may not be Iron Age or Druidic does not seem to bother them.

The second site is about 130yds (120m) to the south, but much harder to find. Take the small footpath from behind the Burrell Collection into the woods. When it turns right leave it and go left for about 22yds (20m) into open woodland (NS55606237). The very low semicircular bank is neither obvious nor spectacular; it has been interpreted, again, as Dark Age or Norman, or possibly late medieval. There is also a fine tree-covered Bronze-Age tumulus in the golf course in the southern part of the park (NS54606164). A dig in 1863 found a cinerary urn with bone fragments and an amber bead.

POLLOKSHAWS

The clock on Pollokshaws Hall has carvings of a winged hourglass and a pair of bearded Victorian gentlemen. Aileen Smart (*Villages of Glasgow: South of the Clyde*) notes that the United Original Secession Church, now the parish church at No. 233 Shawbridge Street, originally had a dwelling for the minister on the upper floor, and when the first minister, Revd James Milne Smith, was in residence, the spare bedroom was haunted by 'a harmless but boisterous ghost'. Smart also records a belief among the folk of the Shaws that the glue produced in the former mill on the cart at the Shaw Bridge had healing or protective properties. As a result, children with whooping cough were held over pots by their mothers while the glue was being stirred.

Eastwood Old Cemetery at No. 200 Thornliebank Road was the site of the original Eastwood church until 1781. Notable structures include the eighteenth-century Maxwell Mausoleum, and the striking Egypto-Greek monument to Revd Robert Wodrow, probably designed by Alexander Thomson. Wodrow's *Analecta*, his history of the Church during the Covenanting times, includes many examples of ministers communicating with divine or angelic voices, and other supernatural-religious incidents.

SHAWLANDS

Aileen Smart notes that the playing fields on the west side of Haggs Road were once called the Common Muir, and that next door was a 2–3 acre (0.8–1.2 hectare) piece of uncultivated ground called the Good Man's Croft. The Good or Guid Man was the flattering term for the Devil, and the land was set aside for his use so he would not need to blight the worked fields. There are many such sites across Scotland. Old maps of Pollok estate also feature the Guid Man's Road and Bridge.

Hagg's Castle, No. 100 St Andrew's Drive, is a much-altered sixteenth-century structure, now residential. A tree in the grounds, planted in Victorian times and lost in the 1980s, acquired a fanciful legend of being a hanging tree. The house was a museum in the 1970s; I suspect the story was concocted by the guides who used to give tours of the grounds. William Barr in *Ghosts of Glasgow* (ironically a social history rather than a ghost book) mentions that the Old Waverley Picture House on Mosside Road, now the bingo club, was haunted by a projectionist, and the Shawlands Hotel, dating from 1967, was visited in spirit by a former head porter. The elaborately sculptured Lloyds TSB bank on the corner of Mosside Road and Pollokshaws Road has a ceiling decorated with pocketfuls of coins. The Gothic Shawlands Cross Church at the junction of Pollokshaws Road and Kilmarnock Road has several gargoyles.

Diabetes robbed Maurice Elder of Shawlands of his sight. Laser treatment failed and he was told he would never see again. In May 1989 the fifty-four-year-old ex-businessman was at home, dozing in an armchair, when he was startled by a loud bang outside his window. He jumped up and found that his vision had been restored. (Source: *Sunday Mail*, 11 June 1989.)

MAXWELL PARK

In 1974-5 a malevolently potent poltergeist plagued a family in a Maxwell Park council house over many months. The phenomena included raps, bangs, scratches, and frequent crashes so percussive it sounded like a sledgehammer hitting the house; floods; inconstant or flickering light bulbs; blown fuses; the random setting off of alarm clocks and musical toys; doors closing; low temperatures; and the telekinetic movement of domestic items, pictures, toys and beds, and even levitation of furniture. By the time Archie Roy, president of the Scottish Society for Psychic Research (see UNIVERSITY OF GLASGOW) took on the case, the polt had already been active for six months and dozens of people had been involved, including initially cynical journalists, town councillors, family doctors, joiners, plumbers, electricians, the GPO, spiritualists, the local minister, neighbours, and the police. The inspector in charge told Roy, 'You know, I had to take some of my men off that case. They were turning in reports like, "The bed was proceeding in a northerly direction".'

Roy wrote the case up in *A Sense of Something Strange*. The targeted family, whose identity and address are cloaked, were a three-generation unit living on the first floor, above another family with whom they had a longstanding vendetta. When the haunted family fled in despair to a relative's house, the phenomena followed them and even continued there after the family returned to their own home, as if in some way the relative's house had been infected. Roy investigated the case along with Revd Max Magee, chaplain to the students of Strathclyde University, and over several months they found themselves offering moral support to the stressed-out and desperate family through staying overnight. Both witnessed the malign phenomena and Magee recorded the sledgehammer-type noises (which were so powerful furniture and walls would shake).

They also noticed that the phenomena seemed mercurially responsive: if after an exasperatingly long succession of noises Magee said, 'This is ridiculous, stop it!' the sounds temporarily ceased. It became clear that the poltergeist was focused on the family's two sons, who were aged about eleven and fourteen, particularly the elder one, who was introspective, had few friends, hated school and was going through a teenage rebel phase. It seemed attempts were being made to control the two boys – they demonstrated extreme strength or unusual skills such as expert sleight of hand card tricks, their limbs became twisted and their bodies contorted involuntarily.

The situation finally came to an end when three things occurred around roughly the same time – Magee carried out a religious service of 'cleansing' in each of the rooms when the family were not there; the hated elderly man below them died of his long-term illness; and the older boy went to stay with his grandparents in the north of Scotland for three weeks. Roy could therefore not come to a conclusion about what had really caused the phenomena to cease. It is possible that the poltergeist, whatever it was, was feeding off the negative feelings connected with the family downstairs, and using the two boys as its vehicle, with the main focus being the troubled teenager (minor phenomena were reported around him up north, and later on a holiday in Spain with his uncle, both of which may have been some kind of residue). The Maxwell Park case joins Britain's infamous list of high-level poltergeists, from Enfield to Sauchie to South Shields.

POLLOKSHIELDS AND STRATHBUNGO

The Bewitching Beauty Salon at No. 670a Pollokshaws Road is run by Pauline Reid, witch, high priestess of the Hearth Coven and organiser of Pagan events. Reid combines conventional beauty treatments, holistic therapies and magic. Each of the three main treatment rooms is themed around the sun, moon or stars. In 2007 several female reporters from national newspapers wrote glowingly about the beneficial effects of the treatments they had taken.

In an interview for the *Daily Express* (29 October 2007), Reid is quoted as saying that her coven performs ceremonies in the salon: 'On full moons and special Wiccan festivals we wash the floor with magical solutions and beat drums to chase away negative vibes. This protects the salon's positive energy so people feel uplifted from the moment they arrive.' In the *Scotsman* (19 June 2007) she told the reporter that some of the products were 'charged' under the full moon to give them power: 'I use magical ingredients and then my coven will stand around and direct energy into the product.' Apart from beauty treatments services include Tarot readings, private magical consultations and a regular spell clinic where clients are taught how to make their own spells. Popular spells include protection from nightmares, preparation for a job interview, fertility, health, friendship, love and lust.

In the *Scotsman* article, Margaret McGee, a care attendant from New Gorbals, said she had bought a spell from Reid to help her sell her house: 'She gave me a little bag which had seeds and a potion in it. It gave an ambiance and, when people came round to see the house, they said it felt very special. The very next day someone wanted to buy it.' Reid subscribes to the Wiccan threefold law, which says that any magical act returns to you three times; as a result she will not perform spells on behalf of clients: that is their own responsibility, empowered by their own energy and desires (*see* www.bewitchingbeauty.co.uk).

St Ninian's Episcopal Church on the corner of Albert Drive and Pollokshaws Road is decorated with an assemblage of gargoyles in the form of saints, prophets and bishops. Pollokshields Burgh Hall at Nos 70-2 Glencairn Drive has Masonic symbols, and the former Southern Christian Institute at the junction of Maxwell Road and Pollokshaws Road has a panel carved with a book, tree, torch and lamp.

QUEEN'S PARK

The area is named after the last flourish of Mary Queen of Scots in Scotland. Having escaped from her island prison in Loch Leven, where she had been held following her abdication in favour of her half-brother, the Earl of Moray, she was heading from Hamilton via Glasgow to the fortress at Dumbarton when her army was blocked by Moray's forces on the north side of the Clyde at the Dalmarnock ford. Wishing to avoid a battle the Queen's troops wheeled through Rutherglen, hoping to circumnavigate the south-west of the city and cross the Clyde at one of the fords further west. Moray, however, crossed the river at the town centre and intercepted Mary's forces at Langside, where Mary was reluctantly forced to fight.

On 13 May 1568 her forces, numbering some 6,000, assembled on Clincart Hill, now roughly where Langside College stands, while Moray fortified the cottages and walls on the tactically-superior higher ground to the west. The lion-topped Langside Monument on Battle Place marks the main site of the fighting. Langside Library has a large mural showing Mary with her standard on a white horse and Moray with the cannons that helped him to victory. The Battle of Langside lasted less than an hour, during which around 300 of Mary's soldiers were killed and several hundred taken prisoner, against minimal loss on Moray's side. Mary, viewing the defeat from near CATHCART CASTLE, fled to England where she threw herself on the dubious mercy of her cousin, Elizabeth I.

The battle, and the unending quasi-religious fascination with Mary, has had a profound effect on the psychogeography of the area, not least in the legend of the 'De'il's Kirkyard', the supposed area where the slain are buried – but do not rest. The story goes that Catholic troops were denied burial in the Protestant graveyard at Cathcart, and so were interred in unhallowed mass graves, either in the area below the semicircle of seats on the terrace, or where the duck and boating ponds now lie, or among the trees on the Queen's Park side of the Camphill Queen's Park Church in Balvicar Drive, or the site known as Dead Man's Lea within Wellcroft Bowling Club. No convincing finds have ever turned up, so although the bodies must have been buried somewhere, there is nothing to anchor them to these locations other than tradition and speculation – and, of course, the ghost sightings.

In *Haunted Scotland* Norman Adams cites the well-known tale that when the Victorian park first opened the wife of the head keeper saw the defeated troops, some minus heads and limbs, march across the park, and there was apparently an ongoing local tradition that spectres loomed out of the boating pond. Adams also mentions the experience of Judith Bowers (*see* BRITANNIA MUSIC HALL), who at midnight on the anniversary of the battle in 1993 allegedly saw a white mist containing the faint outline of heads emerge from the pond; after about twenty minutes the apparitions faded away. Judith gave me a more detailed description of that night. She and several friends had got quite drunk and wanted to see if the stories of ghosts were true. The strange white mist did appear at midnight but she now thought the 'heads' they saw were the result of anticipation and projection – basically, over-interpreting shapes in the mist – rather than anything objective, although the mist did behave strangely, seeming to consciously swerve to avoid touching another person approaching from a different direction.

In my other books I have previously expressed scepticism about ghosts appearing on the anniversaries of battles, largely because of the problem caused by the 'missing 12 days' of the calendrical adjustment of 1752: the 2 September of that year was followed by 14 September. Are we then to assume the ghosts of Langside have also changed their calendar? Or do they turn up on 25 May, and no one notices?

There are further examples of Mary's folkloric influence. Over each entrance of the Corona Bar on the corner of Langside Avenue and Pollokshaws Road in Crossmyloof is a carving of a hand with a red cross on the palm. The story goes that a council of war was held here before the battle. As her generals prevaricated the impetuous Queen, in the words of Hugh MacDonald, 'pulled an ebony crucifix from her breast, and laid it on her snowy palm, saying, at the same time, "As surely as that cross lies on my loof, I will this day fight the Regent."' (Loof = palm).

In a slightly alternative version, when told by her officers she could not reach Dumbarton, she said, 'By the cross in my loof, I will be there tonight in spite of you traitors!' The ridiculously silly tale not only plays fast and loose with local geography – Crossmyloof is far to the west of where Mary's forces were based – it has clearly been concocted solely to explain the curious placename; Aileen Smart suggests it really comes from the Gaelic *crois moaldhuibh*, the Cross of Malduff. There may have been some kind of cross dedicated to this presumed early saint in the area, and may have marked a parish boundary.

The western end of Queen's Park is also home to yet another of Glasgow's enigmatic earthworks, Camphill, situated on one of the best vantage points in the whole area, and an ideal location for some kind of military structure – as well as being one of Harry Bell's key nodes in his network of prehistoric alignments. The low bank and faint outer ditch was initially attributed to the Romans, and later erroneously associated with the Battle of Langside. Excavations in 1867 discovered what was interpreted as a grain kiln. A dig in 1951 unearthed a large collection of cow bones, thought to be a late addition to the site, as well as fourteenth-century pottery, although the excavators were baffled as to what the structure actually was, finally settling for a medieval 'clay castle'.

Another suggestion is that it was a Norman ring work enclosing a small timber castle. Then shards of Samian ware were recovered from the eroding rampart, so possibly the Roman attribution was not too wide of the mark. The most striking contemporary feature is a group of some three dozen boulders in the centre. To the megalithically-minded they immediately suggest some kind of prehistoric structure, but as they are not mentioned in the report of the 1867 exhibition they are probably remnants of some kind of Victorian landscaping activity. The site is on the wooded hill behind the flagpole. There used to be an old pit shaft at the top of Langside Road near the park, which gave access to a network of tunnels.

Victoria Infirmary, like virtually every other hospital in the city, has a reputation for hauntings. On 3 June 2007, on the Hidden Glasgow forum, 'dougie79' posted his experiences of working the nightshift at the infirmary. One night while having a cigarette outside he spotted a strange hooded figure gliding past the incinerator building; it then proceeded through the fence and into Queen's Park. This could be put down to a human trespasser, but the second incident took place on a ward: while waiting for a patient to return from the toilet, dougie saw a 'disgusting and disfigured' dog covered with blood and green fluid. The patient also saw it, crying, 'What the hell is that?' When dougie looked back, the apparition had vanished.

The *Sunday Mail* for 30 August 1987 reported the death of ninety-year-old Grace Jack of Rutherglen in Victoria Infirmary on 23 August; Grace had died at 12.50 p.m., and at exactly the same moment, 7.50 p.m. Eastern Standard time, her ninety-four-year-old sister Agnes Meikle died in a nursing home in Connecticut. The hospital has a carving of a puma above the royal arms on the entrance.

Groups of carved figures in medieval and classical dress punctuate the ground-floor windows and doors on Balmoral Crescent (Nos 78-118 Queen's Drive) while the east corner of the crescent has an exuberant Statue of Liberty. A massive angel with outstretched wings hovers over the front of the church on Balvicar Drive. Gargoyles and heads cluster on the former Institution for the Deaf and Dumb, now Langside College, No. 56 Prospecthill Road.

In 1901, in one of Glasgow's few laudable examples of architectural conservation, a Palladian bank building at No. 57 Queen Street in the city centre was moved stone by stone to No. 1 Langside Avenue, where it was renamed Langside Halls. The carvings include swags of fruit and, on the roof, the royal coat of arms flanked by allegorical figures of Peace (or Britannia) and Plenty. The identity of the bearded faces on the keystones is somewhat disputed. Stephen Terry, in *The Glasgow Almanac*, says they represent the rivers Clyde, Thames, Severn, Tweed and Humber, while Frank Wordsall's architectural guide *Victorian City* agrees with the first three but thinks the others are the Shannon and Wye. Rawcliffe Lodge on Mansionhouse Road has a unique carving of a woman sporting a hat with a large ostrich feather (on the wall to the right of the entrance). This is probably Fanny Stewart, wife of the Victorian businessman who built the grand pile. Since 1919 it has been occupied by Carmelite nuns.

CATHCART

Fifteenth-century Cathcart Castle, off Old Castle Road, was controversially demolished by Glasgow Corporation in 1980 and now only a few walls about 3ft (1m) high survive, a meagre husk barely worth a visit. From the Court Knowe about 100yds (91m) east, Mary Queen of Scots watched the defeat of her forces at the BATTLE OF LANGSIDE. The commemorative stone which used to stand here is now in the KELVINGROVE MUSEUM. Mary was said to have drunk from a well that used to lie near the gate of No. 157 Old Castle Road.

A much more worthwhile visit can be made to the atmospheric old graveyard at Nos 118-120 Carmonnock Road, opposite the current parish church. Contained within is the tower from the previous church (built 1831). A board traces the site's Christian origins to the ninth century, although John Gilmour's 'Notes on some old grave stones in Cathcart churchyard' suggests the name 'Kilmailing' nearby may indicate an earlier Celtic foundation. The original church was dedicated to the Northumbrian St Oswald, and St Oswald's Well existed until filled in when the graveyard was extended in the nineteenth century. Of the graveyard, Hugh MacDonald notes: 'The pensive rambler may here spend a profitable hour ... in meditating among the tombs. Many of the headstones are well worthy the attention of those who love to study the doleful literature of the dead.' Gilmour mentions several flat gravestones with carvings, now difficult to identify: a sword and cross, possibly thirteenth century; a chi rho; a broken stone with a fleur-de-lys; and a coped stone with a sword, spear and foliated cross, which Gilmour thinks might be a Templar grave. An eighteenth-century stone features a pair of sphinxes, an angel, Christ trampling on Death, and Father Time with his sandglass and scythe.

The Hood Mausoleum, a fine example of Victorian Egyptomania, is a replica of a sepulchre in which a Roman governor was buried on an island in the Nile. Hood, a butcher, had visited Egypt and lived in a house designed by Alexander Thomson near Shields Road underground called Nile House (I am grateful to Ronnie Scott for pointing this out).

The Polmadie Martyrs Monument commemorates three Covenanters murdered near Glasgow Green in 1685. The inscription names their killers, Major Balfour and Captain Maitland: 'They murthered them with shots of guns/Scarce time did they to them allow/ Before their Maker their knees to bow.' There is also an anti-bodysnatching iron cage and a watch-house built into the graveyard wall on Kilmailing Road, as well as a lovely mausoleum with Norman decoration over the door and a solid cross atop the dome.

KING'S PARK

In *UFO Scotland* Ron Halliday records two incidents in the King's Park area, the first of which must stand as one of the more extraordinary encounters in the UFO literature. At 8 a.m. on a sunny July morning in 1971, Eleanor Harvey was waiting for her turn in the bathroom in her house in Carmunnock Road. She heard a noise as if something landed on the roof, then 'what sounded like the engine of a small aircraft was switched off.' A broad beam of light came through the window and struck her forehead. She drew back from the window, and then heard a shout. A 'beautiful and sad' face appeared. The beam was shining through the image but she could see brown eyes and 'silver hair ... cut to shoulder length, a moustache and a neat square-cut beard'. As the man looked at her she felt 'as if he was stripping my very soul.' He remained silent and raised his right hand with his palm forward. The image grew stronger so she could see all of the man, who was wearing leather sandals, a long shining white gown with no obvious joins or seams, and a knotted gold cord around the waist. The spellbinding moment was broken by a scratching sound and a noise like a motor starting up, followed by a rattle on the roof as something took off. Rushing to the window Eleanor saw nothing but heard a voice saying, 'I am the light of the world. He that believeth in me shall have everlasting life.' She believed she had been visited by Jesus Christ.

The second episode took place on 15 December 1983. Shortly after 6.25 a.m. on a dry morning Tom Coventry was approaching a bus-stop on Menock Road when he spotted a low-flying object emitting spurts of flame. A zone of silence enveloped him as the grey object hovered 20ft (6m) above his head. It was 'shaped like a railway carriage, but with a curved roof' and gave off an electrical crackle and hum. Three porthole-shaped windows at the front

Dalmarnock Bridge, site of a ghostly suicide.

Sculpture near Dalmarnock Bridge.

revealed yellow smoke swirling within. It moved off towards a nearby railway bridge, paused for a second and then shot upwards and over towards the city centre, at which point the zone of silence vanished and all the ambient street sounds returned in a rush.

'Shammon', a contributor on the www.hiddenglasgow.com website (16 September 2006) revealed that when she was a child her family were forced to sell their house at No. 35 Kings Bridge Crescent because of what sounds like poltergeist activity, although only a few details are given of what may have been extensive phenomena. At the time Shammon was about nine years old and her sister six. The children and their parents had a feeling of being watched and slept with the light on. The neighbour above complained of bangings and other noises when the house was empty. And most spookily, the youngest girl saw lights dancing in her bedroom and a figure float across the lounge. Shammon finishes her post with, 'I'd never go back into that house even if you paid me ...'

In the park itself, the entrance to the walled garden is marked by a wonderfully ornate obelisk sundial, with the dials supported by four squat, winged caryatids, while grotesque heads grin above.

RUTHERGLEN

Andrew Green's *Ghosts of Today* has the earliest mention I can find of the Dalmarnock Road Bridge ghost. David Haggerty, an income tax inspector from Rutherglen, described his experience from July 1972 in a letter to one of Green's friends. He was walking along Dalmarnock Road when he saw, 'A normal looking young man, standing on the bridge looking towards the Clyde. Thinking it may be a suicide attempt, I suddenly found myself shouting, "No, don't" but when only three yards from him, the man jumped, but as I looked over the bridge in horror, I was utterly amazed to see the figure vanish into thin air.' The experience was so powerful Haggerty thought he was going to faint or vomit. Green says that several other

Wolf, Rutherglen Town Hall.

witnesses have described an identical experience. The jumper is described as, 'A youngish man of about 30 wearing a navy-blue three-quarter length coat, and coal black trousers. He has his hair in a crew-cut style.'

Rutherglen was made a royal burgh some years before Glasgow. Its once-important Castle has long gone, and only the tower remains from the medieval kirk, standing alone in the graveyard of the present old parish church on Main Street. The entrance to the churchyard is through a lych gate dated 1663 surmounted by a sundial with the date 1761. The 'sentry boxes' on either side of the entrance were used by the elders when taking collection money from the parishioners.

The Royal Snooker Club across the road from the church apparently has a spook as a customer. Norman Adams (*Haunted Scotland*) describes a series of incidents – cold spots, strange noises, and beer pumps and lights being tampered with – following a refurbishment in 1996. Before the reopening, manager Sam Crawley was standing in the lounge bar when he looked up and saw the figure of a man in the gantry mirror. He seemed sixty to seventy years old, with grey hair tending towards baldness, and was dressed in an old-fashioned grey suit with a waistcoat. When Crawley swivelled around, the figure had vanished.

A female employee working alone in the empty club heard the clicking of snooker balls on a floodlit but unoccupied table. When the former manager popped in for a game he asked for any table apart from No. 8 (which is now table No. 1): 'The ghost plays that table,' he said. Ron Halliday in *The A-Z of Paranormal Scotland* quotes Glasgow psychic Ian Shanes as saying the place is 'jumping with spirits' who are kept under control by 'a tiny priest in black robes and a skullcap.'

The small exhibition in the Town Hall contains a twelfth-century Romanesque stone statue of St Eloi, patron saint of goldsmiths and metalworkers. It was found in 1794 during the demolition of the medieval church and had possibly been buried for safekeeping at the time of the Reformation. The west wall of the Town Hall has a splendid pack of cast iron wolves' heads. A secret tunnel was alleged to run from the church (or castle) to Glasgow Cathedral or to another more local destination. Hugh MacDonald tells of the local tradition of the piper

Gallowflat Mound, Rutherglen, possibly prehistoric, or Roman, or medieval, or …

who went into the tunnel and *never returned* – although his pipes were heard in the vicinity of Dalmarnock repeating the lament 'I doot, I doot, I'll ne'er get oot.' After this event the tunnel was closed up and forgotten about, obviously just waiting for some pesky kids to show up and rediscover it (if it had ever really existed). The story is, of course, yet another 'Piper in the Tunnel' tale, of which there are dozens of examples from throughout Scotland.

The secret tunnel comes into play in a post on the Hidden Glasgow forum on 16 September 2006. 'Shammon' describes several strange events at a residential care home somewhere in the centre of Rutherglen in the mid-1990s. One night a staff member saw all the door handles on a long corridor on the top floor move down and then up in synchronized succession. Shadows were often seen which set off sensor lights. And a room at the end of the corridor was found to have all the furniture – bed, chairs, cupboard – stacked up in the middle of the room.

Apparently a priest from St Columbkille's Church on Main Street was called in to bless or possibly exorcise the upper part of the building. The supposition was that the hauntings derived from the home being built on a tunnel between the medieval church and a 'Roman burial mound' nearby. This latter is probably Gallowflat Mound, a genuine archaeological mystery surrounded by houses 550yds (500m) east of the shopping centre along Main Street, between Hardie Avenue and Richmond Place (NS63206158). No one really knows what this low mound once was – possibilities include a Neolithic burial cairn, a Roman/Iron-Age structure, an early medieval motte, or a 'judgement hill'. *Archaeology Around Glasgow* suggests it may even have been all these things at one time or another.

Charles Kirkpatrick Sharpe, in *A Historical Account of the Belief in Witchcraft in Scotland,* quotes Patrick Walker for events that supposedly took place during the dread Covenanting times of the seventeenth century. Many people at the time clove to the National Covenant in support of Presbyterianism against the then-dominant Episcopalian form of religion favoured by the Stuart Kings. Many Covenanters were brutally persecuted. By 1688 the tide had started to turn in their favour and one of the key dissenting ministers, John Dickson, was released from captivity. Several people on their way to hear him preach at his old parish of Rutherglen saw a hillside covered with people and tents and heard a voice crying out: 'This is the everlasting gospel; if ye follow on to know, believe, and embrace this gospel, it shall never be taken from you.' When the witnesses moved forward to join, the huge group vanished. Others in the area heard voices singing the ninety-third psalm, which 'obliged them to stand still until it was ended.' Others who stayed at home heard the forty-fourth psalm, others again the forty-sixth. Several other examples were reported of phantom congregations and invisible choirs.

The *Anecdotage of Glasgow* has another tale of Revd Dickson. Passing the churchyard at midnight he heard revelry. Investigation revealed 'several of his own congregation, male and female, engaged in some mysterious ceremony, in company with a gentleman in black, whom he at once knew, from *a well-known peculiarity of foot*, as the enemy of mankind.'The evil crew paralysed both the minister and his horse, and refused to de-petrify them unless a solemn pledge was given that identities would not be revealed. Dickson reluctantly agreed, and for this reason the Rutherglen witches were never unmasked in public. A few years previously, as recorded in the memoirs of the Covenanter preacher Donald Cargill, a Rutherglen woman was milking her cows when,

> … two or three of them dropped dead at her feet, and Satan, as she conceived, appeared unto her: which cast her under sad and sore exercises and desertion, so that she was brought to question her interest in Christ and all that had formerly passed betwixt God and her soul, and was often tempted to destroy herself, and sundry times attempted it.

An apparently ancient Rutherglen custom was the baking of sour cakes on St Luke's Eve in November. It was claimed to be of pre-Christian origin, possibly even connected with the worship of Baal (not too much credence should be placed on this; Baal is one of the few non-Christian deities mentioned in the Old Testament, and the Victorians were very keen on mentioning him.) In 1854 Hugh MacDonald recorded the practice as it took place in the Thistle Inn:

> This mystic baking requires for its proper execution the services of some six or eight elderly ladies. These, with each a small bake-board on her knee, are seated in a semicircle on the floor … and pass the cakes, which are formed of a kind of fermented dough, in succession from one to the other, until the requisite degree of tenacity is attained, when they are dexterously transferred to an individual called the Queen, who with certain ceremonies performs the operation of toasting … They are somewhat like a wafer in thickness, of an agreeable, acidulous taste.

The cakes were given to strangers visiting St Luke's Fair, also known as Draigle Dubbs fair, the last market day of the year.

CAMBUSLANG

The area is traditionally associated with St Cadoc, a Welsh saint whose *Life* (written around 1086, some 600 years after his death, so probably not entirely reliable) has him founding a monastery here over the grave of Caw, sub-king of Cwm Cawlwyd. Caw is mentioned in the monk Nennius' eighth-century *History of the Britons* as being one of King Arthur's enemies. Arthur also turns up, twice, in Cadoc's *Life*. Nennius describes Arthur's twelve great battles, one of which, the sixth, was 'on the river called Bassas,' a site that has tentatively been identified as being Cambuslang – although there are at least five other equally credible candidates. Put together, all of this leads to nothing more substantial than monkish conjecture and medieval propaganda and wonder tales, but it is an enticing prospect that some of the great legendary personalities of Dark-Age Britain once spent time here.

Cadoc is supposedly buried at Cambuslang, and there appears to have been a pilgrimage site here, with a shrine containing his relics. In 1379 a chapel dedicated to the Virgin Mary was founded, possibly to cater to the needs of pilgrims. The chapel is long lost but just possibly may be on the site of the current St Bride's Roman Catholic Church of 1902.

In 1928 a Territorial Army soldier sitting in a moving train on the outskirts of Glasgow fired his rifle at a crow. The round killed a young woman walking with her fiancé on Cathkin Braes two miles (3.2km) away. The soldier was jailed for three months (source: Kenna and Sutherland, *In Custody*). W.B. Herbert's *Railway Ghosts* relates an episode from the mid-1970s. James

The blood–chlorophyll labyrinth, Holmbyre Road, Castlemilk.

Tomlinson, a railway guard, was on his last trip of the night, arriving at Kirkhill station terminus around dawn. He saw a man walk along the cross-over and arrive at the platform, obviously waiting for the train. He was around 5ft 5in (1.68m) tall, and was carrying a briefcase and wearing a dark coat and soft trilby hat. Tomlinson changed the indicator board, looked back – but the man was nowhere to be seen, on the platform, in the train, or even under it. Neither the driver nor the booking clerk had seen anyone, but Tomlinson swore he had not imagined the man. Possibly it was a commuter still posthumously keeping to a well-worn travelling schedule.

CASTLEMILK

According to William Barr (*Ghosts of Glasgow*), Mary Queen of Scots slept at Castlemilk House the night before the BATTLE OF LANGSIDE. On the hillside nearby (above Mitchell Hill Road) is her well, with whose waters the children of the Stuart line of Castlemilk were baptised in her memory. The much-altered mansion was purchased by Glasgow Corporation in 1938 and used as children's home until 1969 when the house was demolished. Only fragments of the basement now remain. In *Haunted Castles & Houses of Scotland* Martin Coventry notes sightings of a Green Lady in the grounds and woodlands, a White Lady near a bridge over the burn, an ancient Scottish soldier who wounded a local man in the back of the head with an arrowshot, and 'the Mad Major', who gallops up to the former door on a phantom horse. The horseman has sometimes been identified by as Captain William Stirling Stuart on his return from Waterloo.

In 2007 a labyrinth was created on the south-western side of Holmbyre Road by artist Edwina Fitzpatrick. The design of the stone-lined open labyrinth is based on the similarities between blood haemoglobin and plant chlorophyll – an environmental metaphor for the manifold links between humans and the Green world. For more details see www.castlem-ilkevironmenttrust.org.uk. As part of the site development, dowser Grahame Gardner located the courses of several underground streams so that reintroduction of specific plants could be planned (Grahame maintains that the energies of the site are also profoundly affected by being sandwiched between two graveyards). At the centre of the blood-chlorophyll labyrinth, where two underground streams intersect, a tree was planted – a *Sorbus Embley*, whose leaves are green in summer and blood-red in autumn. One hundred artworks made by local residents are embedded in the stones.

CARMUNNOCK

The recommended booklet by the Carmunnock Preservation Society notes that Nos 8 and 10 Busby Road stand on the site of buildings once occupied by monks, who were reputed to use an underground passage to reach the church. Needless to say, the tunnel has not been found. The 1767 church stands on a site which may stretch back to a sixth-century foundation by St Cadoc. The graveyard contains the burial vault of the Stewarts of Castlemilk and an anti-bodysnatching watchhouse which still retains its set of 1828 Regulations for the Watch, with prohibitions against drinking or firing guns ('Except When There is Cause of Alarm that Any of the Inhabitants in Such Cases May be Able to turn Out to the Assistance of the Watch').

GIFFNOCK

In 1940 George Thomson, as part of his job as an emergency relief officer in the Welfare Department, visited an office in Mauchline, Ayrshire. Inspecting a large cupboard filled with thousands of used business envelopes, he chose a bundle at random, opened the first envelope, and found within a playing card, the King of Clubs. He then opened a large number of the other envelopes; all were empty. In 1960 he was living in Overlee House, Clarkston. His wife, taking the dog for a walk near the house, found, lying on the path, the Jack of Clubs; in 1962, when they were staying at a house in Largs with an enclosed boundary wall and restricted access, she found the Queen of Clubs on the rear step. Towards the end of the same year, having parked in the only space they could find in Blythswood Street in Glasgow, Thomson and his wife exited their respective sides of the car, met at the rear – and found lying behind the car the Ace of Clubs. In 1966 the family moved to No. 273 Fenwick Road, Giffnock. Shortly after they moved in Thomson's wife was walking along their front path when she found the final playing card – the Joker.

All the cards were in good, clean condition, no other cards were found around them, and none of the Thomson family were card players, so they could not have dropped them. The story is told in *A Sense of Something Strange* by Archie Roy. Roy had known Thomson for many years and dismissed any suggestion of lying or fraud. So either the Thomsons had experienced an incredible set of synchronicities over twenty-six years, or, as Roy suggests, the Cosmic Joker had been toying with them, and at the end of the game had actually signed his work.

KENNISHEAD

In 1973 a standing stone was removed in advance of road widening from Boydstone Road (NS541608). Traffic one, Prehistory zero.

NITSHILL

Glasgow Museums Resource Centre (GMRC) at No. 200 Woodhead Road, South Nitshill Industrial Estate, is a storage facility and visitor centre which houses the more than 200,000 items unable to be on display at KELVINGROVE MUSEUM. Although closed for refurbishment at the time of writing, it will offer free access and guided tours, so if you have an interest in,

The war memorial on Nitshill Road, a replica of the ninth-century Pictish Dupplin Cross.

Arthurlie Cross, Barrhead.

say, the collection of cup-and-ring marked stones, you can arrange in advance to see them. Open Monday to Thursday and Saturday, 10 a.m. to 5 p.m., Friday and Sunday, 11 a.m. to 5 p.m. Tel. 01412 769300.

The war memorial on Nitshill Road is an exact replica of the ninth-century Dupplin Cross, currently in St Serf's Church, Dunning, Perthshire, complete with all the Pictish warriors, monsters and other carvings. The 'Darnley Sycamore' at the junction of Nitshill Road and Kennishead Road is supposed to have sheltered Mary Queen of Scots as she nursed Lord Darnley back to health.

BARRHEAD

The Arthurlie Cross, a carved tenth- or eleventh-century cross shaft, stands incongruously in Arthurlie housing estate, at the southernmost junction of Springhill Road and Carnock Crescent. Little is known about the monument – why it was erected, and whether it was ever associated with a church or graveyard. In a 1872 paper to the Society of Antiquaries of Scotland, T. Etherington Cooke gives the site's entirely unsubstantiated folklore:

> ... a combat took place near this spot between two chiefs named Arthur and Neil (giving names respectively to Arthur-lee and Neil's-ton), and that both dying from their wounds, the former was buried here, while the latter was interred at 'Cross-stane Brae,' to the south of Neilston village ... Another conjecture supposes the cross to have marked the burial-place of a chief of the name of Arthur, who may have fallen in conflict with the Danes at the Battle of Crosstab, the scene of which lies about a mile north of Arthurlee.

There is a tradition that a chapel once stood near Chapell House off Chapell Street, and was dedicated to St Connel/Conval. The precise location of this chapel has never been established but the oval stone-lined St Connel's Holy Well still exists on sloping ground 24yds (22m) south of the house (NS49305886).

WHITECRAIGS

About 440yds (400m) north-west of Cathcart Castle Golf Clubhouse is an undated circular enclosure, possibly from a small medieval tower house; the site is known as Druid's Temple Hill (NS55895749).

NEWTON MEARNS

Mearns Kirk on Mearns Road is a fine early nineteenth-century structure on the site of several previous churches, possibly dating back to the Dark Ages. Harry Bell records a visit to the circular graveyard by a group of dowsers – 'The instruments whirled like spinning tops ... one man was so overcome with 'the vibes' that he had to leave the party.' About one and a quarter miles (2km) south-east along the road to Eaglesham is the Devil's Plantation (NS55765357), also known as the De'il's Plantin, Deil's Wood and Bonnyton Mound, a low tree-grown mound chiefly notable for being the starting point for Bell's researches into his Network of Aligned Sites. It is not known what the mound is, or how old it is. The hollows at the crown date from a search for gold conducted by the son of the laird before the First World War.

Time Flies, Buchanan
bus station.

GLASGOW AIRPORT

Ron Halliday's *The A-Z of Paranormal Scotland* quotes oil worker William McRoberts' report of seeing a puma padding by the side of his car as he drove slowly on the A726 perimeter road around the airport. He described it as being fawn-coloured, the size of an Alsatian dog, and moving with the definite gait of a cat. The report was dated 27 December 1992.

In 1996 a pilot named Bob Hambleton-Jones was in the airport foyer when he spotted his friend Robert Macleod. Macleod seemed distracted and after chatting briefly said 'I must go now.' Hambleton-Jones bent down to pick up his luggage – and when he looked back Macleod was gone. The next day Macleod's obituary appeared in the paper; he had died several days earlier. The episode is recounted in Halliday's *Evil Scotland*.

On 30 December 1974 *The Guardian* reported that a young man was found dead in a room of the airport's Excelsior Hotel. His name, passport number and Glasgow address were all false. Despite a '6in (15cm) surgical wound' in his chest a post-mortem failed to reveal the cause of death, and his identity remains a mystery. Glasgow's own Kaspar Hauser?

BIBLIOGRAPHY

Works which have been of especial use are marked with an asterisk★.

NEWSPAPERS

The Big Issue in Scotland: 15-21 May 2003
Carlisle News & Star: 1, 3, 7, 9, 10 & 14 March 2005
Cumberland News: 11 March 2005
Daily Express: 27 December 1971; 26 January 2001; 29 October 2007
Daily Mirror: 22 July 1975
Daily Record: 9 March 2001; 8 December 2003; 11 May 2005
Evening Citizen: 19 August 1971
Evening Times: 14 December 1978; 31 October 2001; 31 October 2006
TheGuardian: 30 December 1974; 22 December 2004; 9 March 2005
Herald (formerly *The Glasgow Herald*): 15 December 1978; 14 November 1979; 12 January 2003; 20
    September 2004; 11 May 2007
News of the World: 14 March 1999; 4 July 1999; 29 September 2002
Scotland on Sunday: 2 September 2007
Scotsman: 19 June 2007; 27 August 2007
Sunday Mail: 30 August 1987; 11 June 1989
Sunday Post: 20 August 1978; 24 June 1990
The Times: 14 February 1985; 9 April 2005
Sun: 19 August 1971; 25 February 1983; 30 October 2007

MAGAZINES

Fortean Times: Winter 1979, May 2002, June 2005, June 2007, March 2008

PROGRAMMES

Charlie Chester Show at the Empire Theatre, 19 November 1956. In the Scottish Theatre Archive at the
    University of Glasgow, reference code GB 247 STA Ae 2/22c, Call Number STA Ae 2/22c

HISTORY, ARCHAEOLOGY AND GENERAL

Addison, Joseph *The Works of Joseph Addison Complete in Three Volumes Embracing the Whole of the
    "Spectator," &c* (Harper & Brothers; New York, 1864)
Aird, Andrew *Glimpses of Old Glasgow* (Aird & Coghill; Glasgow, 1894)
Alcock, Leslie 'The Auld Wives' Lifts' in *Antiquity* 51, 1977
Derek Alexander 'Knappers, Great Western Road (Old Kilpatrick parish, West Dunbartonshire)
    Evaluation' in *Discovery and Excavation in Scotland* New Series, Vol. 1, 2000 (Council for Scottish
    Archaeology, Edinburgh, 2001).

Alison, Robert *Anecdotage of Glasgow Comprising Anecdotes and Anecdotal Incidents of the City of Glasgow And Glasgow Personages* (Morison; Glasgow, and Simpkin, Marshall; London, 1892)★

Barr, William *Ghosts of Glasgow* (Richard Drew Publishing; Glasgow, 1988)

Baxter, Neil (ed.) *A Tale of Two Towns: A History of Medieval Glasgow* (Neil Baxter Associates; Glasgow, 2007)★

Berry, James J. *The Glasgow Necropolis Heritage Trail and Historical Account* (City of Glasgow District Council; Glasgow, 1985)★

Berry, Simon and Hamish Whyte (eds.) *Glasgow Observed* (John Donald; Edinburgh, 1987)

Blair, Robert (ed. Thomas McCrie) *The Life of Mr Robert Blair, Minister of St Andrew's, Containing his Autobiography from 1593-1636* (Wodrow Society; Edinburgh, 1848)

Bowers, Judith *Stan Laurel and Other Stars of the Panopticon: The Story of the Britannia Music Hall* (Birlinn; Edinburgh, 2007)★

Brotchie, T.C. *The History of Govan* (Old Govan Club; Glasgow, 1938)

Buchanan, George (ed. John Watkins) *The History of Scotland* (Henry Fisher & Son and P. Jackson; London, 1831)

Burrowes, John *Great Glasgow Stories* (Mainstream; Edinburgh, 1998)

———— *Glasgow: Tales of the City* (Mainstream; Edinburgh, 2001)

Callant, A.G. *Saint Mungo's Bells; Or Old Glasgow Stories Rung Out Anew* (David Bryce; Glasgow, 1888)

Campbell, George *Eastwood: Notes on the Ecclesiastical Antiquities of the Parish* (New Club; Paisley, 1902)

Cant, Ronald G. and Ian G. Lindsay *Old Glasgow* (Oliver and Boyd; Edinburgh, 1947)

Carmunnock Preservation Society *Carmunnock Conservation Village* (Carmunnock Preservation Society; Glasgow, 2008)

Chalmers, P.M. *The Govan Sarcophagus: The Shrine of St Constantine* (Glasgow, 1902)

Chambers, Robert *Domestic Annals of Scotland from the Reformation to the Revolution* 3 Vols (W. & R. Chambers; Edinburgh and London, 1859)

Cleland, James *Annals of Glasgow* 2 Vols (James Hedderwick/The Glasgow Royal Infirmary; Glasgow, 1816)

Cochrane, Hugh *Glasgow – The first 800 years* (City of Glasgow District Council; Glasgow, 1975)★

Cooke, T. Etherington 'Notice of a Cross-Shaft at Arthurlee, Renfrewshire' in *Proceedings of the Society of Antiquaries of Scotland* Vol. 9 (1870-1872)

Crawford, B.E. *Scandinavian Scotland* (Leicester University Press; Leicester, 1987)

Crawfurd, George *The History of the Shire of Renfrew* (Alex. Weir; Paisley, 1782)

Curl, James Stevens *The Victorian Celebration of Death* (David & Charles; Newton Abbot, 1972)

———— *A Celebration of Death* (BT Batsford; London, 1993)

Davidson, J.M. 'A Bronze Age Cemetery at Knappers, Kilbowie, Dumbartonshire' in *Proceedings of the Society of Antiquaries of Scotland* Vol. 69 (1934-5)

Doak, A.M. and Andrew McLaren Young (eds.) *Glasgow at a Glance* (Robert Hale; London, 1983)

Driscoll, Stephen T. 'Church Archaeology in Glasgow and the Kingdom of Strathclyde' in *Innes Review* 49 (1998)

———— 'Govan: An Early Medieval Royal Centre on the Clyde' in Richard Welander, David Breeze, John Clancy, Thomas Owen (eds.) *The Stone of Destiny: Artefact and Icon* (Society of Antiquaries of Scotland monograph series 22, Society of Antiquaries of Scotland; Edinburgh, 2003)

Eunson, Eric *The Gorbals: An Illustrated History* (Richard Stenlake Publishing; Ochiltree, 1996)

Eyre-Todd, George *Early Scottish Poetry, Thomas the Rhymer, John Barbour, Androw of Wyntoun, Henry the Minstrel* (William Hodge; Edinburgh, 1891)

———— *History Of Glasgow* 3 Vols (Jackson, Wylie & Co.; Glasgow, 1934)

Eyre-Todd, George (ed.) *The Book of Glasgow Cathedral: A History And Description* (Morison Brothers; Glasgow, 1898)

Fairhurst, H. & Scott, J.G. 'The Earthwork at Camphill in Glasgow' in *Proceedings of the Society of Antiquaries of Scotland* Vol. 85 (1950-51)

Fawcett, Richard *Scottish Cathedrals* (BT Batsford/Historic Scotland; London, 1997)

Fisher, Joe *The Glasgow Encyclopedia* (Mainstream; Edinburgh, 1994)★

Foreman, Carol *Glasgow Curiosities* (John Donald; Edinburgh, 1998)

Gibb, Andrew *Glasgow – The Making of a City* (Croom Helm; London, 1983)

Gilmour, John 'Notes on some old grave stones in Cathcart churchyard' in *Transactions of the Glasgow Archaeological Society*, new series, Vol. 11 (1947)

Glasgow Museum and Art Galleries *The Burrell Collection* (William Collins; Glasgow, 1988)

Glenday, David *Anderston As It Was* (Glasgow City Libraries; Glasgow, 1994)

Gray, Muriel *Kelvingrove Art Gallery and Museum: Glasgow's Portal to the World* (Glasgow Museums; Glasgow, 2006)★

Harvey, Wallace *Chronicles of Saint Mungo: Antiquities and Traditions of Glasgow* (John Smith & Son; Glasgow/William Blackwood & Sons; London & Edinburgh, 1843)

Hone, William *The Every-Day Book Table Book; or, Everlasting Calendar of Popular Amusements, Sports, Pastimes, Ceremonies, Manners, Customs, and Events in Past and Present Times* 3 Vols (Thomas Tegg; London, 1827)

Hothersall, Susan *Archaeology Around Glasgow* (Glasgow Museums and Glasgow Archaeological Society; Glasgow, 2007)★

House, Jack *Square Mile of Murder* (W. & R. Chambers; Edinburgh, 1961)★

——————— *Portrait of the Clyde* (Robert Hale & Co; London, 1969)

——————— *The Heart of Glasgow* (Richard Drew Publishing; Glasgow, 1972)★

Johnston, Ruth *Glasgow Necropolis Afterlives: Tales of Interments* (Johnstonedesign; Glasgow, 2007)

Kenna, Rudolph *Heart of the Gorbals* (Fort Publishing; Ayr, 2004)

Kenna, Rudolph and Ian Sutherland *In Custody: A Companion to Strathclyde Police Museum* (Strathclyde Police and Clutha Books; Glasgow, 1998)

——————— *They Belonged to Glasgow: The City from the Bottom Up* (Neil Wilson Publishing; Glasgow, 2001)

Keppie, Lawrence *William Hunter and the Hunterian Museum in Glasgow, 1807-2007* (Edinburgh University Press; Edinburgh, 2007)

Livingstone, Sheila *Confess and Be Hanged: Scottish Crime & Punishment Through the Ages* (Birlinn; Edinburgh, 2000)

MacDonald, Hugh *Rambles Round Glasgow: Descriptive, Historical and Traditional* (John Smith & Son; Glasgow, 1910. Originally published 1854)★

Macgeorge, Andrew *Old Glasgow: The Place and the People, from the Roman Occupation to the Eighteenth Century* (Blackie And Son; Glasgow, 1880)

McKenzie Peter *Reminiscences of Glasgow and the West of Scotland* (John Tweed; Glasgow, 1865-68)

McKenzie, Ray *Sculpture in Glasgow: An Illustrated Handbook* (The Foulis Archive Press; Glasgow, 1999)★

——————— *Public Sculpture of Glasgow* (Liverpool University Press; Liverpool, 2002)★

McLaughlan, Robert *Gifted: Personalities and Treasures of the University of Glasgow* (Mainstream; Edinburgh, 1990)

MacLeod, Innes and Margaret Gilroy *Discovering the River Clyde* (John Donald; Edinburgh, 1991)

McMahon, Andrew J. *A History of Kinning Park and District, Glasgow* (Queen's Nursing Institute of Scotland; Aberdeen, 2003)

MacQuarrie, A. 'The Kings of Strathclyde *c.* 400-1018' in A. Grant and K. Stringer (eds.) *Medieval Scotland: Crown, Lordship and Community* (Edinburgh University Press; Edinburgh, 1993)

McRoberts, David 'The Scottish Catholic Archives 1560-1978' in *Innes Review*, Vol. 28 No. 2 (1977)

McUre, John *The History of Glasgow* (MacVean and Wylie & Co.; Glasgow, 1830)

Marshall, Ian and Ronald Smith *Queen's Park: Historical Guide and Heritage Walk* (Glasgow City Council; Glasgow, 1997)

Matheson, Alex *Glasgow's Other River: Exploring the Kelvin* (Fort Publishing; Ayr, 2000)

Mort, Frederick *Renfrewshire* (Cambridge University Press; Cambridge, 1919)

Pagan, James *Glasgow Past and Present: Illustrated in Dean of Guild Court Reports and in the Reminiscences and Communications of Senex, Aliquis, J.B., etc.* (David Robertson & Co.; Glasgow, 1884)

Primrose, Revd James *Mediaeval Glasgow* (James MacLehose & Sons; Glasgow, 1913)

Radford, C.A.R. 'The Early Christian Monuments at Govan and Inchinnan' in *Transactions of the Glasgow Archaeology Society* Vol. 15 (4) (1967)

Renwick, Robert *Glasgow Memorials* (James Maclehose & Sons; Glasgow, 1908)

Ritchie, Anna (ed.) *Govan and its Early Medieval Sculpture* (Sutton; Stroud, 1994)

Ritchie, J.N. Graham and H.C. Adamson 'Knappers, Dunbartonshire: a reassessment' in *Proceedings of the Society of Antiquaries of Scotland* Vol. 111 (1981)

Roughead, William *Classic Crimes: A Selection from the Works of William Roughead* (New York Review of Books Classics; New York, 2000)

Scott, Ronnie *Death by Design: The True Story of the Glasgow Necropolis* (Black & White Publishing; Edinburgh, 2005)★

Simpson, W.D. 'Crookston Castle' in *Transactions of the Glasgow Archaeological Society*, new series, Vol. 12 (1953)

Slessor, Catherine 'Surreal Polychromy – Water Tower in Glasgow, Scotland' in *Architectural Review* August 1999

Smart, Aileen *Villages of Glasgow: North of the Clyde* (John Donald; Edinburgh, 2002)

——————— *Villages of Glasgow: South of the Clyde* (John Donald; Edinburgh, 2002)

Smith, Bill *Hornel: The Life and Work of Edward Atkinson Hornel* (Atelier Books; Edinburgh, 1997)

Smith, John Guthrie and John Oswald Mitchell *The Old Country Houses of the Old Glasgow Gentry* (James MacLehose & Sons; Glasgow, 1878)★

Smith, Ronald *Pollokshields: Historical Guide and Heritage Walk* (Glasgow City Council; Glasgow, 1998)

———————— The Gorbals: Historical Guide and Heritage Walk (Glasgow City Council; Glasgow, 1999)

Smyth, A.P. Warlords and Holy Men: Scotland AD 80-1000 (Edinburgh University Press; Edinburgh, 1989)

South Glasgow Heritage Environment Trust City of the Dead: A Guide to Glasgow's Southern Necropolis (Culture and Sport Glasgow; Glasgow, 2007)

Spottiswoode, Archbishop John The History of the Church of Scotland 3 Vols (The Spottiswoode Society; Edinburgh, 1851)

Stewart, George Curiosities of Glasgow Citizenship as Exhibited Chiefly in the Business Career of its old Commercial Aristocracy (James MacLehose; Glasgow, 1881)

Strang, John Memories and Portraits of One Hundred Glasgow Men (James MacLehose; Glasgow, 1886)

Stuart, Andrew North Glasgow (Tempus; Stroud, 2004)

Stuart, Robert Views and Notices of Glasgow in Former Times (Robert Stuart; Glasgow / Bell & Bradfute; Edinburgh, 1848)

Terry, Stephen The Glasgow Almanac: An A-Z of the City and its People (Neil Wilson Publishing; Glasgow, 2005)

Todd, Margo The Culture of Protestantism in Early Modern Scotland (Yale University Press; New Haven and London, 2002)

Walker, Frank Arneil 'Origins and First Growths' in Peter Reed (ed.) Glasgow The Forming of the City (Edinburgh University Press; Edinburgh, 1999)

Watson, John Once Upon a Time in Glasgow: The City from the Earliest Times (Neil Wilson Publishing; Glasgow, 2003)

Whittington-Egan, Richard The Oscar Slater Murder Story: New Light on a Classic Miscarriage of Justice (Neil Wilson Publishing; Glasgow, 2001)

Wilson, Daniel The Archaeology and Prehistoric Annals of Scotland (Sutherland and Knox; Edinburgh, 1851)

Wordsall, Frank Victorian City (Richard Drew Publishing; Glasgow, 1982)

Yeoman, Peter Medieval Scotland: An Archaeological Perspective (BT Batsford/Historic Scotland; London, 1995)

———————— Pilgrimage in Medieval Scotland (BT Batsford/Historic Scotland; London, 1999)★

MYSTERIOUSNESS

Adams, Norman Haunted Scotland (Mainstream; Edinburgh, 1998)

———————— Scottish Bodysnatchers: True Accounts (Goblinshead; Musselburgh, 2002)

Aitken, Hannah (ed.) A Forgotten Heritage: Original Folk Tales of Lowland Scotland (Scottish Academic Press; Edinburgh and London, 1973)

Ardrey, Adam Finding Merlin – The Truth Behind The Legend (Mainstream; Edinburgh, 2007)

Automobile Association Secret Britain (Automobile Association; Basingstoke, 1986)

Balfour, Michael Mysterious Scotland (Mainstream; Edinburgh, 1997)

Bell, Harry Glasgow's Secret Geometry: An Account of the Discovery of the Glasgow Network of Aligned Sites (Leyline Publications; Glasgow, 1998)★

Black, Jimmy History's Mysteries (Saint Andrew Press; Carlisle, 1993)

Bord, Janet and Colin Modern Mysteries of Britain: 100 Years of Strange Events (Grafton Books; London, 1987)

Boyce, Chris Extraterrestrial Encounter: A Personal Perspective David & Charles; Newton Abbot, 1979)

Brotchie, T.C.F. 'The Holy Wells in and around Glasgow' in Old Glasgow Club Transactions Session 1919-1920 (Aird and Coghill; Glasgow, 1920)

Buchanan, Dr G. 'Reminiscences of Body Lifting' in unnamed newspaper c. 1867 (Item 250 in Perth Pamphlets Vol. 12, in the A.K. Bell Library, Perth)

Child, Francis James The English And Scottish Popular Ballads 5 Vols (Houghton Mifflin; Boston, 1882-1898)

Cooper, Quentin and Paul Sullivan Maypoles Martyrs & Mayhem (Bloomsbury; London, 1994)

Coventry, Martin Haunted Castles & Houses of Scotland (Goblinshead; Musselburgh, 2004)

Fowler, Alexander 'Old Draw and Drip Wells' in Old Glasgow Club Transactions Session 1913-1914 (Aird and Coghill; Glasgow, 1919)

Fraser, Donald M. Scottish Mysteries (Mercat Press; Edinburgh, 1997)

Frayling, Christopher Nightmare – The Birth of Horror (BBC Books; London, 1996)

Gaskill, Malcolm Hellish Nell: Last of Britain's Witches (Fourth Estate; London, 2001)

Glasgow Museums The St Mungo Museum of Religious Life and Art (Chambers; Edinburgh, 1995)

Goss, Michael The Halifax Slasher: An Urban Terror in the North of England (Fortean Times Occasional Paper No. 3, Fortean Times; London, 1987)

Green, Andrew *Our Haunted Kingdom* (Wolfe; London, 1973)

———— *Ghosts of Today* (Kaye & Ward; London, 1980)

Green, Cynthia Whiddon 'Saint Kentigern, Apostle to Strathclyde: A Critical Analysis of a Northern Saint' M.A. Thesis, The Faculty of the Department of English, University of Houston (1998) online at www.gypsyfire.com/Thesis.htm★

Halliday, Ron *McX: Scotland's X-Files* (B&W Publishing; Edinburgh, 1997)

———— *UFO Scotland* (B&W Publishing; Edinburgh, 1998)

———— *The A-Z of Paranormal Scotland* (B&W Publishing; Edinburgh, 2000)

———— *Evil Scotland* (Fort Publishing; Ayr, 2003)

Hayward, James *Myths & Legends of the First World War* (Sutton; Stroud, 2002)

Hickey, Des and Gus Smith *Miracle* (Hodder & Stoughton; London, 1978)

Laing, Jennifer *Britain's Mysterious Past* (David & Charles; Newton Abbott, 1979)

Lovett, Edward 'The Whitby Snake-Ammonite Myth' in *Folklore*, Vol. 16, No. 3 (1905)

Lunan, Duncan *Man and the Stars: Contact & Communication with other Intelligence* (Souvenir Press; London, 1974)

MacKenzie, Donald A. *Ancient Man in Britain* Senate, London 1996 (first published 1922)

———— *Buddhism in Pre-Christian Britain* (Blackie & Son; London and Glasgow, 1928)

MacKinlay, James M. *Folklore of Scottish Lochs and Springs* (William Hodge; Glasgow, 1893)

MacLagan, Robert Craig *Scottish Myths: Notes on Scottish History and Tradition* (MacLachlan and Stewart; Edinburgh, 1882)

MacQuarrie, A. 'The career of St Kentigern: Vitae, Lectiones and Glimpses of Fact' in *Innes Review* Vol. 37 (1986)

McRoberts, David 'The Death of St Kentigern of Glasgow' in *Innes Review* Vol 24 No. 1 (1973)

Mann, Ludovic Maclellan *Earliest Glasgow: A Temple of the Moon* (The Mann Publishing Company; Glasgow and London, 1938)

———— *The Druid Temple Explained* (The Mann Publishing Company; London and Glasgow, 1939)

Matthews, John *Merlin – Shaman, Prophet, Magician* (Mitchell Beazley; London, 2004)

Monaghan, Andrew *God's People?* (St Andrew Press; Edinburgh, 1991)

Morrison, Grant 'Pop Magic!' in *The Book of Lies: The Disinformation Guide to Magick and the Occult* ed. Richard Metzger (Disinformation; New York, 2003)

Mulholland, Drew 'Magical Cyrkles' in *Strange Attractor Journal One* ed. Mark Pilkington (Strange Attractor Press; London, 2001)

Napier, James 'On Some Popular Superstitions Common in Partick Forty Years Ago' in *Transactions of the Glasgow Archaeological Society* Glasgow Part V (James MacNab; Glasgow, 1868)

———— *Notes and Reminiscences Relating to Partick* (Hugh Hopkins; Glasgow, 1873)★

———— *Folk Lore: Or Superstitious Beliefs in the West of Scotland within this Century* (Alex. Gardner; Paisley, 1879)★

O'Donnell, Elliott *Scottish Ghost Stories* (Jarrold; Norwich, 1975)★

Ramsey, Ted *Don't Walk Down College Street* (Ramshorn; Glasgow, 1985)★

Rannachan, Tom *Psychic Scotland* (Black & White Publishing; Edinburgh, 2007)★

Rattray, W.J. *The Scot in British North America* (Maclear and Co.; Toronto, 1880)

Sharpe, Charles Kirkpatrick *A Historical Account of the Belief in Witchcraft in Scotland* (Hamilton, Adams; London / Thomas D Morison; Glasgow, 1884)

Spence, Lewis 'Mythology and St Mungo' in *Scots Magazine*, 46:2, 1946

Third Eye Centre *St John Ogilvie S.J. 1579-1615 An Illustrated History of his Life Martyrdom and Canonisation* (Third Eye Centre; Glasgow, 1979)

Underwood, Peter *Gazetteer of Scottish Ghosts* (Fontana/Collins; Glasgow, 1975)

———— *Guide to Ghosts & Haunted Places* (Piatkus; London, 1999)

Walker, J. Russel '"Holy Wells" in Scotland' in *Proceedings of the Society of Antiquaries of Scotland* Vol. 17 (1882-3)

'W.G.' 'Legends of Scottish Superstition No. VI. The Laird o' Gawfell and the Witches' in *The Scottish Journal of Topography, Antiquities, Traditions, etc.* Vol. 2 (John Menzies; Edinburgh, March to July 1848)

Williamson, Elizabeth, Anne Riches & Malcolm Higgs *The Buildings of Scotland: Glasgow* (Penguin; London, 1990)★

Wodrow, Robert *Analecta, Or, Materials for a History of Remarkable Providences; Mostly Relating to Scottish Ministers and Christians* 4 Vols. (Maitland Club; Edinburgh, 1842-1843)

Wright, A.R. and E. Lovett 'Specimens of Modern Mascots and Ancient Amulets of the British Isles' in *Folklore*, Vol. 19, No. 3 (Sep. 30, 1908)

FILM AND LITERATURE

Bruce, David *Scotland The Movie* (Polygon; Edinburgh, 1996)
Burgess, Moira *The Glasgow Novel* (Scottish Library Association; Motherwell, 1986)
———————— *Reading Glasgow* (Book Trust Scotland; Edinburgh, 1996)
———————— *Imagine a City! Glasgow in Fiction* (Argyll Publishing; Glendaruel, 1998)
Manlove, Colin *Scottish Fantasy Literature: A Critical Survey* (Canongate Academic; Edinburgh, 1994)

FICTION

Lunan, Duncan (ed.) *Starfield* (Orkney Press; Orkney, 1989)
Mina, Denise *John Constantine Hellblazer: Empathy is the Enemy* (Vertigo; New York, 2006)
———————— *John Constantine Hellblazer: The Red Right Hand* (Vertigo; New York, 2007)
Scott, Sir Walter *Rob Roy* (Signet Classics; Harmondsworth, 1995 – first published 1817)

WEBSITES

Britannia Music Hall/Panopticon: www.glasgowmerchantcity.net/britanniapanopticontrust.htm
Friends of the Glasgow Necropolis: www.glasgownecroplis.org
The Ghost Club: www.ghostclub.org.uk
Ghost Finders Scotland: www.ghostfinders.co.uk
Glasgow – City of Sculpture: www.glasgowsculpure.com
Glasgow Network of Aligned Sites: www.geocities.com/alignedsites
The Glasgow Story: www.theglasgowstory.com
Hidden Glasgow: www.hiddenglasgow.com
The Modern Antiquarian: www.themodernantiquarian.com
Royal College of Physicians and Surgeons of Glasgow: http://www.rcpsg.ac.uk
Royal Commission on Ancient and Historical Monuments in Scotland: www.rcahms.gov.uk
Scottish Ghosts: www.freewebs.com/scottishghosts
Scottish Paranormal Investigations: www.scottishparanormalinvestigations.co.uk
Scottish Society for Psychical Research: www.sspr.org.uk
Tuatha de Bridget: www.tuathadebridget.co.uk
Virtual Mitchell: www.mitchelllibrary.org/virtualmitchell/
West of Scotland Archaeology Service: www.wosas.net

INDEX

Contents

Foreword

The examples in this book have been carefully prepared to demonstrate the many features of Visual Basic. You are encouraged to try out the examples on your own computer to discover the exciting possibilities offered by the Visual Basic programming language. The straightforward descriptions should enable you to easily recreate the examples manually or, if you prefer, you can download an archive containing all the example projects by following these simple steps:

1 Open your web browser and visit our website at **http://www.ineasysteps.com**

2 Navigate to the "Resource Center" and choose the "Downloads" section

3 Find the "From Visual Basic in easy steps, 3rd edition" item in the "Source code" list then click on the hyperlink entitled "Projects" to download the compressed ZIP archive

4 Extract the contents of the ZIP file to any convenient location on your computer – for easy reference these are arranged in sub-folders whose names match each chapter title of this book and each project is named as described in the book. For example, the "GettingStarted" project in the first chapter is located in the "1-Getting started" folder

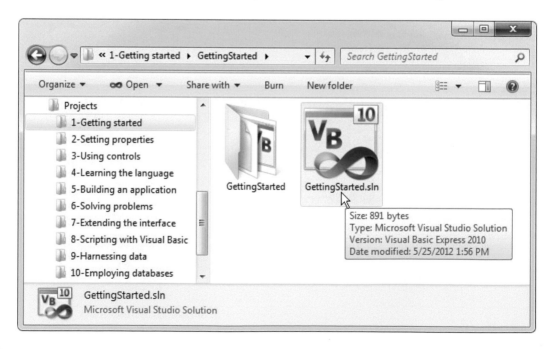

5 Double-click on the Visual Basic solution file (file extension ".sln") in any project folder to launch that example in a Visual Basic Integrated Development Environment

1 Getting started

Welcome to the exciting
world of Visual Basic
programming. This chapter
introduces the Visual Basic
Integrated Development
Environment (IDE) and
shows you how to create a
real Windows application.

Introduction

In choosing to start programming with Visual Basic you have made an excellent choice – the Visual Basic programming language offers the easiest way to write programs for Windows. This means you can easily create your own programs to give maximum control over your computer and automate your work to be more productive. Also, programming with Visual Basic is fun!

Like other programming languages Visual Basic comprises a number of significant "keywords" and a set of syntax rules. Beginners often find its syntax simpler than other programming languages making Visual Basic a popular first choice to learn.

Although writing programs can be complex Visual Basic makes it easy to get started. You can choose how far to go. Another advantage of Visual Basic is that it works with Microsoft Office and on the Internet – so the possibilities are immense...

- Visual Basic (VB) – quite simply the best programming language for the novice or hobbyist to begin creating their own standalone Windows applications, fast

- Visual Basic for Applications (VBA) – an implementation of Visual Basic that is built into all Microsoft Office applications. It runs within a host rather than as a standalone application

- Visual Basic Script (VBScript) – a derivative of Visual Basic that can be used for Windows scripting and client-side web page scripting for Internet Explorer

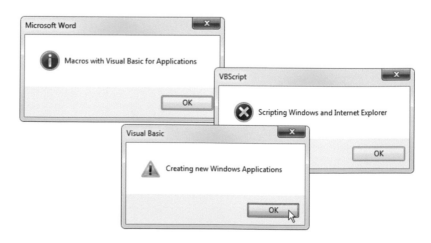

The evolution of Visual Basic

- Visual Basic 1.0 released in May 1991 at the Comdex trade show in Atlanta, Georgia, USA

- Visual Basic 2.0 released in November 1992 – introducing an easier and faster programming environment

- Visual Basic 3.0 released in the summer of 1993 – introducing the Microsoft Jet Database Engine for database programs

- Visual Basic 4.0 released in August 1995 – introducing support for controls based on the Component Object Model (COM)

- Visual Basic 5.0 released in February 1997 – introducing the ability to create custom user controls

- Visual Basic 6.0 released in the summer of 1998 – introducing the ability to create web-based programs. This hugely popular edition is the final version based on COM and is often referred to today as "Classic Visual Basic"

- Visual Basic 7.0 (also known as Visual Basic .NET) released in 2002 – introducing a very different object-oriented language based upon the Microsoft .NET framework. This controversial edition broke backward-compatability with previous versions and caused a rift within the developer community

- Visual Basic 8.0 (also known as Visual Basic 2005) – adding .NET 2.0 language features to the previous edition

- Visual Basic 9.0 (also known as Visual Basic 2008) – adding .NET 3.5 language features to the previous edition

- Visual Basic 10.0 (also known as Visual Basic 2010) – adding more powerful language features from the .NET 4.0 framework to the previous edition

All examples in this book have been created for Visual Basic 10.0 although many of the core language features are common to previous versions of the Visual Basic programming language.

Hot tip

Visual Basic derives from an earlier simple language called BASIC – Beginners All-purpose Symbolic Instruction Code. The "Visual" part was added later as many tasks can now be accomplished visually, without writing code.

Microsoft®
.NET

Installing Visual Basic

In order to create Windows applications with the Visual Basic programming language you will first need to install a Visual Basic Integrated Development Environment (IDE).

Microsoft Visual Studio is the professional development tool that provides a fully Integrated Development Environment for Visual C++, Visual C#, Visual J#, and Visual Basic. Within its IDE, code can be written in C++, C#, J# or the Visual Basic programming language to create Windows applications.

Microsoft Visual Basic Express Edition is a streamlined version of Visual Studio specially created for those people learning Visual Basic. It has a simplified user interface and omits advanced features of the professional edition to avoid confusion. Within its IDE, code can be written in the Visual Basic programming language to create Windows applications.

Both Visual Studio and Visual Basic Express Edition provide a Visual Basic IDE for Visual Basic programming. Unlike the fully-featured Visual Studio product, the Visual Basic Express Edition is completely free and can be installed on any system meeting the following minimum requirements:

Component	Requirement
Operating system	Windows® XP + Service Pack 3 Windows® Server 2003 + Service Pack 2 Windows® Vista + Service Pack 2 Windows® Server 2008 + Service Pack 2 Windows® 7
CPU (processor)	1.6 GHz or faster
RAM (memory)	1024 Mb (1 Gb) minimum
HDD (hard drive)	3 Gb available space, 5400 RPM speed
Video Card	DirectX 9-capable, and a screen resolution of 1024 x 768 or higher

The Visual Basic Express Edition is used throughout this book to demonstrate programming with the Visual Basic language but the examples can also be recreated in Visual Studio. Follow the steps opposite to install Visual Basic Express Edition.

1 Open your web browser and navigate to the Visual Basic Express Edition download page on the Microsoft website – at the time of writing this can be found at **http://www.microsoft.com/express/download**

2 Click the Visual Basic Express Edition "Download" option then click "Save" in the File Download dialog that appears and save the "vb_web.exe" installer file on your computer's desktop

3 Click on the "vb_web.exe" file to run the installer then click Next in the Welcome to Setup dialog and accept the terms in the License Terms dialog – click on Next once more to continue

4 In the Installation Options dialog be sure to check the option to also install Microsoft SQL Server, then click on Next to continue

5 Accept the suggested destination folder, then click on Install to implement the installation of Visual Basic

Hot tip

You can uncheck the option box in the "Welcome to Setup" dialog if you prefer not to share your setup experiences with Microsoft.

11

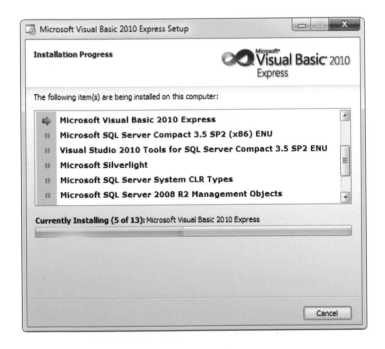

Beware

Choosing a different destination folder may require other paths to be adjusted later – it's simpler to just accept the suggested default.

Exploring the IDE

To launch the Visual Basic Integrated Development Environment click Start, All Programs, then select the Visual Basic menu item:

Almost immediately the Visual Basic Integrated Development Environment (IDE) appears from which you have instant access to everything needed to produce complete Windows applications – from here you can create exciting visual interfaces, enter code, compile and execute applications, debug errors, and much more.

The Visual Basic IDE initially includes a default Start Page, along with the standard IDE components, and looks like this:

Menu
Bar

Tool
Bar

Toolbox

Recent
Projects

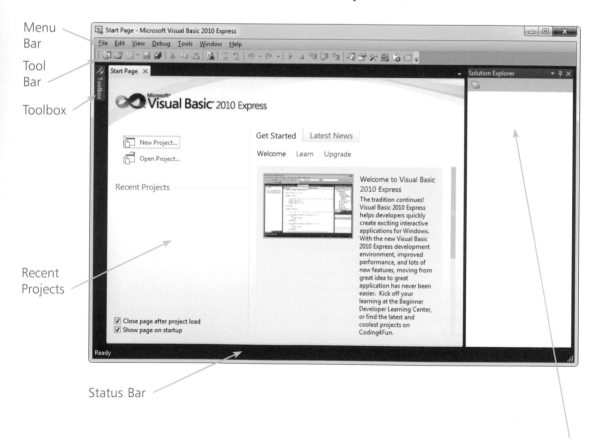

Status Bar

Solution Explorer

Start Page elements

The default start page provides these useful features:

- **Recent Projects** – conveniently lists recently opened projects so you can select one to reopen, or create a brand new project

- **Get Started** – contains helpful hyperlinks offering assistance on Visual Basic topics

- **Latest News** – feeds the latest online news direct from the Microsoft Developer Network (MSDN)

Visual Basic IDE components

The Viual Basic IDE initially provides these standard features:

- **Menu Bar** – where you can select actions to perform on all your project files and to access Help. When a project is open extra menus of Project, Build, and Data, are shown in addition to the default menu selection of File, Edit, View, Debug, Tools, Window, and Help

- **Tool Bar** – where you can perform the most popular menu actions with just a single click on its associated shortcut icon

- **Toolbox** – where you can select visual elements to add to a project. Place the cursor over the Toolbox to see its contents. When a project is open "controls", such as Button, Label, CheckBox, RadioButton, and TextBox, are shown here

- **Solution Explorer** – where you can see at a glance all the files and resource components contained within an open project

- **Status Bar** – where you can read the state of the current activity being undertaken. When building an application a "Build started" message is displayed here, changing to a "Build succeeded" or "Build failed" message upon completion

Hot tip

You can return to the Start Page at any time by selecting View, Start Page on the Menu Bar.

Don't forget

Online elements of the Start Page require a live Internet connection – if the hyperlinks do not appear to work verify your Internet connection.

13

Starting a new project

1 On the Menu Bar click File, New Project, or press the Ctrl+N keys, to open the New Project dialog box

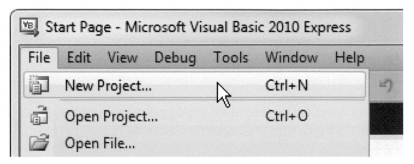

2 In the New Project dialog box select the Windows Forms Application template icon

3 Enter a project name of your choice in the Name field then click on the OK button to create the new project – in this case the project name will be "GettingStarted"

Visual Basic now creates your new project and loads it into the IDE. A new tabbed Form Designer window appears (in place of the Start Page tabbed window) displaying a default Form and a Properties window is added below the Solution Explorer.

Hot tip

The New Project dialog automatically selects the Windows Forms Application template by default as it is the most often used template.

...cont'd

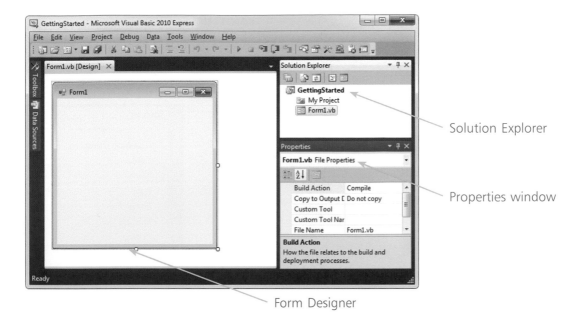

Solution Explorer

Properties window

Form Designer

The Form Designer is where you create visual interfaces for your applications and the Properties window contains details of the item that is currently selected in the Form Designer window.

The Visual Basic IDE has now gathered all the resources needed to build a default Windows application – click the Start Debugging button on the Tool Bar to launch this application.

Start Debugging (F5)

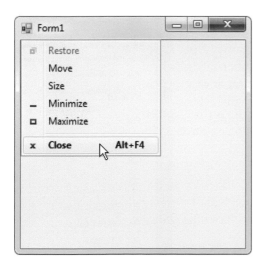

The application simply creates a basic window – you can move it, minimize it, maximize it, resize it, and quit the application by closing it. It may not do much but you have already created a real Windows program!

Hot tip

You can alternatively run applications using the F5 keyboard shortcut key.

Adding a visual control

The Toolbox in the Visual Basic IDE contains a wide range of visual controls which are the building blocks of your applications. Using the project created on the previous page follow these steps to start using the Toolbox now:

1 Place the cursor over the vertical Toolbox tab at the left edge of the IDE window, or click View, Other Windows, Toolbox on the Menu Bar, to display the Toolbox contents. The visual controls are contained under various category headings beside an expansion arrow

2 Click on the Common Controls category heading to expand the list of most commonly used visual controls. Usefully each control name appears beside an icon depicting that control as a reminder. You can click on the category heading again, to collapse the list, then expand the other categories to explore the range of controls available to build your application interfaces

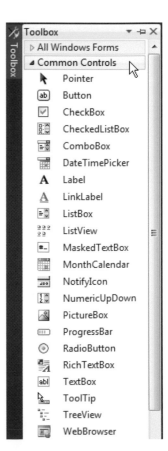

3 Click'n'drag the Button item from the Common Controls category in the Toolbox onto the Form in the Designer window, or double-click the Button item, to add a Button control to the Form

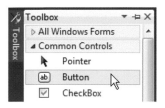
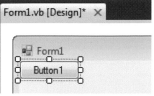

The Button control appears in the Form Designer surrounded by "handles" which can be dragged to resize the button's width and height. Click the Start Debugging button, or press F5, to run the application and try out your button.

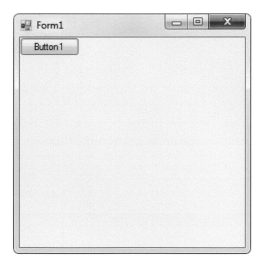

The Button control behaves in a familiar Windows application manner with "states" that visually react to the cursor:

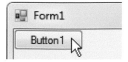
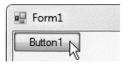

Default State   Hover State   Down State

Adding functional code

The Visual Basic IDE automatically generates code, in the background, to incorporate the visual controls you add to your program interface. Additional code can be added manually, using the IDE's integral Code Editor, to determine how your program should respond to interface events – such as when the user clicks a button.

Using the project created on the previous page follow these steps to start using the Visual Basic Code Editor now:

1 Double-click on the Button control you have added to the default Form in the Designer window. A new tabbed text window opens in the IDE – this is the Code Editor window

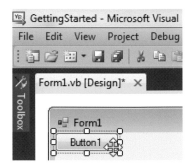

2 The cursor is automatically placed at precisely the right point in the code at which to add an instruction to determine what the program should do when this button is clicked. Type the instruction **MsgBox("Hello World!")** so the Code Editor looks exactly like this:

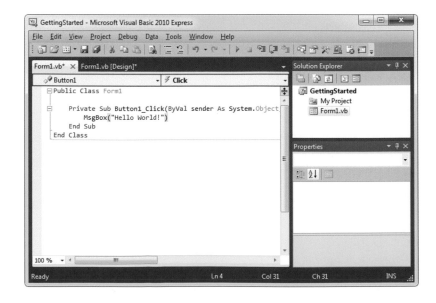

3 Click the Start Debugging button, or press F5, to run the application and test the code you have just written to handle the event that occurs when the button is clicked

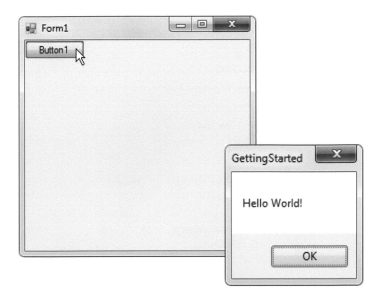

4 Push the OK button to close the dialog box, then click the "X" button on the Form window, or click the Stop Debugging button on the Menu Bar, to stop the program

Each time the button in this application is pressed the program reads the line of code you added manually to produce a dialog box containing the specified message. The action of pressing the button creates a "Click" event that refers to the associated "event-handler" section of code you added to see how to respond.

In fact most Windows software works by responding to events in this way. For instance, when you press a key in a word processor a character appears in the document – the "KeyPress" event calls upon its event-handler code to update the text in response.

The process of providing intelligent responses to events in your programs is the very cornerstone of creating Windows applications with Visual Basic.

Saving projects

Even the simplest Visual Basic project comprises multiple files which must each be saved on your system to store the project.

Follow these steps to save the current New Project to disk:

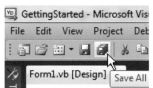

1 Click the Save All button on the Tool Bar, or click File, Save All on the Menu Bar, or press the Ctr+Shift+S keys, to open the Save Project dialog

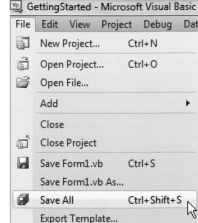

2 In the Save Project dialog you can optionally change the Project name if it is part of a larger Solution – for simple applications just leave the Project name the same as the Solution Name

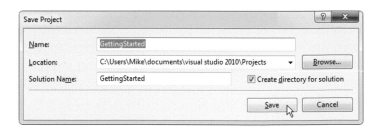

3 Choose a Location at which to save your project, or accept the suggested Location

4 Ensure that the "Create directory for solution" box is checked, then click the Save button to save all your project files

Reopening projects

Use these steps to re-open a saved Visual Basic project:

1 Click File, Open Project on the Menu Bar, or press the Ctrl+O keys, to launch the Open Project dialog

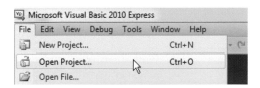

2 In the Open Project dialog navigate to the location at which you saved your project

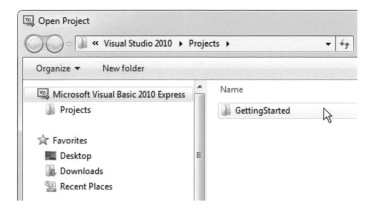

3 Double-click on the Visual Basic Solution file with the extension ".sln", to open the project in the IDE, or open the project named folder then double-click on the Visual Basic Project File with the extension ".vbproj" to open the project in the IDE

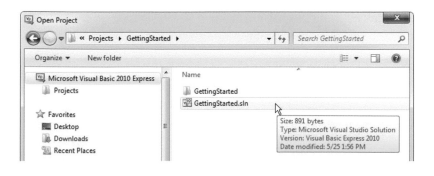

Beware

Only have one project open at any given time to avoid confusion – unless several are needed to be open together for advanced programming.

Hot tip

If you don't see the Form Designer window after reopening a project click the Form1.vb icon in Solution Explorer to make it appear.

Summary

- The Windows Application Template in the New Project dialog is used to begin creating a new Windows application project

- A unique name should be entered into the New Project dialog whenever you create a new Visual Basic project

- The Form Designer window of the Visual Basic IDE is where you create the visual interface for your program

- Visual controls are added from the Toolbox to create the interface layout you want for your program

- A control can be dragged from the Toolbox and dropped onto the Form, or added to the Form with a double-click

- The Visual Basic IDE automatically generates code in the background as you develop your program visually

- The Code Editor window of the Visual Basic IDE is where you manually add extra code to your program

- Double-click on any control in the Form designer to open the Code Editor window at that control's event-handler code

- The Start Debugging button on the Visual Basic Tool Bar can be used to run the current project application

- Pressing a button control in a running application creates a Click event within the program

- Code added to a button's Click event-handler determines how your program will respond whenever its Click event occurs

- Providing intelligent responses to events in your programs is the cornerstone of programming with Visual Basic

- Remember to explicitly save your working project using the Save All button on the Tool Bar to avoid accidental loss

- Select the solution file with the ".sln" extension in your chosen saved project directory to re-open that project

2 Setting properties

This chapter describes how properties of an application can be changed at "designtime", when you are creating the interface, and at "runtime", when the application is actually in use.

Form properties

Most applications created with Visual Basic are based upon a window Form – a canvas on which to paint the user interface. In some cases an application will have more than one Form and Visual Basic lets you display and hide Forms while the application is running. Closing the main Form quits the application.

Like all Visual Basic objects, each Form has several interesting familiar properties, such as those distinguished below.

Icon – a small graphic appearing at the top left corner of the open Form, and when it's minimized

Text – a caption appearing in the title bar of the open Form, and when it's minimized

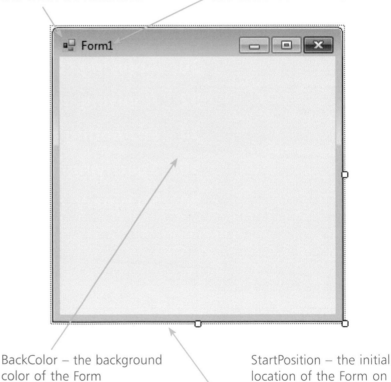

Don't forget

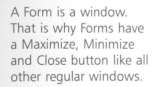

A Form is a window. That is why Forms have a Maximize, Minimize and Close button like all other regular windows.

BackColor – the background color of the Form

StartPosition – the initial location of the Form on the Windows desktop

Size – the height and width of the Form

Meeting the property editor

The Visual Basic IDE provides a Properties window where object properties can be inspected. This displays a list of the currently selected object's properties, along with their present values. The full list of Form properties, for example, is much larger than the few shown opposite and can be inspected in the property editor.

1 Identify the Properties window in the IDE – if it's not visible click View, Properties Window, or press the F4 key, to open it

2 Click on File, New Project to start a new Windows Forms application using the suggested default name

3 Click on the blank Form in the Form Designer window to display its properties in the Properties window

4 Try out the Properties window buttons, immediately above the property list, to explore different types of Categorical and Alphabetical display

5 Use the scroll bar in the Properties window to examine the complete list of Form properties and their present values

25

Hot tip

Every object in Visual Basic has a name – the name of the currently selected object appears in the dropdown list at the top of the Properties window.

Beware

Although "Form1" is the default value for both Text and (Name) properties it is important to recognize that the Text property only sets the Form's caption whereas the (Name) property is used to reference that Form in Visual Basic programming code.

Editing property values

Changing the properties of a Visual Basic object allows you to determine the appearance of that object. When creating an interface, at designtime, an object's Size property can be changed by moving its handles to resize it in the Form Designer window – its new dimension values will then appear in the Properties window. More usefully, the value of each single Form and Control property can be edited directly in the Properties window.

Editing a Form property value

1 Click on a default blank Form in the Form Designer window to display its properties in the Properties window

2 Find the Text property in the Properties window then double-click in the value column alongside it to highlight the present value – this will be "Form1" by default

3 Type "New Caption" to specify that as a new value for the Text property – the text string appears in the value column as you type

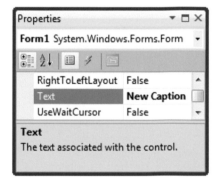

Beware

Although a new value has been assigned to the Form's Text property here its (Name) property still has the default value of "Form1" for reference in Visual Basic programming code.

4 Hit Return, or click anywhere else, to apply the new value – it now also appears on the Form in the Form Designer

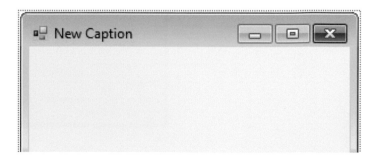

Editing a Control property value

1 Click View, Toolbox on the Menu Bar or press Ctrl+Alt+X, to open the ToolBox

2 Click'n'drag the Label item from the Common Controls category, or double-click on it, to add a Label control to a blank default Form

3 In the Form Designer window double-click on the Label control to display its present property values in the Properties window

4 Find the Text property in the Properties window then double-click in the value column alongside it to highlight the present value – this will be "Label1" by default

5 Type "New Label Text" to specify that as a new value for the Text property – the text string appears in the value column as you type

27

6 Hit Return, or click anywhere else, to apply the new value – it now also appears on the Label in the Form Designer

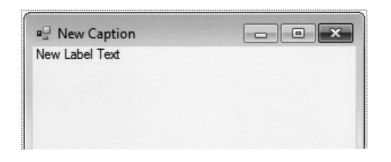

Hot tip

Some properties, such as Icon, provide a browse button when you click on their value column so you can navigate to the location of a local resource to select as the new property value.

Don't forget

Whenever you make changes in the IDE Visual Basic works in the background to make associated changes to the underlying code.

Coding property values

In addition to setting property design values for your application in the Properties window you may also set some text and color values in programming code, so the properties get assigned their initial values (are "initialized") when the Form first loads.

Statements to initialize property values should be placed within the Form's Load event-handler. This executes the statements it contains when it is called by the action of the Form loading – just as the Click event-handler executes its statements when it is called by the action of a user clicking the Button.

Initializing Control properties

Hot tip

Use the Properties window to set design features such as fonts and layout – only use code to initialize text or color values.

1. Cick on File, New Project, or press Ctrl+N, to start a new Windows Forms application and name it "Initialize"

2. Click'n'drag a Label item from the Common Controls category, or double-click on it, to add a Label control to a blank default Form

3. In the Form Designer window double-click anywhere on the default Form to launch the Code Editor – the cursor is automatically placed in the Form's Load event-handler section of code, ready to add statements

Hot tip

The Visual Basic Color object lets you specify a wide range of colors. Try adding an instruction to set this label's ForeColor property to Color.Red.

4. Type the instruction **Label1.BackColor = Color.Yellow** to set the Label's background to yellow, then hit Return

5. Type the instruction **Label1.Text = "Initialized Text"** to set the Label's text content, then hit Return

6. Click on the Start Debugging button, or press F5, to run the application and see that the Label properties initialize with the values you have specified

Initializing Form properties

1 Click the Stop Debugging button to halt the Initialize application and return once more to the Code Editor at the Form's Load event-handler section of code

2 Add the instruction **Form1.BackColor = Color.Blue** to attempt to set the Form's background to blue, then hit Return – notice that a blue wavy underline now appears beneath **Form1.BackColor** on this line of code

3 Place the mouse pointer over the blue wavy line and read the ToolTip message that pops up

```
Form1.BackColor = Color.Blue
```
'WindowsApplication1.Form1' cannot refer to itself through its default instance; use 'Me' instead.

4 The ToolTip message means you cannot refer to the Form by its name within its own event-handler, so change the instruction to **Me.BackColor = Color.Blue** – now hit Return and see the blue wavy underline disappear

5 Type the instruction **Me.Text = "Initialized Caption"** to set the Form's text caption, then hit Return

6 Click on the Start Debugging button, or press F5, to run the application and see that the Form properties initialize with the values you have specified

29

Applying computed values

The Properties window and initialization code technique allows the programmer to specify static property values at designtime. Creating code to calculate further values from known static values allows your application to compute property values at runtime.

1 Cick on File, New Project, or press Ctrl+N, to start a new Windows Forms application and name it "Compute"

2 From the ToolBox add six Label controls and one Button control to the default Form, then drag them into position so the Form looks something like the arrangement below

3 Selecting each item in turn use the Properties window to change the Text property value of the Form, Button, and all Labels, to look like this

4 To avoid confusion with other controls use the Properties window to change the (Name) property of the three Labels down the right-hand side of the form to be **Num1**, **Num2**, and **Sum**, reading from top-to-bottom – the new names can now be used in Visual Basic programming code to refer to these controls

5 Double-click on the Button to open the Code Editor within its Click event-handler section of code. Here's where a statement can be added to calculate the total of the static Text property values of **Num1** and **Num2**.

6 Type **Sum.Text = Val(Num1.Text) + Val(Num2.Text)** then hit Return to add a statement assigning the computed total value to the Sum Label's Text property

7 Click on the Start Debugging button, or press F5, to run the application. Click the button to execute the statement you added and see the **Sum** total value appear

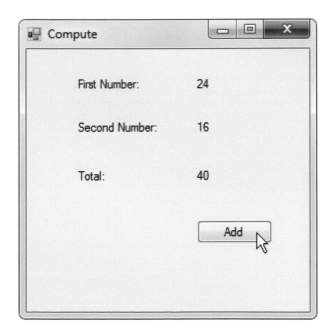

Don't forget

The Visual Basic Val() function is used here to extract the numeric version of the text string values so it can perform arithmetic on them – arithmetic functions are fully explained later.

31

Hot tip

Try adding a further Button to provide a clear facility with the statement Sum.Text="" in its event-handler.

Applying user values

While the Label control works great to display an assigned Text property value it does not allow the user to directly input a value. The TextBox control does both and should be used instead of a Label control where direct dynamic user input is desirable.

Replacing the Label controls named **Num1** and **Num2** in the previous example with TextBox controls of the same name allows the user to dynamically change those values used to compute the Sum total value when the Button is clicked.

1 Cick on File, New Project, or press Ctrl+N, to start a new Windows application and name it "UserInput"

2 From the ToolBox add four Label controls, two TextBox controls, and two Button controls to the default Form

3 Use the Properties window to change the Text property value of the Form, Buttons, and Labels, and arrange their position so the interface looks something like this

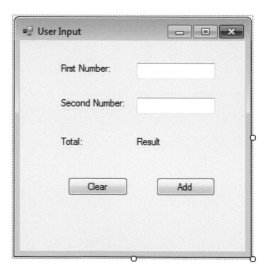

Hot tip

It is good programming practice to give meaningful names to all controls, for easy recognition – the name AddBtn makes a Button more easily recognizable than the name Button1.

4 To avoid confusion with other controls use the Properties window to change the (Name) property of the two TextBox controls to **Num1** and **Num2**, the Button controls to **AddBtn** and **ClearBtn**, and the Label with the "Result" Text value to **Sum** – the new names can now be used in programming code to refer to these controls

5 Double-click on the **AddBtn** to open the Code Editor within its Click event-handler and add the statement
Sum.Text = Val(Num1.Text) + Val(Num2.Text)

6 Double-click on the **ClearBtn** to open the Code Editor within its Click event-handler and add the statements
Sum.Text = "Result" : Num1.Text = "" : Num2.Text = ""

7 Click on the Start Debugging button, or press F5, to run the application. Enter any numeric values you like into the TextBox fields then click the Add button to see the **Sum** total value

 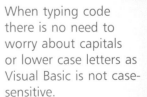
```
User Input
                                          ▢ ▢ ✕

    First Number:       22.5

    Second Number:      47.5

    Total:              70

         Clear                    Add
```

8 Click the Clear button to assign new property values, resuming the application's initial state and ready to add two more input values

Prompting for input

In addition to input via Form window controls, an application can seek user input from an InputBox dialog. This is similar to a MsgBox dialog but also has a text field where the user can type input that will be returned to the application. The user input value can then be assigned to a property in the usual way.

Unlike a simple code statement that calls up a MsgBox, just to advise the user, a statement that calls up an InputBox should make an assignation of the returned value.

1. Cick on File, New Project, or press Ctrl+N, to start a new Windows application and name it "DialogInput"

2. From the ToolBox add a Button control to the Form

3. Double-click on the Button to open the Code Editor within its Click event-handler and add the statement **Me.Text = InputBox("Enter a Caption...")**

4. Click the Start Debugging button, or press F5, to run the application then click the Button to call up the InputBox

5. Enter any text you like into the input field then click the OK button to assign the value of your input to the Form's Text property as a window title caption

InputBox Title and Default Response

Notice that the InputBox title caption assumes the name of the application by default – in this case it's "DialogInput". You may, however, specify your own InputBox title by adding a second string after the message string within the parentheses.

Optionally, you may specify a default response that will appear in the text field when the InputBox is called by adding a third string within the parentheses. All strings must be separated by a comma.

Hot tip

Notice how the special space+underscore characters are used here to allow the statement to continue on the next line.

1. In the DialogInput application double-click on the Button to reopen the Code Editor within its Click event-handler and edit the previous statement to read
Me.Text = InputBox("Enter a Caption..." , _
"Caption Selector" , "Dandy Window Title")

2. Click the Start Debugging button, or press F5, to run the application then click the Button to call up the InputBox

3. Note the InputBox title caption, then click the OK button to assign the default response value to the Form's Text property as a window title caption

Hot tip

Try specifying a message and a default response – separating the two strings by TWO commas.

35

Specifying dialog properties

The features of a MsgBox dialog can be determined by adding a comma and specification value after the message string within its parentheses. This can specify which buttons the dialog will display and what graphic icon, if any, will appear on the dialog.

Button constant	Value
vbOkOnly	0
vbOkCancel	1
vbAbortRetryIgnore	2
vbYesNoCancel	3
vbYesNo	4
vbRetryCancel	5

The dialog button combinations can be specified using the Visual Basic constant values, or their numeric equivalents, in this table. For example, to have the dialog display Yes, No, and Cancel buttons specify the **vbYesNoCancel** constant or its numeric equivalent **3**.

Icon constant		Value
vbCritical	❌	16
vbQuestion	❓	32
vbExclamation	⚠️	48
vbInformation	ℹ️	64

The dialog icon can be specified using the Visual Basic constant values, or their numeric equivalents, in this table. For example, to have the dialog display the question mark icon specify the **vbQuestion** constant or its numeric equivalent **32**.

Hot tip

Always specify a graphic icon when calling a MsgBox dialog to help the user easily understand the nature of the message.

In order to have the MsgBox display both a particular button combination and a certain graphic icon the specification can add the button constant and the icon constant together using the addition + operator. For example, the specification to display Yes, No, and Cancel buttons along with a question icon would be **vbYesNoCancel + vbQuestion**. Alternatively specify the sum total of their numeric equivalents – in this case it's **35** (3 + 32).

The buttons in a MsgBox dialog each return a specific numeric value to the application when they are clicked. This can be assigned to a property in much the same way as the value returned from the InputBox dialog in the previous example.

1 Cick on File, New Project, or press Ctrl+N, to start a new Windows Forms application and name it "MsgBoxDialog"

2 From the ToolBox add a Button, a Label, and a TextBox to the default Form and arrange them to your liking

3 Set the Label's Text property to "Button Value :" and name the TextBox **BtnValue**

4 Double-click on the Button to open the Code Editor within its Click event-handler and add the statement
**BtnValue.Text = MsgBox("Click any button" , _
vbYesNoCancel + vbQuestion)**

5 Press F5 to run the application then, like it says, click any button and note the value it has returned to the TextBox

Beware

Don't confuse the button return values with the Visual Basic constant values used to specify the button combinations.

37

Hot tip

Try changing the MsgBox combination specification using constant or numeric values – and make a note of the value returned by each button.

Summary

- In Visual Basic each object has a name and properties

- When an object is selected in the Form Designer the current value of each of its properties can be inspected in the Properties window

- The value of any property can be edited in the Properties window to assign a new value to that property

- Features determining the appearance of an application, such as Font and Layout, can be set at designtime along with content

- Content, such as Text and Color values, can also be initialized at runtime using the Form's Load event-handler

- Control objects placed on a Form can be addressed by their name but you should use the Me keyword to address the current Form itself

- Programming code can use existing property values in a calculation to compute a further value at runtime

- Label controls merely display text, they do not allow user input

- TextBox controls both display text and allow user input

- It is recommended you give all controls a meaningful name for easy recognition

- Visual Basic is not case-sensitive so no special care is needed to observe capital or lower case letters in code

- An InputBox allows user input to be assigned to any property

- Unlike a MsgBox statement, a call to the InputBox should always assign the value which will be returned

- Optionally, a title and default response can be specified for an InputBox dialog

- Optionally, a button combination and icon can be specified for a MsgBox dialog

3 Using controls

This chapter illustrates how many of the Common Controls within the Visual Basic Toolbox can be used to develop an exciting application interface.

Tab order

When creating an application interface with multiple controls consider how it can be navigated without a mouse, by those users who prefer keyboard navigation. Typically they will expect to be able to move the focus from one control to another by pressing the Tab key. It is, therefore, important to allow the focus to move in a logical order when the Tab key is pressed, by setting the TabIndex property values of your controls.

1 Place several controls on a Form then click on the one you want to be first in the tab order to select it

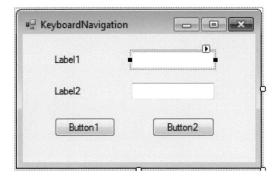

2 Set the TabIndex property value of the selected control to zero so it has first focus

Don't forget

Not all controls can receive focus. The Label controls in this example are not able to get focus so the tab action just skips to the next control.

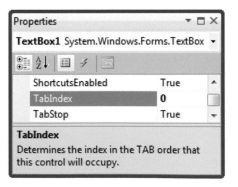

3 Repeat for other controls setting each TabIndex with an ascending value – 1, 2, 3, and so on

Using Button

The Button control provides the user with an easy way to start an operation, confirm or cancel a choice, or get help. In Visual Basic, programming code needs to be added within each Button's event-handler to determine its function. Also its properties need to be set to determine its appearance – Size, Text, Color, Font, etc. When setting the Text property you can easily create an access key shortcut by prefixing the value with an ampersand & character.

Hot tip

The Enabled property can be set to False to prevent a Button being available to the user until your program enables it.

1. Select the Button control in the Form Designer then use the Properties window to modify its Size, and Color

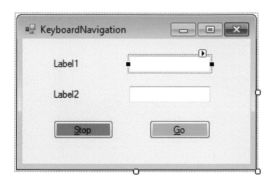

2. Assign a Text property value that is prefixed by an ampersand & character to create an access key shortcut

Beware

The standard Windows look is familiar and comfortable for most users – avoid radical customization of your application.

3. Repeat for other Button controls, setting each Text property with a unique access key shortcut value, then press Alt+G to test this "Go" button's access key

Using TextBox

The TextBox control is an essential part of most applications, typically providing a single-line text input area for the user. Greater amounts of text input can be accommodated in a TextBox if its Multiline property is set to True and its ScrollBars property is set to Vertical.

1. Place a TextBox and a Button control onto a Form

2. Select the TextBox and use the Properties window to set its ScrollBars property to Vertical

3. Click on the Smart Tag arrowed button over the TextBox, or use the Properties window, to set its Multiline property to True

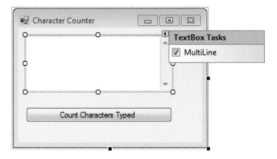

4. Add this statement to the Button's Click event-handler
   MsgBox("You typed: " & _
   Str (Len (TextBox1.Text)) & " characters")

5. Run the application, type some text into the TextBox, then click the Button to test the application

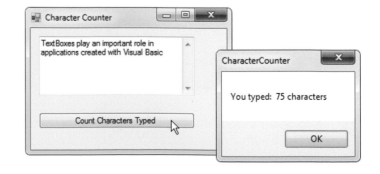

Using ComboBox

A ComboBox control can be used in place of a TextBox to provide an additional range of text values in a dropdown list. The user can choose one of the listed values to insert into the text field or type into it directly, just like a regular TextBox. The ComboBox provides a user-friendly list of anticipated input but occupies only the same space as a single-line TextBox.

1 Select the ComboBox control and find its Items property in the Properties window

2 Click the ellipsis (...) button in its value column to launch the String Collection editor

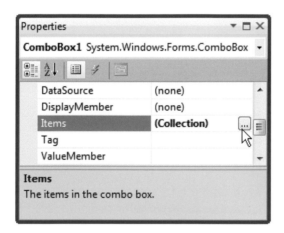

3 Enter a list of alternatives you wish to offer, adding one on each line, then click the OK button

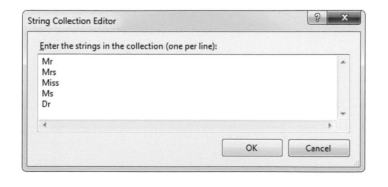

Don't forget

You can discover the value selected by the user from the ComboBox's Text property.

Using Label

A Label control is intended to advise the user and provides a rectangular area that is generally used to provide text information. It can also provide simple rectangular graphics by displaying no text value and setting its AutoSize and BackColor properties.

1 Add three Label controls to a Form

2 Select each Label in turn and, in the Properties window, set the AutoSize property value to False

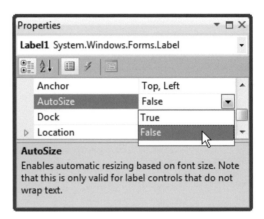

3 Select each Label in turn and, in the Properties window, set the BackColor property value to your preference

4 Select each Label in turn and, in the Properties window, delete the Text property value so it becomes blank

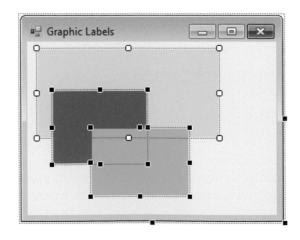

Using PictureBox

The PictureBox control allows images to be added to your application interface. These can be referenced as local files or imported into your application as a resource. Adding an image as a resource ensures your application will be portable when deployed as it includes its own copy of the image.

1 Add a PictureBox control to a Form then select it

2 Find its Image property in the Properties window then click the ellipsis button [...] to launch the Select Resource dialog box

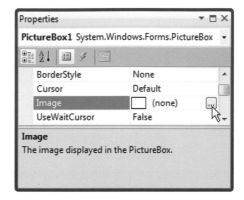

Beware

Acceptable image formats are Bitmap (.bmp), Icon (.ico), GIF (.gif), Metafile (.wmf), and JPEG (.jpg) – other formats cannot be imported unless they are converted first.

3 Click the "Project resource file" radio button then click Import to browse to the location of the image file

Hot tip

Notice after importing an image how the file gets added into the Resources folder in the Solution Explorer window.

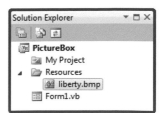

4 Click OK to import the image file into your application and to place the image in the PictureBox control

Using ListBox

The Visual Basic ListBox is one of the most useful controls as it provides a convenient way to present multiple choices to the user. It allows large lists, of even several thousand items, to be displayed in a compact manner. Typically the list data is derived from an external source, such as a database, then incorporated within your application – address books, business records, collections, etc.

Although the Properties window allows items to be added manually to a ListBox Items property, as with a ComboBox, it is often more appropriate to build the list dynamically by adding items at runtime – using the Form's Load event-handler.

1 Add a ListBox, Label, and Button control to a Form

2 Name the ListBox "BookList" and change the Text property values of the Label and Button like this

3 Double-click on the Form to open the Code Editor in the Form's Load event-handler and add the statement **BookList.Items.Add("HTML in easy steps")**

4 Repeat the above statement, each on a new line, substituting a different title within the parentheses for each title you want to add to the list

---

Hot tip

You don't need to worry about setting ListBox scroll bars for longer lists – they get added automatically.

46

Don't forget

The items in this small list example are added in the code one by one. Larger lists, can be added more economically using a code loop – learn more about loops on page 68.

5 To have the list items sorted alphabetically add the
statement **BookList.Sorted = True**

6 To have the first item in the list selected by default add
the statement **BookList.SelectedIndex = 0**

7 To show the list length in the Form caption add the
statement **Me.Text = BookList.Items.Count & _**
" More Books by Mike McGrath"

8 Return to the Form Designer and double-click on the
Button to open the Code Editor in its event-handler. To
display the current selected list item when it is clicked
add the statement **MsgBox(BookList.Text)**

Beware

Remember that the
first item in the index is
numbered as zero, not 1.

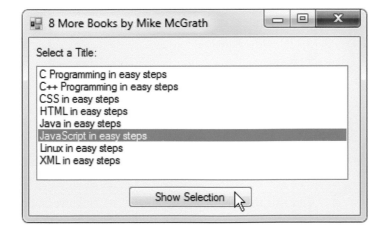

9 Run the application
and see the first item
appear selected. Select a
different item then click
the Button to confirm
the selection

Hot tip

The ListBox's Sorted
property can also be set
in the Properties window.

47

Using CheckBox

A CheckBox control is a small box with a caption. It lets the user select the caption choice by clicking on the box and a check mark appears in the box to indicate it has been chosen. Clicking the box once more deselects the choice and unchecks the box.

CheckBox controls are ideal to present a set of choices from which the user can select none, one, or more than one choice.

1   Add two CheckBox controls to a Form along with a Label, ListBox, and Button

2   Use the Properties window to change the Text property values of the CheckBox controls, Label, and Button to look like the ones below and name the ListBox "Pizza"

3   Add this statement to the Button's Click event-handler to clear the list box when it's clicked **Pizza.Items.Clear()**

4   Now add these statements to add list items for each checked CheckBox control

```
If CheckBox1.Checked = True Then
        Pizza.Items.Add( Checkbox1.Text )
End If

If CheckBox2.Checked = True Then
        Pizza.Items.Add( Checkbox2.Text )
End If
```

Don't forget

The conditional If - Then statements shown here are explained in detail later. For now, just remember that the Checked property is set to True when chosen.

Using RadioButton

A RadioButton control is like a CheckBox, but with one crucial difference – the user can check only one choice in the group. Checking a RadioButton automatically unchecks any others.

RadioButton controls are ideal to present a set of choices from which the user can select only one choice.

1 Add two RadioButtons and a Label to the Form opposite then edit their Text properties so they look like this

2 Insert these statements in the Button's Click event-handler right after the clear instruction

If RadioButton1.Checked = True Then
    Pizza.Items.Add(RadioButton1.Text)
End If

If RadioButton2.Checked = True Then
    Pizza.Items.Add(RadioButton2.Text)
End If

3 Run the application, select various choices, then click the Button to test the selection results

49

Hot tip

When creating radio button groups always set one choice as the default by changing its Checked property value to True in the Properties window.

Hot tip

Try adding a Clear button to the Form that will clear the ListBox and all selected choices when it gets clicked.

Using WebBrowser

The Visual Basic WebBrowser control makes it a snap to quickly add a document viewer to your application that can view HTML documents both online and on your own computer. It can also display plain text and image files – just like Internet Explorer.

1 Add a WebBrowser control to a Form – it will automatically occupy the entire Form area

2 Click on the Smart Tag arrow button and select the link to "Undock in parent container"

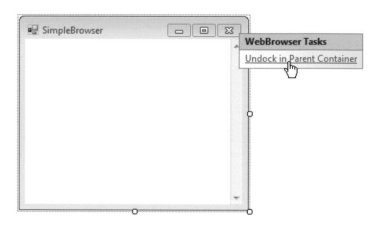

3 Add a TextBox and Button control then arrange the Form controls to look like this

Don't forget

Grab the handles around the controls to resize them on the Form.

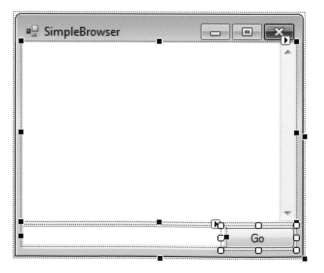

4 Double-click on the Button to open the Code Editor in its event-handler then add the following statement **WebBrowser1.Navigate(TextBox1.Text)**

5 Run the application, type a valid URL into the TextBox field, then click the Button to view the web page

Beware

The Enter key will not activate the Button's click event unless you add an access key shortcut.

6 Now type a valid local file address into the TextBox field and click the Button to view it in the WebBrowser

Hot tip

You can download the projects from this book at www.ineasysteps.com.

Using Timer

The Timer is an invisible control that can be found in the Components section of the Visual Basic ToolBox. When added to your application it fires an event at a regular interval set by you. Statements within the Timer's event-handler are then executed whenever the Timer event occurs.

1 Add two PictureBox controls and a Button to a Form

2 Assign two similar images of the same size to the PictureBox controls then hold down the Shift key while you click on each to select both together

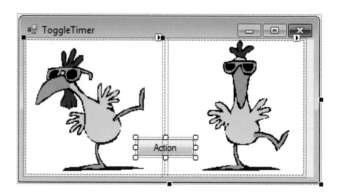

3 On the Menu Bar select Format, Align, Centers to exactly align the PictureBox controls one above the other

4 Select Format, Order, Bring to Front or Send to Back to ensure that PictureBox1 is at the front (on top) of the PictureBox2 control – click on the top one and check the current selected control name in the Properties window

5 Add a Timer control to the Form from the Components section of the ToolBox – its icon appears on the Component Tray at the bottom of the Form Designer

6 Double-click on the Timer icon to open the Code Editor at its event-handler then add these statements

If PictureBox1.Visible = True Then
    PictureBox1.Visible = False
Else
    PictureBox1.Visible = True
End If

This code inspects the Visible property of the top PictureBox and "toggles" its visibility on and off – like flicking a light switch

7 Double-click on the Button to open the Code Editor at its event-handler then add these statements

If Timer1.Enabled = False Then
    Timer1.Enabled = True
Else
    Timer1.Enabled = False
End If

This code inspects the Enabled property of the Timer and "toggles" it on and off when the Button gets clicked

8 Run the application then click the Button to watch the Timer appear to animate the PictureBox images

Don't forget

The popular controls demonstrated in this chapter are just some of the many controls available in the ToolBox – experiment with each one to understand them.

Hot tip

You can adjust the Timer's Interval property value to change the speed of the animation.

Summary

- The TabIndex property determines the order in which a user can navigate around the interface controls with the Tab key

- Access key shortcuts are assigned to Buttons by prefixing the Text property value with an ampersand & character

- TextBox controls can usefully display multiple lines of text if their MultiLine property is set to True and their ScrollBars property is set to Vertical

- A ComboBox control allows typed text input, like a TextBox, plus it offers the user a list of anticipated input items to click

- Label controls contain text information and do not allow focus or direct input. They can, however, be useful to provide simple rectangular graphics

- A PictureBox control allows an image to be incorporated in the application interface

- Importing images as a resource ensure that the application will be portable when it is deployed

- ListBox controls are useful to compactly display numerous data items – both from within the program and from external sources such as a database

- CheckBox controls let the user choose none, one, or more options, whereas RadioButton controls let the user choose just one option from a group

- A WebBrowser control can display HTML documents plus plain text and images – just like your regular web browser

- You can use a Timer control to create an event in your application that fires at a regular interval set by you

- The toggle technique is useful in Visual Basic programming to alternate a Property value

4 Learning the language

This chapter demonstrates the mechanics of the Visual Basic programming language which allow data to be stored, controlled, and manipulated, to progress the application.

Elements of a program

A program is simply a series of instructions that tell the computer what to do. Although programs can be complex each individual instruction is generally simple. The computer starts at the beginning and works through, line by line, until it gets to the end. Here are some of the essential elements in Visual Basic:

Statements

A statement is an instruction that performs an action. For example, the statement **Lbl.BackColor = Color.Blue** sets the background color of **Lbl** to **Blue**.

Functions

A function is a statement that returns a value. For example, the function **InputBox()** returns the value of its dialog text field.

Variables

A variable is a word defined in the program that stores a value. For example, the statement **msg = "Hello World!"** stores a string of characters in a variable called **msg**.

Operators

An operator is an arithmetical symbol. For example, the * asterisk character is the multiplication operator and the / forward slash character is the division operator.

Objects

An object is a program "building block" entity. It can be visible, like a Button control, or invisible like a Timer control.

Properties

A property is a characteristic of an object. For example, the property **Btn.Text** is the **Text** property of the **Btn** object.

Methods

A method is an action that an object can perform. For example, the method **Btn.Click()** is the **Click** method of the **Btn** object.

Comments

A comment is an explanatory line in the program code starting with an apostrophe ' character. It's not actually read by the compiler but exists to explain the purpose of the code. For example, ' **Clear the list.** might explain a **Clear** statement.

Hot tip

The examples in this chapter demonstrate the various elements of a program. Refer back here for identification.

Don't forget

The Visual Basic IDE is a safe environment in which to experiment and learn from your mistakes.

...cont'd

The illustration below shows the Code Editor view of Visual Basic programming code for the Click event-handler of a Button control – line numbering is turned on to aid analysis of the code.

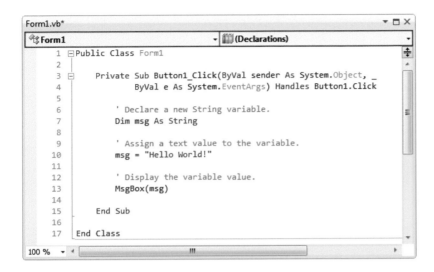

Line-by-line analysis

- Lines 1 and 17 – start and end of the entire Form code
- Lines 3 and 15 – start and end of the Button event-handler
- Lines 6, 9, and 12 – explanatory comments
- Line 7 – creates a variable called **msg** to store String data
- Line 10 – places text value into the **msg** variable
- Line 13 – calls the **MsgBox()** function to show the **msg** value

Syntax high-lighting

- Keywords – Visual Basic core language words appear in blue
- Strings – text values, within double-quotes, appear in red
- Comments – explanatory lines appear in green
- Code – everything else appears in **black**

Hot tip

To turn on line numbering click on Tools, Options, then expand Text Editor Basic. Choose Editor then check the Line Numbers option.

57

Beware

The syntax colors shown here are the default colors. Custom colors can be chosen in the Tools, Options dialog by expanding Environment, Fonts and Colors.

Declaring variable types

A variable is like a container in a program where a data value can be stored. It is called a variable because its contents can change during the course of the program.

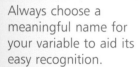
You can create a variable by typing a declaration comprising the Visual Basic **Dim** keyword followed by a unique variable name of your choice. For example, **Dim msg** declares a new variable with the name **msg**.

The variable declaration should also specify the type of data the variable can store using the As keyword followed by one of the Visual Basic data types. So, **Dim msg As String** declares a new variable called **msg** that can store a string of characters.

There are many data types available in Visual Basic programming but those most frequently used are listed in the table below.

Data type	Possible value
Boolean	True or False
String	Characters
Integer	Whole number
Double	Floating-point number

After a variable has been created with a specified data type it can only store data of the type specified in the declaration. For example, you cannot assign a String to an Integer variable.

Data, of the appropriate type, can be assigned to the variable at any point in the program. A variable declaration can also initialize a variable. For example, **Dim msg As String = "Hello"** initializes a new String variable called **msg** with the value **Hello**.

...cont'd

Specifying data types for variables has several advantages:

- It lets you perform specialized tasks for each data type – character manipulation with Strings, validation with Booleans, and arithmetic with Integers and Doubles

- It enables IntelliSense to pop up their features as you type

- It takes advantage of compiler type checking to prevent errors

- It results in faster execution of your code

You can easily display the value stored in any variable by assigning it to the text-based property of a visual control, such as a ListBox.

1 Add a ListBox control and a Button control to a Form

2 Double-click on the Button to launch the Code Editor in its event-handler

3 Add these lines to declare and initialize four variables
```
Dim bool As Boolean = False
Dim str As String = "Some text"
Dim int As Integer = 1000
Dim num As Double = 7.5
```

4 Now add these lines to display the stored values
```
ListBox1.Items.Add( "bool value is " & bool )
ListBox1.Items.Add( "str value is " & str )
ListBox1.Items.Add( "int value is " & int )
ListBox1.Items.Add( "num value is " & num )
```

5 Run the application and click the Button to see the value stored in each variable

Hot tip

IntelliSense is the pop-up box that appears as you type in the Code Editor, showing code features.

59

Beware

Two useful functions are Str(), that converts a number to a string, and Val(), that converts a string to a number. The Str() function was seen in action on page 42 and Val() back on page 31.

Understanding variable scope

The accessibility of a variable is known as its "scope" and depends upon where its declaration is made in the program. A variable's scope determines which parts of the program are able to inspect or change the value stored in that variable.

Variables that are declared within a Sub routine section of code, such as an event-handler, are only accessible within that routine. Reference to them from outside that routine will result in an error as they will not be visible from other routines. A variable declared within a Sub routine is, therefore, said to have "local" scope – it is only accessible locally within that routine.

Local variables are generally declared with the **Dim** keyword, a given name, and a data type specification. The given name must be unique within its own scope but can be used again for another local variable of different scope. For example, two different event-handler Sub routines may both declare a local variable called msg. There is no conflict here as each one is invisible to the other.

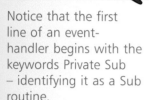

Hot tip

Notice that the first line of an event-handler begins with the keywords Private Sub – identifying it as a Sub routine.

1. Add three Buttons to a Form

2. Double-click on Button1 to open the Code Editor in its event-handler and add this code
   ```
   Dim msg As String = "Hello from the Button1 Sub"
   MsgBox( msg )
   ```

3. Now double-click on Button2 and add the following code to its event-handler, also declaring a msg variable
   ```
   Dim msg As String = "Hello from the Button2 Sub"
   MsgBox( msg )
   ```

4. Run the application and click these Buttons to confirm the value in each **msg** variable is retrieved without conflict

Beware

Visual Basic projects have a compiler setting called Option Explicit that can enforce proper variable declaration, as described here – always leave this set to On (its default setting) so you will be obliged to declare variables correctly.

You may often want a variable to be accessible by more than one Sub routine in your program so its declaration will need to be made outside of any Sub routine code. It should, instead, appear in the Form Declarations section, right after the Form Class line at the start of the code. Variables may be declared here with either the **Private** or **Dim** keyword to become accessible throughout the entire Form scope – so any Sub routine can reference them.

The Form Declaration section may also contain variable declarations made with the **Public** keyword to be accessible throughout the entire project, including other Form modules. These are known as "global" variables because they are accessible from absolutely anywhere.

Don't forget

Variable names must be unique within their visible scope.

5 In the Code Editor type these declarations into the Form Declarations section, at the top of the code
Public globalVar As String = "Hello from the Project"
Private formVar As String = "Hello from this Module"

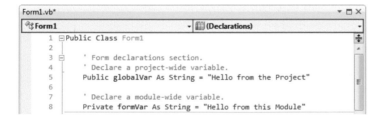

6 Add this line to the Button3 event-handler subroutine
MsgBox(globalVar & vbCrLf & formVar)

7 Run the application and click on Button3 to retrieve the values from the project-wide and module-wide variables

Hot tip

In deciding where best to declare a variable always make it as local as possible to avoid errors – your first choice should be a local Dim declaration, then a Private module declaration, then a Public global declaration.

Working with variable arrays

The variables introduced so far let you store just one value, but sometimes it's more convenient to deal with a set of values. For example, you might want to store the monthly sales figures for a quarterly period. Rather than create three separate variables named JanSales, FebSales, and MarSales, you can create a single variable array named Sales with three elements – one for each month. You can refer to them as Sales(0), Sales(1), and Sales(2).

1 Add a Button to a Form then create an array variable of 3 elements in its Click event-handler with this code
```
Dim Sales(2) As Double
```

2 Assign values to each element in turn
```
Sales(0) = 5245.00
Sales(1) = 4785.00
Sales(2) = 7365.50
```

3 Create a regular variable then assign it the total value of all three array elements
```
Dim Quarter As Double
Quarter = Sales(0) + Sales(1) +Sales(2)
```

4 Finally, add a statement to display the total value, formatted by the computer's regional currency settings
```
MsgBox("Quarter Sales:" & FormatCurrency(Quarter) )
```

5 Run the application to test the result. It is shown here producing the total value formatted in dollars but the formatting depends on the regional settings of the computer on which the application is running.

VarArray

Quarter Sales: $17,395.50

OK

You may, if you wish, initialize the array elements in its declaration without explicitly specifying the number of elements. The values should be assigned as a comma-separated list within curly braces. In this example the declaration would be
```
Dim Sales() As Double = { 5245.0, 4785.0, 7365.5 }
```

Multi-dimensional arrays

Arrays can have more than one dimension. For example, you could create a 2-dimensional array to store the monthly sales of two stores over a quarterly period with **Dim Sales(2,1) As Double**. Individual elements can then be referenced as **Sales(0,0)**, **Sales(1,0)**, **Sales(2,0)**, **Sales(0,1)**, **Sales(1,1)**, and **Sales(2,1)**.

1 Add a Button to a Form then create an array variable of 3x2 elements in its Click event-handler with this code
Dim Sales(2,1) As Double

2 Assign values to each element in turn
Sales(0,0) = 1255 : Sales(1,0) = 1845.5 : Sales(2,0) =1065
Sales(0,1) = 2175 : Sales(1,1) = 2215.5 : Sales(2,1) = 2453

3 Create two regular variables. Assign one the total value of all elements in the array's first dimension and the other the total value of all elements in its second dimension
Dim Store1, Store2 As Double
Store1 = Sales(0,0) + Sales(1,0) +Sales(2,0)
Store2 = Sales(0,1) + Sales(1,1) +Sales(2,1)

4 Finally, add a statement to display the total values, formatted by the computer's regional currency settings
MsgBox("Quarter Sales..." & vbCrLf & _
"Store 1 : " & FormatCurrency(Store1) & vbCrLf & _
"Store 2 : " & FormatCurrency(Store2))

5 Run the application to test the result. It is shown here producing the total values formatted in dollars but the formatting depends on the regional settings of the host computer.

Beware

Arrays of two dimensions represent a square and those of three dimensions represent a cube but arrays of more than three dimensions are best avoided as they are difficult to visualize.

Hot tip

Notice how the underscore character and vbCrLf constant are used here to format the MsgBox message.

Performing operations

The Visual Basic arithmetic operators listed in the table below are used to return the result of a calculation.

Operator	Description	Example
+	Addition	16 + 4
-	Subtraction	16 - 4
*	Multiplication	16 * 4
/	Division	16 / 4

In statements using more than one arithmetic operator it is important to specify operator precedence to clarify the expression. For example, the expression **6 * 3 + 5** could return **48 (6 * 8)** or **23 (18 + 5)** – depending which arithmetic is performed first. Adding parentheses around the part to perform first clarifies the expression so that **(6 * 3) + 5** assures the result will be **23** (18 + 5).

The Visual Basic comparison operators listed in the table below are used to test an expression and return a True or False result.

Operator	Description	Example
=	Equality	**num = 10**
<>	Inequality	**num <> 10**
>	Greater than	**num > 10**
>=	Greater than or equal to	**num >= 10**
<	Less than	**num < 10**
<=	Less than or equal to	**num <= 10**

Beware

In Visual Basic the = symbol is used both to assign values and to test for equality – other programming languages have a separate == equality operator.

The Visual Basic arithmetic operators can be used to easily create simple calculation functionality in your application.

1 Add two TextBox controls, four Buttons, and three Labels to a Form and arrange them as below

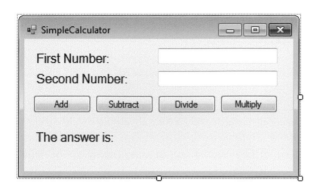

2 Double-click on the Add button to open the Code Editor in its event-handler then type the following statement
Label3.Text = "The answer is : " & _
Str(Val(TextBox1.Text) + Val(TextBox2.Text))

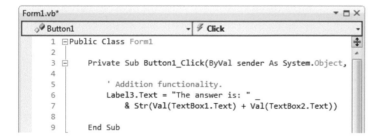

3 Repeat step 2 for the other Button controls but replace the + operator with the appropriate arithmetic operator - for Subtract, / for Divide, and * for Multiply

4 Run the application and enter two numbers, say 16 and 4, into the TextBox fields then click each Button control

Don't forget

Other Visual Basic operators include the ampersand & which is used to concatenate (join) code, and the underscore _ which lets statements continue on the next line.

65

Branching code

Making statements that test an expression allows the program to perform one action or another, according to the result of the test. This important technique is known as "conditional branching" – the code will branch one way or another depending whether a condition is **True** or **False**. In Visual Basic conditional branching can be performed by an **If** statement, using this syntax

```
If ( test-expression-returns-True ) Then
        execute-this-statement
Else
        execute-this-alternative-statement
End If
```

Optionally, multiple expressions can be included in the test using the **And** keyword, where both expressions must be **True**, or the **Or** keyword where either one of the expressions must be **True**.

Don't forget

An If statement must always end with the End If keywords.

1 Add a Label control to a Form

2 Double-click on the Form to open the Code Editor in the Form's Load event-handler

3 Type the following If statement to assign an appropriate value to the Label control according to whether either of the two tested expressions is True

```
If ( WeekDay( Now ) = vbSaturday ) Or _
( WeekDay( Now ) = vbSunday ) Then
        Label1.Text = "Relax – it's the weekend"
Else
        Label1.Text = "Today's a working weekday"
End If
```

4 Run the application – the message will vary depending if the current day is a weekday or a weekend day

Hot tip

If statements were used back on page 53 to toggle property values, and on page 48, without the optional Else part, to test the status of CheckBoxes and RadioButtons.

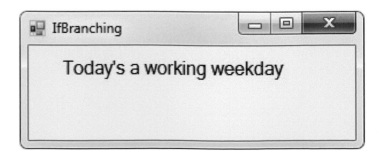

Conditional branching can also be performed with a **Select Case** statement, to provide multiple possible branches, using this syntax

Select Case *expression-to-test*
Case Is *test-returns-True*
      execute-this-statement-then-exit
Case Is *test-returns-True*
      execute-this-statement-then-exit
Case Else
      execute-this-default-statement
End Select

You can add as many **Case** tests as you wish and, optionally, use **Case Else** to provide a final default statement to be executed when none of the tests return **True**.

1. Add a Label control to a Form

2. Double-click on the Form to open the Code Editor in the Form's Load event-handler

3. Type the following Select Case statement to assign an appropriate value to the Label control according to which of the tested Case expressions is True
```
Select Case WeekDay( Now )
Case Is = vbSaturday
        Label1.text = "It's a Super Saturday"
Case Is = vbSunday
        Label1.Text = "It's a Lazy Sunday"
Case Else
        Label1.text = "It's just another working day"
End Select
```

4. Run the application to see an appropriate message

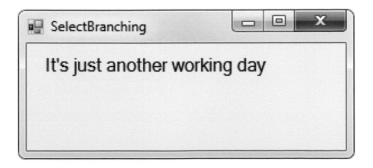

Hot tip

Try using a Select Case statement to branch code according to the value returned from a MsgBox dialog with Yes, No, and Cancel buttons – as seen on page 36/37.

Beware

An If statement must always end with End If keywords and a Select Case statement with the End Select keywords.

Looping code

Programming loops allow statements within the loop to be executed repeatedly until the loop ends. They must always include a test expression to determine when to end – or they will run forever! The most popular loop in Visual Basic is the **For Next** loop which uses a counter to test the number of times it has executed (iterated) its statements, and has this syntax:

For *counter* = *start* **To** *end*
        execute-this-statement
Next *update-the-counter*

It is often useful to incorporate the increasing value of the counter into the statement/s executed on each iteration of the loop.

1 Add a TextBox, Button, and ListBox control to a Form

2 Double-click on the Button to open the Code Editor in its Click event-handler then type this For Next loop

```
Dim amount As Double = Val( TextBox1.Text )
Dim counter As Integer
For counter = 1 To 10
        ListBox1.Items.Add( "At " & counter & _
        "% interest is " & _
        FormatCurrency( (amount * counter) / 100 ) )
Next counter
```

3 Run the application, enter a number in the TextBox, then click the Button to run the loop

Beware

The counter variable stores the loop index – do not assign it any other value in the loop.

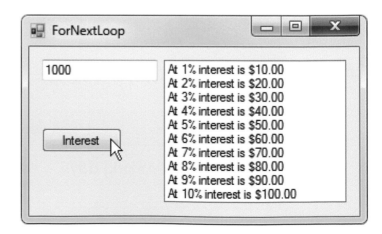

Other types of loop possible in Visual Basic are the **Do Until** loop and the **Do While** loop. Although similar, these two loops are subtly different – a **Do Until** loop executes its statements until the test expression becomes **True**, whereas the **Do While** loop executes its statements until the test expression becomes **False**.

All loops work great to iterate lists of data and are especially useful to iterate the values contained in array elements.

1 Add a ListBox control to a Form

2 Double-click on the Form to open the Code Editor in its Load event-handler then create this array
**Dim Sales() As Double = { 5601, 8502, 6703, 4204, _
7605, 8206, 9107, 6508, 7209, 5010, 8011, 7012 }**

3 Create a String variable with **Dim sum As String**

4 Now type this Do Until loop then run the application
```
Dim counter As Integer
Do Until counter = Sales.Length
        sum = FormatCurrency( Sales( counter ) )
        counter = counter + 1
        sum = sum & vbTab & MonthName( counter )
        ListBox1.Items.Add( sum )
Loop
```

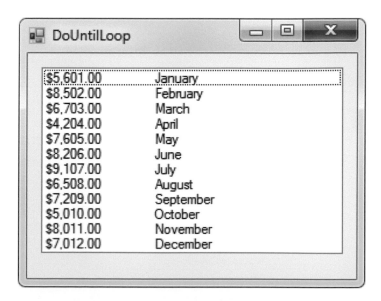

Don't forget

Choose the Do loop which offers greater clarity for your particular purpose – but remember they must both contain a statement to change the counter, and end with the Loop keyword.

Hot tip

The limit of this loop is specified by the Length property of the array. The counter references each element (0-11) from the Sales array and also each month name (1-12) from the Visual Basic MonthName function.

Calling object methods

Visual Basic objects have methods that can be called in code to make the object perform an action at runtime. This works in much the same way that you can write code to assign property values to dynamically change an object's characteristics.

To view any object's available properties and methods type its name followed by a period into the Code Editor. An "IntelliSense" pop-up window will appear showing all that object's properties and methods. Scroll down the list then double-click on an item to add that property or method into the code.

1 Add two Label controls and five Buttons to a Form

2 In the Properties window set each Label's AutoSize to False, and delete their default Text value

3 Make the BackColor of one Label red and name it **RedLbl**, then set the other Label's BackColor to yellow

4 Edit the Text property of each Button then arrange the controls so the Form looks like this

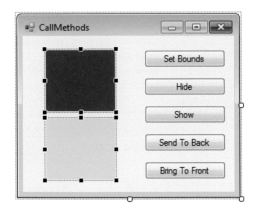

Beware

Leaving the AutoSize property set to the default of True prevents the Label being resized.

5 Double-click on the Set Bounds Button to open the Code Editor in its event-handler then type **RedLbl**.

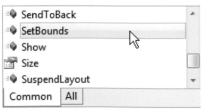

6   Find the **SetBounds** method in the IntelliSense window then double-click it to add it to the code

7   The **SetBounds** method sets the size and position of the control using X, Y, Width, and Height. Add the settings **(45, 45, 45, 100)** to the code, right after the method name

Don't forget

When you select an item in the IntelliSense window a Tooltip appears containing that item's definition.

8   Repeat for the other Buttons adding calls to the **Hide()**, **Show()**, **BringToFront()**, and **SendToBack()** methods – no settings are required for any of these

9   Run the application and click each Button to try its action – see the stacking order change from back to front

71

Using the With block shorthand

When creating code addressing several properties or methods of an object it can be tedious to repeatedly type the object name.

```
BlueLbl.AutoSize = False
BlueLbl.BackColor = Color.Blue
BlueLbl.Width = 50
Blue.Lbl.Height = 50
BlueLbl.SendtoBack()
```

Usefully, a With block can neatly specify all the values and calls

```
With BlueLbl
        .AutoSize = False
        .BackColor = Color.Blue
        .Width = 50
        .Height = 50
        .SendToBack()
End With
```

Hot tip

Try adding another Label to the Call Methods example then set its properties and methods in the Form's Load event using a With block.

Creating a sub method

When you double-click on a Form or Button to open the Code Editor you see that each event-handler begins and ends like this:

Private Sub ... End Sub

"Sub" is short for "subroutine" and each event-handler subroutine is a Private method of that Form's class. You can create your own subroutine method from scratch that can be called from other code in your application as required.

1 Add Labels, Buttons, and TextBox controls to a Form, then arrange them like this

2 Click on View, Code, or press F7, to open the Code Editor then type this code into the Declarations section

```
Private Sub ClearForm()
        TextBox1.Text = ""
        TextBox2.Text = ""
        TextBox3.Text = ""
End Sub
```

3 Click on View, Designer, or press Shift+F7, to return to the Form Designer then double-click on the Clear Button to open the Code Editor in its Click event-handler

4 Type **Me.** and notice that the new ClearForm method has been added to the IntelliSense window. Double-click on it to add **Me.ClearForm()** to the code

5 Run the application, type some text into all three text fields, then click the Button to clear the fields

Sending parameters

A powerful feature of Sub routines is the ability to receive information as they are called. This information is known as "parameters" and is sent from the parentheses of the calling statement to the parentheses of the Sub routine.

In order for a Sub routine to handle parameters it must specify a name and data type for each parameter it is to receive. For example, **str As String** would receive a single string parameter from the caller – it cannot be called unless one string is passed. The Sub routine code can then refer to the passed value using the given name, in this case **str**. Multiple parameters can be passed if the Sub routine specifies the correct number and data types.

1 Click Stop Debugging to return to the Form window shown opposite

2 Now click on View, Code, or press F7, to open the Code Editor then type this code into the Declarations section
```
Private Sub Customer(name As String, addr As String)
        TextBox1.Text = name
        TextBox2.Text = addr
End Sub
```

3 Edit the Customer Button's Click event-handler to include this call to the new Sub routine
```
Me.Customer( "Mike McGrath", "1 Main Street, USA" )
```

4 Run the application and click the Customer Button

Creating a function

A Function is similar to a Sub routine, but with one important difference – a Function returns a value to the caller. This means that you must specify the data type of the return value, in addition to specifying parameters, when creating a Function.

1 Add three Labels, a Button, and a TextBox to a Form then arrange them like this

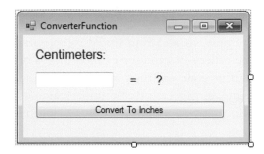

2 Click on View, Code, or press F7, to open the Code Editor then type this code into the Declarations section

```
Private Function Inches(ByVal Cm As String) As Double
        Inches = Cm / 2.54
        Inches = FormatNumber( Inches , 2 )
        Return Inches
End Function
```

The parentheses specify the parameter Inches must be a String data type – this value is used in the calculation. The result is assigned to the Function name for return as a Double data type, formatted to just two decimal places.

3 Add a call to the Inches Function in the Button's Click event-handler Sub routine

```
Label1.Text = Inches(TextBox1.Text) & " Inches"
```

4 Run the application, enter a number, then click the Button to use the Function

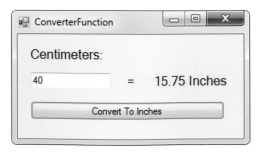

Doing mathematics

The Visual Basic Math object has many methods that are useful when performing mathematical calculations. The most frequently used methods are listed below together with examples returns.

Data type	Description
Math.Ceiling()	Rounds a number up eg: Math.Ceiling(3.5) returns 4
Math.Floor()	Rounds a number down eg: Math.Floor(3.5) returns 3
Math.Round()	Rounds to the nearest integer eg: Math.Round(3.5) returns 4
Math.Sqrt()	Returns the square root eg: Math.Sqrt(16) returns 4
Math.Max()	Returns the larger of two numbers eg: Math.Max(8, 64) returns 64
Math.Min()	Returns the smaller of two numbers eg: Math.Min(8, 64) returns 8
Math.Pow()	Returns a number raised to the specified power. eg: Math.Pow(5, 2) returns 25
Math.Abs()	Returns an absolute value eg: Math.Abs(10.0) returns 10
Math.Cos()	Returns a cosine value eg: Math.Cos(10.0) returns -0.839
Math.Log()	Returns a natural logarithm eg: Math.Log(10.0) returns 2.303
Math.Sin()	Returns a sine value eg: Math.Sin(10.0) returns -0.544
Math.Tan()	Returns a tangent value eg: Math.Tan(10.0) returns 0.648

Hot tip

The Math class also has a Math.PI constant representing the value of π – approximately 3.142.

Don't forget

The returns shown here for Cosine, Log, Sine, and Tangent are rounded to three decimal places – the actual returns provide greater precision.

Generating a random number

Random numbers can be generated by the Visual Basic **Rnd()** function that returns a floating-point value between 0.0 and 1.0. Multiplying the random numbers will specify a wider range. For example, a multiplier of 20 will create a random number between zero and twenty. To make the generated random number more useful you can round it up to the nearest higher integer value with the **Math.Ceiling()** method so the range, in this case, becomes from 1 to 20.

The numbers generated by **Rnd()** are not truly random but are merely a sequence of pseudo random numbers produced by an algorithm from a specific starting point. Whenever an application loads, a call to the **Rnd()** function will begin at the same starting point – so the same sequence will be repeated. This is not generally desirable so the application needs to create a new starting point when it loads to avoid repetition. This can be achieved by calling the **Randomize()** function in the Form's Load event to "seed" the **Rnd()** function with a starting point based upon the system time when the application gets loaded – now the sequence of generated numbers is different each time.

Beware

The numbers generated by the algorithm for Randomize() and Rnd() may be predicted so this technique should not be used for cryptography.

Don't forget

Text in a label will not wrap to the next line unless AutoSize is False.

1 Add a Label, TextBox, and Button control to a Form and arrange them like this

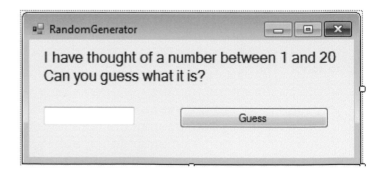

2 Name the Label control **Msg**, set its AutoSize property to False, then assign its Text property to the illustrated text

3 Name the TextBox control **Guess** and set the Text property of the Button likewise

4 Click on View, Code, or press the F7 key, to open the Code Editor then create a variable in the Declarations

Dim num As Integer

5 Still in the Declarations section add a Sub routine to assign a random number 1-20 to the **num** variable

```
Private Sub GetNumber()
        num = Math.Ceiling( Rnd() * 20 )
End Sub
```

Don't forget

The integer value must be extracted from the TextBox by the Val() function before making any comparison.

6 In the Form's Load event-handler add a call to seed the random number generator and a call to set the **num** variable with an initial pseudo random value

```
Randomize()
GetNumber()
```

7 Now add some logic to the Button's Click event-handler

```
Select Case ( Val( Guess.Text) )
Case Is > num
        Msg.text = Guess.Text & " is too high"
Case Is < num
        Msg.Text = Guess.Text & " is too low"
Case Is = num
        Msg.Text = Guess.Text & " is correct" & _
        "I have thought of another number - Try again!"
        GetNumber()
End Select
Guess.Text = ""
```

8 Run the application and guess the random number

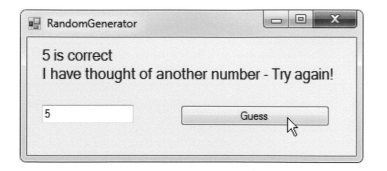

Hot tip

You can use the vbCrLf constant to format the contents of the Label.

77

Summary

- A program's essential elements are Statements, Variables, Functions, Operators, object Properties, and object Methods

- Comment lines help to explain the purpose of the code

- Variable declarations create a variable and can begin with the **Dim, Public,** or **Private** keywords

- Each variable declaration should specify the type of data that variable may contain with the **As** keyword and a data type

- **String, Integer, Double,** and **Boolean** are common data types

- Numbers can be extracted from a string by the **Str()** function and a String converted to a number with the **Val()** function

- The **Private** and **Dim** keywords allow local scope – where the variable is only accessible within a procedure or module

- The **Public** keyword allows global scope – where the variable is accessible across an entire program

- A variable array stores values in elements numbered from zero

- Operators are used to perform arithmetic and comparison

- Code can be made to conditionally branch using **If Else** statements or **Select Case** statements

- **For Next** and **Do Until** statements perform code loops

- Object properties and methods can be addressed in code

- A **Function** returns a value but a **Sub** does not

- Values can be sent to a **Sub** routine or a **Function** if they are of the correct data type and of the number specified

- The **Math** object provides many useful methods for performing mathematical calculations

- Pseudo random numbers can be generated by the **Rnd()** function when seeded by the **Randomize()** function

5 Building an application

This chapter brings together elements from previous chapters to build a complete application – from the initial planning stage to its final deployment.

Beware

Omission of the planning stage can require time-consuming changes to be made later. It's better to "plan your work, then work your plan".

Hot tip

Toggle the value of a Button's Enabled property to steer the user. In this case the application must be reset before a further series of numbers can be generated.

The program plan

When creating a new application it is useful to spend some time planning its design. Clearly define the program's precise purpose, decide what application functionality will be required, then decide what interface components will be needed.

A plan for a simple application to pick numbers for a lottery entry might look like this:

Program purpose

● The program will generate a series of six different random numbers in the range 1 – 49, and have the ability to be reset

Functionality required

● An initial call to start the random number generator

● A routine to generate and display six different random numbers

● A routine to clear the last series from display

Components needed

● Six Label controls to display the series of numbers – one number per Label

● One Button control to generate and display the numbers in the Label controls when this Button is clicked. This Button will not be enabled when numbers are on display

● One Button control to clear the numbers on display in the Label controls when this Button is clicked. This Button will not be enabled when no numbers are on display

● One PictureBox control to display a static image – just to enhance the appearance of the interface

Having established a program plan means you can now create the application basics by adding the components needed to a Form.

1 Open the Visual Basic IDE and create a new Windows Forms Application project called "Lotto"

2 In the Form Designer, add six Label controls to the Form from the Toolbox

3 Now add two Buttons and a PictureBox to the Form

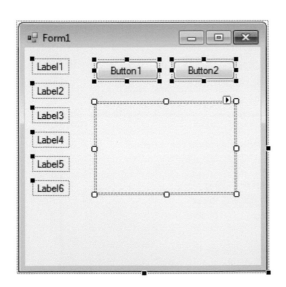

Don't forget

You can drag'n'drop items from the Toolbox or double-click them to add them to the Form.

Assigning static properties

Having created the application basics, on the previous page, you can now assign static values using the Properties window.

1 Click anywhere on the Form to select it then, in the Properties window, set the Form's Text property to "Lotto Number Picker"

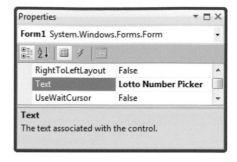

2 Select the Button1 control then, in the Properties window, change its [Name] property to **PickBtn** and its Text property to "Get My Lucky Numbers"

3 Select the Button2 control then, in the Properties window, change its [Name] property to **ResetBtn** and its Text property to "Reset"

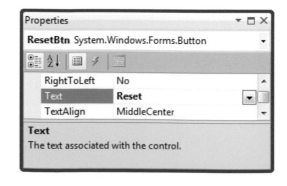

4 Select the PictureBox1 control then, in the Properties window, click the Image property ellipsis button to launch the Select Resources dialog

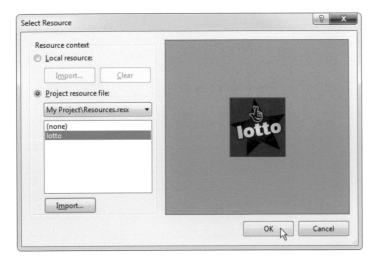

Hot tip

You can use the dropdown list at the top of the Properties window to select any control.

5 Click the Import button, browse to the image location, then click OK to import the image resource – this action automatically assigns it to the PictureBox1 Image property

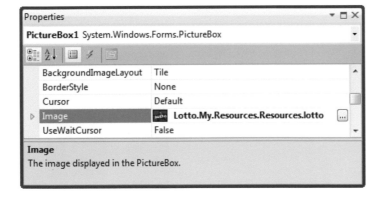

Beware

Remember to save your project periodically as you build it using File, Save All on the Menu Bar or Ctrl+Shift+S keys.

Designing the interface

Having assigned static property values, on the previous page, you can now design the interface layout.

The size of both the PictureBox1 control and the **PickBtn** control first needs to be adjusted to accommodate their content. This can easily be achieved by specifying an AutoSize value so that Visual Basic will automatically fit the control neatly around its content.

1 Select the PictureBox1 control then, in the Properties window, change its SizeMode property to "AutoSize"

2 Select the **PickBtn** control then, in the Properties window, set its AutoSize property to "True"

Now you can use the Form Designer's Format menu and Snap Lines to arrange the interface components to your liking.

3 Hold down the left mouse button and drag around the Labels to select all Label controls

4 Click Format, Align Tops on the Menu Bar to stack the Labels into a pile

5 Click Format, Horizontal Spacing, Make Equal to arrange the pile of Labels into a row

Don't forget

In this case it does not matter in what order the Labels appear in the row.

6 Use the Form's right grab handle to extend its width to accommodate the row of Labels and PictureBox1, then drag the row and both Buttons to top right of the Form

7 Drag the PictureBox1 control to top left of the Form, then use the Form's bottom grab handle to adjust its height to match that of the image

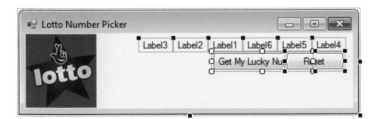

85

8 Use the Snap Lines that appear when you drag controls around the Form to position the row of Labels and the Buttons to make the interface look like this

Hot tip

Set the Form's MaximizeBox property to False if you do not wish to have Maximize and Minimize buttons on the interface.

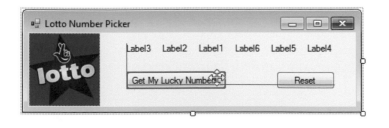

Initializing dynamic properties

Having designed the interface, on the previous page, you can now add some functionality to dynamically set the initial Text properties of the Label controls and the initial Button states.

1 Click View, Code on the Menu Bar, or press F7, to open the Code editor

2 Type the following code into the Declarations section then hit the Return key
Private Sub Clear

The Visual Basic IDE recognizes that you want to create a new subroutine called **Clear**. It automatically adds parameter parentheses after the Sub name and an **End Sub** line to create a subroutine code block.

3 With the cursor inside the new subroutine code block press Ctrl+J, to open the IntelliSense pop-up window

4 Scroll down the list of items in the IntelliSense window and double-click on the "Label1" item to add it into the **Clear** subroutine code block

Don't forget

The technique described here demonstrates how to use IntelliSense – but you can, of course, just type the code directly.

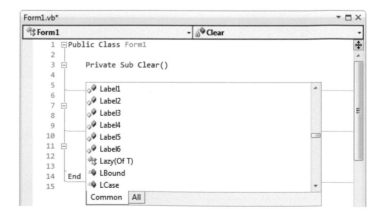

5 Type a period, then double-click the "Text" item when the IntelliSense window reappears to add that code

6   Now type = "..." to complete the line so it reads like this
Label1.Text = "..."

7   Repeat this procedure for the other Label controls – so that the **Clear** subroutine assigns each an ellipsis string

8   With the cursor inside the **Clear** Subroutine code block use IntelliSense in the same way to add these two lines
PickBtn.Enabled = True
ResetBtn.Enabled = False

This completes the **Clear** subroutine functionality by setting the Button states. All that remains is to add a call to the **Clear** subroutine to execute all its instructions when the program starts.

9   In the Form Designer double-click on the Form to open the Code Editor in its Load event-handler, then press Ctrl+J to open the IntelliSense window

10   Scroll down the list in the IntelliSense window and double-click on the "Clear" item you have just created

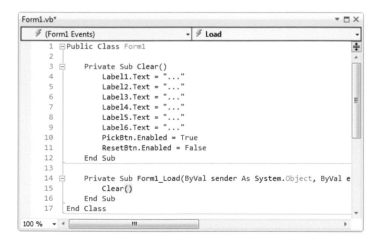

Hot tip

Add some line breaks and comments to make the code more friendly.

Adding runtime functionality

Having created code to initialize dynamic properties, on the previous page, you can now add runtime functionality to respond to clicks on the Buttons.

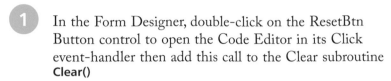

1 In the Form Designer, double-click on the ResetBtn Button control to open the Code Editor in its Click event-handler then add this call to the Clear subroutine
Clear()

This is all that is needed to provide dynamic functionality for the ResetBtn control. The main dynamic functionality of this application is provided by the PickBtn control which requires the random number generator to be started when the program starts

2 In the Form Designer, double-click on the Form to open the Code Editor in its Load event-handler then add this code to start the random number generator
Randomize()

Now you can create the code to provide dynamic functionality for the PickBtn control itself.

3 In the Form Designer, double-click on the PickBtn Button control to open the Code Editor in its Click event-handler then add this line to declare some variables
Dim i, r, temp, nums(50) As Integer

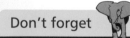

Don't forget

You don't need to understand in detail the algorithm that is used to shuffle the values.

4 Add a loop to fill the nums array elements 1-49 with the integer values 1 to 49
For i = 1 To 49
    nums(i) = i
Next

5 Add a second loop to shuffle the values contained in num elements 1-49 – an algorithm to randomize their order
For i = 1 To 49
    r = Int(49 * Rnd()) + 1
    temp = nums(i)
    nums(i) = nums(r)
    nums(r) = temp
Next

6 Now add the following lines to display the integer values contained in nums elements 1-6 in the Label controls
Label1.Text = nums(1)
Label2.Text = nums(2)
Label3.Text = nums(3)
Label4.Text = nums(4)
Label5.Text = nums(5)
Label6.Text = nums(6)

7 Finally, add these two lines to set the Button states ready to reset the application
PickBtn.Enabled = False
ResetBtn.Enabled = True

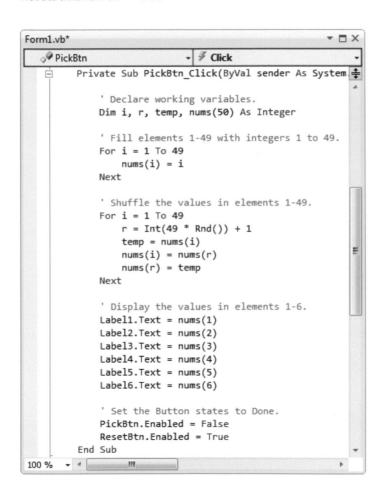

Beware

The variable declaration creates integer variables called "i", "r", and "temp", along with an integer array called "nums" of 50 elements. Element nums(0) is not actually used though.

Hot tip

Add comments and line breaks like these to clarify the intention of your code when read by someone else – or when you revisit the code later.

69

Testing the program

Having worked through the program plan, on the previous pages, the components needed and functionality required have now been added to the application – so it's ready to be tested.

①   Click the Start Debugging button, or press F5, to run the application and examine its initial start-up appearance

The Form's Load event-handler has set the initial dynamic values of each Label control and disabled the reset button as required.

②   Click the **PickBtn** Button control to execute the instructions within its Click event-handler

Hot tip

Notice that no number is repeated in any series.

A series of numbers within the desired range is displayed and the Button states have changed as required – a further series of numbers cannot be generated until the application has been reset.

③   Make a note of the numbers generated in this first series for comparison later

④   Click the **ResetBtn** control to execute the instructions within that Click event-handler and see the application return to its initial start-up appearance as required

5 Click the **PickBtn** Button control again to execute its Click event-handler code a second time

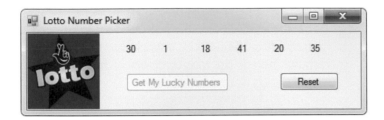

Another series of numbers within the desired range is displayed and are different to those in the first series when compared – good, the numbers are being randomized as required.

6 Click the Stop Debugging button then the Start Debugging button to restart the application and click the **PickBtn** Button control once more

The generated numbers in this first series of numbers are different to those noted in the first series the last time the application ran – great, the random number generator is not repeating the same sequence of number series each time the application runs.

Beware

Failing to call the Randomize() method to seed the Random Number Generator will cause the application to repeat the same sequence each time it runs.

Deploying the application

Having satisfactorily tested the application, on the previous page, you can now create a stand-alone version that can be executed outside the Visual Basic IDE and that can be distributed to others for deployment elsewhere.

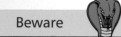

Beware

An application cannot be published unless it has been built first.

1. Click Debug, Build Lotto on the Menu Bar to build a release version of the application

2. Click Project, Publish Lotto to launch the Publish Wizard dialog

3. Use the wizard's Browse button to select a location where you wish to publish the application – the chosen location shown here is the root directory of removable drive G

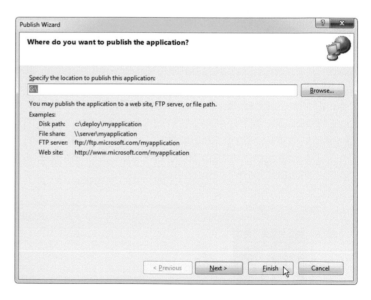

Hot tip

When choosing a publish location use the Create New Folder button in the File System dialog to make a folder to contain all the application files.

4. Click the Next button then select whether the user will install the application from a website, network, or portable media such as CD, DVD, or removable drive – in this case accept the default portable media option

5. Click the Next button then select whether the installer should check for application updates – accept the default option not to check for updates in this case

6 Click the Next button to move to the final dialog page, confirm the listed choices, then click the Finish button to publish the application at the specified location

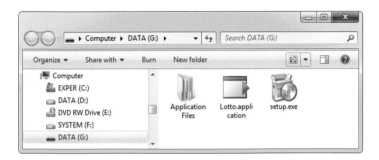

The Publish Wizard generates a number of files including a familiar "setup.exe" executable installer.

7 Move the portable media to the system where it is to be deployed then run **setup.exe** to install the application

When the application is installed on the client system a shortcut is automatically added to the Start Menu which can be used to launch the application. The user can then run the release version of the application just as it performed during testing of its debug version in the Visual Basic IDE.

The installer also adds an item to the client system's Add/Remove Programs list which can be used to uninstall the application – just like any other Windows program.

Summary

- Always make an initial program plan to avoid the need for time-consuming changes later

- A program plan should clearly define the program purpose, functionality required, and components needed

- Static properties, that will not change when the application is running, can be set at Designtime in the Properties Window

- An AutoSize property value makes Visual Basic automatically fit a control neatly around its content

- The Form Designer's Format menu contains useful features to quickly align and space multiple interface controls

- Snap Lines help you to easily align a selected control to others in the interface at Designtime

- Dynamic properties, that will change when the application is running, can be initialized with the Form's Load event-handler

- The pop-up IntelliSense window lets you easily add program code when using the Code Editor

- Runtime functionality responds to user actions by changing dynamic properties

- A Debug version of an application allows its functionality to be tested as the application is being created in text format

- The Build process compiles a Release version of an application in binary format

- The Publish process creates a final Release version with an installer so the application can be deployed elsewhere

- Applications created with the Visual Basic IDE can be installed and uninstalled just like other Windows applications

6 Solving problems

This chapter describes how to fix errors, debug code, handle exceptions, and get assistance from the Visual Basic Help system.

Real-time error detection

As you type code in the Code Editor window the Visual Basic IDE is constantly monitoring your code for possible errors. When you hit the Return key at the end of each line it examines the line you have just typed and provides realtime feedback of possible errors by adding a wavy underline to questionable code.

Warnings of potential problems are indicated by a green wavy underline. These are not critical and will not prevent execution of the application. A rollover ToolTip explains the warning.

1 In the Code Editor type the following variable declaration in a subroutine block, then hit Return
Dim num As Integer

```
Dim num As Integer
```

2 Place the cursor over the green wavy underline to discover that the warning is merely indicating of a potential problem as the variable has not yet been assigned a value

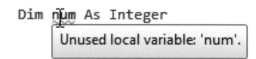

Errors are indicated by a blue wavy underline. Unlike warnings these are critical and will prevent execution of the application. A rollover ToolTip explains the error.

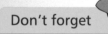

Don't forget

Warnings can be ignored but errors must be corrected.

1 In the Code Editor type the following variable declaration in a Sub routine block, then hit Return
Dim num As Integer =

```
Dim num As Integer =
```

2 Place the cursor over the blue wavy underline to discover that the error is due to a missing value in the expression

Real-time error detection in the Visual Basic IDE is a fantastic
tool to help prevent errors when you are writing code. It not only
indicates errors but can even provide a list of correction options.

1 In the Code Editor type the following variable
declaration in a Sub routine block, then hit Return
Dim num As Integr

```
Dim num As Integr
```

2 Notice that the blue wavy underline ends with a red box
to indicate possible corrections are available. Place the
cursor over the blue wavy underline to discover that the
error is due to an unknown data type specification

```
Dim num As Integr
```
Type 'Integr' is not defined.

3 Move the cursor over the red box to see an arrow button
appear offering error correction options

```
Dim num As Integr
```
Error Correction Options

97

4 Click the arrow button then choose an option to rectify
the error – see your code get corrected accordingly

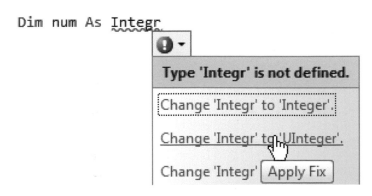

```
Dim num As Integr
```

Type 'Integr' is not defined.

Change 'Integr' to 'Integer'.

Change 'Integr' to 'UInteger'.

Change 'Integr' | Apply Fix

Hot tip

With the cursor over the
wavy underline you can
press Shift+Alt+F10
to reveal the list of
correction options.

Fixing compile errors

While syntax errors like those on the previous page can be detected by the Code Editor in realtime, other errors that employ correct syntax cannot be detected until the code is compiled. Compile errors are typically errors of logic and they cause the execution to halt when an "exception" occurs. For example, when incompatible data types appear in an expression an "InvalidCastException" occurs and execution stops immediately.

1 In the Code Editor type the following lines into a subroutine code block
Dim num As Double = 7.5
Dim str As String = "five"
MsgBox(num * str)

2 Click the Start Debugging button, or press F5, to run the Sub routine and see execution is soon halted. The line causing the exception becomes highlighted in the Code Editor and an Exception Assistant pop-up window appears with a list of possible solutions

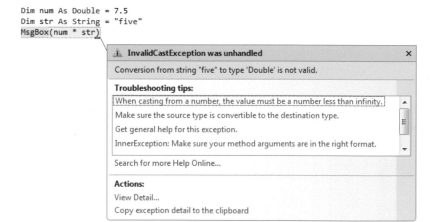

Hot tip

You can click on the View Details item in the Exception Assistant's Actions list for more error information.

To fix this InvalidCastException the code would obviously need amendment so both expression values are of the Double data type.

The cause of other compile errors may be less obvious without some further investigation. For example, when a loop that is reading array elements attempts to address an element index that does not exist, causing an "IndexOutOfRangeException".

Execution halts immediately so it is useful to examine the counter value to identify the precise iteration causing the compile error.

1 In the Code Editor type the following variable declaration and loop into a Sub routine code block
```
Dim i, nums(10) As Integer
For i = 1 to 20
        nums(i) = i
Next
```

2 Click the Start Debugging button, or press F5, to run the Sub routine and see execution is soon halted. The code causing the exception becomes highlighted in the Code Editor and an Exception Assistant pop-up window appears with a list of possible solutions

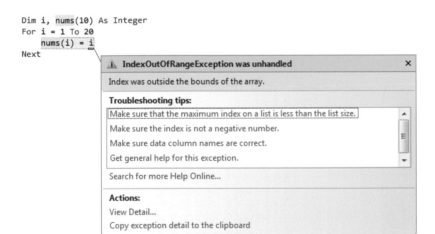

3 Place the cursor over the counter variable to see a pop-up appear showing its current value

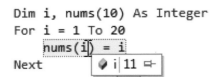

It's now clear that execution halted when the loop attempted to address nums(11) – beyond the bounds of last element nums(10). To fix this IndexOutOfRangeException the code would need amendment to end the loop after ten iterations.

Beware

Another common compile error is the FileNotFoundException that occurs when a file is missing or its path name is incorrect.

Debugging code

It is sometimes useful to closely examine the progression of a program by watching its execution line by line to locate any bugs. Progress is controlled by clicking the Step Into button on the Menu Bar, or by pressing the F8 key, to move through the entire program one line at a time. When you begin debugging you can also open a Watch window to monitor the value of particular variables as execution proceeds.

1 Double-click on a Form to open the Code Editor in its Load event-handler then add the following code
```
Dim i As Integer
Dim pass As Integer = 0
Dim base As Integer = 2
For i = 1 To 2
        pass = pass + 1
        base = Square( base )
Next
```

2 Now add the Square function into the Declarations section of the code with these lines
```
Function Square(ByVal num As Integer)
        num = num * num
        Return num
End Function
```

3 Click the Step Into button once, or press F8, to begin debugging

Don't forget

You can click the Stop Debugging button at any time to return to normal Code Editor mode.

4 Click Debug, Windows, Watch on the Menu Bar to launch the Watch window

5 Type the variable name "pass" into the Name column and hit Return, then repeat to add the "base" variable name

Watch		▾ □ ✕
Name	Value	Type ▲
◈ pass	0	Integer
◈ base	0	Integer
		▾

6 Click Step Into five times to reach the Square function call in the first loop iteration and note the variable values

```
For i = 1 To 2
    pass = pass + 1
    base = Square(base)
Next
```

Watch			▼ ❏ ✕
Name	Value	Type	▲
⬦ pass	1	Integer	
⬦ base	2	Integer	
			▼

7 Click Step Into eight more times to progress through each line of the Square function and the loop, returning to the function call on the second iteration

```
For i = 1 To 2
    pass = pass + 1
    base = Square(base)
Next
```

Watch			▼ ❏ ✕
Name	Value	Type	▲
⬦ pass	2	Integer	
⬦ base	4	Integer	
			▼

8 Click Step Over once to execute the function without stepping through each line

```
For i = 1 To 2
    pass = pass + 1
    base = Square(base)
Next
```

Watch			▼ ❏ ✕
Name	Value	Type	▲
⬦ pass	2	Integer	
⬦ base	16	Integer	
			▼

Hot tip

The Step Out button is used to return to the function caller when you are stepping through lines of a called function.

Setting debug breakpoints

In all but the smallest of programs stepping through each line is very tedious when debugging. Instead, you can quickly reach the part you wish to examine by setting a "breakpoint" to halt execution on a particular line. Setting one or more breakpoints is useful to help you understand how certain Visual Basic code constructs work – such as the nested loop construct shown here.

1 Double click on a Form to open the Code Editor in its Load event-handler and type this code

```
Dim i, j, k As Integer
Dim pass As Integer = 0
For i = 1 To 3
        For j = 1 To 3
                For k = 1 To 3
                        pass = pass + 1
                Next
        Next
Next
```

2 In the Code Editor click in the gray margin against each line containing the Next keyword to set three breakpoints – a red dot will appear in the margin and each Next statement is highlighted to indicate the set breakpoints

3 Click the Start Debugging button, or press F5, and the application will run to the first breakpoint it meets

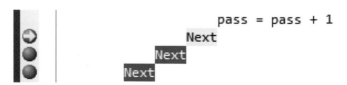

4 Click Debug, Windows, Locals to launch the Locals window and notice the current value of each variable

...cont'd

Watch			
Name	Value	Type	
⊞ ◆ me	{WindowsApplication 🔍 ▾	WindowsApplication	
⊞ ◆ e	{System.EventArgs}	System.EventArgs	
◆ i	1	Integer	
◆ j	1	Integer	
◆ k	1	Integer	
◆ pass	1	Integer	
⊞ ◆ sender	{WindowsApplication 🔍 ▾	Object	

5. Watch the variable values change as you repeatedly click the Start Debugging button to move to each next breakpoint until you reach the third outer **Next** statement, then click Step Into to reach the end of the subroutine

```
              Next
          Next
      Next

   End Sub
```

Watch			
Name	Value	Type	
⊞ ◆ me	{WindowsApplication 🔍 ▾	WindowsApplication	
⊞ ◆ e	{System.EventArgs}	System.EventArgs	
◆ i	4	Integer	
◆ j	4	Integer	
◆ k	4	Integer	
◆ pass	27	Integer	
⊞ ◆ sender	{WindowsApplication 🔍 ▾	Object	

At the end of the subroutine each counter variable has been incremented beyond the upper limit set in the For statements, to exit each loop, and there has been a total of 27 iterations (3x3x3).

6. Click Stop Debugging to finish, then click Start Debugging to once more run to the first breakpoint

7. Click Debug, Windows, Immediate, or press Ctrl+G, to launch the Immediate window

8. In the Immediate window type i = 3 and hit Return, then use the Step Into button to step through each line of the final complete outer loop iteration

Don't forget

The locals window shows all variables in current scope as the program proceeds.

103

Hot tip

Any code you type into the Immediate window is dynamically applied to the application being debugged but does not change its code. Try typing MsgBox("Hi") into the Immediate window, then hit the Return key.

Detecting runtime errors

While the Code Editor provides real-time detection of syntax errors, and the compiler provides detection of logic errors, it is the responsibility of the programmer to anticipate user actions that may cause runtime errors when the application is in use. Consideration of all different ways a user could employ your application is important to predict potential runtime errors.

1. In a new project add Label, TextBox, and Button controls to a Form so it looks like this

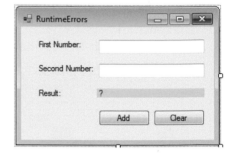

2. Name the yellow Label "ResultLbl"

3. Double-click on the Add button to open the Code Editor in its Click event-handler then type the code below to create a simple adding machine

```
Dim num1 As Integer = Val( TextBox1.Text )
Dim num2 As Integer = Val( TextBox2.Text )
ResultLbl.Text = num1 + num2
```

4. Click Save All, note the location where the project is being saved, then close the Visual Basic IDE

5. Navigate to the project location and double-click on the executable file in its /bin/Debug folder to run the application outside the Visual Basic IDE

6. Enter numeric values into each text field then click the Add button to see the application perform as expected

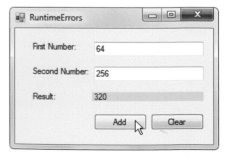

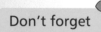

Don't forget

Adding floating point values with this application will produce a result rounded to the nearest integer.

7 Now try adding large numbers like those shown here – an error will occur and the system will halt the program, complaining of an overflow

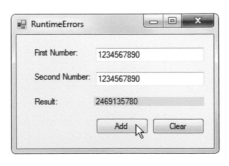

```
ResultLbl.Text = num1 + num2
```

OverflowException was unhandled   ×

Arithmetic operation resulted in an overflow.

Troubleshooting tips:

Make sure you are not dividing by zero.

Get general help for this exception.

Search for more Help Online...

Actions:

View Detail...

Copy exception detail to the clipboard

While the programmer may not have intended the application to be used to add such large numbers it is possible the user may wish to do so – and this possibility should have been considered in order to predict this type of runtime error. The overflow has, in fact, occurred because the Integer data type can only store numeric values up to around two billion. This problem can be fixed by changing the variables to use a Long data type instead.

8 Quit the application then edit the Add button's Click event-handler to read like this
Dim num1 As Long = Val(TextBox1.Text)
Dim num2 As Long = Val(TextBox2.Text)
ResultLbl.Text = num1 + num2

9 Save the amended project then run the application and try to add the two long numbers again

Hot tip

The precise value range of the Integer data type is -2,147,483,648 through 2,147,483,647.

Catching runtime errors

When you are able to predict potential runtime errors by considering all eventualities you can provide code to handle exceptions that may arise with a Try Catch code block. Your program can supply information to the user about the error, should you wish to do so, then proceed normally. This technique could be used to provide code to handle the exception that arose in the previous example instead of the fix suggested.

1 Repeat steps 1, 2 and 3 on page 104 to recreate the simple adding machine application then click the Start Debugging button, or press F5, to run the application in Debug mode

2 Enter two long numbers then click the Add button to attempt the addition – the compiler reports that an OverflowException has occurred

```
Dim num1 As Integer = Val(TextBox1.Text)
Dim num2 As Integer = Val(TextBox2.Text)
ResultLbl.Text = num1 + num2
```

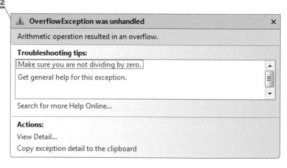

Hot tip

You can use the right-click context menu to quickly switch between the Code Editor and Form Designer.

3 Click the Stop Debugging button so you can edit the code

4 Right-click in the Add button's Click event-handler code block then choose Insert Snippet, Common Code Patterns, Error Handling from the context menu

5 Double-click Try...Catch..End Try Statement to paste a Try Catch code block into the Code Editor

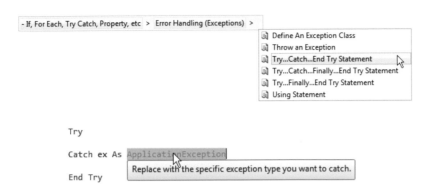

Hot tip

Insert Snippet contains lots of useful pieces of code to paste into the Code Editor – take some time to explore its contents.

6 Type OverflowException in place of ApplicationException in the pasted code block

7 Cut'n'paste the original lines of code to put them between the Try and Catch lines

8 Add this code between the Catch and End Try lines MsgBox("Only numbers up to 2 Billion are allowed")

```
Try
    Dim num1 As Integer = Val(TextBox1.Text)
    Dim num2 As Integer = Val(TextBox2.Text)
    ResultLbl.Text = num1 + num2

Catch ex As OverflowException

    MsgBox("Only numbers up to 2 Billion are allowed")

End Try
```

Hot tip

Try adding code to handle the exceptions on page 98 and 99 instead of the suggested fixes.

9 Click Start Debugging then enter long numbers as before and click the Add button to see the exception handled

10 Click OK to close the Message Box then change the numbers to be within the range allowed and click the Add button to proceed normally

Getting help

The Visual Basic Help system is a Library providing an extensive source of reference to help resolve most problems. The Help Library can be accessed from the Help menu or by pressing the Ctrl+F1 keys. But before the Help Library can be accessed for the very first time you must choose whether to use local or online sources – online is best unless you don't have a broadband Internet connection. You can edit the sources you prefer to use at any time.

1 Press Ctrl+Alt+F1 to start the Help Library Manager

2 In the Help Library Manager window click the link to "Choose online or local help"

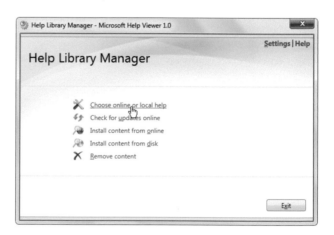

Hot tip

The Help Library Manager also allows you to download the Help Library for offline use, check for available updates, and install the Library locally if you have it on a disk.

3 Now check the option stating "I want to use online help", then click the OK button to apply that setting

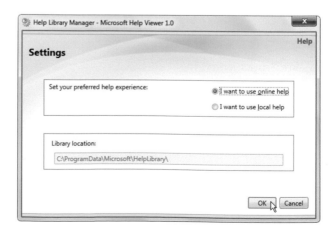

The Help Library documentation can be searched for answers to your Visual Basic coding questions. For example, you might need to discover all data types available in Visual Basic programming.

1 With an Internet connection click Help, View Help on the Menu Bar, or press Ctrl+F1, to open the Help Library start page in your default web browser

2 Type **data types visual basic** into the search box then click the search button to perform the search

3 When the search returns the results click on the link to "Data Types in Visual Basic"

109

Hot tip

You can also click the "MSDN Forums" item on the Help menu to ask programming questions on the MSDN forums, and CodeZone Community websites specialize in Microsoft coding – take a look at VBCity.com for help with Visual Basic.

Beware

The Help Library is common to other Microsoft programming products – be sure that search results relate to Visual Basic only.

Summary

- The Code Editor constantly monitors your code to provide realtime error detection

- Warnings are not critical and are indicated by a green wavy underline – whereas errors are critical and are indicated by a blue wavy underline

- A red box at the end of a blue wavy underline indicates that a list of possible corrections is available

- Typically, real-time errors are errors of syntax and compile errors are errors of logic

- When a compile error occurs in Debug Mode execution stops and the Exception Assistant offers a list of possible fixes

- In Debug Mode you can discover the current value of any variable simply by placing the cursor over the variable name

- The Step Into button lets you walk through a program one line at a time

- The Step Over button lets you bypass the lines of a called function and the Step Out button lets you return to the line where that function is called

- Variable values can be monitored as a program proceeds using the Watch window or the Locals window

- Breakpoints halt the execution of a program to allow examination of the part of the program where they are set

- In Debug Mode code can be dynamically applied using the Immediate window

- Runtime errors occur when the user action has not been anticipated by the programmer

- Use a Try Catch block to handle anticipated exceptions

- The Help Library system provides extensive reference sources and online assistance

7

Extending the interface

This chapter demonstrates how applications can incorporate dialogs, menus, multiple forms, and Windows Media Player.

Color, Font & Image dialogs

The Visual Basic IDE makes it simple to add the ability to call upon the standard Windows selection dialogs so the user can choose options within your applications. For example, selection of colors, fonts, and images.

1 Start a new Windows project and add a PictureBox, TextBox, and three Button controls to the Form

2 Name the Buttons **ColorBtn**, **FontBtn**, and **ImgBtn**

3 From the Dialogs section of the Toolbox add a ColorDialog, FontDialog, and OpenFileDialog component to the Form – see them appear in the Component Tray at the bottom of the Form Designer

4 Double-click on the **ColorBtn** Button and add this code to its Click event-handler
```
If ColorDialog1.ShowDialog = _
        Windows.Forms.DialogResult.OK Then
        Me.BackColor = ColorDialog1.Color
End If
```

5 Double-click on the **FontBtn** Button and add this code to its Click event-handler
```
If FontDialog1.ShowDialog = _
        Windows.Forms.DialogResult.OK Then
        TextBox1.Font = FontDialog1.Font
End If
```

6 Double-click on the **ImgBtn** Button and add this code to its Click event-handler

```
If OpenFileDialog1.ShowDialog = _
        Windows.Forms.DialogResult.OK Then
  Try
        PictureBox1.Image = _
        New Bitmap(OpenFileDialog1.FileName)
  Catch ex As ArgumentException
        MsgBox("Not an image")
  End Try
End If
```

7 Click on the Start Debugging button, or press F5, to run the application then click the **ColorBtn** Button to launch the familiar Windows Color selection dialog

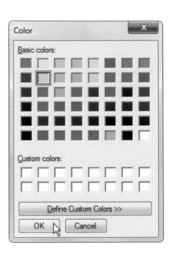

8 Choose a color then click the OK button to apply it to the Form's background

Beware

The OpenFileDialog allows the user to select any file. The Try Catch statement handles the ArgumentException that is thrown if the user chooses a file type that is not an image.

9 Type some text in the TextBox then click the **FontBtn** Button and choose a Font for that text

10 Click the **ImgBtn** Button then browse to select an image to assign to the PictureBox control

Open, Save & Print dialogs

Applications created with Visual Basic can call upon the standard Windows selection dialogs to allow the user to open, save and print files.

1 Start a new Windows project and add a RichTextBox control and three Buttons to the Form – name the Buttons **OpenBtn**, **SaveBtn**, and **PrintBtn**

2 From the Dialogs section of the Toolbox add an OpenFileDialog and SaveFileDialog component, then add a PrintDialog component from the Printing section of the Toolbox – see them appear in the Component Tray at the bottom of the Form Designer

3 Double-click on the **OpenBtn** and add this code to its Click event-handler

```
With OpenFileDialog1
        .Title = "Open File"
        .Filter = "Rich Text Files | *.rtf"
        .FileName = ""
        .CheckFileExists = True
End With

If OpenFileDialog1.ShowDialog = _
        Windows.Forms.DialogResult.OK Then
RichTextBox1.LoadFile(OpenFileDialog1.FileName, _
RichTextBoxStreamType.RichText)
End If
```

Hot tip

Always define filter options to determine which file types the OpenFileDialog can see.

4 Double-click on the **PrintBtn** and add this code

```
If PrintDialog1.ShowDialog = _
        Windows.Forms.DialogResult.OK Then
        ' Insert code here to process and print.
End If
```

5 Double-click on the **SaveBtn** and add this code to its
Click event-handler

```
With SaveFileDialog1
        .Title = "Save File"
        .Filter = "Rich Text Files | *.rtf"
        .DefaultExt = ".rtf"
        .OverWritePrompt = True
End With

If SaveFileDialog1.ShowDialog = _
        Windows.Forms.DialogResult.OK Then
RichTextBox1.SaveFile(SaveFileDialog1.FileName, _
        RichTextBoxStreamType.RichText)
End If
```

6 Click on the Start Debugging button, or press F5, then
use the **OpenBtn** Button to launch the Windows Open
File dialog

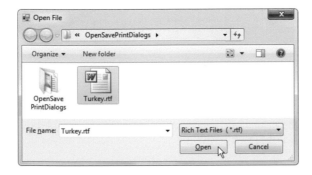

7 Choose a Rich Text Format file then click Open to load
it in the RichTextBox control

8 Click the **SaveBtn**
Button to launch
the Save File dialog
and save the loaded
file with a different
name

9 Click on the PrintBtn Button to launch the familiar
Windows Print dialog where you can select Printer
preferences before printing

Beware

The Print dialog does not
automatically know how
to print the document
– you need to provide
code to enable printing.
See page 151 for an
example of how to print
plain text documents.

115

Creating application menus

Dropdown menus, toolbars, and status bars, like those found in most Windows applications, can easily be added to your own Visual Basic applications from the Toolbox.

1 Find the Menus & Toolbars section of the Toolbox then double-click the MenuStrip item to add it to the Form

2 Click the MenuStrip's arrow button on its Smart Tag then select the option to **Insert Standard Items**

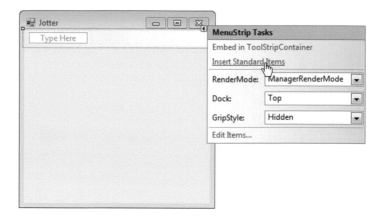

3 When the familiar headings and items have been added to the MenuStrip right-click on any item and use the context menu to edit that item. Also type new custom items into the Type Here boxes as required

Don't forget

You can create your own custom menus using the Type Here boxes instead of Insert Standard Items.

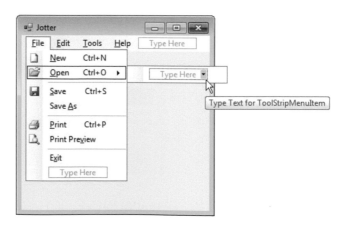

4 In the Toolbox, double-click on the ToolStrip item to add it to the Form then click its Smart Tag button and once more select **Insert Standard Items**

5 When the familiar icon buttons have been added to the ToolStrip right-click on any item and use the context menu to edit that item. Also add further custom items from the dropdown list as required

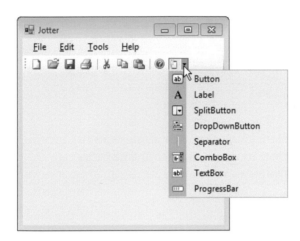

6 In the Toolbox, double-click on the StatusStrip item to add it to the Form

7 Select the StatusLabel item from the StatusStrip's dropdown list, then set its text property to "Ready"

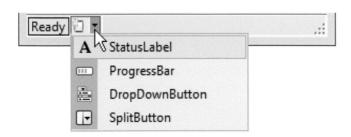

Hot tip

Use StatusBar messages to provide feedback to the user.

8 Add a RichTextBox control to the center of the Form, click its Smart Tag button and select the option to **Dock in parent container**, then ensure that its ScrollBars property is set to **Both**

Making menus work

The menu items and toolbar buttons created on the previous page will not perform their desired actions until you add some code to make them work. For actions that feature both in a menu and on a toolbar button it is best to create a Sub routine that can be called from the menu item's Click event-handler and the button's Click event-handler – to avoid duplication.

1. In Form Designer click File, New to select the New menu item

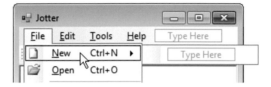

2. Double-click on the New menu item to open the Code Editor in its event-handler and add this call
NewFile()

3. Immediately below the End Sub line of the New menu item's event-handler add this custom Sub routine
Private Sub NewFile()
RichTextBox1.Text = ""
ToolStripStatusLabel1.Text = "Ready"
End Sub

4. Return to the Form Designer then double-click on the New toolbar button to open the Code Editor in that event-handler and add a call to the custom Sub routine
NewFile()

5. Add an OpenFileDialog and SaveFileDialog component from the Dialogs section of the Toolbox

6. In the Click event-handlers of both the Open menu item and the Open toolbar button add this code
OpenFile()

7 Immediately below the End Sub line of the Open menu item's event-handler add this custom Sub routine

```
Private Sub OpenFile()
OpenFileDialog1.Filter = "Text Files | *.txt"
If OpenFileDialog1.ShowDialog = _
        Windows.Forms.DialogResult.OK Then
RichTextBox1.LoadFile(OpenFileDialog1.FileName, _
        RichTextBoxStreamType.PlainText) End If
End Sub
```

8 In the Click event-handlers of both the Save menu item and the Save toolbar button add this code

```
SaveFile()
```

9 Immediately below the End Sub line of the Save menu item's event-handler add this custom Sub routine

```
Private Sub SaveFile()
SaveFileDialog1.Filter = "Text Files | *.txt"
If SaveFileDialog1.ShowDialog = _
        Windows.Forms.DialogResult.OK Then
RichTextBox1.SaveFile(SaveFileDialog1.FileName, _
        RichTextBoxStreamType.PlainText)  End If
End Sub
```

10 Run the application and test the functionality of the New, Open, and Save file menu items and toolbar buttons

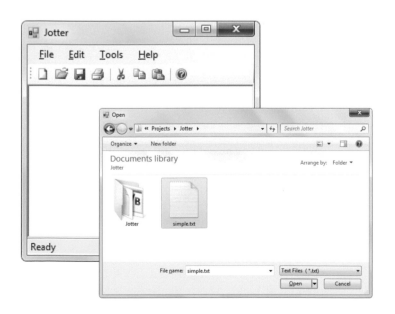

Adding more forms

Most Windows applications have more than one Form – even the simplest application usually has an About dialog, and perhaps a Splash Screen, to provide version information to the user. These can easily be added to your applications in Visual Basic.

1 Click Project, Add New Item on the Menu Bar, to launch the Add New Item dialog, then select the About Box icon and click the Add button – see a new Form file called **AboutBox1.vb** get added in the Solution Explorer

2 In Solution Explorer right-click on the top project icon then select Properties from the context menu, or click Project, Properties on the Menu Bar, to open the Project Designer window

3 In the Project Designer's Application tab, click the Assembly Information button and modify the Copyright, Description, and Company fields to your preference, then click the OK button

4 In Form Designer double-click on the About item in the Help menu then add this code to its Click event-handler
AboutBox1.ShowDialog()

5 Click Start Debugging, or press F5, to run the application then click Help, About to see the About dialog

Adding a Splash Screen

1 Click Project, Add New Item on the Menu Bar, to launch the Add New Item dialog, then select the Splash Screen icon and click the Add button – see a new Form called **SplashScreen1.vb** get added in Solution Explorer

2 In Solution Explorer right-click on the top project icon then select Properties from the context menu, or click Project, Properties on the Menu Bar, to open the Project Designer window

3 Open the Splash Screen dropdown list at the bottom of the Project Designer window and select **SplashScreen1**

Splash screen:

(None)	▼
(None)	
AboutBox1	
SplashScreen1	

4 Click Start Debugging, or press F5, to run the application and see a splash screen display for about two seconds before the main Form appears

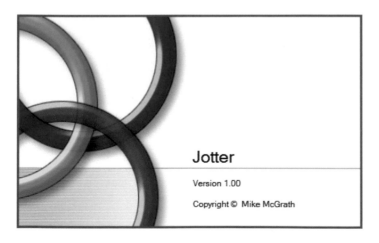

Jotter

Version 1.00

Copyright © Mike McGrath

Don't forget

The Splash Screen and About dialog are similar – both display information from the Assembly Information but less detail is shown in the Splash Screen because it is only displayed briefly.

Controlling multiple forms

Applications sometimes need more than one Form to accommodate the user interface. When the user moves to the second Form the first one can be hidden so any information it contains will remain in memory and reappear when the user returns to that Form. Similarly, the second Form can be hidden so any user input it contains is available to the program when the user returns to the first Form. Alternatively the second Form can be closed when the user returns to the first Form but any user input will then be lost unless it has been stored in variables.

1 Add two Buttons and Labels to a Form so it looks like this and name the yellow Label **ValueLbl**

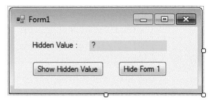

2 Click Project, Add New Item and add another Windows Form to the project

3 Add two Buttons and a TextBox to this Form, naming the Buttons as **CloseBtn** and **HideBtn**

Hot tip

Consider using multiple Forms when the application interface becomes cluttered with many controls.

4 In Form Designer double-click on the "Hide Form 1" Button in Form 1 and add this code to its Click event-handler
Me.Hide()
Form2.Show()

5 Now double-click on the "Show Hidden Value" Button in Form 1 and add this code to that Click event-handler
ValueLbl.Text = Form2.TextBox1.Text

6 In Form Designer double-click on the "Hide Form 2" Button in Form 2 and add this code to its Click event-handler
Me.Hide()
Form1.Show()

7 Now double-click on the "Close Form 2" Button in Form 2 and add this code to that Click event-handler
Me.Close()
Form1.Show()

8 Click Start Debugging, or press F5, to run the application and click the "Hide Form 1" Button – Form 1 disappears and Form 2 appears

9 Type something into the TextBox then click on the "Hide Form 2" Button – Form 2 disappears, and Form 1 reappears

10 Click the "Show Hidden Value" Button in Form 1 – the text you typed into the TextBox in Form 2 gets copied into the **ValueLbl** Label in Form 1

11 Click "Hide Form 1" once more then type something else in the TextBox and click the "Close Form 2" button

12 Click the "Show Hidden Value" Button in Form 1 again – nothing is displayed in the **ValueLbl** Label as your input has been lost

123

Hot tip

Try creating a variable to store the value in the TextBox when Form 2 gets closed so the user input can be recalled.

Playing sounds

Sound files can be included within an application as a resource, in much the same way that image files can be imported as a resource, to enhance the application. These can then be played, as required, by calling upon the Windows Media Player on the local system.

1 Start a new Windows Application project and add a single Button control to the Form

2 In Solution Explorer, right-click on the top project icon then choose Properties from the context menu to open the Project Designer window

3 In Project Designer select the Resources side tab, then the Audio item from the dropdown list

4 Select the Add Existing File... item from the Add Resource dropdown list to launch the Add File dialog

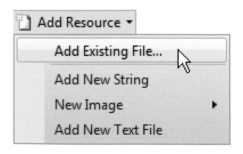

5 Browse to the location of the sound file you wish to add then click the Add button – see the sound file **tada.wav** get added to the Resources folder in Solution Explorer

6 Click the X button to close the Project Designer and click Yes when asked if you want to save changes

7 Click View, Code, or press F7, to open the Code Editor then add this line to the Declarations section
Friend WithEvents player _
      As New System.Media.SoundPlayer

8 In Form Designer double-click on the Button then add the following code to its Click event-handler
player.Stream = My.Resources.tada
player.Play()

9 Click Start Debugging, or press F5, to run the application, then click the Button to play the sound

Playing multimedia

A Visual Basic application can employ an ActiveX instance of the Windows Media Player to play all types of local media files within the application interface.

1 Start a new Windows Application and add a Button control to the Form and an OpenFileDialog component

2 In the Toolbox right-click on the Components section and select Choose Items from the context menu

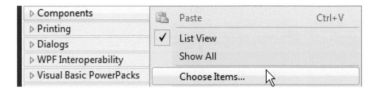

3 When the Choose Toolbox Items dialog appears click its **COM Components** tab, then check **Windows Media Player** and click OK – a new Windows Media Player item gets added to the Toolbox Components section

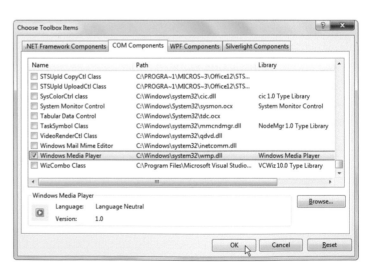

Don't forget

The Common Object Model (COM) is a standard platform that allows components to be easily shared.

4 From the Toolbox, add a Windows Media Player component to the Form and resize it so its display and controls are fully visible – note that the component is called **AxWindowsMediaPlayer1**

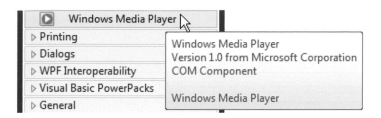

5 In Form Designer, double-click on the Button to open the Code Editor in its Click event-handler and add the following code

```
With OpenFileDialog1
  .Title = "Media File Browser"
  .Filter = "Media Files (*.wmv;*.mp3)|*.wmv;*.mp3"
  .FileName = ""
  .CheckFileExists = True
End With

If OpenFileDialog1.ShowDialog = _
        Windows.Forms.DialogReult.OK Then
AxWindowsMediaPlayer1.URL = _
        OpenFileDialog1.Filename
End If
```

6 Run the application then click the Button control to launch the OpenFileDialog and choose a valid media file – see it start playing in the application interface

Summary

- The Dialogs section of the Toolbox contains components that can be added to an application to call upon the standard Windows dialogs to select Colors, Fonts, Images, and Files

- Open File and Save File dialogs can be configured to filter file types so they only display files of a specified file extension

- A Print dialog allows the user to select printer options but it cannot automatically print

- Familiar menus can easily be added to an application using the Insert Standard Items option of the MenuStrip component

- The ToolStrip component provides familiar toolbar icons

- You can add a StatusStrip component to provide an application status bar to display feedback to the user

- Where both MenuStrip and ToolStrip components appear in an application it is best to create Sub routines to be called when the user chooses a menu item or associated icon

- A MenuStrip component automatically provides keyboard shortcuts for each of its menu items

- The Add New Item option on the Project menu can be used to add a Form, About Box dialog, and Splash Screen

- Multiple forms can be controlled using their **Show()**, **Hide()**, and **Close()** methods

- Applications can be enhanced by including audio files in their Resources folder to provide sound

- Windows COM components can be added to the standard selection of components on the Visual Basic Toolbox

- An ActiveX instance of Windows Media Player can be added to an interface to allow the application to play multimedia files

8

Scripting with Visual Basic

This chapter illustrates how Visual Basic may be used outside the Visual Basic IDE to add functionality to Microsoft Office applications and to add interactive features to web pages.

An introduction to VBA macros

Visual Basic for Applications (VBA) is the programming language built into Microsoft Office applications. It shares the same core Visual Basic language as that in the Visual Basic IDE but has different available objects in each application – Word has an ActiveDocument object and Excel has an ActiveSheet object.

Where Microsoft Office is installed on a system all Office objects are available across all versions of Visual Basic. So you can program Word from Excel, or from a standalone application created in the Visual Basic IDE.

VBA has a Form Designer and Debugger much like those in the Visual Basic IDE but with a more limited set of features.

Hot tip

Most VBA keyboard shortcuts are the same as in the Visual Basic IDE – F5 to run, etc.

Form Designer

Toolbox

Code Editor

Run Button   Properties Window   Project Window

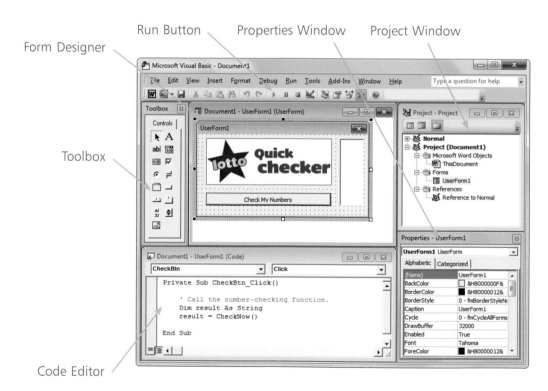

You cannot create standalone executable applications with Visual Basic for Applications, as it has no native code compiler, but you can create a script, hidden within the document file, to execute a series of instructions upon the document. This is known as a "macro" and is typically used to automate a task you perform regularly that requires multiple commands. For example, to insert a table with a specific style and number of rows and columns.

1 Launch Microsoft Word, or any other Office 2007 application, then click the Developer tab and choose the Visual Basic ribbon icon to launch the Visual Basic Editor

2 In the Visual Basic Editor, click Insert, Module to open the Code Editor window

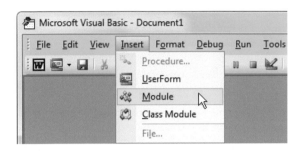

3 In the Code Editor, type this Visual Basic subroutine
Private Sub Hello()
  MsgBox("Hello from VBA!")
End Sub

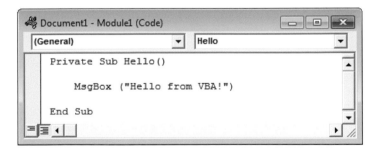

4 In the Visual Basic Editor, click the Run button or press F5 to execute the subroutine – the Visual Basic Editor gets minimized until you click the OK button in the Message Box

Hot tip

If the Developer tab is not visible click the Office button, then Word Options, and select the "Show Developer tab in the Ribbon" checkbox from Popular options.

Hot tip

For earlier versions of Office the Visual Basic Editor is launched from the Tools, Macros menu.

131

Creating a Word macro

Bookmarks can be inserted into a Word document to indicate the position at which a macro should insert content.

1 Open a new document in Word, type this book's title, then use Insert, Links, Bookmark to add a bookmark – and name it "mark"

2 Click Developer, Visual Basic, or press Alt+F11, to launch the Visual Basic Editor

3 In the Visual Basic Editor, click Insert, Module to open the Code Editor window

4 Now type the following code into the Code Editor

```
Sub AddTable()
  If ActiveDocument.Bookmarks.Exists("mark") Then
  ActiveDocument.Bookmarks("mark").Select
  Set tbl = ActiveDocument.Tables.Add(Range:= _
    Selection.Range, NumRows:=3, NumColumns:=9)
  tbl.AutoFormat Format:=wdTableFormatClassic2
  End If
End Sub
```

5 Click the Run button, or press F5, to run the macro – see a formatted table appear at the bookmark position

Hot tip

You can use the Undo button in Word to reverse the two steps performed by VBA to Add and Format this table.

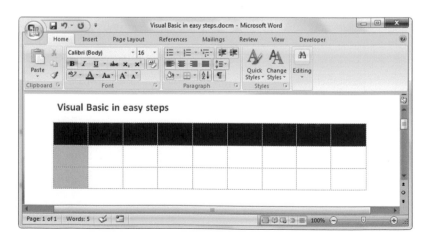

When you have created a macro that you wish to make available for use in other documents the macro can be stored inside Word's master template **Normal.dotm** and added as a Word menu item.

1 Select Developer, Macros to open the Macros dialog, then click the Organizer button

2 Choose the Macro Project Items tab, select the macro module from the current document list, then click the Copy button to copy the macro to **Normal.dotm**

3 Close the Organizer and the current document then start a new document and insert a bookmark named "mark"

4 Click the Word Quick Access toolbar button and choose "Customize Quick Access Toolbar", "More Commands" to launch the Options dialog

5 In the Options, Customize dialog, select to Choose Commands from Macros, then Add the **AddTable** module and click OK to add an icon to the Quick Access Toolbar

6 Click the newly added **AddTable** macro icon on the Quick Access Toolbar to run the macro – once more adding a formatted table at the bookmark position

Hot tip

The Run button on the Macros dialog can be used to run any macro stored in Normal.dotm – without creating a custom menu item.

Creating an Excel macro

Values can be inserted into cells of an Excel spreadsheet by a macro that uses a loop to move through a range of cells.

1 Open a worksheet in Excel then click Developer, Visual Basic, or press Alt+F11, to launch the Visual Basic Editor

2 In the the Visual Basic Editor, click Insert, Module to open the Code Editor window

3 Now type the following code into the Code Editor

```
Private Sub AddMonthNames()
Dim i As Integer
i = 0
Do Until i = 12
        Set currentCell = ActiveSheet.Cells( _
          ActiveCell.Row + i , ActiveCell.Column)
        i = i + 1
        currentCell.Font.Bold = True
        currentCell.Font.Color = vbRed
        currentCell.Value = MonthName( i )
Loop
End Sub
```

4 Select any cell in the worksheet then click the Run button, or press F5, to run the macro – see bold red month names appear in cells down the current column, starting at the selected cell

Don't forget

VBA has a small range of color constants, like the vbRed constant seen here. Refer to VBA Help to discover a full list.

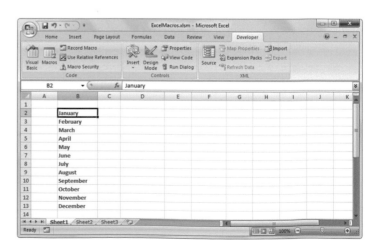

Excel macros can be run automatically when a Worksheet gets loaded, or manually using a keyboard shortcut or Button control.

1 In the Project Window, right-click on the **ThisWorkbook** icon and choose View Code from the context menu

2 From the dropdown list at the top of the Code Editor select the Workbook item then add this code
Private Sub Workbook_Open()
MsgBox("Workbook opened at "+ Str(Time))
End Sub

3 Close the Visual Basic Editor then click Macros, Options and add a shortcut key letter of your choice to the **Ctrl+** statement in the Options dialog

4 On the Developer tab click Insert, ActiveX button control then click an empty cell to place a Button control there

5 Double-click the Button control to open the Code Editor in its Click event-handler then add this Call statement
Call AddMonthNames()

6 Save the changes and close the worksheet – reopen the worksheet to see the MessageBox appear then use the Button, or your keyboard shortcut, to run the macro

Hot tip

Use the Design Mode button on the Developer tab when you want to edit or move controls on a worksheet.

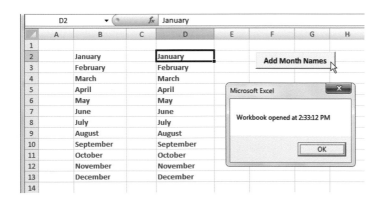

Running advanced macros

More advanced macros can be created to control one Office application from within another. Typically you may want to include information from an Excel spreadsheet within a Word document using a macro to get the information automatically.

1 Open Excel and add some data in cell B2. Name this cell "Total", then save the Workbook as "Sales.xlsx" in your Documents folder and close Excel

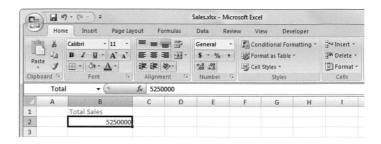

2 Start a new Word document then insert a Bookmark and also name it "Total" – it doesn't need to have the same name as the Excel cell but it is convenient

3 Open the Visual Basic Editor then click Tools, References to launch the References dialog – check the reference for the Microsoft Excel Object Library then click OK

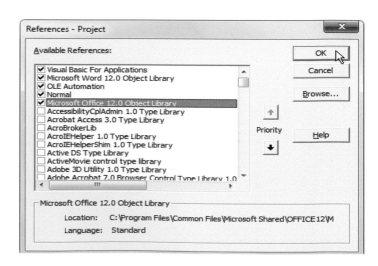

4 In the the Visual Basic Editor, click Insert, Module to open the Code Editor window

5 Now type the following code into the Code Editor, modifying the path to suit the location of your "Sales.xlsx"

```
Private Sub GetTotal()
Set xl = CreateObject("Excel.Application")
xl.Workbooks.Open ("C:\Users\Mike\Documents\Sales.xlsx")
xl.Worksheets("Sheet1").Activate
ActiveDocument.Bookmarks("Total").Select

Dim sum As String
sum = FormatCurrency( _
        xl.ActiveSheet.Range("Total").Value, 0)
Selection.InsertAfter (sum)

xl.Workbooks.Close
Set xl = Nothing
End Sub
```

Hot tip

The named cell in this example can alternatively be addressed as xl.ActiveSheet.Cells(2,2) – row 2 and column 2.

6 Click the Run button, or press F5, to run the macro and see the value retrieved from the Excel cell get formatted into the local currency and appear in the Word document

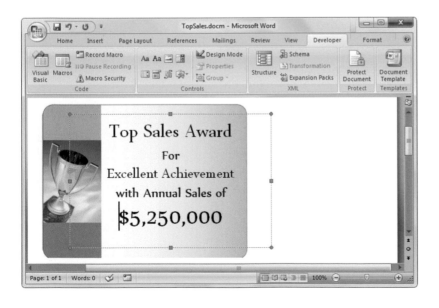

Beware

Remember to have the macro close the Workbook and release Excel after it has retrieved the cell value.

An introduction to VBScript

VBScript is a scripting language that, like VBA, shares the same core Visual Basic language as that found in a Visual Basic IDE. Scripts written in VBScript are interpreted by a script "engine" that processes the instructions to execute the script. The script engine can be invoked either from within the Windows GUI, or at a Windows Command Prompt, or by Internet Explorer.

Unlike the Visual Basic IDE, and VBA, there is no development environment for VBScript – you simply create your scripts in any plain text editor.

Don't forget

Notice that VBScript does not have any parentheses in this statement.

1 Open a plain text editor, such as Windows Notepad, then type the following code
MsgBox "Hello from VBScript!", vbExclamation

2 Name this file "Hello.vbs" and save it on your Desktop

3 Double-click on the file icon to invoke the script engine from the Windows GUI to execute the script – see the Message Box appear

4 Launch a Command Prompt window, then use the CD command to navigate to your Desktop directory

5 Now type the command **Hello.vbs** and hit Return to invoke the script engine from the Command Prompt – see the Message Box appear again

6 Open Notepad, or your favorite HTML editor, then type the web page source code shown below

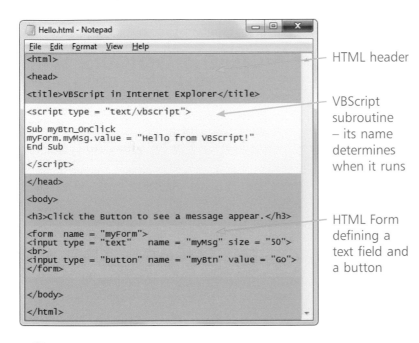

HTML header

VBScript subroutine – its name determines when it runs

HTML Form defining a text field and a button

Beware

The <script> tag must include the attribute type = "text/vbscript" or Internet Explorer may not recognize the script.

7 Save the file as "Hello.html" then open it in Internet Explorer and click the button to run the script

Hot tip

Use JavaScript rather than VBScript if you want your scripts to run on browsers over the web. If you are developing an Intranet where everyone uses Internet Explorer then you can use VBScript.

Scripting for Internet Explorer

In order to make scripts respond to events within Internet Explorer each subroutine must be carefully named using the object name and event name, separated by an underscore character. Clicking an HTML button fires its **onClick** event – so a subroutine to respond when a button called "myBtn" is clicked would have to be be named **myBtn_onClick**.

Common events are listed in the table below with brief descriptions and example subroutine names.

Event	Description	Example Sub Name
onClick	Object is clicked	**myBtn_onClick**
onChange	Text is changed	**myTxt_onChange**
onFocus	Object gets focus	**myTxt_onFocus**
onBlur	Object loses focus	**myTxt_onBlur**
onSelect	Text is selected	**myTxt_onSelect**
onMouseOver	Mouse hovers	**myObj_onMouseOver**
onSubmit	Form is submitted	**myForm_onSubmit**

Beware

VBScript cannot read or write files for security reasons. Its power has nevertheless been abused by virus writers – always treat an unknown VBS file with suspicion.

Objects available to VBScript in Internet Explorer are arranged hierarchically, following its Document Object Model (DOM). Uppermost is the **Window** object that has properties and methods concerning the current browser window. For example, you can call the **Window.Open()** method to launch a new pop-up window.

The **Document** object on the first tier level of the DOM hierarchy has properties and methods about the current document page. For example, the **Window.Document.Title** property contains the page title, as stated between the HTML **<title>** tags.

Optionally, you may omit the uppermost part when addressing any first-tier object, so the **Window.Document.Write()** method, for example, can be addressed simply as **Document.Write()**.

Lower-level objects can be addressed using the DOM hierarchy or by the value assigned to their HTML **name** attributes. For example, if the first HTML form in a document is named "myForm", and the first element in that form is named "myMsg", the value in that element can be addressed as **myForm.myMsg.Value** or as **Window.Document.Forms(0).Elements(0).Value**.

1. Make a copy of the **Hello.html** file, listed on page 139, and save it as **Dom.html**

2. Delete all the previous VBScript code in the script block – everything between the **<script>** and **</script>** tags

3. In the script block type the following new subroutine to address objects using the DOM hierarchy
```
Sub Window_onLoad
Window.Document.BgColor = vbGreen
Window.Document.Forms(0).Elements(0).Value = _
"Welcome to " & Window.Navigator.AppName
End Sub
```

4. In the script block type the following new subroutine to address objects by their HTML **name** attribute values
```
Sub myBtn_onClick
MsgBox myForm.myMsg.Value
End Sub
```

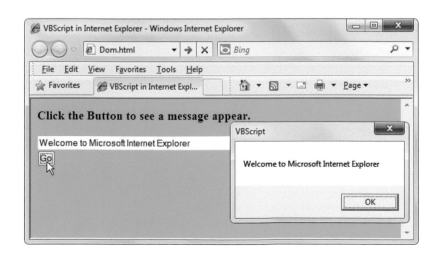

141

Scripting ActiveX objects

Internet Explorer is able to include ActiveX controls within an HTML document and VBScript can be used to address their properties and methods. ActiveX controls used in this way do perform well, because they run as native code on the user's system, but only if the user has first installed and registered those controls. It is, therefore, best to only use ActiveX controls in HTML documents on an Intranet – where you can be sure users will already have the required ActiveX controls.

Each ActiveX control has a unique identification number. This is hidden from you in the Visual Basic IDE but must appear in the source code of an HTML document so Internet Explorer can recognize the ActiveX control. The number must first be assigned to the **classid** attribute of an HTML **<object>** tag then VBScript can address its properties and methods, as with any other object.

1 Copy the following code between the body tags of a new HTML document, to add an ActiveX Calendar control to the body section of the page

```
<div>
<object id = "Calendar1" classid =
  "CLSID:8E27C92B-1264-101C-8A2F-040224009C02">
</object>
</div>
```

2 Next in the document body add a paragraph to display a background image and provide an initial message to the user when the page first loads

```
<div id="pic">
<p id="msg">
Click the ActiveX calendar to choose a date</p>
</div>
```

3 Now add this script in the head section of the document to dynamically display a message confirming the date selected by the user from the ActiveX Calendar control

```
<script type = "text/vbscript">
Sub Calendar1_Click
msg.innerHTML = "Thanks for choosing<br>"
& MonthName(Calendar1.Month) & " "
& Calendar1.Day & ", " & Calendar1.Year
End Sub
</script>
```

Hot tip

The Calendar ActiveX control is included in the code archive for this book – along with this example's HTML document, stylesheet, and image file. All available for download at www.ineasysteps.com.

4 Save the document then open it in Internet Explorer

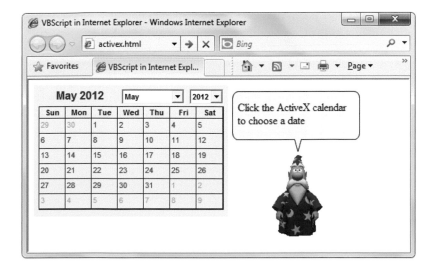

Don't forget

ActiveX scripting only works with Internet Explorer.

Providing the user has the appropriate ActiveX control Internet Explorer will display the Calendar.

5 Click on any date in the Calendar control to see the confirmation message replace the initial default message

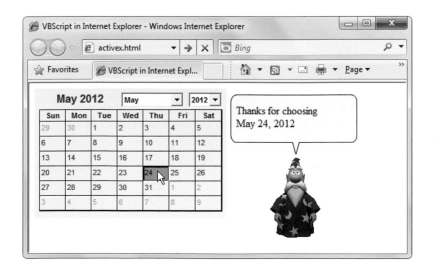

Hot tip

The background image illustrates a "talking" Microsoft Agent character that was a popular ActiveX control. Microsoft Agent is not however supported by default in Windows 7 – see more details at microsoft.com/msagent.

Running dynamic web scripts

Dynamic HTML (DHTML) effects can be achieved using VBScript in Internet Explorer to respond to user actions on the page. This simply requires event-handlers to change some aspect of the page to provide feedback to the user.

The most common DHTML effect uses the **onMouseOver** event to change the appearance of an item on the page when the user places the mouse cursor over that item. Similarly, the **onMouseOut** event can revert the item to its original appearance when the user moves the cursor off the item. This is often called a "rollover" effect from its resemblance to a pinball machine action.

Taking this effect further, additional changes can be applied in response to the **onMouseDown** and **onMouseUp** events that occur when the user clicks and releases the mouse button when on the item – so the item can have four possible dynamic states.

Individual elements of an HTML document can usefully be addressed simply by the unique value assigned to their **id** attribute and their appearance modified by changing their styles to provide rollover effect feedback to the user.

Beware

Be sure to copy the style sheet rules accurately – omitting a colon or semi-colon may not apply all the styles correctly.

1   Type the following code into the body section of a new HTML document to create an item for the rollover effect

```
<div id = "r1">OUT</div>
```

2   Copy the following style sheet into the head section of the document to define the item's initial appearance

```
<style type = "text/css">
#r1     { width:150px; height:30px; text-align:center;
          font-size:20pt; padding:10px; color: red;
          background:silver; border:8px outset red }
</style>
```

3   Add this subroutine to the HTML document's script block to handle the item's **onMouseOver** event

```
Sub r1_onMouseOver
r1.innerHTML = "OVER"
r1.style.color = "green"
r1.style.background = "lime"
r1.style.border = "8px outset green"
End Sub
```

4 Add this subroutine to the HTML document's script block to handle the item's **onMouseOut** event

```
Sub r1_onMouseOut
r1.innerHTML = "OUT"
r1.style.color = "red"
r1.style.background = "silver"
r1.style.border = "8px outset red"
End Sub
```

Hot tip

Routines that await events are sometimes referred to as "listeners".

5 Add this subroutine to the HTML document's script block to handle the item's **onMouseDown** event

```
Sub r1_onMouseDown
r1.innerHTML = "Down"
r1.style.color = "olive"
r1.style.background = "yellow"
r1.style.border = "8px inset olive"
End Sub
```

6 Add this subroutine to the HTML document's script block to handle the item's **onMouseUp** event

```
Sub r1_onMouseUp
r1.innerHTML = "Up"
r1.style.color = "blue"
r1.style.background = "aqua"
r1.style.border = "8px outset blue"
End Sub
```

7 Save the file then run it in Internet Explorer and test the rollover as your mouse creates four dynamic states

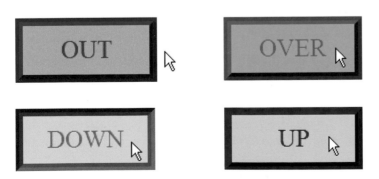

Don't forget

You can also create image rollovers, that swap the image assigned to the src attribute of an <img> tag. Other popular dynamic effects change the location, or visibility of items.

Summary

- Visual Basic for Applications (VBA) is built into all Microsoft Office applications, but each application has unique objects

- The VBA environment is similar to that of the Visual Basic IDE but it can't produce standalone executable applications

- A macro can insert content into a Word document at the position indicated by an inserted bookmark

- Saving macros in the **Normal.dotm** master template makes them available for use in other Word documents

- Loops can be used in a VBA macro to read or write a range of cells within an Excel spreadsheet

- Advanced macros allow one Office application to be controlled from within another one

- There is no development environment for VBScript – scripts are created in any plain text editor such as Windows Notepad

- The script engine that interprets VBScript instructions can be invoked from within the Windows GUI, at the Command Prompt, or by Internet Explorer

- VBScript subroutines for Internet Explorer must be named using the object name and event name, separated by an underscore, so the browser can recognize the event handler

- Internet Explorer's Document Object Model (DOM) arranges its objects hierarchically, with the Window object at the top

- Lower-level objects can be addressed either by their full DOM address, **name** attribute value, or **id** value

- ActiveX controls can be included in an HTML document if that control is available on the user's system

- VBScript can create Dynamic HTML (DHTML) effects by changing the appearance of items in response to user actions

9 Harnessing data

This chapter shows how Visual Basic applications can import data from a variety of external sources.

Reading text files

The **My.Computer.FileSystem** object has methods that make it easy for Visual Basic applications to work with local files. Text can be imported using its **ReadAllText()** and exported using its **WriteAllText()** method to append text to an existing file, or create a new file. Files can be removed with the **DeleteFile()** method or their existence confirmed with the **FileExists()** method.

1 Start a new Windows Forms Application then add two TextBox controls and three Button controls to the Form

2 Set the Multiline property of Textbox2 to True then name the buttons **WriteBtn**, **ReadBtn**, and **DeleteBtn**

3 Press F7 to open the Code Editor then create a path variable in the Declarations section, modifying the path to suit the Documents directory location on your system
Dim myFile As String = "C:\Users\Mike\Documents\log.txt"

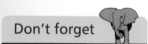

Don't forget

Remember to include the third True parameter to append text to a file.

4 Double-click on the **WriteBtn** to open the Code Editor and add the following code to its Click event-handler
```
My.Computer.FileSystem.WriteAllText( _
        myFile, TextBox1.Text & vbCrLf, True)
TextBox1.Text = ""
```

5 Return to the Form Designer then double-click the **ReadBtn** and add this code to its Click event-handler
```
Try
TextBox2.Text = _
My.Computer.FileSystem.ReadAllText( myFile )
Catch ex As Exception
TextBox2.Text = "Unable to read from  " & myFile
End Try
```

6   Return to the Form Designer then double-click the
DeleteBtn and add this code to its Click event-handler
TextBox1.Text = ""
TextBox2.Text = ""
If My.Computer.FileSystem.FileExists(myFile) Then
My.Computer.FileSystem.DeleteFile(myFile)
End If

Beware

Ensure that the
application has
permission to write to
the log file location.

7   Click the Start Debugging button, or press F5, to run the
application then enter some text into the top TextBox

8   Click the **WriteBtn** to have your text written into a new
file and see the top TextBox become cleared

9   Click the **ReadBtn** to have the file contents read and see
your text appear in the bottom TextBox

Hot tip

Remove the log file then
click the ReadBtn to
attempt to read from the
missing file – the Catch
statement will appear.

10   Repeat steps 7 and 8 to append more lines of text then
click the **DeleteBtn** to remove the file and text content

Streaming lines of text

The Visual Basic **System.IO** class can be used to import data and files into an application as a "stream". A stream is more flexible than a file as it can be searched and manipulated. A stream is first created as a new **System.IO.FileStream** object that specifies the file to work with and the operation to perform as its parameters. A new **System.IO.StreamReader** object can then be created to read from an opened file in a variety of ways – its **ReadToEnd()** method will read the entire file. It is important to then release the StreamReader and FileStream using their **Dispose()** method.

1. Add to a Form an OpenFileDialog, a TextBox and two Button controls named **OpenBtn** and **PrintBtn**

2. Double-click on the **OpenBtn** to open the Code Editor then add this code to the Declarations section
Dim txt As String

3. Now add the following code to the **OpenBtn** control's Click event-handler
```
If OpenFileDialog1.ShowDialog = _
        Windows.Forms.DialogResult.OK Then
Dim stream As New System.IO.FileStream _
(OpenFileDialog1.FileName, System.IO.FileMode.Open)
Dim reader As New System.IO.StreamReader(stream)
txt = reader.ReadToEnd()
reader.Dispose() : stream.Dispose()
TextBox1.Text = txt
End If
```

Hot tip

Two statements can appear on a single line if they are separated by a colon character, as here.

4. Run the application then click the **OpenBtn** and browse to select a text file for display in the TextBox

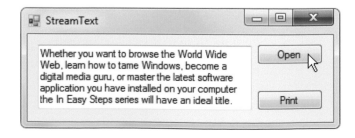

150

Adding Print ability

1 Add both a PrintDialog and PrintDocument component from the Printing section of the Toolbox

2 Double-click on the PrintBtn and add the following code to its Click event-handler

```
PrintDialog1.AllowSomePages = True
PrintDialog1.ShowHelp = True
If PrintDialog1.ShowDialog = _
        Windows.Forms.DialogResult.OK Then
        If txt <> "" Then
        PrintDocument1.Print()
        End If
End If
```

This Sub routine configures the Print dialog then, if the **txt** variable is not empty, calls the **Print()** method of the PrintDocument1 component. This is not enough to print by itself – it merely fires a **PrintPage** event whose event-handler must be coded to make the application print out the text.

3 Double-click on the PrintDocument1 icon in the Form Designer's component tray to open the Code Editor in its PrintPage event-handler and type this code

```
e.Graphics.DrawString(txt, Me.Font, Brushes.Black, _
e.MarginBounds, StringFormat.GenericTypographic)
```

In this code the letter "e" is specified in the event-handler's parameters to represent a **PrintPageEventArgs** object that uses the **Graphics.DrawString()** method to print the text.

4 Click the Start Debugging button, or press F5, to run the application and use the **OpenBtn** to choose a text file then click the **PrintBtn** to send it to your printer

Don't forget

The PrintDialog component lets your application launch the Windows Print dialog – but you need to add a PrintDocument component to actually print anything.

Beware

Further code would need to be added to the PrintPage event-handler to allow the printer to handle multiple pages.

Reading Excel spreadsheets

Data contained within an Excel spreadsheet can be imported into an application where the value of each cell can be conveniently stored in a two-dimensional array, representing rows and columns. This allows each individual cell to be addressed using the same row and column number that it has in the spreadsheet – for instance, cell(2,3) could address the third cell on the second row.

1 Create an Excel Workbook called "Data.xlsx", enter values like those below, then save it in your Documents directory

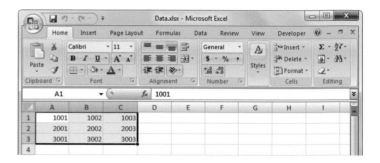

2 Start a new Windows Forms Application and add three ListBox controls, three Labels, and a Button to the Form

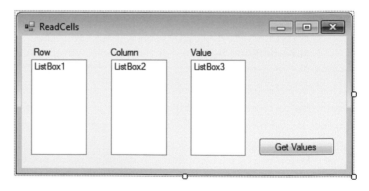

Hot tip

Refer to page 136 for an illustration of the References dialog – compare the similarities in this example with the VBA example listed there.

3 Click Project, Add Reference to launch the Add Reference dialog then choose the Microsoft Excel Object Library item on the COM tab and click OK

4 Press F7 to open the Code Editor then create a path variable to the spreadsheet in the Declarations section
Dim mySS As String = "C:\Users\Mike\Documents\Data.xlsx"

5 Double-click on the Button control to open the Code Editor and type this code into its Click event-handler

```
Dim row, col, finalRow, finalCol As Integer
Dim xl = CreateObject("Excel.Application")
xl.Workbooks.Open( mySS )
xl.Worksheets("Sheet1").Activate()
finalRow = xl.ActiveSheet.UsedRange.Rows.Count
finalCol = xl.ActiveSheet.UsedRange.Columns.Count
Dim vals(finalRow, finalCol) As String
```

This opens the Worksheet, counts the number of used rows and columns, then create a two-dimensional array of the same size.

6 Add this loop to assign the cell values to the array elements and to display them in the ListBoxes

```
For row = 1 To finalRow
        For col = 1 To finalCol
        vals(row, col) = _
                Str(xl.ActiveSheet.Cells(row, col).Value)
        ListBox1.Items.Add(row)
        ListBox2.Items.Add(col)
        ListBox3.Items.Add( vals(row, col) )
        Next col
Next row
```

7 Finally, add these two lines to release the resources then run the application and click the Button

```
xl.Workbooks.Close()
xl = Nothing
```

Don't forget

Many examples in this book benefit by enclosure in a Try Catch statement but they are not listed in order to save space – add one to this example to catch the exception that would be thrown if the Worksheet could not be read.

153

Hot tip

See page 63 for more on multi-dimensional arrays.

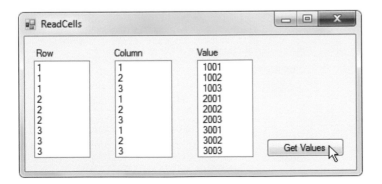

Reading XML files

The Visual Basic **System.Xml** object can be used to easily import data into an application from an XML document. A container for the data is first created as a **System.Xml.XmlDocument** object then the data is loaded into it using its **Load()** method to copy data from the XML document file.

A **System.Xml.XmlNodeList** can then create an **Item()** array of all the elements in the XML document. Individual elements can be addressed by stating their name as the parameter to the **SelectSingleNode()** method of the **Item()** array, and the value contained within that element retrieved by its **InnerText** property.

 Open any plain text editor, such as Notepad, and create an XML document with elements like those below – name it **books.xml** and save it in the Documents folder

Don't forget

You can download the XML document, along with all the other files used in this book, from www.ineasysteps.com.

```
books.xml - Notepad

File  Edit  Format  View  Help
<?xml version="1.0" encoding="utf-8" standalone="yes" ?>

<shelf>

        <book>
                <isbn> 978-1-84078-396-4</isbn>
                <title>Linux In Easy Steps</title>
                <author>Mike McGrath</author>
                <class>Operating Systems</class>
        </book>

        <book>
                <isbn>978-1-84078-381-0</isbn>
                <title>Windows 7 In Easy Steps</title>
                <author>Harshad Kotecha</author>
                <class>Operating Systems</class>
        </book>

        <book>
                <isbn>978-1-84078-346-9</isbn>
                <title>Java In Easy Steps</title>
                <author>Mike McGrath</author>
                <class>Programming</class>
        </book>

        <book>
                <isbn>978-1-84078-314-8</isbn>
                <title>Web Design In Easy Steps</title>
                <author>Richard Quick</author>
                <class>Web Development</class>
        </book>

        <book>
                <isbn>978-1-84078-337-7</isbn>
                <title>XML In Easy Steps</title>
                <author>Mike McGrath</author>
                <class>Web Development</class>
        </book>

</shelf>
```

2 Start a new Windows Forms Application and add a
ListBox and a Button to the Form

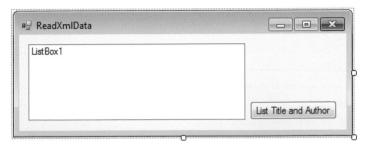

3 Double-click on the Button to open the Code Editor and
type this code into its Click event-handler to create an
XmlDocument object from the XML file
Dim doc As New System.Xml.XmlDocument
doc.Load("C:\Users\Mike\Documents\books.xml")

4 Add the following code to create an XmlNodeList from
the <book> elements and their nested elements
Dim nodes As System.Xml.XmlNodeList
nodes = doc.SelectNodes("shelf/book")

5 Now add a loop to display the text contained in each
<title> and <author> element, then run the application
Dim counter = 0
Do Until counter = nodes.Count
ListBox1.Items.Add(nodes.Item(counter) _
** .SelectSingleNode("title").InnerText & " by " _**
& nodes.Item(counter) _
** .SelectSingleNode("author").InnerText & vbCrLf)**
counter += 1
Loop

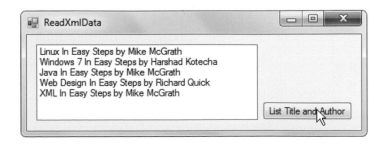

Hot tip

Notice how the
Count property of the
XmlNodeList is used to
set the limit of the loop.

155

Creating an XML dataset

Visual Basic provides specialized components for working with data in table format, such as that contained in XML elements or database tables. These components can be found in the Toolbox under the "Data" heading.

The DataSet component can be added to an application to create a table in the system memory that can be loaded with data from any suitable source. Most often it is convenient to display the table data in the interface using a DataGridView component. This allows the data stored in memory to be dynamically manipulated within the application then written back to a file.

1. Start a new Windows Forms Application and add a DataGridView component and two Buttons to the Form – name the Buttons **ReadBtn** and **WriteBtn**

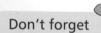

Don't forget

The document file books.xml must be located in the Documents directory – adjust the path to suit your system.

2. Double-click on the **DataSet** item in the Toolbox then choose the **Untyped DataSet** option in the Add DataSet dialog and click OK – see the DataSet icon appear on the component tray in the Form Designer

3. Double-click the **ReadBtn** to open the Code Editor then type this code into its Click event-handler to create a DataSet from the XML document shown on page 154
   DataSet1.ReadXml("C:\Users\Mike\Documents\books.xml")

4. Add this code to load those elements nested under the <book> element from the DataSet into the DataGridView control
   DataGridView1.DataSource = DataSet1
   DataGridView1.DataMember = "book"

5   Return to the Form Designer then double-click the **WriteBtn** and add this code to its Click event-handler
DataSet1.WriteXml("C:\Users\Mike\Documents\books.xml")

6   Click Start Debugging, or press F5, to run the application then click the **ReadBtn** to load the DataSet data into the DataGridView control

Hot tip

You can set a DataGridView's AutoSizeColumnsMode property to AllCells to automatically show all text content in each cell.

isbn	title	author	class
978-1-84078-396-4	Linux In Easy Steps	Mike McGrath	Operating Systems
978-1-84078-381-0	Windows 7 In Easy Steps	Harshad Kotecha	Operating Systems
978-1-84078-346-9	Java In Easy Steps	Mike McGrath	Programming
978-1-84078-314-8	Web Design In Easy Steps	Richard Quick	Web Development
978-1-84078-337-7	XML In Easy Steps	Mike McGrath	Web Development

The DataGridView control displays the element name as the heading for each column and the element content on each row of that column. Initially the first cell on the first row is in focus but you can click on any other cell to move the focus. When you double-click the cell in focus it changes into edit mode where you can update its content.

7   Add another row of data to the last row of the table then click the **WriteBtn** control to save the amended data

isbn	title	author	class
978-1-84078-396-4	Linux In Easy Steps	Mike McGrath	Operating Systems
978-1-84078-381-0	Windows 7 In Easy Steps	Harshad Kotecha	Operating Systems
978-1-84078-346-9	Java In Easy Steps	Mike McGrath	Programming
978-1-84078-314-8	Web Design In Easy Steps	Richard Quick	Web Development
978-1-84078-337-7	XML In Easy Steps	Mike McGrath	Web Development
	Visual Basic in easy steps	Mike McGrath	Programming

Beware

ScrollBars will, by default, automatically appear when the cell content overflows the DataGridView control. Setting its ScrollBars property to None can hide content from view.

8   Restart the application then click the **ReadBtn** to once more load the XML data into the DataGridView control – see that the row you added has been preserved

Reading RSS feeds

Live XML data can be imported from outside the local system into a Visual Basic application using a Really Simple Syndication (RSS) feed. This delivers the XML data as a stream that can be stored within a **System.Xml.XmlDocument** object, like that used to store data from an XML file on page 155.

Hot tip

You can find the GroupBox control in the Containers section of the Toolbox.

1. Start a new Windows Application then add a GroupBox Label, Button, and TextBox control to the Form

2. Name the TextBox as "ZipCode" and set its Text property to "10021" – a New York City Zip code. Arrange the controls so your Form looks like this

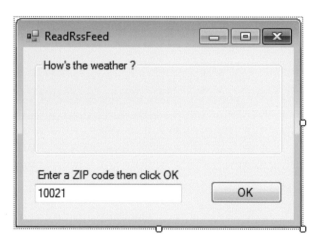

Beware

This example relies upon the format of an external XML document – if the format gets changed it may need amendment to run correctly. You can discover the latest details about the Yahoo RSS weather feed online at http://developer.yahoo. com/weather.

3. To create a request to the Yahoo Weather RSS Feed for the Zip code above double-click on the Button and type the following code into its Click event-handler

```
Dim rssUrl = _
        "http://xml.weather.yahoo.com/forecastrss?p=" _
        + ZipCode.Text
Dim rssRequest As System.Net.WebRequest = _
        System.Net.WebRequest.Create(rssUrl)
```

4. Save the response data into a Stream object by adding these two statements

```
Dim rssResponse As System.Net.WebResponse = _
        rssRequest.GetResponse()
Dim rssStream As System.IO.Stream = _
        rssReponse.GetResponseStream()
```

5 Type the code below to load the saved data stream into an XMLDocument object

```
Dim rssDoc As New System.Xml.XmlDocument
rssDoc.Load(rssStream)
```

6 Create an XmlNodeList under the <channel> element of the XmlDocument object by adding these lines

```
Dim nodes As System.Xml.XmlNodeList
nodes = rssDoc.SelectNodes("/rss/channel")
```

7 Now add this code to display the content contained in the <title> element of the XmlDocument object

```
GroupBox1.Text = _
nodes.Item(0).SelectSingleNode("title").InnerText
```

8 Run the application and click the OK button to test the RSS request – after a short delay see the GroupBox Text property change to the title of the response document

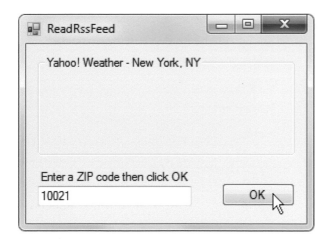

When the application is able to retrieve the title from the XML response document you can proceed to add further code, as described on the next page, to extract information from the document about the current weather conditions.

Hot tip

You need an Internet connection to run this application successfully.

Don't forget

Change the value in the TextBox to any other valid US Zip code then click OK to see the title change again – for instance, try 90021.

159

Addressing XML attributes

The XML response document sent from Yahoo Weather, in response to the RSS request made by the application on the previous page, contains information about the current weather conditions for the specified Zip code.

The details are assigned to attributes of XML elements that each have a **yweather:** namespace prefix. To access XML namespace elements in Visual Basic it is necessary to first create an **XmlNamespaceManager** object then specify the namespace name and URL as parameters to its **AddNamespace()** method. Once an **XmlNamespaceManager** has been created you simply add its name as a second parameter to each **SelectSingleNode()** call.

1 Add three TextBoxes and three Label controls to the Form in the previous example

2 Name the TextBox controls **Climate**, **Temperature**, and **Humidity** then set the Text property of each Label control accordingly

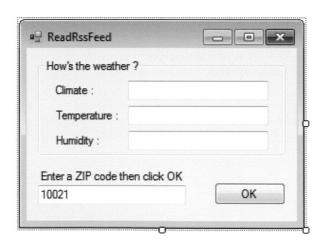

Hot tip

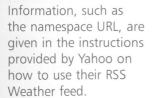

Information, such as the namespace URL, are given in the instructions provided by Yahoo on how to use their RSS Weather feed.

3 Double-click on the OK Button to open the Code Editor and append the following code after the earlier code in its Click event-handler to create an XmlNamespaceManager

```
Dim nsMgr = New _
System.Xml.XmlNamespaceManager(rssDoc.NameTable)
nsMgr.AddNamespace("yweather", _
        "http://xml.weather.yahoo.com/ns/rss/1.0")
```

4 Add this code to display the current weather condition
```
Climate.Text = rssDoc.SelectSingleNode( _
"/rss/channel/item/yweather:condition/@text", _
        nsMgr).InnerText
```

5 Add this code to display the current temperature
```
Temperature.Text = rssDoc.SelectSingleNode( _
"/rss/channel/yweather:wind/@chill", _
        nsMgr).InnerText + " F"
```

6 Add this code to display the current humidity
```
Humidity.Text = rssDoc.SelectSingleNode( _
"/rss/channel/yweather:atmosphere/@humidity", _
        nsMgr).InnerText + " %"
```

7 Surround the entire code inside the Click event-handler with a Try Catch statement – to catch the exception that will be thrown in the event that the RSS feed is not accessible

8 Run the application then click the OK button to retrieve the current weather information for the specified Zip code from the RSS feed

Hot tip

Notice how the @ character is used here in the URL to denote the name of an attribute.

161

Don't forget

You can see more about Try Catch statements on page 106.

Summary

- The **My.Computer.FileSystem** object can be used to read and write files on your computer

- A **System.IO.Stream** object can store text that has been read from a local file or external source, such as a web response

- It is important to dispose of **System.IO.Stream** and **System.IO.StreamReader** objects after they have been used

- The **Print()** method of a **PrintDocument** component does not actually send data to your printer – it only fires a **PrintPage** event whose event-handler must be coded in order to print

- Data imported from an Excel spreadsheet can best be stored in a two-dimensional array representing rows and columns

- The **System.Xml.XmlDocument** object is used to store a representation of an XML document

- A **System.Xml.XmlNodeList** object creates an **Item()** array of elements selected from a **System.Xml.XmlDocument**

- The **InnerText** property of a node contains the actual content of that element

- A **DataSet** component creates a table in system memory that can be loaded with data from any suitable source

- It is often convenient to display **DataSet** table data in a **DataGridView** component – where it can be modified then written from system memory back to the original source

- An application can request an RSS feed using a **System.Net.WebRequest** object

- A **System.Net.WebResponse** object handles the response received after requesting an RSS feed

- XML elements that have a namespace prefix can be addressed after creating a **System.Xml.NamespaceManager** object

10 Employing databases

This chapter introduces databases and demonstrates how to add powerful database functionality to a Visual Basic application with SQL Server.

An introduction to databases

Databases are simply convenient storage containers that store data in a structured manner. Every database is composed of one or more tables that structure the data into organized rows and columns. This makes it easy to reference and manipulate the data. Each database table column has a label to identify the data stored within the table cells in that column. Each row is an entry called a "record", that places data in each cell along that row like this:

MemberID	Forename	Surname
1	John	Smith
2	Ann	Jones
3	Mike	McGrath

The rows of a database table are not automatically arranged in any particular order so they can be sorted alphabetically, numerically, or by any other criteria. It is important, therefore, to have some means to identify each record in the table. The example above allocates a "MemberID" for this purpose and this unique identifier is known as the **Primary Key** for that table.

Storing data in a single table is useful but relational databases with multiple tables introduce more possibilities by allowing the stored data to be combined in a variety of ways. For example, the table below could be added to the database containing the table shown above.

VideoID	Title	MemberID
1	Titanic	2
2	Fantasia	3
3	Star Wars	1

The table lists video titles sorted numerically by "VideoID" and describes a relationship linking each member to the video they have rented – John (MemberID 1) has Star Wars (VideoID 3), Ann (MemberID 2) has Titanic (VideoID 1) and Mike (MemberID 3) has Fantasia (VideoID 2). In this table the

Beware

Spaces are not allowed in label names – so you should use "MemberID" instead of "Member ID".

VideoID column has the **Primary Key** values identifying records in this table and the **MemberID** column in this table contains **Foreign Key** values that reference records in the first table.

SQL Server

The SQL Server DataBase Management System (DBMS) that is bundled with Visual Basic adheres to the relational model like other Relational DataBase Management System (RDBMS) software, such as Oracle or IBM DB2. This means that it observes "normalization" rules that you need to be aware of when designing a database.

Data normalization

Normalization rules insist that data is organized efficiently, and without duplication or redundancy, in order to reduce the potential for anomalies when performing data operations. They require each table to have a Primary Key column and permissable data types must be defined for all other columns. This determines whether cells in the column may contain text or numbers, within a specified range, and whether cells may be left empty or not.

In considering the design of a database, normalization sensibly requires data to appear only once – so any repeated data should be moved into its own table then referenced where required. For example, where customer name and address details are repeated in two tables they should be moved to their own table which can then be referenced from each of the two original tables. This makes it easier to update the customer details without the possibility of creating an anomaly by updating just one set of data.

Data integrity

Another important aspect of RDBMS software concerns the preservation of data integrity by prohibiting "orphaned" records. This means that records that are referenced in another table cannot be deleted unless the reference is first deleted. Otherwise the reference would become orphaned as it could not find the data in its "parent" table. For example, where a table of customer order details contains a reference to a record in a table of products the RDBMS software will not allow the product record to be deleted as doing so would render the customer order reference useless.

Hot tip

A Foreign Key always references a Primary Key in another table – name them both alike for easy recognition.

Don't forget

SQL Server gets installed along with Visual Basic – see the installation components on page 11.

Designing a database

The process of database design is typically one of refinement to recognize the rules of normalization. Start out with a single table design for all data fields then move those which are repeating into their own table.

Consider the design for a database to store data about an imaginary range of motorcycles comprising "Sport", "Cruiser", and "Touring" models that are selectively available in "Standard", "Deluxe" and "Classic" versions, and where each model/version has a unique price. A single **Bikes** table of the entire range, plus a column for individual notes, might look like this:

BikeID	Model	Version	Price	Note
1	Sport	Standard	4995	
2	Sport	Deluxe	5495	
3	Cruiser	Standard	7995	
4	Cruiser	Deluxe	8495	
5	Cruiser	Classic	8995	
6	Touring	Standard	9495	
7	Touring	Classic	9995	

Don't forget

A Primary Key uniquely identifes a row within a database table – so a Primary Key value should never be changed.

The **BikeID** column provides a unique identifier for each row and can be set as the **Primary Key** for the table. The **Price** column contains unique values and all cells in the **Note** column are initially empty. **Model** and **Version** columns both contain repeating data in contravention of the normalization rules so they should each be moved into separate tables like those below:

ModelID	Model
1	Sport
2	Cruiser
3	Touring

VersionID	Version
1	Standard
2	Deluxe
3	Classic

The **ModelID** and **VersionID** columns provide a unique identifier for each row and can be set as the **Primary Key** (PK) for their table – and they can also be used as a **Foreign Key** (FK) in the refined Bikes table below:

BikeID [PK]	ModelID [FK]	VersionID [FK]	Price	Note
1	1	1	4995	
2	1	2	5495	
3	2	1	7995	
4	2	2	8495	
5	2	3	8995	
6	3	1	9495	
7	3	3	9995	

In considering permissable data types for each column, in line with normalization rules, the **BikeID, ModelID, VersionID,** and **Price** columns should each allow only integer values. The **Model** and **Version** columns should only allow up to ten characters and the **Note** column should allow up to, say, fifty various characters. All except the **Note** column are required to contain data – in database terms they should be "Not Null". The Database Diagram below illustrates these data constraints and the table relationships:

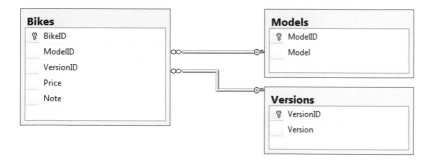

Beware

In setting data constraints consider future eventualities – might a new Model or Version perhaps have a name longer than 10 characters?

167

This design is used on the ensuing pages to create a SQL Server database and a Visual Basic application that can communicate with it to dynamically retrieve and manipulate data.

Creating a database

SQL Server is well integrated with Visual Basic so you can easily create a new database from within the IDE.

1 Start a new Windows Forms Application in Visual Basic and name it **BikesApplication**

2 Click View, Other Windows, Solution Explorer, or press Ctrl+Alt+L, to open the Solution Explorer window

3 In the Solution Explorer window, right-click on the top project icon then choose Add, New Item from the context menu to launch the Add New Item dialog

4 In the Add New Item dialog select the "Service-based Database" icon, type BikesDatabase.mdf in the name field, then click the Add button

Beware

Be sure to click the Cancel button to close the Data Source Configuration Wizard dialog – not the Finish button.

5 When the Data Source Configuration Wizard dialog appears just click its Cancel button for now

Connecting to a database

1 In Solution Explorer, right-click the **BikesDatabase.mdf** icon that has been added, then choose Open from the context menu to open the Database Explorer window

2 Examine the **BikesDatabase.mdf** icon in Database Explorer and you should see it has an "electric-cord"  below it to indicate you are connected to that database

3 Right-click the **BikesDatabase.mdf** icon in Database Explorer then choose Close Connection from the context menu – see the icon change to have a red X below it

4 Right-click the **BikesDatabase.mdf** icon in Database Explorer then choose Refresh to reconnect to the database – see the icon has the "electric-cord" below it once more to indicate you are connected again

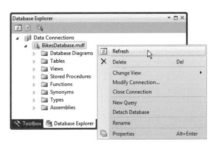

5 To test the connection right-click the **BikesDatabase.mdf** icon again then choose Modify Connection to launch the Modify Connection dialog and click its Test Connection button – see the Connection Succeeded confirmation dialog appear

6 Click the OK button on both dialogs to close them

Hot tip

You can also open the Database Explorer window by choosing View, Database Explorer on the Menu Bar, or with a double-click on the BikesDatabase.mdf icon in Solution Explorer.

169

Beware

This chapter builds a complete database application. To recreate this application it is important you carefully follow each step, in the same sequence, in order to avoid errors later.

Adding database tables

Having created the **BikesDatabase** database on the previous page, you can begin to add the **Bikes, Models**, and **Versions** tables from the database design on page 167 by creating the tables and setting the Primary Key column for each table.

1 In Database Explorer right-click on the Tables icon and choose Add New Table from the context menu to open the Table Designer window and tool bar

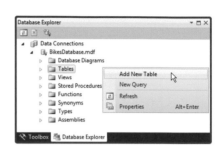

2 In Table Designer, type **BikeID** in the field below the Column Name heading to name the column

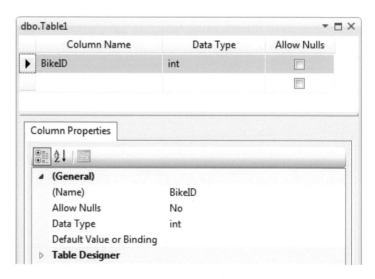

Don't forget

When working with Table Designer you can close the Form Designer window to tidy the IDE.

3 Click below the Data Type heading then choose the **int** item from the dropdown options to allow only integer data in this column

4 Ensure that the Allow Nulls checkbox is not checked so empty cells will not be allowed in this column

5 Click the **Set Primary Key** button on the Table Designer toolbar to make this column the table's Primary Key

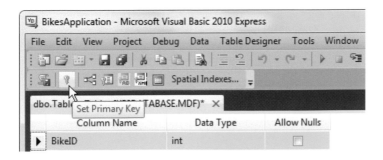

6 In the Column Properties window, expand Identity Specification under the Table Designer menu then set the **Is Identity** property to Yes – to have the column automatically number its rows

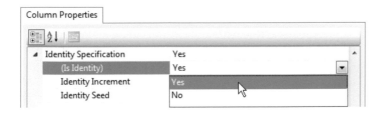

7 Click File, Save Table1, or press Ctrl+S, to launch the Choose Name dialog then name this table **Bikes** and click the OK button

8 Repeat these steps to create the **Models** table with **ModelID** and the **Versions** table with **VersionID** – and see icons appear in Database Explorer for each new table

Defining table columns

Having created the **Bikes**, **Models**, and **Versions** tables on the previous page, you can begin to define other columns for each table, setting their Column Name, Data Type and Allow Nulls.

1 In Database Explorer, right-click on the **Bikes** table icon in the Tables folder then choose Open Table Definition from the context menu to open it in Table Designer

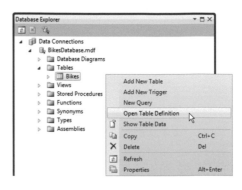

2 Click the next line under the Column Name heading, below the box containing the **BikeID** name, then type **ModelID** to name that column, set the data type to **int** and uncheck the Allow Nulls checkbox

3 Repeat step 2 to define the **VersionID** and **Price** columns

4 Add a column named **Note**, set the data type to **varchar(50)** and do check the Allow Nulls checkbox so the completed table definition looks like this

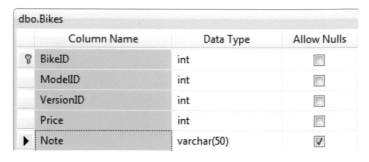

dbo.Bikes		
Column Name	Data Type	Allow Nulls
🔑 BikeID	int	☐
ModelID	int	☐
VersionID	int	☐
Price	int	☐
▶ Note	varchar(50)	☑

5 In Database Explorer, double-click on the **Models** table icon to open it in Table Designer

Don't forget

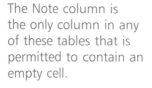

The Note column is the only column in any of these tables that is permitted to contain an empty cell.

6 Click the next line under the Column Name heading, below the box containing the **ModelID** name, then type **Model** to name that column, set the data type to **char(10)** and uncheck the Allow Nulls checkbox

| dbo.Models | | |
Column Name	Data Type	Allow Nulls
🔑 ModelID	int	☐
▶ Model	char(10)	☐

Hot tip

When a table is open in Table Designer you can click View, Properties Window to discover properties of that table.

7 In Database Explorer, double-click on the **Versions** table icon, or choose Open Table Definition from the right-click context menu, to open it in Table Designer

8 Click the next line under the Column Name heading, below the box containing the **VersionID** name, then type **Version** to name that column, set the data type to **char(10)** and uncheck the Allow Nulls checkbox

| dbo.Versions | | |
Column Name	Data Type	Allow Nulls
🔑 VersionID	int	☐
▶ Version	char(10)	☐

173

9 Click File, Save All, or press the Save All button, to save the project and all the updated table definitions – expand the tables in Database Explorer to see all the defined columns you have created

Hot tip

If the IDE complains about saving with table recreation click Tools, Options then check Show All Settings. Now expand Database Tools, Table and Database Designers then uncheck "Prevent saving changes that require table recreation" and click OK.

Making table relationships

Having defined all the table columns on the previous page, you can now establish the relationship between the tables to recognize the links for the **Bikes** table's **ModelId** column to the **Models** table, and its **VersionID** column to the **Versions** table.

1. In Database Explorer, right-click on the Database Diagrams icon then choose Add New Diagram from the context menu

2. When a dialog box appears asking if you want to create required objects click the Yes button – after a short delay the Add Table dialog will appear

3. Select all three tables (**Bikes, Models, Versions**) in the Add Tables list then click the Add button to create a diagram – click Close to close the Add Tables dialog

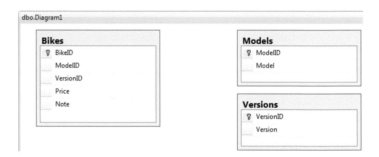

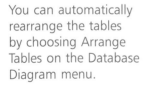

You can automatically rearrange the tables by choosing Arrange Tables on the Database Diagram menu.

4. Click the Save All button, or press Ctrl+Shift+S, to save the diagram and the Choose Name dialog will request a name – type **BikesDiagram** then click OK

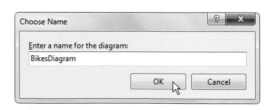

The relationship to be established in this case is to create a Foreign Key for the **ModelID** and **VersionID** columns in the **Bikes** table, linking them to their respective tables.

5 In the Database Diagram click on the yellow key button in the **Models** table then drag the cursor to the **ModelID** column in the **Bikes** table – a line gets drawn between the two points indicating the linked relationship

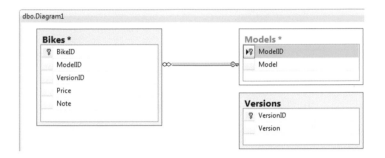

Beware

The order in which you create the link is important – always first click the yellow key in the table from which you are taking the Primary Key, then drag to the Foreign Key column in the other table.

6 Release the mouse button and see two dialogs appear. In the Tables and Columns dialog check that **ModelID** is the common link then click OK in both dialogs to close them

7 Now click the yellow key button in the **Versions** table and drag the cursor to the **VersionID** column in the **Bikes** table – see another line get drawn in the diagram

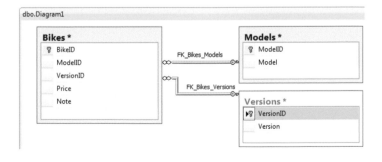

Hot tip

On the Database Diagram menu choose Show Relationship Labels to add text above the link lines describing the relationships, as seen in this illustration.

175

8 Close both dialogs again then click the Save All button, or press Ctrl+Shift+S, to add the relationships to the database and click Yes when asked if you want to save

Entering table data

Having established the tables relationship on the previous page, you can now begin to enter actual data records into each table.

1 In Database Explorer, expand the Tables tree then right-click on the **Models** table icon and choose Show Table Data from the context menu to open the **Models** table in the Table Data window

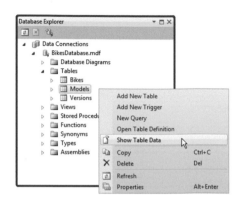

2 Click under the **Model** heading and type **Sport** then press Tab to move to the **Model** column on the next row – see numbering automatically appear in the **ModelID** column as you specified when creating the table

3 Type **Cruiser** on the second row and **Touring** on the third row so the table looks like this – then click the X button to close this window

Models

	ModelID	Model
▶	1	Sport
	2	Cruiser
	3	Touring
✱	*NULL*	*NULL*

4 Open the **Versions** Table Data window then, under the **Version** column, enter **Standard** on the first row, **Deluxe** on the second and **Classic** on the third row

Versions

	VersionID	Version
▶	1	Standard
	2	Deluxe
	3	Classic
✱	*NULL*	*NULL*

5 Open the **Bikes** table in the Table Data window then click under the **ModelID** heading and enter the data from the colored table on page 167 – use the Tab key to move through the cells to enter **ModelID**, **VersionID**, and **Price** data so that the table looks like this:

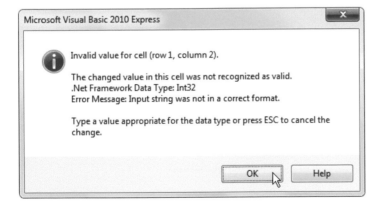

	BikeID	ModelID	VersionID	Price	Note
▶	1	1	1	4995	NULL
	2	1	2	5495	NULL
	3	2	1	7995	NULL
	4	2	2	8495	NULL
	5	2	3	8995	NULL
	6	3	1	9495	NULL
	7	3	3	9995	NULL
*	NULL	NULL	NULL	NULL	NULL

6 To test that the table constraints are working correctly click the **ModelID** cell on row 1 and change its value to text then press the Tab key – an error dialog should appear complaining that this entry is invalid

Microsoft Visual Basic 2010 Express

Invalid value for cell (row 1, column 2).

The changed value in this cell was not recognized as valid.
.Net Framework Data Type: Int32
Error Message: Input string was not in a correct format.

Type a value appropriate for the data type or press ESC to cancel the change.

OK   Help

7 Press the Esc key to revert back to the original cell value then click the X button to close the Table Data window

Hot tip

If you encounter an error message when entering table data it is probably because the table constraints do not allow that entry – check the table definition to correct the problem.

177

Don't forget

You can test the Foreign Key constraints are working by trying to delete any row from the Models or Versions table – you should see a dialog appear saying you cannot do so.

Creating a database dataset

Having created a database with related tables and data entries, over the last few pages, you can now proceed to develop the **BikesApplication** program to incorporate the data as a dataset.

1 Click Data, Add New Data Source on the Menu Bar to launch the Data Source Configuration Wizard dialog

2 Select the Database icon then click Next to proceed

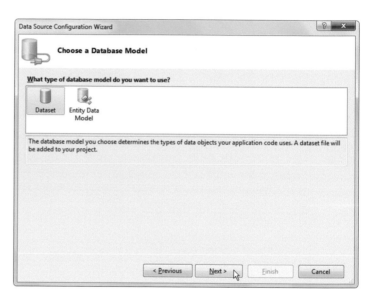

3 Select **BikesDatabase.mdf** as the chosen connection in the dropdown list, then click Next

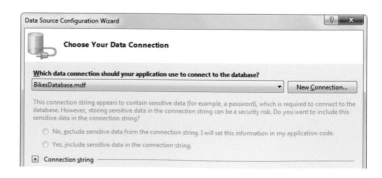

4 Check the "Yes, save the connection as" checkbox, then click Next again

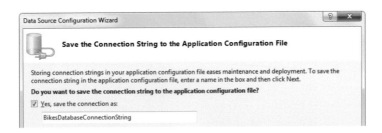

5 Check the Tables checkbox to include all the database tables in the dataset, then click the Finish button

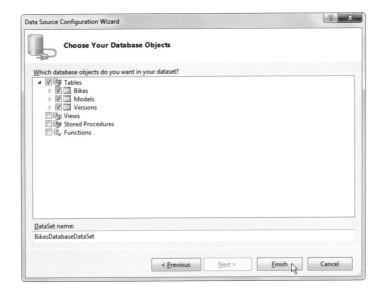

6 In Solution Explorer see that the dataset has been created as a new XML Schema Document and the application configuration is stored in an XML document named **app.config**

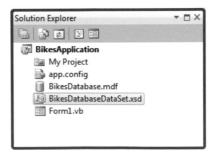

Don't forget

A dataset is an in-memory representation of the tables in the database which can be manipulated before writing data back to the tables.

Adding form data controls

Having created a database dataset on the previous page you are now ready to add controls to the Form to display the data.

1 Ensure Form Designer is open then click Data, Show Data Sources to open the Data Sources window

2 Select the **Bikes** icon then click on the dropdown arrow button that appears and choose the Details option

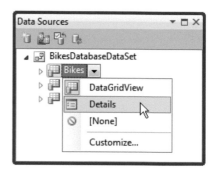

3 Expand the **Bikes** tree, select any item then click the arrow button that appears to see a list of possible controls. Choose ComboBox for **ModelID** and **VersionID**, and Textbox for the rest

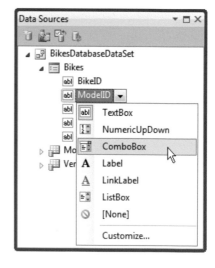

180

4 Get ready to experience one of the most stunning features in Visual Basic! Click on the **Bikes** icon in the Data Sources window then drag it across the IDE and drop it onto the Form in Form Designer – see lots of controls get automatically added to the Form and see these five items get added to the Component tray

BikesDatabaseDataSet   BikesBindingSource   BikesTableAdapter
TableAdapterManager   BikesBindingNavigator

Two ComboBox controls and three Textbox controls are added to the Form, as specified in the Data Sources dropdown list, plus a navigation ToolStrip and labels matching the column headings.

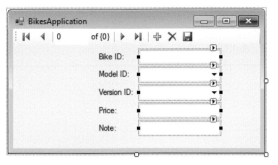

The items added to the Component Tray are non-visual components to manage the data flow:

● **TableAdapterManager** is the top-level component that coordinates the update operations of TableAdapters

● **TableAdapter** is the data access object that has Fill and GetData() methods to actually supply data to the controls

● **DataSet** contains data tables of the in-memory representation of the database tables

● **BindingSource** is an intermediate manager between the dataset and Form controls

● **BindingNavigator** supports the navigation ToolStrip to move through the records, and allows data to be added or deleted

5 Run the application and try out the navigation controls – see the data appear from the Bikes table

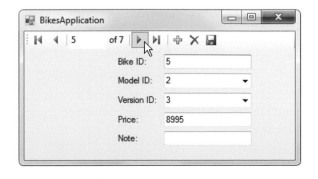

Hot tip

You can view a graphic representation of the DataSet – right-click on the DataSet icon in the Data Sources window and choose Edit DataSet with Designer.

Binding meaningful data

Having added data controls to the Form on the previous page you can now display the data contained in the **Bikes** table but the **ModelID** and **VersionID** fields are still displaying the ID number – not the associated value from the linked table. To correct this so the application displays meaningful data it is necessary to bind the linked tables to those controls.

1 Click on the **Models** table icon in the Data Sources window then drag it to Form Designer and drop it onto the **ModelID** ComboBox control – see **ModelsBindingSource** and **ModelsTableAdapter** items get added to the Component Tray

    ModelsBindingSource   ModelsTableAdapter

2 Click on the **Versions** table icon in the Data Sources window then drag it to Form Designer and drop it onto the **VersionID** ComboBox control – see **VersionsBindingSource** and **VersionsTableAdapter** items get added to the Component Tray

    VersionsBindingSource   VersionsTableAdapter

3 Click the arrow button on each ComboBox control to reveal their new data binding settings on the Smart Tag

Don't forget

All the data binding settings are made automatically when you bind the linked tables to the ComboBox controls.

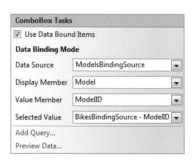
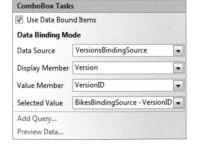

The **ModelID** ComboBox control is now bound to **ModelsBindingSource** so will now display the **Model** value, rather than its ID number.

Similarly, the **VersionID** ComboBox is now bound to the **VersionsBindingSource** so will now display the **Version** value, rather than its ID number.

4   Edit the Label control alongside each ComboBox to remove the "ID" text – reflecting the new value these controls will display

5   As the BikeID is not really meaningful to the user set its Visible property to False in the Properties window then delete its Label control

6   Run the application and see meaningful values appear

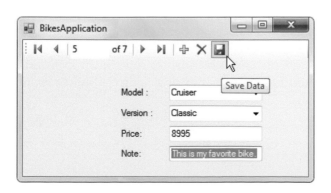

7   To test the ability to save data permanently back to the database enter some text in the Note field and click the Save Data button – restart the application and see that your text has been preserved

Hot tip

You can also go the projects bin/debug folder and run the executable application there to see that the data is preserved in the database.

Building custom SQL queries

Having added the ability to display meaningful data on the previous page you can now exploit the true power of databases by building custom SQL queries to extract only specific data.

 Select the **BikesTableAdapter** icon in the Component Tray then choose Add Query from its Smart Tag options to launch the Search Criteria Builder dialog

The Search Criteria Builder dialog displays an SQL query named **FillBy** that is executed by the Form's Load event-handler to populate the navigation ToolStrip and Form fields. This query selects all columns and rows of the **Bikes** table. It can be recreated as a custom SQL query that can be executed to perform the same service whenever the user requires all data to be selected.

2 Change the New Query Name field to "GetAll", then click OK – see another ToolStrip get added to the Form containing a button labelled **GetAll**

3 Select the new ToolStrip then, in the Properties window, set its AutoSize to False and change its MaximumSize and Size properties to resemble a single button 100, 30

To create custom SQL queries that select specific data you can simply edit the default query by appending a qualification clause.

4 Click the **BikesTableAdapter** component icon and choose Add Query to open Search Criteria Builder again

5 Change the New Query Name field to "GetClassics", then append this statement to the Query Text statement **WHERE VersionID = 3**

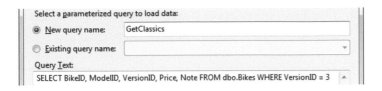

Select a parameterized query to load data:
- ⦿ New query name: GetClassics
- ○ Existing query name:

Query Text:
SELECT BikeID, ModelID, VersionID, Price, Note FROM dbo.Bikes WHERE VersionID = 3

6 Click OK to create a ToolStrip for this query and resize it as before to resemble a single button

7 Reopen Search Criteria Builder and create a new Query named "GetCruisers" appending this to the Query Text **WHERE ModelID = 2**

8 Resize the new ToolStrip as before, then run the application and click the **GetClassics** button to select data on all **Classic** versions only

BikesApplication

◄◄ ◄ | 2   of 2 | ▶ ▶◄ | ⊕ ✕ 🖫

GetAll

GetClassics	Model :	Touring ▼
GetCru ̮sers	Version :	Classic ▼
GetClassics	Price:	9995
	Note:	

9 Click the **GetAll** button to select all data once more, then click **GetCruisers** to select data on all **Cruiser** models only

BikesApplication

◄◄ ◄ | 1   of 3 | ▶ ▶◄ | ⊕ ✕ 🖫

GetAll

GetClassics	Model :	Cruiser ▼
GetCruisers	Version :	Standard ▼
GetCruisers	Price:	7995
	Note:	

Hot tip

The navigation ToolStrip shows the number of records selected by that query – in this case two Classic versions and three Cruiser models.

Summary

- Databases store data in structured rows and columns making it easy to reference and manipulate data

- Each row in a database table is called a record and must have a **Primary Key** to uniquely identify that record

- A table in a relational database can address its own records by **Primary Key** and address other tables by **Foreign Key**

- Normalization rules insist that data must not be duplicated within a database and column data types must be defined

- Data integrity is preserved by database constraints

- SQL Server is integrated with Visual Basic to allow databases to be created from within the IDE

- Table constraints are established in the Table Definition

- Setting the **Primary Key** column's **Is Identity** property to Yes will automatically number each row

- Table relationships can be established graphically in a **Database Diagram**

- Table constraints are tested in realtime as Table Data is input

- A database dataset is an in-memory representation of the data contained within the database tables

- Drag'n'drop a table from the **Data Sources** window onto a Form to automatically create data controls

- A **BindingSource** manages the data flow between a dataset and Form controls

- Drag'n'drop a table from the **Data Sources** window onto a control to bind meaningful data from the table to that control

- A **TableAdapter** has methods to supply data to Form controls and can add custom SQL queries to exploit the true power of databases by selecting specific data

Index

187